RISKS AT SEA

The Bourse in Amsterdam

The east side of the Bourse in Amsterdam, from an engraving by Hermanus Petrus Schoute published in the Atlas of Pierre Fouquet Jnr (1783). An arcade surrounded the central courtyard with forty-six numbered pillars, the first portrayed here on the right. They often carried posters and notices; or served as meeting-points for dealers in different sections of the market. The engraving is reproduced by kind permission of the Director of the Rijksprentenkabinet.

RISKS AT SEA
Amsterdam insurance and
maritime Europe, 1766–1780

FRANK C. SPOONER

Professor of Economic History
University of Durham

CAMBRIDGE UNIVERSITY PRESS

Cambridge
London   New York   New Rochelle
Melbourne   Sydney

PUBLISHED BY THE PRESS SYNDICATE OF THE UNIVERSITY OF CAMBRIDGE
The Pitt Building, Trumpington Street, Cambridge, United Kingdom

CAMBRIDGE UNIVERSITY PRESS
The Edinburgh Building, Cambridge CB2 2RU, UK
40 West 20th Street, New York NY 10011–4211, USA
477 Williamstown Road, Port Melbourne, VIC 3207, Australia
Ruiz de Alarcón 13, 28014 Madrid, Spain
Dock House, The Waterfront, Cape Town 8001, South Africa

http://www.cambridge.org

First published 1983
First paperback edition 2002

A catalogue record for this book is available from the British Library

Library of Congress catalogue card number: 82-22000

ISBN 0 521 25275X hardback
ISBN 0 521 89387 9 paperback

'But ships are but boards, sailors but men . . .
and then there is the peril of waters,
winds, and rocks'

Shylock in *The Merchant of Venice*,
Act I, Scene iii.

CONTENTS

ILLUSTRATIONS

MAPS

ATLAS

TABLES

ABBREVIATIONS

AAE : Archives des Affairs Etrangères, Paris (CP = Correspondence Politique; MD = Mémoires et Documents)

AC : Archivio Comunale (and place)

AER : American Economic Review

Annales : Annales: économies, sociétés, civilisations

ARA : Algemeen Rijksarchief, The Hague (KA = Koloniaal Archief; WIC = West-Indische Compagnie)

AS : Archivio di Stato (and place)

BMG : Bijdragen en Mededelingen betreffende de Geschiedenis der Nederlanden

EcHR : Economic History Review

EHA : Economisch-Historisch Archief, formerly in The Hague and now in Amsterdam

EHJ : Economisch- (en Sociaal-) Historisch Jaarboek

EJ : Economic Journal

GA : Gemeentearchief (and place)

HSA : Hauptstaatsarchiv (and place)

KVA : Kamer van Assurantie en Avarij, Amsterdam

PRO : Public Record Office

QJE : Quarterly Journal of Economics

RAZ : Rijksarchief in Zeeland, Middelburg (MCC = Middelburgsche Commercie Compagnie)

RH : Revue Historique

SA : Staatsarchiv (and place)

Seville, Indias : Archivo General de Indias, Seville

Simancas : Archivo General de Simancas

TVG : Tijdschrift voor Geschiedenis

VOC : Verenigde Oost-Indische Compagnie

CHAPTER 1

Introduction

The history of marine insurance, *lato sensu*, has still to be written. This should not imply that one of the venerable forms of commercial protection has suffered from neglect, that scholars have passed the challenge of the subject. Rather the reverse, for the collections in libraries are eloquent and deal with many countries. A few names mentioned and the contribution becomes substantial. Classic authors such as Enrico Bensa and J.-M. Pardessus have a well-deserved reputation in the field.[1] And different countries have not been backward in producing a wealth of talent: Violet Barbour, P. J. Blok, E. L. G. den Dooren de Jong, J. E. Elias, W. H. A. Elink Schuurman, I. Schöffer, H. G. Schuddebeurs, Z. W. Sneller and J. P. Vergouwen for The Netherlands;[2] R. Ehrenberg, G. A. Kiesselbach, and J. F. Plass for Hamburg;[3] C. Thorsen for

---

[1] Enrico Bensa, *Il contratto di assicurazione nel medio evo* (Genoa, 1884); J.-M. Pardessus, *Collection des lois maritimes antérieures au XVIIIe. siècle* (6 vols., Paris, 1828–45).

[2] Violet Barbour, 'Marine risks and insurance in the seventeenth century', *Journal of Economic and Business History*, I (1928–29); P. J. Blok, 'Het plan tot oprichting eener Compagnie van Assurantie', *Bijdragen voor Vaderlandsche Geschiedenis en Oudheidkunde*, 4e. Reeks, I (1900); E. L. G. den Dooren de Jong, 'De pratijk der Amsterdamsche Zeeverzekering in de 17e. eeuw', *Het Verzekeringsarchief*, VIII (1927); J. E. Elias, *Schetsen uit Geschiedenis van ons Zeewesen* (6 vols., The Hague, 1916–30), and *De Vlootbouw in Nederland in de eerste helft der 17e. eeuw, 1596–1655* (Amsterdam, 1933); W. H. A. Elink Schuurman, 'Korte aanteekeningen betreffende verzekering in de dagen der Republiek', *EHJ*, III (1917); I. Schöffer, 'De vonnissen in averij-grosse van de Kamer van Assurantie en Avarij te Amsterdam in de 18e. eeuw', *EHJ*, XXVI (1956); H. G. Schuddebeurs, 'Het Nederlandsche verzekeringsbedrijf gedurende de laatste twee eeuwen, voorsoover dit werd uitgeoefend door naamlooze vennootschappen', *EHJ*, XIV (1928), and 'Vier eeuwen verzekering in Nederland', *Het Verzekeringsarchief*, XXX (1953); Z. W. Sneller, 'Die drie cargasoenen rogge van Daniel van der Meulen c.s. anno 1592 en hun verzekering', *Amstelodamum*, XXXI (1935); J. P. Vergouwen, *De geschiedenis der Makelaardij in Assurantiën hier te lande tot 1813* (The Hague, 1945).

[3] R. Ehrenberg, 'Studien zur Entwicklungsgeschichte der Versicherung', *Zeitschrift für die gesamte Versicherungswissenschaft*, I (1901); G. A. Kiesselbach, *Die wirtschafts- und rechtsgeschichtliche Entwickelung der Seeversicherung in Hamburg* (Hamburg, 1901); J. F. Plass, *Geschichte der Assecuranz und der hanseatischen Seeversicherungsbörsen, Hamburg – Bremen – Lübeck* (Hamburg, 1902).

Denmark;[4] Giuseppe Felloni, Jacques Heers, Federigo Melis, Giuseppe Stefani, C. Schwarzenberg, and Alberto Tenenti for Italy;[5] L. A. Boiteux, J. Delumeau, and H. Lafosse for France;[6] M. B. Amzalak, N. Arié, and J. Piedade for Portugal;[7] A. H. John, F. Martin, J. Trenerry, C. Wright and C. E. Fayle for London;[8] and across the Atlantic, H. E. Gillingham and S. S. Huebner for the United States.[9] The on-going bibliography already has remarkable distinction and there is much more besides.[10]

The areas of enquiry have been no less extensive, particularly for the history of companies, institutions, and procedures of marine insurance: the evolution of legal forms, corporations, and concepts of property; the status and privileges of insurers, the types and conditions of ships, their personnel, cargoes and destinations; the capital investments, risks and claims for accidents and losses. All, or almost all, these aspects have passed under close scrutiny. Sometimes the range of information reflects the formation and direct interests of the scholars themselves; at other times, the haphazard survival of the documents has decided in advance the scope of conclusions reached. The nature of the transactions and the

[4] C. Thorsen, *Det Kongelig Oktroierede Sø-Assurance Kompagni, 1726–1926: et Bidrag til dansk Søforsikrings Historie* (Copenhagen, 1926).

[5] G. Felloni, 'Una fonte inesplorata per la storia dell' economia marittima in età moderna: i calcoli di avaria', in *Wirtschaftskräfte und Wirtschaftswege, Festschrift für Hermann Kellenbenz*, ed. Jürgen Schneider (5 vols., Nuremberg, 1978), II; J. Heers, *Gênes au XVe. siècle: activité économique et problèmes sociaux* (Paris, 1961); F. Melis, *I primi secoli delle assicurazione (sec. XIII–XVI)* (Rome, 1965); G. Stefani, *L'assicurazione a Venezia dalli origini alla fine della Serenissima* (2 vols., Trieste, 1956); C. Schwarzenberg, *Ricerche sull'assicurazione marittima a Venezia* (Rome/Milan, 1969); A. Tenenti, *Naufrages, corsaires et assurances maritimes à Venise (1592–1602)* (Paris, 1959), and English edition (London, 1967).

[6] L. A. Boiteux, *L'assurance maritime à Paris sous le règne de Louis XIV* (Paris, 1945), *Cinq années d'assurances maritimes à Marseille (1631–1636)* (Sète, 1958), and *La fortune de la mer* (Paris, 1968); J. Delumeau, 'Exploitation d'un dossier d'assurances maritimes du XVIIe. siècle', in *Mélanges en l'honneur de Fernand Braudel* (2 vols., Toulouse, 1973), I, pp. 135–163; H. Lafosse, *La jurisdiction consulaire de Rouen, 1556–1791* (Rouen, 1922).

[7] M. B. Amzalak, *O tratado de seguros de Pedro de Santarém* (Lisbon, 1958); N. Arié and J. Piedade, 'The Portuguese contribution in the field of insurance', *Versicherungswissenschaftliches Archiv*, III (1957).

[8] C. E. Fayle, 'Shipowning and marine insurance', in C. N. Parkinson (ed.), *The Trade Winds* (London, 1948); A. H. John, 'The London Assurance Company and the marine insurance market of the eighteenth century', *Economica*, XXV (1958); F. Martin, *History of Lloyd's and Marine Insurance in Great Britain* (London, 1876); J. Trenerry, *The Origin and Early History of Insurance* (London, 1926); C. Wright and C. E. Fayle, *A History of Lloyd's* (London, 1928).

[9] H. E. Gillingham, *Marine Insurance in Philadelphia, 1721–1800* (Philadelphia, 1933); S. S. Huebner, *Marine Insurance* (New York, 1920).

[10] Important introductions to the extensive bibliography in Stefani, *L'assicurazione a Venezia*; and J. Halpérin, *Le rôle des assurances dans les débuts du capitalisme moderne* (Neuchâtel, 1945); H. A. L. Cockerill and E. Green, *The British insurance business and guide to historical records in the United Kingdom* (London, 1976).

regulations within which institutions functioned have exerted a decisive influence – especially for new types of high risk. Then, as now, decisions tended to rely pre-eminently on intuitions and experience rather than on manuals and theories of practice. Unlike fire and life protection where information analysed over long years has brought insurance operations to an actuarial science and calculated probabilities, marine insurance for centuries appears to have remained highly personal, guided by prudence. The keynote has been *caveat assecurator!* and it leaves scholars to take the subject from the twilight of history.

The following study does not intend to put such excellent work aside; but rather to pursue a line of enquiry from the stand-point of a well-established, focal market. It is possible to assess the handling of marine risks from the central tendency of prices and premiums, and then to pass beyond these to a much larger reality of navigation in the international economy. On this occasion the chosen market is Amsterdam and there is much in its favour. The explosive force unleashed by Spain and Portugal in opening the oceans soon transmitted itself to other countries, above all to The Netherlands. The golden age of the early Republic saw the Dam grow to astonishing wealth and prestige. Waves of fertile innovations created further opportunities in an expanding Atlantic economy. As decade followed decade, initiatives of enterprise ripened into a high summer of affluence – impressive, pervasive, rich in advantages, yet at the same time fraught with attendant tribulations. With the passing years fortunes accumulated like coral but became perhaps less mobile, more committed. By the eighteenth century the capital base of the Dam was broad and diversified in complex social structures, nourished by high propensities to save. Any attempt to assess the international economy of the *ancien régime* must take measure of the compelling advantages of Amsterdam. Long experience at the heart of affairs endowed it with institutions and refined techniques; business acumen and a sense of enterprise; a reputation which brought flows of reports in which Europe generally could actively share.

That multilateral flow of information has bequeathed a basis for the present study. The early regulation of the Amsterdam Bourse prescribed official price-lists, the famous *prijscouranten*, established by the sworn brokers. In time, these double-sided lists of commodity prices, regularly issued in print, came to include further sections for the means of settlement: money, exchanges, and insurance.[11] The important section of *Assurantiën* listed premiums for voyages to and from destinations in Europe and the West Indies. The price-lists circulated widely, they even

---

[11] W. P. Sautijn Kluit, *De Amsterdamsche Prijs-Courantiers in de 17e. en 18e. eeuw* (Amsterdam, 1872); Vergouwen, *De geschiedenis der Makelaardij*, pp. 48–49.

reached the Far East through the correspondence of the United East India Company.[12] Their survival in the archives has been uncertain, and scholars must be thankful for the enterprise of Nicolaas Posthumus in making the initial collection.[13] Even now, the sequence of these lists is disappointing. As often happens, history and archives are not always of the same mind: *scribitur ad narrandum, non ad probandum*. However, as we shall see later, the years covered by this study, at first sight a random choice based on surviving documents, have in effect the exceptional advantage of coinciding with a pause, a stage in the long-term evolution of the insurance market.

Similar series exist, of course, for other commercial centres in Europe. There are the important *Preis-couranten* of Hamburg;[14] but the great port of the Elbe won full independence, and attained to focal international prominence in the late eighteenth century, and that in time of war. The great archive of the Maatschappij van Assurantie, Discontering, en Beleening der stad Rotterdam,[15] founded in 1720, has remarkable records of registered insurance, but such information is not precisely the same as the concerted quotations of an international market. *Lloyd's Lists* are another outstanding source for London, available from 1740,[16] giving a wealth of information on ships' movements. But they are silent on premiums: these remained the highly personal enterprise of the under-writers, so that it is difficult to detect the concerted action of the market.

Amsterdam, nevertheless, retains the persuasive advantage of having an established position in the economy of Europe. Within the limits of the period 1766–80, the data provide an opportunity to contrast external peace, in the years following the close of the Seven Years' War (1756–63), with growing hostilities in North America after 1775 and in Europe after 1778, which finally embroiled The Netherlands in open

---

[12] N. W. Posthumus, *Inquiry into the History of Prices in Holland* (2 vols., Leiden, 1946–64), I, and esp. pp. xxv–xxviii.

[13] The collection in the Economisch-Historisch Archief originally in The Hague and now in the Economisch-Historische Bibliotheek, Amsterdam. When I first worked on the series, a number of the lists seemed to have disappeared. A subsequent survey by post of archives in The Netherlands, Europe and Indonesia proved unsatisfactory, indeed, two letters to the State Archives in Jakarta went without reply. However, the series has now been extensively surveyed and established by the welcome research of J. J. McCusker and Cora Gravesteijn.

[14] This remarkable series is in the Commerzbibliothek, Hamburg; and see E. Baasch, 'Aus der Entwicklungsgeschichte der Hamburger Kurszettels', *Bank-Archiv*, V (1905), and 'Geschichte der hamburger Waren-Preiscourant', *Forschungen zur hamburger Handels-geschichte*, III, 3 (1902).

[15] The archives of the Maatschappij van Assurantie, Discontering, en Beleening der stad Rotterdam (hereafter cited as Maatschappij van Assurantie), in the Gemeentearchief, Rotterdam. Dr R. A. D. Renting, the Director, has been particularly generous in making material available.

[16] *Lloyd's List*, begun in 1734, available in facsimile for the period 2 January 1740 to 29 December 1826, published Farnborough, 1969.

conflict (1780). However, the first period of relative international peace was marked by serious upheavals at home: 1763 saw a severe financial crisis from which recovery was slow and arduous. Then came the bankruptcies of 1772–73 to interrupt the operations of the market. These two breaks, together with the involvement of The Netherlands in active war from December 1780, may be said to reflect a moment in the history of The Netherlands in general, and of Amsterdam in particular. That city of prestige had achieved so much in co-ordinating the trade and navigation of the continent. And yet, like other precocious pioneers, it was obliged to come to terms with a stern reality: competition from other markets in Europe.

★

My interest in marine insurance has developed over the years, from many influences and almost unintentionally, in the margin of my main research into monetary development; in part from spending some long spells at sea, of seeing the destructive force of gales and typhoons; and in part from a curiosity about the risks of transferring high-value cargoes from one market to another. For the latter, the margins of profit in the eighteenth century were often astonishingly narrow – as low as one-sixteenth percent on bullion dealings if we are to believe a report of August 1749. This, it should be noted, at a time when the insurance premium between Amsterdam and London was running at one and a half percent.[17] If such conditions were typical of the period under study, then changes in the cost of protection at sea could pass on important costs to the consumer and inevitably set constraints on monetary and financial operations.

These interests grew with study in different universities. The Ecole Pratique des Hautes Etudes (VIe. Section) in Paris, under Lucien Febvre and Fernand Braudel, was active in the maritime history of early modern Europe. In 1955 in Chicago, I attended the lectures of Frank Knight, with his wide-ranging discussion of risk and profit, of Earl J. Hamilton and Milton Friedman; and later in New York, the Securities Research Department of Merrill Lynch. At Harvard, I was fortunate to be able to follow the teaching of Alexander Gerschenkron, Simon Kuznets, and Wassily Leontief. These were remarkable opportunities indeed; and I remain grateful for the ideas discussed and the perspectives opened.

In 1960, en route for the economic history conference in Stockholm, I went to survey documents in Amsterdam for a project on rates of interest, planned at that time by Earl J. Hamilton and T. S. Ashton. The scheme did not materialise; and instead of going to Stockholm, I continued to study the *prijscouranten*, then kept in The Hague.[18] Long

[17] *ARA, Generaliteits Muntkamer*, 21, fo. 208 vo.
[18] See notes 12 and 13 above.

delays intervened, partly from a protracted attempt to find more price-lists in the archives; partly from other pressing work in the mainstream of my research; and partly from the inevitable procession of academic duties. The material was assembled and checked, and the series of data finally in place, the maps, graphs and tables ready. Then, in 1975 I decided to enlarge the sections on the uncertainties which disrupted the market in 1763, 1772–73, and the prologue to war in 1780.

At the outset, as in much research, the subject appeared to be simple enough. Here was a great market, in the late splendour of early prosperity, enjoying the fruits of a long and diverse expansion among the Atlantic economies. If some lines of its trade in the eighteenth century no longer passed without serious challenge from other centres of growth such as Hamburg and London, it nevertheless had the substantial assets and business ramifications won by creative enterprise. A broad stream of inherited wealth percolated the activity of the Dam, seeking or creating opportunities for investment. Refined techniques and established institutions served to encourage mutual risk-aversion, to shift risks and spread prospective losses: the traditional *rederij*, for example; the great commercial companies with shares quoted on the market; the Wisselbank and Bourse; the precocious system of puts and calls, of forward buying so accurately displayed by Don Josseph de la Vega (1688).[19] These were powerful instruments to diversify finance and spread the risks of trading across the seas.

At the same time, the market was important for insurance in another direction. The payment of premiums created net risk capital – that is, the sum of premiums less management costs. These became part of the financial assets of the market, and generated a flow of funds ready for short-term investment. The insurance market was thus sensitive to both long- and short-term factors.

However, the problems of insurance were not just those of a working market, closed on itself, concerned with domestic activity. Marine insurance belonged implicitly to the international economy. Navigation followed expected utility preferences, similar to those which John von Neumann and Oscar Morgenstern discerned in the theory of games. In one sense, maritime trade was a continuum of income – exports of goods and the repatriation of profits, providing a progressive addition of value realised in the final sales in markets and to consumer. The prospect of losing cargoes which progressively appreciated as they approached market, but carried in ships which depreciated on the voyage, was not

---

[19] Don Josseph de la Vega, *Confusión de Confusiones (1688)*, ed. M. F. J. Smith and trans. G. J. Geers (The Hague, 1939); see also the excellent Introduction by H. Kellenbenz, Publication no. 13, *Kress Library of Business and Economics* (Cambridge, 1957).

easy to countenance in early modern Europe.[20] At least, this could be assumed if all the consignments of merchandise came sailing home on the flood, or the lines of trade moved in direct voyages from Amsterdam to their destinations. The reality was much more complex: ships often dropped in from port to port – Balthazar-Marie Emerigon referred to this as *la caravane*;[21] tramp shipping would be a convenient but anachronistic term. And so preconceived notions of continuous functions became mixed with discontinuities. Each of the major lines of trade to the regions of Europe – the Mediterranean, Portugal and Spain, the British Isles, the Baltic, Scandinavia, and the North – enjoyed varying income expectations and probabilities. Colonial transactions, especially with America and the West Indies, relied on their highly favourable land–labour ratios – at least by comparison with Europe – and were exceptional examples. Nevertheless, a central theme of this study is that insurance operations reveal a *leitmotif* of continuity. The multilateral system found expression in the rôle of Amsterdam as a central market co-ordinating a through-put of commodities. It is a problem germane to any analysis of insurance, and of those risks and uncertainties which confronted maritime trade in pre-industrial Europe.

How, then, to take stock of the complex trading patterns of Amsterdam? One approach – and it does not exclude other possible methods – can start with the array of trade as an input–output matrix, a transactions table for commercial flows to and from the different regions of Europe, and indeed the world. The insurance sections of the *prijscouranten* in the 1760s listed twenty groups of destinations for Europe and two for the West Indies,[22] and so – at least formally – were heavily biased in favour of navigation about the continent. Such a matrix offers a point of departure to discuss the performance of Amsterdam at two levels: on the one hand, considering *structural risks*; and on the other hand, *event uncertainties*.[23] I prefer to use the term *structural risks* since this can group marine risks into packages which seem to have conformed at the time to appraisals of conventional probabilities. Shipowners and merchants were in the market for protection in their dealings ranging to the frontiers of speculation, with a prime objective to maximise average income and minimise variations in that income. The assumption underlying the

---

[20] Original publication in 1722; references in this study to J.-P. Ricard, *Le Négoce d'Amsterdam, contenant tout ce que doivent savoir les Marchands et Banquiers, tant ceux qui sont établis à Amsterdam, que ceux des Pays étrangers* (Rouen, 1723), p. 268.

[21] B.-M. Emerigon, *Traité des Assurances et des Contrats à la Grosse* (2 vols., Marseilles, 1783), II, p. 20. Shippers usually insured for part of the *caravane*, taking out further insurance as the occasion arose.

[22] See below, Chapter 6, p. 165.

[23] For an excellent survey of the problems and bibliography, see J. Hirschliefer and J. G. Riley, 'The analytics of uncertainty and information – an expository survey', *Journal of Economic Literature*, XVII (1979).

concept of structural risks is that from experience and business acumen, insurance dealers could base their portfolios of policies and short-term investments, not on random variables but on average values. The scalars derived from long acquaintance with the frequency and volume of claims on different routes of navigation. In this study, I have concentrated on two major packages which emerge from the data. They are the dynamic seasonal movement, and the linearity of distance on the high seas. Such a formulation of the theory of risk – such as it existed – may be said to point to a closed system of transactions concerned with factors endogenous to the market.

Naturally, it is necessary to look beyond these packages to the interdependence of risks deriving from a number of profound *states* of the world. I use the conventional term *state* to simplify the explanation, but few historians alert to structural history would wish to ignore the slowly changing realities of human ecology. At the forefront of preoccupations at the time were the perils of the sea. For those who went down to the sea in ships, eyes could rarely leave the weather-vane and the quarter of the wind, the clouds forming in the sky, the capriciousness of the waves. Waiting on weather was an immemorial concern, and W.O.W. still remains a laconic label for a harsh reality when oilmen drill at sea. With a brusque change in weather, there were treacherous shoals and sand-banks to strand a ship – such as the *Pampus* at the entrance to Amsterdam, or the *Goodwins* in the Channel – and uncharted rocks or ice-floes to break the hulls. Navigation was thus a dialogue with the adjacent land. Perils of landfall, perils of the sea. For the navigator there were choices in finding the correct course, dead-reckoning on the high seas and cautious observation in coastal waters. If an example is required, we have only to turn to Willem Janz. Blaeu's *Het Licht der Zeevaert* (1620). There the dichotomy is set out with clarity on the title page: two figures – the stylish mariner with his cross-staff and chart, and the practical seaman with his lead and line. Much of the sailing around Europe was 'in soundings' and more than a vestige of an immemorial navigation survived in the reliance on testing the sea-bed. 'Vada co lo scandallio' was a precept of *Lo Compasso da Navigare* (c. 1250)[24] and after half a millenium the advice held good. Such perils were a mariner's heritage, uncertain at first sight but in sum exercising a latent control of navigation.

That dichotomy was not precisely the same for the insurer. Leaving harbour and sailing close inshore set problems different from those of

---

[24] For a discussion of the early techniques, see E. G. R. Taylor, *The haven-finding art* (London, 1956), esp. pp. 104–108. Fra Mauro (1450) noted the problem in the case of the Baltic, P. Dollinger, *The German Hansa* (London, 1970), p. 145.

the oceans. 'Brouwershaven', it was said in Rotterdam, 'lies half-way to Java.'[25] It is part of the discussion in this study that a ship had to overcome the risk-trap of entering and leaving port before attaining to the continuity of the high seas.

Another *state* was technology, or the arts if we return to the convenient phrase of classical economists. The perils of the sea were one thing; the construction, condition, and management of ships to cope with them were another, and of an entirely different complexion. Some related to the ship and the conduct on board. The techniques of sailing, the going information in maps and tables were one aspect of the problem. So, too, were the skills, training, and probity of the crew, not least when it came to jettison cargo and fittings, or when ill-secured stores were taken by the sea in flotsam; or when there was conniving in barratry . . . Innovation in ocean navigation brought potential for growth – and for stagnation – and concerned directly the adoption of 'best-practice techniques'.[26] There was the quality of design, construction, and equipment, for every hour in the water subjected the hull to stresses ranging from the buffeting of the seas to the attrition of rotting timbers.[27] Cost-effective shipping played a crucial rôle in early modern Europe. However, the eighteenth century was a phase of inflation, and rising costs brought pressures to use cheaper materials. Design could have its say. The Netherlands had made a substantial contribution to economical navigation: the famous *fluit* showed this at its best in the seventeenth century.[28] But as the years passed, such novelties gathered the patina of vintage procedures. If anything, sea-navigation under the *ancien régime* tended to a limit, settling for a stage in materials, design and ship-handling,[29] which only industrialisation could fundamentally change. There were, to be sure, signs here and there of improvement, but for our general purpose it may be said that the system in the late eighteenth century assumed many of the characteristics of conformity.

If these were some of the perils from the ships themselves and the conduct on board, there were others arising outside. These constituted

[25] P. D. J. van Iterson, 'Havens', in G. Asaert, Ph. M. Bosscher, J. R. Bruijn, W. J. Hoboken (eds.), *Maritieme geschiedenis der Nederlanden* (4 vols., Bussum, 1976–), III, p. 72.

[26] The theoretical concepts of best-practice techniques can be found in W. E. G. Salter, *Productivity and Technical Change*, 2nd edn (Cambridge, 1966).

[27] R. C. Albion, *Forests and Seapower* (Cambridge, Mass., 1926), esp. pp. 161–162.

[28] R. W. Unger, *Dutch Shipbuilding before 1800* (Assen, 1978), pp. 36–38; J. van Beylen, 'Scheepstypen', in G. Asaert et al., *Maritieme geschiedenis der Nederlanden*, II, pp. 28–32; H. J. Koenen, *Voorlezingen over de geschiedenis van scheepsbouw en zeevaart* (Amsterdam, 1854), pp. 160–161.

[29] G. M. Walton, 'Obstacles to technical diffusion in ocean shipping, 1675–1775', *Explorations in Economic History*, XX (1967).

another *state* of pervading importance, and fell within the scope of government protection. The geopolity of Europe combined climatic zones, resources, endowments, aptitudes, and not least spheres of domination and influence. Between the founding of the Amsterdam Bourse (1611) and Adam Smith's *Wealth of Nations* (1776), western Europe – and it was still predominantly an agrarian Europe – looked to the seas. Navigation offered access to more land and more resources. Nations with access to the Atlantic hotly pursued territorial gain outside the continent, and as the colonial world emerged even trading companies turned slowly from trade to settlement. No less prompt were the claims to territorial waters, the ambitions to define the political and legal constraints of marine frontiers. That competence slowly declared itself, for a direct application of the law of the land to harbours and estuaries left the law of pursuit to hold sway on the high seas. The issues were clear enough in England where the frontier was the sea: the common law courts ruled on the first but the Admiralty court on the second.[30] In The Netherlands, the definition of concepts was crucial, projected into debate in 1609 with the *Mare liberum* of Hugo Grotius (de Groot), and notably advanced in the *De dominio maris dissertatio* of Cornelis van Bynkershoek (1703 and 1744),[31] which set guidelines for posterity. Disputes in the Zuiderzee, for example, would come under the courts of Holland, those 'beyond the dunes' under the *admiraliteiten*.[32] The high seas opened opportunities for profit with the linear freedom of distance. In contrast, coastal waters raised sharply the lines of political dependence and obligation. Taken together, high seas and territorial waters combined into a complex of claims and pressures, formal in exercising control near the coasts, informal in the display of naval power across the oceans and the bids for colonial empire.

Structural risks, such as they were, imply that eighteenth-century Europe approached another mathematical moment in economic develop-ment – that is, an inflexion point rather than stability or equipoise – as one phase or epoch marked the close of an agrarian world and another launched the destiny of industrialisation.[33] A part of the concern of this study is the degree to which insurance dealings in Amsterdam settled

---

[30] C. Molloy, *De Jure Maritimo et Navali* (London, 1676), p. 197.

[31] H. Grotius, *Mare liberum* (Leiden, 1609); C. van Bynkershoek, *De dominio maris dissertatio* (The Hague, 1703), and 2nd edn (Leiden, 1744, repr. New York, 1923); for an ample discussion of these problems of sovereignty and territorial waters, see J. K. Oudendijk, *Status and extent of adjacent waters* (Leiden, 1970).

[32] A. Korthals Altes has kindly clarified the relevant issues for me; see his *Prijs ter zee* (Zwolle, 1973). For the negotiations over the Scheldt (1785), B. Vitányi, *The internation-al régime of river navigation* (Alphen aan den Rijn, 1979), pp. 170–171.

[33] S. Kuznets, *Modern economic growth* (New Haven, Conn., 1967), pp. 2–3.

into a pattern, and came to terms with the economic ecology of the *ancien régime*.

As for the second panel of the diptych, the category of event uncertainties considers the system of transactions as open and relating to exogenous and other stochastic variables. They derive from unforeseen disturbances, ruptures, and catastrophes outside the normal sequence of events. Our concern is to review the effects on the market. Prudent seafarers had to contend with the 'acts of God', the sudden disasters to ship and cargo: the gale to put vessels on the rocks, a hurricane to devastate warehouses, ruin return consignments, 'shift' the cargoes loaded in the holds. Claims under general average – such as those which came for settlement before the Kamer van Assurantie en Avarij in Amsterdam – naturally reshaped expectations of income. At another level, the financiers, insurance agents, and insurers could fall into disarray during a financial upheaval or liquidity crisis. Bankruptcies disrupted the system of mutual risk-aversion. A third and major event uncertainty was political decision. A declaration of war, for example, at once defined loyalties and hardened obligations. But the path to war was littered with minor calamities for international trade: the blockade of a port, the seizure of ships, the raising of tariffs and harbour dues, the long law-suits from which there seemed to be no redress. In the formalities of the *ancien régime*, the games of governments introduced an element of uncertainty which filled the gazettes and troubled the well-laid plans of merchants and financiers.

In effect, event uncertainties faced insurance dealers with exceptional situations in which small changes provoked augmented turbulence in the spectrum of risks. The imperfections of the system, the shortcomings in information, and the inadequacies of scientific knowledge left the market in general and dealers in particular ill-equipped to predict the incidence or even handle the scale of resulting losses. They found themselves unable to meet claims or even continue to write policies. The underwriting losses in 1780–81 were a case in point.[34] These had powerful effects on the supply side of the insurance market and imposed abrupt shifts away from the central tendency. The crux of the matter in event uncertainties was an inability to assign fixed probabilities. Ultimately, there could be 'no market'.

It would be attractive indeed to isolate the commercial system of Amsterdam into dualities of transactions both open and closed. However, in the larger perspective of explanation it is necessary to underline the interaction of structural and event uncertainties, to concentrate on the dominant characteristics of continuity and interdependence. Catastrophe

[34] See below, Chapter 2, Graph 3.

11

theory formulated by René Thom[35] could, perhaps, provide an apt synthesis: the forms of structural stability and interdependence of the system of navigation countenance the *formes informes* of events either unstable and 'chaotic' in themselves or composed of a few elements in mutual contradiction and disharmony. Under such conditions, small changes could provoke violent turbulence. As a market, Amsterdam was not necessarily perfect in the sense that it always cleared, but dealers were able to combine packages of credit, freight, and insurance[36] which strengthened opportunities for risk-aversion. Its function as a staple for the inter-regional flows of goods can be seen in the insurance quotations in the *prijscouranten* for twenty-two groups of destinations. And these were only part of the panorama of trade. Colonial produce from the West Indies found markets in Germany and the Baltic. Grain from Danzig sailed direct to cover shortages in the Mediterranean. These were lines in a well-founded commercial web, but insurance premiums quoted now for one region, now for another, were inter-related through the market.

This pervasive interdependence contended with a spatial problem. Europe represented a complex of climatic zones, which imposed their necessities. In the hierarchy of priorities, The Netherlands concentrated on the Baltic and the strategic commodities from that inclement sea: food, naval stores, metals. In many respects, the timetable of coastal navigation in Europe conformed to the special requirements of the North, where hard winters and the freeze transformed patterns of risk for the rest of the continent. In order to enter the Baltic and northern waters during the propitious months of the summer and complete deals before the onset of winter when ice-floes closed the ports, cargoes were often despatched from the temperate South in the less-favourable months of winter and early spring. In this we can again see structural interdependence between different lines of inter-regional trade. Minimising risks in the Baltic trade imposed more than minimal risks in trade with other

---

[35] R. Thom, *Stabilité structurelle et morphogénèse* (Reading, Mass., 1972), esp. pp. 29–32, 55–70, 108–116; for the cusp catastrophe and the problem of finding single mathematical concepts for market instabilities and crashes under modern conditions, see E. C. Zeeman, 'On the unstable behaviour of stock exchanges', *Journal of Mathematical Economics*, I (1974), 39–40, 47–48; 'Catastrophe theory', in draft (Warwick, 1976), pp. 1–2, 28–31, and in *Scientific American*, CCXXXIV (April, 1976), p. 65. For a remarkable critique of the debate on catastrophe theory, see the review by S. Smale of E. C. Zeeman, *Catastrophe theory: selected papers, 1972–77* (London, 1977), in *Bulletin of the American Mathematical Society*, LXXXIV (November, 1978), 1362–1368. I am grateful to Tom Willmore for his friendly and unstinted advice on this extensive field.

[36] S. Ricard, *Traité générale du commerce* (3 vols., Paris, An 7/1799–1800), esp. I, pp. 80–82, 440–448. Published in Amsterdam in 1781, a further edition appeared in Paris during the Revolution. References are to the latter.

parts of Europe. At least, this could be one set of factors to be taken into account.

★

What, then, are the salient problems to examine from the viewpoint of Amsterdam in the years 1766–80? In the first section of the study, I propose to look at the market itself and review three examples of event uncertainties. These are the crisis of 1763 from which recovery was slow; the bankruptcies of 1772–73; and the concerted almost unavoidable drift into war from the events leading to the declaration of American independence (July 1776) to the immersion in war with Britain (December 1780) long avoided and soon a costly reality.

Then follows the discussion of structural risks. The alternation of the seasons, a regular irregularity, became accepted in practice. The influences of regions, climate, weather, combined in moving the produce of the land to market. The typology of seasonal movements was sufficiently powerful to push the annual forecasts from the realm of the uncertain to that of the approximate.

And then there was the problem of distance. On the high seas, the incidence of winds, tides, and other risks tended to linearity. Merchants could work on conventional probabilities. Ocean navigation benefited from new, refined technology, charts and chronometers, techniques of sailing in prevailing winds, crew-skills and recruitment. Near the coasts, there were different hazards: finding harbours and leaving ports were subject to the vagaries of pilotage and the whims of political economy, the smouldering conflicts of nations, the power tensions of the continent. Here, the risks became highly variable. The spatial context implied a matrix of maritime trade characteristic of early modern Europe and a basis for converging markets. Political constraints often cut through normal operations.

In retrospect, it seems that by the late 1760s and early 1770s the economy of Europe under the *ancien régime* may have reached a mathematical moment; but as a long phase culminated and new growth potential emerged, that attainment became relatively short-lived. After 1775–76, in spite of all, trouble piled on trouble, from which ultimately there was no return. The ensuing conflicts succeeded in demolishing an elegant but creaking façade, criticised by intellectuals and eroded by change. At the same time, it was capable, as Adam Smith was quick to show, of new initiatives, of fresh departures in international activity. Amsterdam, with so many widely scattered commitments, was both exposed and vulnerable. The following study proposes to investigate this position at risk, which touches on the *grande histoire* of Europe. Naturally, it does not claim to give the final answer.

★

13

In completing this research, I have received a great deal of help and kindness. Especially in the archives of The Netherlands: from the late S. Hart in the Gemeentearchief, Amsterdam; from S. H. M. Plantinga and G. W. van der Meiden in the Algemeen Rijksarchief, The Hague; and from P. C. Emmer, A. J. Looijenga and Cora Gravesteijn in the Economisch-Historisch Archief, formerly kept in The Hague and a model of hospitality. Allan Wilson and Michael Turner assisted in tabulating the material. George Brown transformed my maps and graphs. Margaret Hall took special care of the typing. In addition, my research advanced with substantial help from the Leverhulme Trust, the British Academy, and not least the University of Durham. Publication received generous finance. The Twenty-Seven Foundation Awards in London provided a subsidy. The Association Internationale pour l'Etude de l'Economie de l'Assurance in Geneva kindly made me an Ernst Meyer Award. I am grateful to all of them.

CHAPTER 2

The Amsterdam market and marine insurance

The centre, then, is Amsterdam and the period from 1766 to 1780. In this context, commercial finance and marine insurance found a natural identity. They had long since developed those manifest forms of risk-shifting which characterised the general growth of The Netherlands economy. Almost by definition. The institutions of the market had evolved in close harmony to give the Republic the initial gloss of a golden century. With the spreading opportunities of navigation, it is worth noting that the regulation of insurance came early, and survived at leisure: the great ordinance of 1598 formalised procedures, and remained in force until the revision of 1744.[1] If we take the mere factual sequence of dates, it preceded even the foundation of important corporate bodies such as the Verenigde Oost-Indische Compagnie (1602),[2] The Wissel-bank (1609)[3] and the Bourse itself (1611), that pulsating heart of the great city, a clearing-house for Europe. All floated, flourished on a surge of expansion which accompanied the formation of the United Provinces.[4] As the impressive structures matured and deepened, embellished with experience and enlarged by business acumen, the pre-eminent reputation of the Dam penetrated through the arteries of the trading world. Samuel Ricard (1780) could point with understandable partiality to the

---

[1] The text has been widely published: J.-M. Pardessus, *Collection des lois maritimes antérieures au XVIIIe. siècle* (6 vols., Paris, 1828–45), IV, pp. 122 et seq.; as also J.-P. Ricard, *Le Négoce d'Amsterdam* (Amsterdam, 1723), p. 250 et seq. (see above, p. 7, note 20); J. Accarias de Sérionne, *La Richesse de la Hollande* (2 vols., London (Leiden), 1778), I, pp. 89 et seq. For the clarifications of 1756 and 1775, see S. Ricard, *Traité générale du commerce* (3 vols., Paris, An 7/1799–1800), II, pp. 461 et seq.

[2] Hereafter cited as VOC.

[3] J. G. van Dillen, 'The bank of Amsterdam', in *History of the Principal Public Banks* (The Hague, 1934), pp. 79–84; and 'Bloeitijd der Amsterdamse Wisselbank, 1607–1701', in *Mensen en Achtergronden* (Groningen, 1964).

[4] J. G. van Dillen, 'Amsterdam, marché mondial des métaux précieux au XVIIe. et au XVIIIe. siècle', *RH*, CLII (1926). The expansion and range of Netherlands economic power in the seventeenth century has detailed examination in M. Aymard (ed.), *Dutch Capitalism and World Capitalism* (Cambridge, 1982). This collection appeared after the present study had gone to press.

15

prompt sense of affairs which enlivened those tall counting-houses lining the tranquil canals of Amsterdam, to the astuteness of merchants combining credit, freight and insurance.[5] These three services, often provided in concert by the same firms, strengthened the market and co-ordinated flows of cargoes through Europe. They belonged to the same spirit of flexible enterprise displayed in *rederijen*. Commercial risks were implicit in a world which traded and grew in the fringe of territorial discovery. Indeed, speculation was another name for trade itself.

This sets the direction of the chapter to follow. Before dealing with the movement of insurance, it is necessary first to review the market which gave it form and reality. As a meeting-place of business, Amsterdam provided, on the one hand, a framework for underwriting; and on the other hand, a dynamic capacity to cover risks of navigation, mitigated by event uncertainties. In brief, both the potential of the market and its susceptibility to economic trends and fluctuations call for special comment. However, the undertaking is far from easy. Even to-day, the range and volume of business in a financial market is difficult to assess. And how much more so for Amsterdam in the eighteenth century,[6] still set in an age of high transport-costs.

In this chapter, I propose to look in turn at three aspects of its activity. Firstly, the market, its institutions, and regulations. Secondly, the structures and economic trends which shaped its performance. And thirdly, the thriving capital market focused in the Bourse. The payment of premiums created a flow of funds ready for short-term investment which found a place in the aggregate finance of corporate equities, consolidated funds, annuities. The speed with which lenders took up issues of public debt on the market can be seen as one indicator of prevailing liquidity. Buying and selling bonds, servicing loans, paying out dividends, satisfying coupon-holders, all belonged to the financial service. The ample funds in search of investment and high income were like honey to the waspish rulers of Europe, whose agents appeared regularly on the Dam. But high profits for creditors brought attendant dangers. International lending faced a distinct possibility of loss.

THE MARKET OF AMSTERDAM

To many spectators in the 1760s, the Dam still remained the emporium of Europe *par excellence*. There was a potential sale for most things: like London in the nineteenth century, all was supposed to clear at a price.[7]

---

[5] S. Ricard, *Traité*, I, pp. 69, 200–203.

[6] M. Morineau, 'La balance du commerce franco-néerlandais et le reserrement économique des Provinces-Unies au XVIIe. siècle', *EHJ*, XXX (1965).

[7] Charles Kindleberger uses the striking analogy to Filene's Basement in Boston to describe the market of London in the nineteenth century which could always dispose of

Although the reality may have been far from such perfection, the outward appearances offered much to enthral the stray observer. The Atlas of genre engravings published by Pierre Fouquet (1760–83) portrays an enviable serenity of life – elegant houses and spacious public buildings, purposeful activity, canals in the changing seasons, strolling couples.[8] Urban opulence adopted a style of life underpinned by habits of thrift over many generations – Henry Hope, as James Riley underlines, put annual savings at 25 percent of income.[9] Alice Carter maintains that investments which ranged abroad into the national debt in England came all too often in a range of tranches between f. 20,000 and 90,000, from the upper 5 percent of the propertied burghers of Amsterdam.[10] Substance there was, but problems of structural change and the stern realities of economic transformations also lurked close to the surface. Affluence came to contend with maturity. Crises brought uncertainties and a restrained outlook for the future. In retrospect, it seems that in the 1760s and 1770s, the *ancien régime* was turning to the new perspectives of a future industrial world. Both economies and empires responded to a dichotomy of establishment and impending change.

These problems, however, were on the larger canvas of Europe. Our immediate objective is to look for the format of the market in which the business of insurance found its expression. How did it perform?

★

The sequence of events is not too difficult to follow. The struggle for independence carried Amsterdam to the fore. The immemorial rôle of the Low Countries in co-ordinating the trade of northern and southern

---

goods, in theory at least, even at zero price, *International Economics*, 3rd edn (Homewood, 1963), p. 252; see also S. Ricard, *Traité*, I, p. 36.

[8] P. Fouquet, *Nieuwe Atlas van de voornaamste gebouwen en gezichten der stad Amsterdam* (Amsterdam, the completed series, 1783), but first edition as *Afbeeldingen van de wijd vermaerde koopstad Amsterdam* (c. 1770). P. C. Jansen kindly sent me a catalogue of 115 prints (1760–83) edited, with introduction, by I. H. van Eeghen. Fouquet also traded internationally in prints, as is shown by the parcel of engravings brought in *'t jonge Willem*, which sailed from London on 16 January 1775, Kamer van Assurantie en Avarij, Amsterdam (hereafter cited as KVA) transcript XVI, 582. In this study, references are to the excellent collection by Ivo Schöffer in the Economisch-Historische Bibliotheek, Amsterdam.

[9] J. C. Riley, *International government finance and the Amsterdam capital market, 1740–1815* (Cambridge, 1980), pp. 11–14, 27.

[10] Alice Carter, 'Dutch foreign investment, 1738–1800', *Economica*, XV (1953), 328, 340. The benevolence of 1742 rated five *assuradeurs* between f.4,000 and f.10,000 – clearly an unsatisfactory assessment of the assets of underwriters – see W. F. H. Oldewelt (ed.), *Kohier van de personeele quotisatie te Amsterdam over het jaar 1742* (2 vols., Amsterdam, 1945), I, p. 14 and II, lists. Samuel Ricard (1780) remarked on the smaller number of guilder millionaires than supposed, but also on the broad distribution of assets among the wealthy which they held for investment, *Traité*, I, p. 207; see also above, p. 3 and below, Chapter 7, p. 246.

Europe[11] fell to the lot of eager merchants in the United Provinces. 'On the ruins of the trade of Antwerp lately so flourishing and commercial', reported Vicenzo Gussoni to Venice in 1635, 'has been built the wealth and splendour of Amsterdam.'[12] It was a frontier of risk and profit, but the new institutions drew on the accumulated expertise here of the Hansa cities, there of Antwerp with its rich heritage in Flanders. And stretching far beyond these urban achievements were the opportunities of the sea. The readiness of marine insurance in Amsterdam was both remarkable and precocious. The earliest surviving policy bears a date of 20 January 1592.[13] The famous regulations of 31 January 1598 set out procedures, drawing heavily on the practices of Antwerp. They contained little that was particularly new, but nevertheless set the norms for business which survived for a century and a half, until the reform of 1744. In the interval, as Violet Barbour has so admirably shown,[14] marine insurance grew in splendid competence, virtually came of age.

Two institutions to play a leading rôle in this development call for special comment. The *Kamer van Assurantie en Avarij*, prescribed in the regulations of 1598 and established in 1612.[15] Three *Commissarissen* or adjusters heard the depositions and settled the claims for compensation and general average – the term average, if we follow Lord Mansfield's definition, being used to signify 'a contribution to a general loss'. The rules applied in Amsterdam as elsewhere in Europe to come to terms with the perils of the sea. Their decisions are a chronicle of tribulation. Ivo Schöffer has given a remarkable survey of the sequence of settlements.[16] They mark out a panorama of trade, its movement, its riches, and to be sure, its shortcomings.

The Kamer van Assurantie, as Jean-Pierre Ricard reported (1722) exercised its jurisdiction in the Stadhuis within a stone's throw of that other great institution on the Dam, the Bourse. The latter established in 1611,[17] grew in prestige and flourished in commercial dominance.

[11] S. Ricard, *Traité*, I, pp. 388–391; A. Christensen, *Dutch trade to the Baltic about 1600* (The Hague, 1941), p. 18; Accarias de Sérionne, *La Richesse de la Hollande*, I, p. 25.

[12] P. J. Blok, *Relazione Veneziane* (The Hague, 1909), p. 250.

[13] H. L. V. de Groote, 'Zeeverzekering', in G. Asaert, Ph. M. Bosscher, J. R. Bruijn, W. J. Hoboken (eds.), *Maritieme geschiedenis der Nederlanden* (4 vols., Bussum, 1976–), I, p. 218.

[14] V. Barbour, 'Maritime risks and insurance in the seventeenth century', *Journal of Economic and Business History*, I (1928–29), 595–596.

[15] J. P. Vergouwen, *De geschiedenis der Makelaardij in Assurantiën hier te lande tot 1813* (The Hague, 1945), p. 45; I. Schöffer, *Toelichting bij de registers op de vonnissen*, KVA, I.

[16] I. Schöffer, 'De vonnissen in averij-grosse van de Kamer van Assurantie en Avarij te Amsterdam', *EHJ*, XXVI (1956).

[17] J.-P. Ricard, *Le Négoce d'Amsterdam*, p. 8; Joh. C. Breen, 'De juiste datum der opening van Amsterdam's eerste Beursgebouw', *Amstelodamum*, VII (1909), 209–214; Vergouwen, *De geschiedenis der Makelaardij*, pp. 45 et seq.

During the allotted hours of business, dealers found their customary places under the arcades, or near one of the forty-six numbered pillars, or in fair weather in the central courtyard itself (see Frontispiece and Plate 1).[18] The prestigious *Heeren Assuradeurs*[19] appeared at three named locations:

(a)   in the north-east arcade between pillars 4 and 5, alongside dealers in bullion, tobacco, and the West Indian trade.

(b)   in the centre courtyard at the level on one side of pillar 8 and on the other of 40, close to one of the groups of ship-brokers or *cargadors* and the merchants dealing with Hamburg/Bremen, France, Archangel, and whaling.

(c)   in the north-west arcade between pillars 43 and 44, next to the merchants concerned with Norway and part of the Baltic – Riga, Reval, Lübeck, Courland.

The location of interests on the *floor* of the Bourse thus pointed to one of the great strengths of the market of Amsterdam noted by many observers: the confluence of services. It was a powerful aid in combating competition. The flows of short-term capital through payments of premiums – since 1620, they were stipulated in cash[20] – were quickly absorbed into package deals of credit and freight. Take, for example, the case of Frederik Dibbetz, whom we shall encounter again as broker for insurance cover raised in Amsterdam by the Commercie Compagnie of Middelburg.[21] The *Naamen en Woonplaatsen van de Heeren Assuradeurs zo binnen als buyten deze Stad* published by Hendrik Sligtenhorst in 1757,[22] in the early days of the Seven Years' War, lists him in junior partnership with Sappius. In 1764, he acted alone for the Amsterdam policy on the *Haast U Langzaam* on its first voyage from Middelburg.[23] The Sligten-

---

[18] *GA, Amsterdam, Collectie van Bouwtekeningen Rokin van der Historisch-Topografische Atlas van Amsterdam*, 1801, Platte Grond van de Beurs te Amsterdam, met Aanwyzing van de standplaatsen der Kooplieden op de gewoone Beurstyden, volgens de nommers der Pilaaren, als mede de byzondere soort van Koopmanschappen waar in Jeder Dagelyks Handelt (J. C. Philips), see below, Plate 1, reproduced by kind permission of the Director, Gemeentelijke Archiefdienst, Amsterdam. It should be noted that, according to this plan, the *Assuradeurs* congregated at the north end of the Bourse, closest to the Damrak and the harbour. For an explanation of the development of this organisation of the Bourse, see N. W. Posthumus, *Inquiry into the History of Prices in Holland* (2 vols., Leiden, 1946–64), I, pp. lxvi–lxxiii.

[19] See below, p. 25. For a discussion of brokers, both Christian and Jewish, see S. Ricard, *Traité*, I, pp. 71–72.

[20] Ibid., I, p. 195; Accarias de Sérionne, *La Richesse de la Hollande*, I, p. 88.

[21] These policies are in *RAZ, Middelburgsche Commercie Compagnie* (hereafter *MCC*), 509.

[22] These directories were published regularly, originally by Hendrik Sligtenhorst (hereafter cited as *Sligtenhorst lists*). The list for 1767 already consigns the publication to his successor, Erve Hendrik Sligtenhorst en Pieter van Rees; this continues for the series used in this study.

[23] For the case-study of the *Haast U Langzaam* see below, Chapter 4.

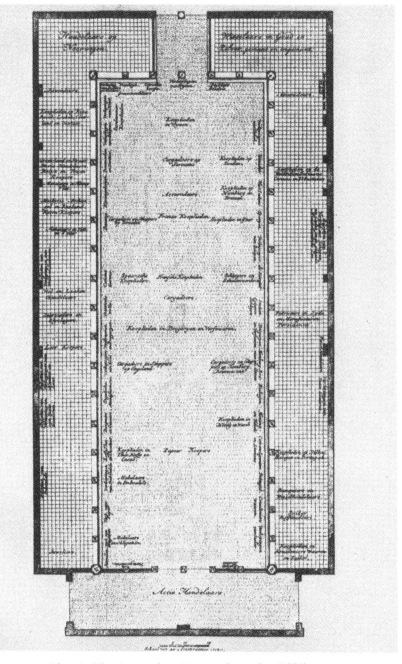

Plate 1. The Amsterdam Bourse: floor plan (1801)

horst lists for 1767 and 1768 enter him first in the partnership with Schorer. Then, at the end of 1768 he emerges, proudly no doubt, in partnership with his son; but no longer features in the Sligtenhorst lists from 1769, even though he continued for almost a decade to act as broker for the policies of the Middelburg Commercie Compagnie. The interests of Dibbetz stretched well beyond marine insurance brokerage. Cargoes from Surinam carried his finance. So did freight and warehousing.[24] He was on hand to take care of bills of exchange, accepted or protested. And when it came to lending cash to the needy planters of the colony – loans which were virtually share-cropping – the firm acted as issue-house to place the bonds on the Amsterdam market. The famous loan (before 1776) to the *Welbedagt* plantation provided for f.40,000 at 6 percent.[25] The business finance of Frederik Dibbetz en Zoon was one example among many of the complex affairs which gained strength and profit from diversity. It left insurance not alone and simple, but spliced into the finance and merchandise trading of the market.

At the same time, it would be misleading to assume that business was restricted to those two powerful institutions, on the one hand of the rulings in the Kamer, and on the other of the business of the Bourse. Effectively there was a market 'in the street'. The later lists of Sligten-horst gave details of days for underwriting. For example, the list of 1809: some firms were open for business every day – G. Bonnike en Zoonen, and Faesch en Compagnie; some wrote lines on set days, as J. H. Eickhoff, on Mondays and Thursdays; and others were not available on Saturdays, as Jan van Loen Janz. – 'every day except Saturday'. Even on the Bourse, it should be noted, the attendance was far from continuous.[26] On Saturdays, naturally, Jewish merchants were conspicuous by their absence: it was noted to be a thin day. Feast-days likewise took their toll. 'The jobbing in English funds is at a standstill', wrote Grand to Vergennes from Amsterdam on 8 April 1778, 'due to the Jewish feasts.'[27] And then again, business went according to the season. Already at the approach of autumn some dealers were ready to withdraw into commercial hibernation. It was much the same in London where the month of August sounded a retreat which gathered momentum in the late autumn and early winter.[28] The image of perfection was not easy to sustain on a

---

[24] *RAZ, MCC*, 508, fo. 38.

[25] J. P. van de Voort, *De Westindische plantages van 1720 tot 1795: financiën en handel* (Eindhoven, 1973), p. 285; see also his survey 'Nederlands kapitaal voor West-Indië in de 18de eeuw', *Spiegel historiael*, IX (1974).

[26] S. Ricard, *Traité*, I, p. 69.

[27] *AAE, CP, Hollande*, 536, fo. 43 vo., letter, Grand to Vergennes, Amsterdam, 8 April 1779.

[28] *British Parliamentary Papers, Report of the Parliamentary Committee, 1810* (226), IV, pp. 253, 316.

day-to-day basis. The market did not always 'clear' according to the classic formula; rather there were imperfections and these in time of crisis carried weight.

Further, the institutions of Amsterdam could not remain oblivious to change. Systems established in the early seventeenth century often did not accord with needs and performances in the late eighteenth. The tribulations of the older staples came to the surface in growing friction between staid organisations – companies, guilds, corporations, accredited brokers – and the swelling numbers of private, free-lance dealers. The growing importance of the commission trade in Amsterdam imposed a silent, profound re-orientation in the level and efficiency of the market. Such a complex movement seems to have had much in common with the invasion by 'private marketing' of formal commercial procedures, which Alan Everitt has observed in the case of England.[29]

The general rôle of brokers pointed to the salient issues. At the formal level of the market, their development was clear. Officially, they had an established position. Eleven took the oath in 1531.[30] And, at the founding of the Bourse, the city of Amsterdam set out their duties in an *Instructie voor de Makelaars* (31 January 1613).[31] From among them the Burgermeester was instructed to choose deputies and they 'made' the market for they reported the going rates and set up the price-currents. Through the seventeenth and eighteenth centuries, however, the operation of free-lance dealers – the *beunhazers* or unsworn *commies* – grew in significance.[32] They created a more volatile element, ready to go to earth when crisis loomed, as in 1763, again in 1772–73; and later too, in the growing hostilities after 1775–76. J. P. Vergouwen has shown how these changes were often slow, but the numbers of brokers grew with the expansion of the market. According to J.-P. Ricard (1722) they numbered 395, and, in addition, some 700 or 800 free-lance dealers joined in the daily business. They were exceptionally prompt in settling claims in insurance; he knew of only three who had demurred in settling claims for compensation.[33] Later, as we shall see, less than a hundred underwriters were engaged in insurance.

[29] A. Everitt, 'The marketing of agricultural produce', in J. Thirsk (ed.), *The Agrarian History of England and Wales*, IV (Cambridge, 1967), pp. 506–563; Accarias de Sérionne, *La Richesse de la Hollande*, II, p. 129.

[30] Vergouwen, *De geschiedenis der Makelaardij*, p. 34.

[31] Ibid., p. 49, citing H. Noordkerk, *Handvesten . . . der Stad Amstelredam* (3 vols., Amsterdam, 1748).

[32] Ibid., pp. 36, 52; *De Koopman, of Bydragen ten opbouw van Neerlands koophandel en zeevaard* (Amsterdam, 1770), II, pp. 34–35.

[33] Vergouwen, *De geschiedenis der Makelaardij*, pp. 52–53, giving the figure of about 100 brokers; J.-P. Ricard, *Le Négoce d'Amsterdam* (1723), pp. 248–249 settles for 50 to 60, presumably underwriters. Samuel Ricard (1780) in *Traité*, I, p. 194, supposes a group of about a hundred underwriters, see below, p. 29.

However, the sworn dealers lost more and more ground. In 1784, at the outcome of war, there were hardly 30; and just before French troops overran the country (1794) apparently only eight.[34] The growth in numbers of free-lance dealers no doubt created an element of uncertainty, for as we shall see later the turnover in numbers was marked.[35] Throughout the century, the official brokers ferociously defended their privileges against the 'beunhazerij' and pressed to form a guild. The bouts of bickering over demarcation lines may be seen as a response to change, but such divisions also indicated a degree of weakness. When the market fell into the disarray of crisis, each fissure soon widened into a crevasse. The strains to the structure altered the time-horizons of financiers and the risks they were prepared to share.

The themes of public office and private enterprise found their way into the formulation of insurance policies. The public nature of established office served a purpose. It could ensure the registration of policies, with attendant advantages and disadvantages. A declaration could give notice of sailing, preferred course, destination, cargo value – valid for any claims for compensation. But once on the books, details could filter out and attract the attention of pirates and privateers to try the main chance. Such fears of loss were often enough to make insurance a private affair, but this carried a penalty. Subsequent claims for compensation which failed to give the destination and value of the cargo were not necessarily valid. In the eighteenth century, the gap between public and private policies tended to close, if not disappear. To all intents and purposes, the form of the insurance policy was largely routine, set out in print with blank spaces to be completed. In England, Lord Mansfield judging the classic case of Carter v. Boehm (1766) declared that a claim for compensation required all the facts to be known. However, it was only in 1779 that the underwriters in London finally agreed on the form of the famous Lloyd's Policy, which was to last so long.[36] It belonged to a substantial settlement in procedures, largely shared by the hierarchies of insurance dealings in The Netherlands and elsewhere in Europe.

The early pre-eminence of Amsterdam implied a hierarchy. The federal system of the Republic and a natural individualism exercised a profound influence on the diversification of economic institutions, but the pyramid was clear by comparison with other maritime cities. In Middelburg, which dominated Zeeland, insurance was regulated on 30

---

[34] Vergouwen, *De geschiedenis der Makelaardij*, pp. 52–53, 75–77.

[35] See below, pp. 29–33.

[36] C. Molloy, *De Jure Maritimo et Navali* (London, 1676), p. 241; B.-M. Emergion, *Traité des Assurances et des Contrats à la Grosse* (2 vols., Marseilles, 1783), I, p. 33. For variations in printing, see below, Plates 2, 3, and 5. I. Kimura compares the form of the Lloyd's Policy to that of Florence (1523), see 'Die Entstehung der Lloyd's Seeversicherungspolice', *Hitotsubashi Journal of Commerce and Management*, VII (1972), 18–20.

September 1600, on the lines of the Amsterdam Act of 1598;[37] this lasted until the amplification of 1719. The officers of the Kamer were to change annually in March, and so at the beginning of the favourable season for navigation. In Rotterdam, the important *ordonnantie* of 12 March 1604 set out rules for insurance and average. Thus a Kamer van Assurantie existed to settle claims. An abortive attempt was made in 1635 to set up a joint-stock company – on the lines of a similar proposal seven years earlier in Amsterdam,[38] but such moves were realised only in 1720–21 with the establishment of the first important insurance company in The Netherlands, the famous Maatschappij van Assurantie, Disconteering en Beleening der Stad Rotterdam,[39] which has survived after two and half centuries.

The Maatschappij van Assurantie had a share capital of f.12 million, largely drawn from local finance, for 316 out of the 388 subscribers came from the city itself.[40] In the absence of a broadly based association of underwriters, the Maatschappij spread risks by bringing together capital from a wide range of local sources. At the same time, it should be noted that its activity was not confined to marine insurance: it had more of the character of a commercial bank or finance house, discounting bills of exchange, advancing credit on the security of goods stored in ware-houses, with keys in the hands of the secretary of the city. A list of 31 December 1728,[41] for example, gave pride of place to the stock-piles of iron (24.7 percent). Pepper and cinnamon took another 18.1 percent; linens 12.2 percent; tea and coffee 8.6 percent; tobacco 7.9 percent; wheat and other grain another 7.2 percent. All these in total accounted for more than three-quarters of the f.614,600 stored. As for insurance, the company also dealt in life and fire cover which were more susceptible to

---

[37] Vergouwen, *De geschiedenis der Makelaardij*, p. 110; A. J. E. Jolles, *Bijdrage tot de kennis van de ontwikkeling de zee-assurantie in de Vereenigde Nederlanden* (Leiden, 1867), pp. 46–48.

[38] Vergouwen, *De geschiedenis der Makelaardij*, pp. 32, 78–82; Jolles, *Bijdrage tot de kennis van de ontwikkeling de zee-assurantie*, p. 45; C. H. Slechte, 'De Maatschappij van Assurantie, Discontering en Beleening der stad Rotterdam van 1720, bekekenen naar haar productie factoren over de periode 1720–1874', *Rotterdams Jaarboekje*, 7e.R, VIII (1970), 254; H. C. Hazewinkel, *Geschiedenis van Rotterdam* (3 vols., Rotterdam, 1940–42), II, p. 223.

[39] Accarias de Sérionne, *La Richesse de la Hollande*, I, p. 96; Vergouwen, *De geschiedenis der Makelaardij*, pp. 32, 88–95; G. van Rijn, 'De Actienhandel in 1720 te Rotterdam en de Maatschappij van Assurantie, Disconteering en Beleening dezer Stad', *Rotterdamsch Jaarboekje*, VI (1899), p. 11 et seq.; Hazewinkel, *Geschiedenis van Rotterdam*, II, pp. 223–226, 229; Slechte, 'De Maatschappij van Assurantie, Discontering en Beleening der stad Rotterdam van 1720', p. 253; F. Kracht, *Die Rotterdamer Seeversicherungs-Börse: ihre Entwicklung, Bedeutung, und Bedingungen* (Weimar, 1922), pp. 61–64.

[40] C. H. Slechte, 'Het aandeel van de Rotterdamse Regenten in de actie-handel van 1720', *Rotterdams Jaarboekje*, 7e.R, X (1972), p. 234.

[41] *GA, Rotterdam, Maatschappij van Assurantie, Discontering en Beleening der Stad Rotterdam* (hereafter cited as *Maatschappij van Assurantie*), 53, 31 December 1728.

fixed probabilities. These became profitable lines of business as the century drew to its close. The rôle of the company was thus both complex and profound.

In contrast, Amsterdam continued to rely on private insurers, and this system held sway for as long as the financial resources of the Dam rested on personal fortunes. Abbé Desnoyers, an alert observer, had few doubts when he wrote from Amsterdam to the Comte de Vergennes on 20 February 1776. 'The *Corps des Assureurs*', he declared, 'is the most powerful to intervene in the trade of Europe and the one whose conduct exerts most influence on public opinion . . .'[42] In contrast, the insurers in Rotterdam tended to keep to customary upper limits – Philipp Nemnich travelling in The Netherlands (1809) noted that for higher cover, shippers and ship-owners were obliged to go to Amsterdam.[43] The accounts were settled by internal bill of exchange.[44] At the fall of the Republic, the Dam prevailed in substance[45] but new ideas also came from Rotterdam; for example, the Regulations of the Maatschappij van Assurantie (28 January 1721) proved a model for the reform in Amsterdam in 1744.

Thus, although Amsterdam emerged at the top in the profile of markets, there were dependent sub-hierarchies, encouraged by distance, the flows of trade, and the proximity of other ports. The capital base of the Maatschappij gave it a widening zone of influence. It could act as a good *lead*, appearing first on a policy, for brokers no doubt found it convenient to approach first the Maatschappij van Assurantie before other private insurers followed in writing their lines. There was a 'pecking order' within the city.

At the same time, the Delta showed growth and convergence. In Middelburg there was an Assurantie Compagnie. This was cited in *Het groote tafereel der dwaasheid* (1720) with a capital of f.1.2 million, along with nineteen other insurance companies formed in The Netherlands;[46] but the subsequent history of this and the others is not entirely clear. Certainly a company of the same name acted as *lead* in the 1764 policy for the *Haast U Langzaam* on its first voyage in the slave trade.[47] Gradually

---

[42] *AAE, CP, Hollande*, 528, fo. 221 ro., letter, Desnoyers to Vergennes, The Hague, 20 February 1776.
[43] S. Ricard, *Traité*, I, p. 192; P. A. Nemnich, *Original-Beiträge zur eigentlichen Kenntniss von Holland* (Tübingen, 1809), p. 395.
[44] *RAZ, MCC*, 509 passim: the accounts of the Middelburgsche Commercie Compagnie in Amsterdam were settled by internal bill of exchange.
[45] Vergouwen, *De geschiedenis der Makelaardij*, pp. 31–33.
[46] G. van Rijn, 'Die Actienhandel in 1720 te Rotterdam en de Maatschappij van Assurantie, Disconteering en Beleening dezer Stad', *Rotterdamsch Jaarboekje*, VI (1899), p. 10. H. G. Schuddebeurs lists this as Maatschappij tot het Asseureeren van Schepen en Goederen binnen de Stad Middelburg, *EHJ*, XIV (1928), p. 62.
[47] *RAZ, MCC*, 509 (1764).

there were further signs of conformity in the delta of Meuse/Rhine/ Scheldt. The Societeit van Assurantie, established in Rotterdam in 1770 with a capital of f.400,000, offered cover from f.5 to 10,000 for ships' cargoes and against fire.[48] An agent was appointed in Amsterdam and the Societeit proposed to underwrite in conjunction with companies in Antwerp and Middelburg to a limit of liability of f.20,000. The risks were therefore spread and the maximum increased. There were, to be sure, hierarchies within hierarchies!

STRUCTURES OF INSURANCE MARKETS

The task implied in this discussion is to examine the nature of the ascendency of Amsterdam. The strength of the insurance market depended on the large number of underwriters, their wealth and resources, their ability to continue in business – such magnitudes are difficult to assess. Some of the information can be found in the Sligtenhorst lists. Those surviving must, however, be accepted with some serious reservations as records of insurers in The Netherlands. They appear to have been collated principally for Amsterdam, and there are clearly shortcomings for other cities. For the latter, entries in the lists tended to be random and probably reflected the existence or absence of business with Amsterdam. The Sligtenhorst list for 1757, for example, gives 15 names for Rotterdam, and they include the notable Joan Ozy en Zoon. However, none of the names appear for the four brokers who delivered business that year to the Maatschappij van Assurantie.[49] These included the substantial Gregorius Mees en Zoon who contributed f.18,300 of the total of f.26,000 on which brokerage fees were paid. Similarly, J. Witkop has commented on the 1779 list that it included 14 entries for Rotterdam, but none of the 24 underwriters who wrote lines on a policy for a slave-ship sailing that year from the port.[50] Again, the 1778–79 balance of the Maatschappij van Assurantie[51] gave commissions on f.144,230 written for eight brokers, including R. Mees en Zoon (re-styled from Gregorius Mees) for f.43,010; none appeared in the Sligtenhorst list. Another brokerage partnership entered in the Maatschappij accounts for 1778–79, Dubbledemuts and Van Dijk, finally won an entry in the Sligtenhorst lists for 1786–89; but by 1792 they had disappeared. Franco and Adriaan Dubbledemuts, it should be noted, also did business in chandling for ships sailing from Middelburg – they supplied bread, for

---

[48] Hazewinkel, *Geschiedenis van Rotterdam*, II, pp. 223–226,
[49] GA, Rotterdam, *Maatschappij van Assurantie*, 348, fo. 19.
[50] J. Witkop, *De ontwikkeling van het Verzekeringswezen te Rotterdam* (Rotterdam, 1928), p. 24.
[51] GA, Rotterdam, *Maatschappij van Assurantie*, 358, 30 June 1779.

example, for the third voyage of the *Haast U Langzaam* (1769–70);[52] and they finally made the Sligtenhorst lists for 1786–88. They were entered as underwriting agents for the Assurantie Compagnie of Bruges.

The same shortcomings emerge for Middelburg: the entries do not correspond with the existing facilities. In the first place, the Assurantie Compagnie of Middelburg receives an entry in 1769 and 1771; and again in 1792. The agent in Amsterdam was Pieter van den Broeke. He too had entries only in the lists of 1769, 1771, and 1792. The Assurantie Compagnie was, after all, the *lead* in all the policies written in Middelburg for the eight voyages of the *Haast U Langzaam* (1764–79). Most of the 17 underwriters and two brokers concerned do not appear in the Sligtenhorst lists. In the hull and cargo insurance of 15 October 1766, for example, Scheyderuyt de Vos, van Nieuwvliet wrote lines for f.1,200 in both policies,[53] with Daniel van den Berg acting as agent. He is entered in the Sligtenhorst lists for 1767 and 1768 at the house of Ambrosius Tulleken in Amsterdam, who clearly held the agency. Again, Jacobus Frederik Landsheer and Jan Joseph Negre began to write lines in the policies of 1766 and 1770 respectively but finally make the Sligtenhorst lists for 1782, and then apparently became a fixture. As a sign of the diversity of business, Landsheer was one of the commissioners for the loan to the planters of Essequibo and Demerara raised in Middelburg in 1772.[54]

In addition to Amsterdam, Rotterdam, and Middelburg, there are entries in the Sligtenhorst lists for other towns, mainly in the province of Holland and the Noorderkwartier. The entries are for various periods:

Broek in Waterland (1757–92)
Edam (1778–92)
Groningen (1786)
Haarlem (1777–86)
Jisp (1757–83)
Maassluis (1782–83)
Oostzaan (1757)
De Rijp (1757–79)
Utrecht (1786–92)
Zaandam (1777–89)

In the insurance business of Amsterdam, the underwriters in the small towns of North Holland clearly had a part to play. Not least, no doubt, that they were close to the ventures of whaling to Greenland and the Davis Strait. Zaanstreek was virtually an industrial estate and included

[52] *RAZ, MCC*, 508, fo. 57; Vergouwen, *De geschiedenis der Makelaardij*, pp. 98–99.
[53] See below, Chapter 4.
[54] *GA, Amsterdam, Familie-Papieren, Archief Heshuysen*, B. 221. 170, 171, 178.

factories – the *traan-kokerijen* – to process the oil and blubber returning from the Arctic.[55] As we shall see later in this study, the *prijscouranten* of Amsterdam did not quote premiums for whaling, but the service may have been offered through these satellite agencies. Whaling flourished less after the 1770s,[56] and this no doubt contributed to the palpable decline of the Noorderkwartier for which A. M. van der Woude is such an excellent guide.[57] One sign among others for our purpose here was the shrinking number of these insurers in the Sligtenhorst lists: eleven in 1757 and in 1779; only eight in 1787; and five in 1792. Of the last, there were three important names to be noted in Broek in Waterland: Harmen Bakker, Cornelis Dekker and Claas Ploeger, the last continuing a long line of underwriters over the preceding 35 years.

The Sligtenhorst lists undoubtedly have many shortcomings in surveying insurance dealers for the whole of The Netherlands; they nevertheless point out the underwriters rather than the brokers of Amsterdam. In this, they give some insights into two important aspects of the market – its hinterland and its continuity.

THE HINTERLAND OF AMSTERDAM INSURANCE

The insurance market in Amsterdam drew firstly from a pool of financial assets wider than the city itself. Underwriters resident in satellite towns had agents on the Dam. This emerges when the lists are composed with the lines written in the policies for the *Haast U Langzaam*. Scheyderuyt de Vos, van Nieuwvliet (in the Middelburg policies of 1766) appears, as we have already seen, in the Sligtenhorst lists of 1767 and 1768 in the house of Ambrosius Tulleken on the Herengracht. Tulleken himself also wrote lines in the Middelburg policies of 1764 and 1766, with Daniel van den Berg acting as agent there. He also appeared in the Sligtenhorst lists of 1767–68. In the important Amsterdam policy of 3 May 1777 on the cargo of the *Haast U Langzaam*, there were 17 underwriters, two from outside the city: Jan de Wit entered in the Sligtenhorst list for De Rijp (1767–69); and Nicolaas des Amories of Rotterdam appeared in the lists of 1777–82 with De Vries en Zoonen acting as agents in Amsterdam. Jan de Wit, it should be noted, wrote the line himself in the 1779 policy; but De Vries en Zoonen accepted on behalf of Des Amories. In the 1786

---

[55] P. Dekker, *De laatste bloeiperiode van de Nederlandse arctische walvis- en robbevangst, 1761–1775* (Zaltbommel, 1971), pp. 19, 27; C. de Jong, 'Walvisvaart', in G. Asaert et al., *Maritieme geschiedenis der Nederlanden*, II, pp. 309–315.

[56] P. Dekker, 'De bloeitijd van de walvisvaart op onze wadden eilanden', *Ons Zeewezen*, LXIII, 9 (1974), 26; J. R. Bruijn, 'Zeevarenden', in G. Asaert et al., *Maritieme geschiedenis der Nederlanden*, III, p. 150; C. de Jong, 'Walvisvaart', ibid., III, p. 340.

[57] A. M. van der Woude, *Het Noorderkwartier. Een regionaal historisch onderzoek in de demografische en economische geschiedenis van westelijk Nederland van de late middeleeuwen tot het begin van de negentiende eeuw*, AAG, Bijdragen, XVI, Wageningen, 1972.

Sligtenhorst list: D. E. van Berkel in Amsterdam acted as agent for Adriaan Steen en Zoon of Rotterdam, and vice versa. Each received separate entries. A final example, this time for 1787: P. C. van Baggen, living on the Prinsengracht, was agent for Lambert Vossenberg of Utrecht. And there were others. Clearly, the net of Amsterdam under-writing stretched well beyond the confines of the city itself.

AMSTERDAM UNDERWRITERS: A PROBLEM OF CONTINUITY

The *corps* of marine underwriters in Amsterdam was composed of individuals, family firms, partnerships. As such, the market contended with that classic problem of continuity faced all too often by institutions of the *ancien régime* when they depended on blood, family and dynasty. This great reality of history combined with another: the effective presence of underwriters active in the market. Samuel Ricard (1780) cites some hundred 'particuliers'.[58] The numbers of entries in the Sligtenhorst lists approximate to this (see Graph 1). In order to assess the profile of this body of underwriters and their continuity, it is possible to select the entries in a number of the Sligtenhorst lists and follow their survival in subsequent lists. This gives what may be called, for the purpose in hand, a survival rate. It is expressed here as a percentage of the original list (see Table 1 and Graph 1). These survival (or loss) rates are primarily related to the performance of each group, and not to the rise or fall in the total numbers, although naturally both respond to the same pressures. The samples (or cohorts) divide into two groups:

(a) 1757, 1767, and 1771: these appear to have lost on average about 7 percent annually over the period of a decade, falling then to about half. The 1771 cohort reached 43 percent at the ten years' mark, this being due to a sharp loss in 1778–79.

(b) 1777, 1782, and 1786: here the cohorts lost at least 11 percent annually over the decade and in the case of 1777 about 12½ percent. The losses were marked during the prelude and onset of the Fourth Anglo-Dutch War, particularly in the years 1779–82, and were even more for the cohorts of 1782 and 1786; there was a clear disaster in 1787. The commotion of the Patriots, their revolt and subsequent surrender to the Prussian army (10 Octo-ber), must no doubt carry the responsibility.[59] The cohort of 1786 lost a third in a year.

[58] S. Ricard, *Traité*, I, p. 194. The numbers of private underwriters and agents in the Sligtenhorst lists fluctuated (see Graph 1): from 77 in 1757, they fell to 68 in 1771 but reached 91 in 1782. In 1787, the entries had fallen to 57; in 1792, they were 52.

[59] S. Schama, *Patriots and Liberators: Revolution in the Netherlands, 1780–1813* (London, 1977), pp. 110–131.

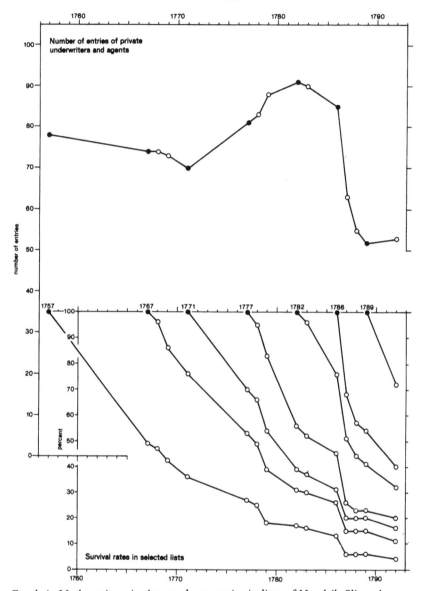

Graph 1. Underwriters in Amsterdam: entries in lists of Hendrik Sligtenhorst

The fortunes of these different groups, if the Sligtenhorst lists are reasonably correct for Amsterdam, point out two sets of conclusions. Firstly, that the heaviest turnover of underwriters in the market of Amsterdam responded not so much to financial crises – severe though they were in the bankruptcies of 1763 and 1772–73 – but rather to war

Table 1. *Underwriters in Amsterdam: survival rates* (in percentages)

Year of the original list = 100	Interval in years			
	1	2	5	10
1757	93	87	70	49
1767	96	86	72	53
1771	94	89	73	43
1777	95	83	56	26
1782	96	89	51	32
1786	68	57	44	30

and political instability in 1779–83 and in 1786–87. Upheavals of such magnitudes required an arbiter but it seemed that neither the federal system of The Netherlands nor the market of the Dam could at once provide enough control to ensure equilibrium.

Secondly, the total number of entries appears to have fallen between the lists of 1757 and 1771, from 77 to 68 respectively. This coincided with a period of the low premiums of relative peace and augmented international competition which followed the Peace of Paris (1763). The lists from 1777 to 1782, however, show the number of underwriters and their agencies to rise to a peak (91 in 1782). The rise in war-risks increased the demand for insurance; and the concomitant element of speculation. This and the spate of high premiums and smuggling may have attracted many 'sleeping' underwriters to re-enter the market in active business. And it may have been these insurers, listed in 1777, 1778, and 1779, who suffered most in the war and in 1787.

For the period as a whole of 35 years, however, the salient characteristic is mobility. The family firms surviving in 1792 from the original list of 1757 carry names to be counted on the fingers of one hand: such as Abraham Bruyn, Jacob de Clerq en Zoon, Adriaan Scharff. Mobility and adaptability were in many respects signs of strength; but for insurance it held a core of weakness in that, at the first signs of trouble, the 'particuliers' would go to earth. It was not the least of problems faced by the market in the late 1770s.

The turnover in membership also emerges from the lists of insurers writing lines in the policies for the eight voyages of the *Haast U Langzaam*. These belong to the case-study discussed later in the book. Of the 39 Amsterdam underwriters (or partnerships) in thirteen policies over 14 years (1764–77), five listed in 1764–68 remained active in 1775–77 (see Graph 2).

Underwriters:	1764 H	1764 C	1766 H	1766 C	1768 H	1768 C	1770 H	1770 C	1772 H	1772 C	1775 H	1775 C	1777 H	1777 C	1777 C
Nic. en Aren. van STAPHORST	●	●			●	●	●	●			●	●			
A. SCHARFF	●														
Wed. Dan. Hen. van HAMEL	●														
Gerard CLIFFORD	●		●		●	●									
Jan Fred. ALBRECHT en Zoon	●														
Paulus van DRIEST	●		●		●	●									
Jan van de POLL en Comp.	●		●				●	●	●	●	●	●	●	●	
Jac. van de POLL	●		●		●	●			●	●			●	●	
Barent LUBELEY	●				●	●	●	●	●	●					
A. SCHARFF Jnr.	●														
Jean NEEL en Zoon			●		●	●									
Dirk VERSTEEGH en Zoon					●	●									●
C. J. van der LYN					●	●									
Christiaan van NOORLE					●	●	●	●	●	●					
VALCKENIER en Comp.					●	●			●	●					●
Pieter ENGELEN en Comp.					●	●	●	●							
Hendrik NIEULANDT					●	●									
Wed. Jan BRUYN Abrmz.							●	●	●	●	●	●			
J. PAUW							●	●							
Pieter SWAANENBURGH									●	●	●	●			●
Ysbrand SEVERIJN									●	●	●	●			
J., D., en W. van VOLLENHOVEN											●	●			
Nic. en Jac. van STAPHORST											●	●			
Anthonij MEIJNTS													●	●	
Christiaan van ORSOIJ													●	●	
Harman van de POLL													●	●	●
SEVERIJN en BRUYN													●	●	●
Abraham BRUYN Jansz.													●	●	●
Jacob LUDEN															●
Johannes LUDEN															●
Dirk LUDEN															●
Jurriaan BARTELSE															●
Jan WILS															●
Gerrit VERSTEEGH en Zoon															●
SWAAN en SWART															●
Jan de WIT															●
P. de VRIES Clsz.															●
De VRIES en Zoon															●
N. des AMORIES															●

H = hull
C = cargo

Graph 2. Underwriting in Amsterdam for the *Haast U Langzaam*

Jacobus van de Poll
Jan van de Poll en Compagnie
Nicolaas en Arend van Staphorst (Arend only from 1768)
Valckenier en Compagnie
Dirk Versteegh en Zoon

The first belonged to the well-established group who survived from 1757 to 1787. Also in this group but signing policies over shorter periods were:

Barent Lubeley
Christiaan van Noorle (1768–72)
Wed. Jan Bruyn Abrmz. (1770–75)
Abraham Bruyn Jansz. (1777)

The last and supplementary cargo policy of 3 May 1777 is particularly remarkable, for it included eleven new underwriters. This may have arisen from the widening opportunities for smuggling through the West Indian islands to the American Republic, then at war.[60] In sum, the changing sequence of policies for the *Haast U Langzaam* underlines a progressive turnover among underwriters, if not always in the market, at least in the type of business they were willing to accept.

Two basic themes, then, emerge for Amsterdam in the 1760s and 1770s: the market was dominated by a large assembly of private insurers or partnerships; and the capital resources were broad, in the sense that investments found opportunities for choices which could diversify. In addition, insurers could restrict their commitments – withdrawing from the market in 'off-seasons', underwriting for a large number of limited sums, combining influential firms with a *peleton* of capable dealers. There is little surprise to find that the names of substantial merchants appearing in the Sligtenhorst list for 1768 continued for a number of years: for example, Jean Etienne Fizeaux (entered last in the list of 1783); Raymond de Smeth (listed until 1778); and Jan en Joseph Texier (still in the list for 1786). The last proved to have a special interest in delivering naval stores to ports in western France in order to provide for return cargoes of colonial goods. For example, *'t goed Fortuyn* sailed from Bordeaux on 16 May 1777 with 47 casks of sugar on account for Jan Texier.[61] He was also the principal shipper in the fatal convoy of December 1779, to be discussed later. Yet important though these names were, none survived in the lists after the francophile Patriot upheaval in the city in 1787.

FURTHER COMMENTS ON CONTINUITY AND RESOURCES: AMSTERDAM, ROTTERDAM, AND MIDDELBURG

Some further aspects of the problem of continuity and contingent resources emerge from the policies for the *Haast U Langzaam*. These have the advantage of being related to the same ship and were placed in three great commercial centres: Middelburg, naturally, for the whole sequence; Amsterdam for 1764–77; Rotterdam for the last voyage of

[60] See below, pp. 100–102.
[61] *KVA*, XVI, 520.

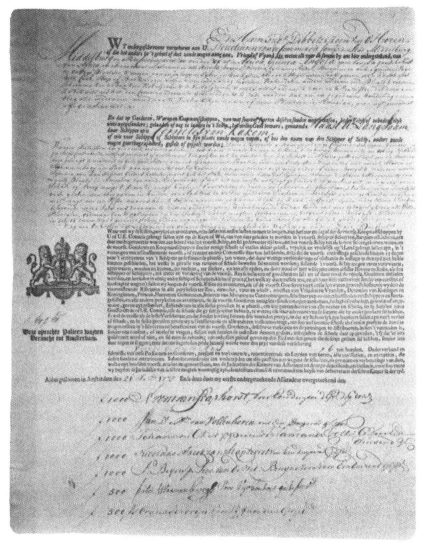

Plate 2. Amsterdam cargo policy (21 January 1775)

1779–81. Examples of the forms of cargo policies used in Amsterdam (1775), Rotterdam (1779), and Middelburg (1772), are given in Plates 2, 3, 4, 5, and 6. It will be noted at once that although the general form of underwriting was similar, there were nevertheless significant differences in the printed and handwritten sections. There were, therefore, the possibilities of ambiguity to be construed. I have not been able to ascertain whether the principle of *contra preferentum* prevailed; but

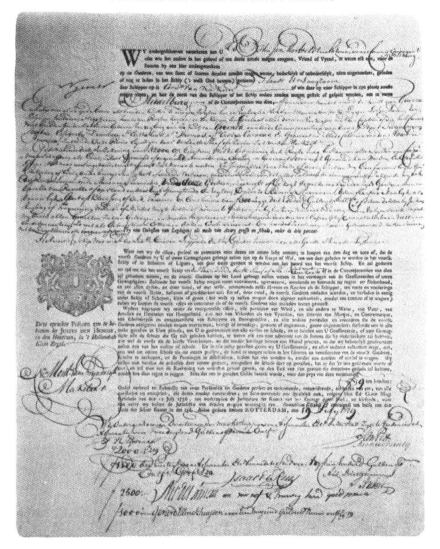

Plate 3. Rotterdam cargo policy (19 July 1779), recto

presumably the employment of brokers implied that ambiguities would
have been construed to the advantage of the insurer. In Amsterdam, it
appeared to be a regular procedure that an underwriter wrote lines on
both hull and cargo policies. The second cargo policy of 3 May 1777 was
an exception, in which 14 of the 17 underwriters were not committed to
insurance on the hull.

The details of this underwriting in three markets appear in Table 2. In

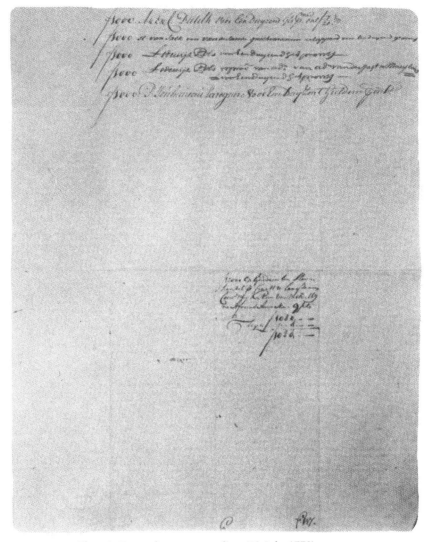

Plate 4. Rotterdam cargo policy (19 July 1779), verso

Amsterdam 39 underwriters handled thirteen policies compared with only 17 underwriters for sixteen policies in Middelburg.[62] It should be noted that the policies for cargo insurance in 1764 and 1766 in Amsterdam appear to be missing; and the policies for 1779 were not taken out there. This sequence is summarised in Graph 2. The turnover in Amsterdam shows each underwriter on average to have been concerned with only three policies. Middelburg had two and a half times that perform-

<hr>

[62] *RAZ, MCC,* 509.

Table 2. *The structure of insurance policies for the* Haast U Langzaam[a]

	Amsterdam (1764–77)	Middelburg (1764–79)	Rotterdam (1779)
No. of policies	13	16	2
Total lines	115	128	11
No. of underwriters	39	18[b]	11[c]
Average lines per underwriter	2.9	7.1	1.0
No. of lines per policy:			
minimum	6	1	2
maximum	17[d]	11	9
most frequent	7 (in six policies)	10 (in seven policies)	–
Range of sums accepted:			
minimum	f.400	f.180	f.1,000
maximum	f.2,000	f.10,800	f.2,500
Sums accepted:			
most frequent	f.1,000	f.300	f.1,000
% of total	46.5	3.8	40.0

[a] For hull and cargo policies outward from Middelburg.
[b] Includes the Assurantie Compagnie te Middelburg.
[c] Includes the Maatschappij van Assurantie, Discontering en Beleening der stad Rotterdam and the Societeit van Assurantie, together with J. F. Landsheer and J. J. Negre of Middelburg for the hull policy.
[d] Excluding this supplementary cargo policy for May 1777, the maximum is twelve.

ance, so that it appears to have been relatively easier to drum up support on the Dam. The minimum number of underwriters per policy was six; and the maximum 17 (for the supplementary cargo policy in 1777; otherwise a maximum of 12). The most frequent was a policy with seven underwriters. In Middelburg, the range was lower, between one and 11, with the most frequent being 10 underwriters (in eight policies).

Similar differences in the capital structure emerge. Samuel Ricard (1780) noted that it was a maxim of prudent underwriting to limit lines to between f.1,000 and f.2,000, although sums outside these norms could be arranged. In Amsterdam, the amounts ranged in the policies from f.400 to f.2,000. In Middelburg, they started at f.180 and went as high as f.10,800. The distribution can be seen in Table 2. While Amsterdam appeared measured and compact – 46.5 percent of the total came from lines of f.1,000, Middelburg had a wide and uneven spread. The most frequent line was for f.300 (3.8 percent of the total), although other amounts favoured were f.600 and f.1,200 (these, it should be noted were round amounts of £50, £100, and £200 vlaams). The large amounts came from two underwriters: Jan Frederik Landsheer and Jan Joseph Negre. Both, clearly, were men of substance; they survived the troubles of the 1780s, and re-emerged in the Sligtenhorst lists of 1787 and 1792. From the details of the policies, it is clear they worked in association, for Negre acted as *procureur* for Landsheer in the policies from 1775 to 1779. Jan Joseph Negre appears twice in the Sligtenhorst lists, first in Middelburg and then in Rotterdam. There he had as agent the important broker Jan Martveldt, with his office in the Boompjes. However, Landsheer and Negre were not alone in taking the larger unit risks. There was also the Assurantie Compagnie of Middelburg, which acted as *lead* and provided most of the higher performance. For amounts of f.6,000 and over, only Landsheer put up f.24,000 (the total of three policies); but the Assurantie Compagnie f.46,800 (the total of six policies). On average, the differences were not great, but the ability to repeat the performance clearly lay with the Compagnie. This insurance, it should be noted, referred to cargo, not hull, policies.

There remains the contribution of Rotterdam, the stand-in for Amsterdam in the 1779 policies. The hull insurance was signed in Rotterdam on 20 July 1779 by Jan Martveldt on behalf of Landsheer and Negre. For the cargo insurance, there were nine underwriters in all. The directors of the companies signed as company underwriters: the Maatschappij van Assurantie for f.2,000 and the Societeit van Assurantie for f.1,500. The private underwriters included Nicolaas des Amories, who signed for f.2,500. He also appears in the last policy in Amsterdam (3 May 1777), with P. de Vries Clsz. acting as *procureur* or agent. In the Sligtenhorst list for 1768, the pair appear in partnership, with their office located at the Raampoort. With Des Amories signing in person in Rotterdam and by proxy in Amsterdam, the partnership or syndicate appears to have straddled the two cities. We have already seen similar flexibility between Middelburg and Rotterdam, and between Amsterdam and the Zeeland city. For the latter in 1764–67, Frederik Dibbetz appeared in partnership with Schorer for the policies taken out on the Dam. From January 1775, Daniel Steven Schorer was underwriting policies for the Commercie Compagnie in Middelburg. If the two were the same person, the liaison between the markets is clear.

The insurance market in Amsterdam before the Fourth Anglo-Dutch War, therefore, appears to have had distinct characteristics and undoubted strengths. It relied on a broad spread of private insurers, able to enter and leave the market with a capability to put up the necessary capital. This flexibility so important in expansion and in time of peace, came under severe testing in wartime conditions. The year July 1780 to

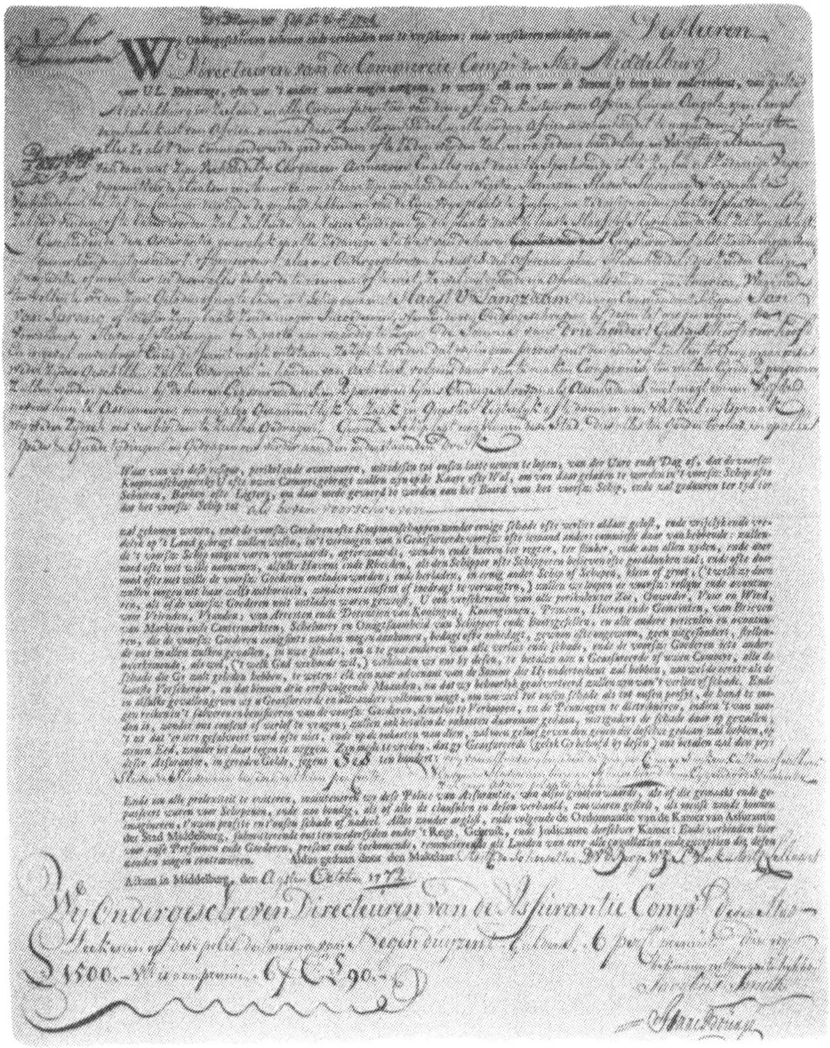

Plate 5. Middelburg cargo policy (8 October 1772), recto

June 1781 proved to be a year of heavy losses: the accounts of the Maatschappij van Assurantie in Rotterdam turned in a deficit on underwriting of f.82,350,[63] of an order unknown in at least the preceding half century (see Graph 3). For Amsterdam, the same no doubt prevailed and it served to underscore weaknesses in structure. The formation of companies and acceptance of agencies offered a solution in keeping with

[63] *GA, Rotterdam, Maatschappij van Assurantie*, 360, fo. 99 ro., 30 June 1781.

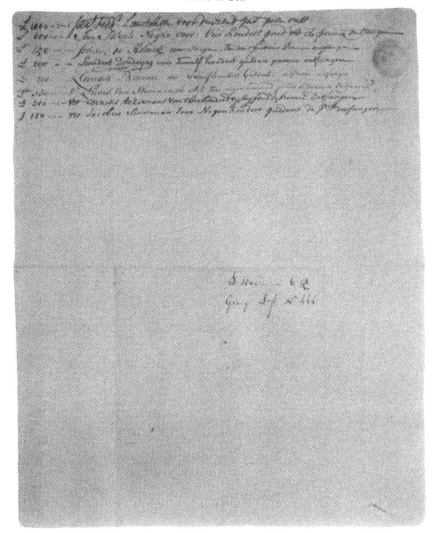

Plate 6. Middelburg cargo policy (8 October 1772), verso

the developments of the eighteenth century. These provide an indicator of subtle but complex pressures at work.

CONTINUITY IN AMSTERDAM INSURANCE: THE ARRIVAL OF COMPANIES

In the late eighteenth century, corporate companies made their appearance in Amsterdam alongside the family firms and partnerships, but

40

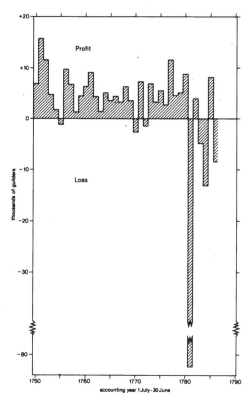

Graph 3. Rotterdam: underwriting profits of the Maatschappij van Assurantie

mainly in the growing business of fire and life insurance. These lines of business were naturally susceptible to actuarial valuations more precise than those prevailing in marine insurance. However, in spite of this bias, their presence added to the substance of the market. C. H. Slechte noted the establishment of the Assurantie Compagnie voor Brand in 1771,[64] and this appears in the Sligtenhorst list for 1777 (the lists are missing for 1772–76) alongside the new entry for the Nederlandse Assurantie Compagnie te Amsterdam voor Brand. The list of 1783 gives the Amsterdamse Assurantie Maatschappij. The list for 1786 includes the Assurantie Maatschappij op Brand, making in all for that year four companies by name; and in addition there were eight agencies for foreign companies.[65] The important characteristic of the companies was, for our purposes here, continuity. Unlike individual underwriters, they survived

[64] C. H. Slechte, *Geschiedenis van de Brandverzekering in Nederland* (Amsterdam, 1971), p. 2; and see above, note 46.
[65] See below, p. 46.

41

the troubles of 1787, but as their titles disclose, their business was notably in the more predictable fire and life insurance. Later, in the early nineteenth century, companies specifically concerned with marine insurance made their appearance: the Zee-risico Societeit, the Tweede Zee-risico Societeit, the Zee-verzekering Societeit.[66] But that, for our purpose, was much later. Outside Amsterdam, companies and company agencies gathered momentum, strengthened the market, and augmented competition. Rotterdam and Middelburg spread connections for themselves in the southern Netherlands. The zone of the Delta offered opportunities for trade and finance which easily crossed boundaries and surmounted divided political obligations.

The long-term trend indeed favoured a broader capital structure in corporate finance, and this put the acid test on the system prevailing in Amsterdam. There was no shortage of underwriting talent on the Dam – Samuel Ricard indicated a figure of about a hundred; the Sligtenhorst list for 1782 gives 91 names of private underwriters and agents. Moreover, they were prudent in the operations – in the normal run of business underwriters signed lines for moderate sums ranging from f.1,000 to f.2,000; and spread their risks in a variety of ways which the system of the market promoted. However, Ricard was also alert to the structure of their capital resources: there were fewer guilder millionaires than often supposed, although the general distribution of wealth was broad. It was relatively easy to set up in business in Amsterdam, but nevertheless difficult to sustain it without considerable assets. In the long-run this may have been a powerful disadvantage at least by comparison with Rotterdam, leaving the Dam less well disposed to dominate new challenges. By the mid nineteenth century, the realities were increasingly evident. If we consult the state of affairs in marine insurance in 1851,[67] Amsterdam had more individual underwriters than Rotterdam (53 against 41) and more companies (70 against 30); but the average capital assets in Rotterdam were higher: f.205,000 against Amsterdam's f.137,000. Rationalisation had no doubt been at work but from a corporative point of view Rotterdam enjoyed a larger structure and implicitly a more substantial and effective capital base.

THE WIDENING INSURANCE MARKET OF EUROPE

These intricate developments in The Netherlands must naturally find a place in the context of other ports and trading centres of the continent.

---

[66] *Sligtenhorst list* (B. Sligtenhorst van Rees), 1820.
[67] F. J. A. Broeze, 'Rederij', in G. Asaert et al., *Maritieme geschiedenis der Nederlanden*, III, p. 127.

As the economy of Europe deepened and commercial systems converged, competition became that much more effective. The founding of joint-stock companies pointed to both the growing demand for protection and the widening requirements of capital and organisation. Europe, to be sure, had a long experience in the insurance business, continuing the early developments in medieval Italy. Those developments continued in spite of obstacles. In a great port such as Venice, propensities remained alert. After all, in May 1682, the Senate finally allowed insurance brokers to write policies for any destination in the world, and that after a century of agitation.[68] Elsewhere, commercial centres with access to the Atlantic grew in competence. To the north, the *alter ego* of Amsterdam, Hamburg, founded the Verein Hamburger Asseceuradeurs in the 1670s; and the first of the Assekuranz-Compagnien, in 1720. The Senate set out important regulations in the Assekuranz- und Havereiordnung on 10 September 1731 which followed the Dutch pattern; later, it chartered the *Assekuranz-Kompagnie* of 1763.[69] The growth in business on the Elbe can be seen in the quotations of insurance premiums which appear in the eighteenth century and survive regularly in the famous *Preis-courant* from 10 September 1762.[70] In 1770, in the thriving *Hafenstadt* of Berlin, the business of the Assekuranzkammer was separated from that of the recently established bank, and given important monopolies.[71] In Copenhagen, similar developments with the important Kongelig Oktroierede Sø-Assurance Kompagni established in 1726. At the outset, it provided insurance for the Far East (at annual rates of 8 percent on the hull and 7 percent on specie), Africa, Greenland/Davis Strait and destinations in Europe. In 1778, as the outlook darkened for The Netherlands, it enjoyed a rapid expansion, its 'glimrende Periode', when dividends rose to an extraordinary 8 percent. The list of premiums of 11 January 1782 quoted China, East and West Indies and 21 destinations in Europe – the

---

[68] N. Magens, *An Essay on Insurances* (2 vols., London, 1755; original publication *Versuch über Assecuranzen, Havereyen und Bodmereyen*, Hamburg, 1753), II, pp. 1 et seq.; G. Stefani, *L'assicurazione a Venezia dalli origini alla fine della Serenissima* (2 vols., Trieste, 1956), I, pp. 108–109, 179–190.

[69] O. von Stritzky, *Verein Hamburger Assecuradeure, 1797–1972* (Hamburg, 1972), p. 10; C. Amsinck, 'Die ersten hamburgischen Assecuranz-Compagnien und der Aktienhandel im Jahre 1720', *Zeitschrift des Vereins für hamburgische Geschichte*, IX (1894); E. von Lehe and F. Böer, *Ein deutscher Seehafen im Dienste der Schiffahrt*, in *750 Jahre Hamburger Hafen* (Hamburg, 1939), p. 34; see also J. Feitama, *Franciscus Roccus' merkwaardige aanmarkingen, alsmede het Reglement der Assurantiën en Haverijen van de Stad Hamburg* (Amsterdam, 1737), pp. 58–68, which lists seven types of insurance policies, including whaling, life, capture by Turks and ransom.

[70] *Commerzbibliothek, Hamburg, S/49, Preis-Courant*, 10 September 1762, and subsequent lists. There are, of course, earlier lists – that for 13 April 1736 being reprinted in E. Achterberg, *Kleine Hamburger Bankgeschichte* (Hamburg, 1964), pp. 32–33.

[71] G. Buss, *Berliner Boerse von 1685–1913* (Berlin, 1913), p. 67.

lowest for Jutland and Holstein (2–2½ percent) and the highest for Venice (8–9 percent), the farthest in the Mediterranean.[72]

To the south, developments in insurance were no less significant. In the southern Netherlands first under Spanish and then Austrian rule, the regulations were old and long-lasting; the famous ordinance of Brussels (31 October 1563); and the *plakaten* of 27 October 1570 and 20 January 1571 virtually settled matters until the end of the eighteenth century. An Insurance Chamber was established by charter on 29 November 1754, and the Keyserlijke en Koninklijke Geoctroyeerde Compagnie van Assurantie renewed in 1779;[73] in Bruges, the Vlaamsch-Oostenrijksche Zeeverseckerings Compagnie (c. 1780); and in Ghent similar developments. Further south again in Rouen, the *bourse couverte* (1556), found a sequel in the Bureau des Assurances (1720).[74] In Paris, the Chambre des Assurances (1668); the Compagnie of 1686 following Colbert's great *ordonnance de la marine* of 1681; and the project of 1746 emerging in the Compagnies of 1750 and 1753.[75] In Spain, the Pragmaticas of Valladolid (notably of 1556, 1588, 1618) continued in the formation of insurance companies. In 1777, they could take care of the policies when it came to moving cannon from Dunkirk to Cádiz or El Ferrol in ships chartered in Amsterdam.[76] In Portugal, King Pedro II created the Casa dos Seguros by royal charter (22 February 1684), with the Junta do Comercio Geral.[77] In London, too, the growth of maritime trade created further demand and the sharpest competition. The early moves in Richard Candler's Office of Assurance (21 February 1575)[78] led on to Elizabeth's Marine Insurance Act (14 December 1601) which referred to insurance 'time out of mind, an usage amongst merchants'. Then came the great departure in 1691 when the coffee-house of Edward Lloyd moved to Lombard Street,

---

[72] C. Thorsen, *Det Kongelig Oktroierede Sø-Assurance Kompagni, 1726–1926* (Copenhagen, 1926), pp. 114, 234–242.

[73] See, in particular, L. Couvreur, 'De eerste verzekerings-compagnie te Antwerpen (1754–1793?)', *Tijdschrift voor Economie en Sociologie*, Ghent, II (1936), pp. 145–174, and 'Recht en zeeverzekerings-practijk in de 17 de. en 18 de. eeuwen', *Tijdschrift voor Rechtsgeschiedenis*, XVI (1938–39), pp. 184–314; H. L. V. de Groote, *De Zeeassurantie te Antwerpen en te Brugge in de zestiende eeuw* (Antwerp, 1975), p. 169.

[74] L. A. Boiteux, *La fortune de la mer* (Paris, 1968); H. Lafosse, *La jurisdiction consulaire de Rouen, 1556–1791* (Rouen, 1922). For the activity of a syndicate in Rouen in the early eighteenth century, see W. R. Dawson, *Marine underwriting at Rouen 1727–1742* (London, 1931), esp. pp. xiii–xv.

[75] *AAE, MD, Hollande*, 1333, fos. 348 ro.-349 vo., 366 ro.-vo., 377 ro.-384 vo., the capital for the company being estimated at £4 million *tournois*.

[76] *Simancas, Estado, Holanda*, Leg. 6369, letter, Herreria to Floridablanca, The Hague, 26 August 1777; for early insurance in Burgos, see M. Basas Fernández, 'El seguro maritimo en Burgos (siglo XVI)', *Estudios de Deusto*, XI (1963).

[77] N. Arié and J. Piedade, 'The Portuguese contribution in the field of insurance', *Versicherungswissenshcaftliche Archiv*, III (1957), p. 161.

[78] J. Trenerry, *The Origin and Early History of Insurance* (London, 1926), pp. 280–281; see also the discussion in C. Molloy, *De Jure Maritimo et Navali* (London, 1676), p. 246.

a turning-point in an already spectacular development.[79] Business grew fast; and weathered the speculation of the South Sea Bubble. The Act of 1720 set up two companies – the London Assurance and the Royal Exchange Assurance – and soon provided for a commission under the Lord Chancellor to settle differences arising out of policies.[80] The form of the A1 policy emerged more clearly in the 1760s and was finally adopted in 1779. To round out this synopsis of companies and institutions in the eighteenth century, we should also look across the Atlantic to New York. There, too, proposals were in the air in 1721; an insurance office appeared in 1759 during the disruptions of the Seven Years' War; it was further enlarged in 1778 (this time in the War of Independence).[81] All these developments made for diversity, and for Amsterdam increasingly keen competition.

The trend towards economic convergence in Europe modified the format of trade and insurance. Spanish merchants were already accustomed, if we follow Jean-Pierre Ricard (1722), to arrange insurance in Amsterdam for consignments to Vera Cruz or other destinations in colonial America.[82] A Rouen syndicate in the second quarter of the eighteenth century had dealings in Holland.[83] The Commercie Compagnie of Middelburg (1720–21) found it convenient to supplement cover raised in Middelburg and Amsterdam with policies written in London: Herman Berens and Sons acted as agents. In March 1742, for example, the Compagnie was quoted insurance for Africa at 12 to 14 percent by the London Assurance Company.[84] The purpose behind the project of December 1746 in Paris during the War of the Austrian Succession to set up an insurance company was the inability of local financiers to provide adequate cover, so that merchants 'were daily obliged to turn to the Royal Assurance Company in London, to Holland, or elsewhere to have insurance'. Insurance and re-insurance between one country and another in the eighteenth century had become a matter of

---

[79] C. Wright and C. E. Fayle, *A History of Lloyd's* (London, 1928), pp. 15–17.

[80] *Parliamentary Committee (1810)*, IV, p. 247; A. H. John, 'The London Assurance Company and the marine insurance market of the eighteenth century', *Economica*, XXV (1958), 126–127; for the Royal Exchange Assurance Company and the related growth of private underwriters and Lloyd's, see the excellent study by B. Supple, *The Royal Exchange Assurance* (Cambridge, 1970), esp. pp. 186–191; and B. Drew, *The London Assurance* (London, 1949), pp. 7–16.

[81] S. S. Huebner, 'The development and present status of marine insurance in the United States', *The Annals of the American Academy of Political and Social Science*, XXVI (1905), 432–433.

[82] J.-P. Ricard, *Le Négoce d'Amsterdam*, p. 251.

[83] For dealing between Rouen and The Netherlands, see W. R. Dawson, *Marine underwriting at Rouen, 1727–1742* (London, 1931), pp. 55–58.

[84] *RAZ, MCC*, 74, letters of 7 August 1730 and 16 March 1742; see also below, Chapter 4.

course.[85] These flows of business sketched out the early days of an international insurance market.

Some of the eddies and flows can be detected by the agencies on the Dam for foreign companies. In 1786, eight had put in an appearance in the Sligtenhorst list for that year. They came mainly from Austria and the southern Netherlands:

Oude Trieste Compagnie, Vecchia compagnia d'assicurazione (Austria)
Assurantie Compagnie te Trieste, Camera mercantile dell'assicurazione marittima (Austria)
Gendse Societeit (Ghent)
Assurantie Compagnie (Ghent)
Tweede Compagnie (Ghent)
Assurantie Maatschappij (Bruges)
Assurantie Societeit (Brussels)
Assurantie Compagnie (Spain)

The presence of these agencies was not necessarily continuous; they were not, presumably, in the first place, solely for marine insurance; but they indicate a certain widening of the market and the opportunities for insurance arbitrage. Corporate companies were, after all, institutions and in a position to offer a decided measure of continuity.

Although competition was often imperfect, the nature of trade tended to bring a rough conformity in maritime jurisdiction. Emerigon had few doubts on the subject. Samuel Ricard (1780) was naturally eager to praise the reliability of Amsterdam insurers and the services they offered.[86] But so, too was Malachy Postlethwaite (1751–56) for London.[87] Both pointed to the excellence of each system of transactions, above all to the reliance on *uberrima fides*, the key to successful underwriting. In time of peace, competition between markets could be direct, and so the differentials between premiums narrowed. War, in contrast, brought disruption and pushed premiums away from the point of central tendency towards wider fluctuations. The reasons were clear enough: insurance taken out abroad at once published ship movements and exposed the value of cargoes; it was contrary to best national interests and was discouraged. For Amsterdam, Samuel Ricard (1780) was categorical that during hostilities a greater degree of variance prevailed.[88] And writing some

---

[85] See above, note 75; E. L. G. den Dooren de Jong, 'Reassurantie in de Zeeverzekering, 1500–1800', *Het Verzekeringsarchief*, X (1929), 103–105; Thorsen, *Det Kongelig Oktroierede Sø-Assurance Kompagni, 1726–1926*, p. 239.

[86] S. Ricard, *Traité*, I, p. 198; Emerigon, *Traité des Assurances*, I, p. 21; J. P. Vergouwen, 'De makelaardij in assurantiën in Italië, Spanje en Vlaanderen voor 1575', *Het Verzekeringsarchief*, XXV (1944).

[87] M. Postlethwaite, *The Universal Dictionary of Trade and Commerce* (2 vols., London, 1751–55), I, p. 145; see also John, 'The London Assurance Company', p. 127.

[88] S. Ricard, *Traité*, I, p. 194.

thirty years' later Philipp Nemnich (1809) commented in the same vein: low rates in peacetime turned to prudence and caution in time of war, which in the final count resulted in high premiums.[89] In the long-term, the interruptions of war in 1780–84 proved to be a serious hindrance; and in the wake of this Amsterdam suffered from the Patriot revolt (1786–87), the fall of the Republic (1795), the continental wars. According to F. J. A. Broeze – and the data for 1836 are convincing – the situation in the early nineteenth century was clear. Amsterdam could outdistance Antwerp, but was hardly a match for the low premiums of London.[90] This was for marine underwriting; but it should not obscure the development of insurance business over a wide range. According to Pascoe Grenfell, the director of the Royal Exchange Assurance Company of London, giving evidence to the Select Committee of 1810, the volume of fire and life insurance already exceeded that of marine underwriting.[91]

MARINE INSURANCE AND ECONOMIC GROWTH

The performance of the insurance market belonged to the general activity and development of Amsterdam as a commercial and financial centre. Inevitably, this raised the difficult but still unresolved problem of the economic growth and stagnation of The Netherlands. The general lines are clear enough. The astonishing expansion into the Atlantic and the ocean trades which illuminated the golden age brought high profits to hard-lipped enterprise and carried the Dam to the forefront of Europe. At three levels it bore the hallmark of success: in the commodity trades – and what could be more eloquent than the lists in the *prijscouranten* themselves which ran the gamut of rich and strategic goods from the four corners of the world? In foreign exchange, which for a time cleared a large share of the settlements of Europe through the bulky but laconic ledgers of the Wisselbank. And in finance, all too evident as investors in The Netherlands gave power of attorney abroad, and with no less ease catered for the improvident rulers of Europe whose ministers came trooping to the Dam with briefs to cover rising debts with Dutch wealth. At all three levels, Amsterdam excelled but the multipolar expansion of Europe in the eighteenth century progressively restricted its degrees of freedom. At the same time that expansion brought competing rates of

---

[89] P. A. Nemnich, *Original-Beiträge zur eigentlichen Kenntniss von Holland* (Tübingen, 1809), p. 392. See also, P. J. Blok, 'Het plan tot oprichting eener Compagnie van Assurantie', *Bijdragen voor Vaderlandsche Geschiedenis en Oudheidkunde*, 4 e. reeks, I (1900); and F. Snapper, *Oorlogsinvloeden op de handel van Holland, 1551–1719* (Amsterdam, 1959).

[90] F. J. A. Broeze, 'Rederijn', in G. Asaert et al., *Maritieme geschiedenis der Nederlanden*, III, p. 127.

[91] *Parliamentary Committee (1810)*, IV, p. 364.

growth, new economic structures as Europe debouched into industrialisation, and new foci of material and technical advance. For The Netherlands the arguments about stagnation ride uneasily on the analysis of growth both absolute and relative to other economic regions in Europe.

It is not our purpose here to launch into the detail of this huge debate, only to take up some of the more restricted issues which impinge on the scale and direction of insurance operations. This is a prologue to the explanations later in the study. Three merit special attention: first, the format of shipping, which held a key to navigation; second, the flows of goods, in other words, the cargoes carried; and third, by no means least, the range and regional structure of The Netherlands economy itself.

First, then, to consider: shipping. The typology of modern growth demands a shift in the structure of trade and industry at the expense of the rural sector.[92] The early development of The Netherlands canted towards maritime trade; it emerged as the precocious common carrier of Europe. There were, after all, exceptional opportunities to be seized: on the one hand, the 'frontier' of the Atlantic, and on the other hand, the north/south coastal trade in general and to the north and Baltic in particular. The golden age was a phase of diverse invention and innovation – this is clear from the studies of P. W. Klein and R. Unger. In many respects, the famous cargo-carrying *fluit* was the symbol of such opportunities and achievement.[93] The coastal trade required a ship designed to handle well with small crews in the shallow estuaries and delta systems of The Netherlands; to make the ports of the North and settle on the mud flats when the tide was out; to ride the changeable winds and currents of Europe's coasts rather than the pitching and tossing on the Atlantic rollers. Such sailing conditions tended to encourage underwater design to combine cargo capacity with minimal draught. The *moeder-commercie* of the Baltic focused these constraints when the trip through the Sound presented dangers off Jutland, ungenerous channels and currents between Sjaeland and southern Sweden. Even more, there were the customs tolls to pay at Helsingør, under the muzzles of the cannon of Kronborg. These tolls were at first levied according to tonnage measured by the length and breadth on deck, the draught of the ship at the beam, and multiplied by 0.65.[94] Out of such constraints came the *fluit* – longer than usual (a ratio of length to beam

[92] S. Kuznets, *The economic growth of nations* (Cambridge, Mass., 1971), p. 153.
[93] R. W. Unger, *Dutch shipbuilding before 1800* (Assen, 1978), pp. 26, 30, 44, 109; J. van Beylen, 'Scheepstypen', in G. Asaert et al., *Maritieme geschiedenis der Nederlanden*, II, pp. 28–32; J. R. Bruijn, 'De vaart in Europa', ibid., II, p. 203.
[94] C. J. W. van Waning, 'Schepen en luiden uit vroeger tijd', *Ons Zeewezen*, L, 12 (1961), 77.

of some 5 to 1); gaining cargo capacity with bulging bows and stern; with a tendency to a flat bottom to pass the shoals and bars of ports; and showing a sharp 'tumble-home', that is, a marked inward curve upwards from the waterline designed to minimise the demands of the Customs measurers. The basic design, so successful as it turned out, came with various modifications to suit different trades – the timber-ships, grain-carriers, the special whaling-vessels, and those on the Archangel run. The bigger versions sailed for the Mediterranean, Spain, and France. Even in the Far East, the VOC used this class of vessel, usually much larger, with room enough to house soldiers and marines, the force of colonial rule.[95]

After 1700, however, the tolls at Helsingør introduced new measurements, notably that the breadth was taken at the widest point of the beam. This reduced much of the value of the 'tumble-home'.[96] However, the surge of invention was diminishing. After 1630, certainly after 1670, there was less general drive in The Netherlands to invent and innovate.[97] Changes came slowly in the vintage field, but could on occasion be significant in the eighteenth century.[98] With the cut-back in naval expenditures, the ship-building yards had less current experience in scale construction. In some respects they failed to maintain the cost-effectiveness of Dutch shipping. Nevertheless, the designs evolved to meet current needs: the *bootschip* with its broader deck, square on the waterline, used especially for whaling; the *galjoot* and *kof* for the Baltic and Mediterranean; and above all the *katschip*, a type of *fluit*, apt for bulky cargoes such as timber from the Baltic. It managed to overcome its lack of speed with the undeniable advantages of easy handling.[99] These were important developments, but they emphasised that ship-building in The Netherlands tended towards the improvement of existing types rather than to innovation. In Dordrecht, ship-building in the eighteenth century concentrated on smaller ships, destined to work the inland waterways.[100] It did not pass without comment that England and France developed ship-designs better suited to ocean-sailing, with greater

---

[95] Van Beylen, 'Scheepstypen', in G. Asaert et al., *Maritieme geschiedenis der Nederlanden*, II, pp. 31–32; Bruijn, 'De vaart in Europa', ibid., II, p. 201.

[96] See above, note 94.

[97] Unger, *Dutch shipbuilding before 1800*, pp. 44, 109.

[98] B. E. van Bruggen, 'Schepen, ontwerp en bouw', in G. Asaert et al., *Maritieme geschiedenis der Nederlanden*, III, p. 15; P. W. Klein, 'Gouden eeuw en pruikentijd: een beeld van contrasten?' *Spiegel historiael*, II, 10 (1967), 547.

[99] Van Bruggen, 'Schepen, ontwerp en bouw', III, pp. 24–26; Simancas, Estado, Holanda, Leg. 6371, letter, Herreria to Floridablanca, The Hague, 22 April 1779: from the ships built in 1765–78 and surviving in 1779, the largest carried 54 guns.

[100] R. W. Unger, 'Wooden shipbuilding at Dordrecht', *Mededelingen van de Vereeniging voor Zeegeschiedenis*, XXX (1975), 11.

length, draught and keel patterns.[101] The waterways of The Netherlands in effect set constraints; but the resulting vessels were often admirably suited to the coastal trades of the continent.

A second set of considerations concerns cargoes. The transfers of bulky commodities lay at the core of Dutch commercial success. At one level, it resolved into the concept of the *staple*; at another, it related to the share of the volume trade of Europe. Such realities touched the heart of Amsterdam's prosperity. The function as a staple languished under taxes and high port dues and in consequence an unwillingness on the part of the authorities, notably in 1751, to establish a *porto franco*.[102] Trade could easily by-pass Holland, sailing directly from origin to destination: Samuel Ricard thought that it could account for as much as half the total of ships routed from the Baltic.[103] However, he found difficulty in estimating the volume of Amsterdam's tonnage which could have been much less than often inferred – perhaps some 500 ships registered in the city suitable for foreign trade, and a majority of ships coming from Friesland.[104] Dutch ships were busy in the trade of Europe, but from the figures available claimed a smaller share of the total. It is difficult to assess the precise nature of this reality for often the flag was not a correct indicator; and in any case, when adjusted for size of population, the share of The Netherlands was far from negligible. From the simple figures, however, the indicators were clear: at Cádiz in the 1760s, for example, still the major link-point for access to the Spanish colonies and the flow of bullion, the Dutch flag covered about a quarter of the ships entering the Bay.[105] In the Baltic trade, Amsterdam's *moeder commercie*, the port movement of St Petersburg soared in the second half of the eighteenth century; but Dutch tonnage played a subordinate rôle.[106] By contrast, in 1787, Britain claimed as much as a quarter of Europe's tonnage.[107]

[101] L. van Zwyndregt, *Verhandeling van den Hollandschen Scheepbouw raakende de verschillende charters der oorlogschepen* (The Hague, 1759), p. 4.

[102] *Simancas, Estado, Holanda*, Leg. 6345, Letter, Rodriguez to Quadra, Amsterdam, 13 March 1738; ibid., letter, Rodriguez to Carvazal, Amsterdam, 14 September 1752; Wilson, *Anglo-Dutch Commerce*, p. 22; J. Hovy, *Het voorstel van 1751 tot instelling van een beperkt vrijhavenstel in de Republiek (Propositie tot een gelimiteerd porto-franco)* (Groningen, 1966).

[103] S. Ricard, *Traité*, I, pp. 183, 214.

[104] Ibid., I, p. 186.

[105] *Seville, Indias, Contratación*, 4935, 4936, 4937, *Total de las embarcaciones de guerra y marchantes de todas Naciones que han entrado en esta Bahía de Cádiz*.

[106] S. Ricard, *Traité*, I, p. 282; Accarias de Sérionne, *La Richesse de la Hollande*, II, p. 46; Joh. de Vries, *De economische achteruitgang*, p. 76: since 1763, in addition to Amsterdam, exchange rates extended to London and Hamburg; Faber, *De achttiende eeuw*, p. 135; Wilson, *Anglo-Dutch Commerce*, p. 65; G. E. Munro, *The development of St. Petersburg as an urban center during the reign of Catharine II (1762–1796)* (Ann Arbor, 1974), p. 209.

[107] Unger, *Dutch shipbuilding before 1800*, p. 110; R. Davis, *The rise of the English shipping industry* (Newton Abbot, 1962), pp. 78–79.

As for the composition of cargoes, the tentacles of trade touched all levels of the economy. Consignments drawn from the various destinations were often simple and consisted of a high proportion of raw materials and primary products. The outward cargoes from The Netherlands, in contrast, were mixed, with a wide range of important manufactures. At one level, this gap in trade put the competitiveness of Dutch industry in question. At another level, it related to the swelling trade in colonial products from termini of other national colonial corporations with their protected, mercantilist industries; or colonial products from the small ports which clustered the Atlantic coasts but did not give immediate access to an extensive hinterland. Ports such as Lorient, St Malo or Dunkirk.[108] Little wonder that merchants such as Jan Texier pressed to deliver timber, masts, hemp, tar and other stores to nearby naval depots.[109] They created credits to be laid out in return cargoes. A few examples will set out the problem for trade, navigation, and not least marine insurance. The trade with St Petersburg was one. The *St Anna*[110] left the port of Kronstadt on 22 October 1773 with a cargo of six items: hemp, sailcloth, canvas, wax, bar-iron and bristles, for a value of f.21,250. One shipper was involved. In return, the cargo of the *Werkhoven*[111] which sailed from the Texel on 4 September 1773 bound for St Petersburg. Among the 46 shippers were such redoubtable firms as Andries Pels en Zoonen (it was albeit September 1773), Hope and Company, and Blaauw en Compagnie. The 50 different types of cargo came to an estimated value of f.156,200 and included a wide variety of primary materials, colonial products, and manufactured goods: raisins, lemons, herring, cheese, bulbs, wine, and spa-water; cochineal, chocolate, coffee, indigo, pepper, camelhair, and sandalwood; cotton, linen and woollen textiles, books, iron-ware, and not least to balance the accounts, two thousand *rijksdaalders* and a small parcel of 65 gold *dukaten*.

In another direction, the transfers with Smyrna. The *St Thadoro*[112] sailed from the port in convoy on 2 April 1775 with a cargo valued at f.101,250 for 29 shippers. There were 10 types of commodities but predominantly cotton and cotton goods. An outward cargo in the *Spridion*[113] bound for Smyrna and Constantinople on 16 July 1774 had 37 shippers. There were 19 types of cargo specified and seven entries for unspecified merchandise and manufactures, for a total estimated value of f.182,775.

From Cádiz, the ship *Portugal*[114] sailed for Amsterdam on 12 October 1774 with a cargo valued at f.76,325 for 15 shippers. It consisted of hides,

---

[108] J. M. Fuchs, *Beurt- en Wagenveren* (The Hague, 1946), pp. 231–232.
[109] See below, Chapter 3, note 179 and Table 6.
[110] *KVA*, XVIII, 519.   [111] *KVA*, XVIII, 515.   [112] *KVA*, XVIII, 703.
[113] *KVA*, XVIII, 542.   [114] *KVA*, XVIII, 586.

wool, cochineal, indigo, drugs, and 30 bales of jalap. In addition, six shippers had consignments of gold and silver bullion and specie which they valued at f.39,506. In contrast the *Vrouwe Barbara Hendrina*[115] carried from Amsterdam on 25 October 1774 for Cádiz, on behalf of 19 shippers, cargo to the value of f.59,025. It included iron-wares, woollen cloth, Silesian linen, thread, butter, cheese, white beans, linseed oil, paper, saffron, cloves.

A last example: the trade from St Eustatius. The *Concordia*[116] sailed from the island on 29 January 1774 with a cargo valued at f.78,450 for 41 shippers. It consisted mainly of coffee, with some sugar, tobacco, cacao, dye-wood, cassia fistula and a small parcel of specie. The outward cargo in the *Amsterdamse Galey*[117] which left for the island on 5 November 1774 was consigned by 78 shippers and for an estimated value of f.124,950. Again the range of commodity was wide: 25 types and numerous entries of general cargo. There were manufactures such as linen, nails, iron-ware, paper, rope, sail-cloth, pottery, bricks and tiles (perhaps as ballast); a heavy lacing of beer, wines and gin; products of the farms, notably cheese; and colonial wares from Asia: tea and pepper.

These few examples do not close the immense and bulky dossier of The Netherlands' trade. But they point to a number of the salient issues: the problem of outward cargoes and their returns. Amsterdam acted as a clearing-house, collecting and distributing a wide range of products both European and colonial. In addition, there was the crucial rôle of manufactures, which all too often underpinned the high value of the consignments. The finger of contention thus pointed to the industrial competitiveness of The Netherlands economy.

At this level, it is all too easy to detect shortcomings. The provinces were highly urbanised – 60 percent of the population of South Holland living in cities of 10,000 inhabitants or more; 30 percent for the country as a whole.[118] According to Adna Weber, the Republic at its fall was at the top of the league of urbanisation in Europe.[119] The cities and their guilds had much to say in the organisation of industry. But urban labour costs were high – in 1816 still more than half again as high as those in the southern Netherlands.[120] Johannes de Vries has shown that in the difficulties of the eighteenth century the labour-intensive sectors suffered more heavily than most.[121] A skilled urban work-force indeed held many advantages; but as the classic case of Lancashire during industrialisation

---

[115] *KVA*, XVIII, 585.   [116] *KVA*, XVIII, 523.   [117] *KVA*, XVIII, 624.
[118] Faber, 'De achttiende eeuw', p. 121.
[119] A. F. Weber, *The growth of cities in the nineteenth century* (New York, 1899), pp. 144–145.
[120] J. Mokyr, *Industrialization in the Low Countries* (New Haven, Conn., 1976), pp. 188–189.
[121] Joh. de Vries, *De economische achteruitgang*, pp. 83–118.

was to show, growth often required the 'novelty' of re-location away from the staid and restricting towns of customary form and output. At the time, there were few signs of this, only cries of distress, rising in a shrill chorus for help and government protection. Some urban industries were vulnerable, the woollen textiles of Leiden, for example, and the bleach-works of Haarlem.[122] They felt the cold draught of competition from the cloths of France, of neighbouring Juliers or Aix-la-Chapelle, the fine linens of Silesia. There were troubles in store for paper-makers, merchants in timber floated down the Rhine, saw-millers and ship-builders on Zaanstreek,[123] hat-makers, sugar-refiners . . . and not least the fishers for herring. Symptoms of outward decay seized the headlines. Urban crafts vied with rural manufactures. Cities once set like jewels in a golden age seemed to passing travellers already to have dimmed in desolation. And these cities often held the key to provide and assemble outward cargoes.

A third dimension must be the spatial network of navigation, implicitly crucial for insurance and the concept that The Netherlands offered a point of balance in Europe. Again the eighteenth century projected a mix of problems for the performance of the economy. As will be seen from the cast of the chapters to follow, The Netherlands promoted a comprehensive trade around the coasts of Europe. At one level, it was made explicit in the regular shuttle services – virtually as a common carrier – to a variety of coastal destinations. Thus there were the famous *beurtvarten*[124] to Hamburg (1613); Bremen (1647); London (1611) and northwest France; to Cologne and Düsseldorf (1641). In the eighteenth century, there were further developments to Antwerp, the prelude to the opening of the Scheldt (1791); and to the southern Netherlands where access to the hinterland came with canals either dug or refurbished, to Leuven (1750); Ghent (1760); Bruges, Ostend, Dunkirk (1770).[125]

In a larger perspective, the great ports of The Netherlands were selective in their orientation, and were not all concerned with the same commercial structures. Amsterdam looked particularly to the dialogue of north and south – an old equation in the inter-regional trade of Europe.[126] Rotterdam in contrast was destined to favour more east–west relations in association with French, English, and Scottish ports. It retained a natural partiality for the Rhine–Meuse trade and the German

---

[122] Faber, 'De achttiende eeuw', pp. 137, 142–143.
[123] Ibid., p. 144; Accarias de Sérionne, *La Richesse de la Hollande*, I, pp. 260–261; II, pp. 37–38.
[124] E. Baasch, 'Die Bortfahrt zwischen Hamburg, Bremen und Holland', *Forschungen zur hamburger Handelsgeschichte*, II (1898), pp. 3–6, 40.
[125] Fuchs, *Beurt- en Wagenveren*, p. 228.
[126] S. Ricard, *Traité*, I, pp. 195, 397; Accarias de Sérionne, *La Richesse de la Hollande*, I, p. 25.

hinterland, so that the Baltic often came in second place.[127] However, this comparison should not obscure the weight of Amsterdam interests in the hinterland. One indication of this was the insurance of trips on inland waterways: J. P. Vergouwen points to the beginning of this business in 1759, during the Seven Years' War.[128] The Rhine trade clearly offered a potential market, and this received further regulation in the important *ordonnantie* of 14 May 1791.[129] At that time, Amsterdam had 36 *beurten* assigned with the Rhineland, 16 for Dortrecht and 10 for Rotterdam.[130] This system continued to prevail in the days of sail of the early nineteenth century.

Such balances of interest, however, must not obscure the changes and fluctuations in the second half of the eighteenth century. These carry weight when it comes to assessing the insurance business. In this period, normally taken as a phase of expansion, economic indicators were not always smooth and pointing in the same direction. For France, an important trading partner of The Netherlands, Ernest Labrousse[131] has detected a long reflux, an *intercycle* of falling rents and prices lasting from 1770 to 1787. The commercial activity of Britain faced adverse gross barter terms of trade: after a spell of improvement in the two decades 1730–50, the trend changed into decline lasting to 1786–87, and this situation did not improve until the last decade of the century.[132] In The Netherlands, the income of the Directie van de Oosterschen Handel en Rederijen in 1770 entered a long phase of decline from which it had apparently not escaped when the century closed.[133]

These summary indicators widen the scope of the problem. And if we turn to the trade of Europe, the value systems of regional markets are at once in question. Few will doubt the complexity of settlements and flows of cash in the third quarter of the century – the end to the great expansion of the Brazilian gold trade;[134] the relay offered by the renewed

---

[127] J. V. Th. Knoppers, 'De vaart in Europa', in G. Asaert et al., *Maritieme geschiedenis der Nederlanden*, III, p. 237.

[128] Vergouwen, *De geschiedenis der Makelaardij*, pp. 62–69; Joh. de Vries, *De economische achteruitgang*, pp. 1–10, 41; Faber, *De achttiende eeuw*, p. 136.

[129] See above, note 125.

[130] Ibid.; J. Op den Hooff, *Iets over de vaart op den Rijn* (Amsterdam, 1826), p. 16.

[131] C.-E. Labrousse, *La crise de l'économie française à la fin de l'Ancien Régime et au début de la Révolution* (Paris, 1944), pp. 9–12.

[132] P. Deane and W. A. Cole, *British economic growth, 1688–1959*, 2nd edn (Cambridge, 1967), Appendix I; and see above, Chapter 3, and note 45.

[133] GA, Amsterdam, *Directie van de Oostersche Handel en Rederijen*, 376, 377; M. Gideonse, *Dutch Baltic Trade in the Eighteenth Century* (diss.), Harvard, 1932, pp. 370–373; and for the early development of the *Directie*, see S. van Brakel, 'De Directie van den Oosterschen Handel en Reederijen te Amsterdam', *Bijdragen voor Vaderlandsche Geschiedenis en Oudheidkunde*, 4e. R., IX (1910).

[134] V. Noya Pinto, *O ouro brasiliero e o comércio anglo-português* (São Paulo, 1972), p. 123, cited and with graph, F. Braudel, *Civilisation matérielle, économie et capitalisme XVe.– XVIIIe. siècle* (3 vols., Paris, 1979), II, p. 304.

production of the silver mines of Central and South America. The latter may have stemmed, even reversed for a while the trend towards price convergence observed in the first half of the century.

As for insurance business, there is little quantitative evidence on aggregate performance. Some partial evidence can be found in the accounts of the companies. In Rotterdam, the Maatschappij van Assurantie enjoyed a very successful year in 1750–51, both for trading in general and for underwriting in particular. The net profits of the latter were f.15,780 – not matched in the next 35 years (see Graph 3).[135] After a sharp drop in 1752–53, and a net loss of f.1,190 in 1754–55, the directors prudently drew in their horns and took risks with caution – 'it is too dangerous' they often decided.[136] But afterwards, business picked up, in spite of war. In the following 25 years, with net annual losses only in 1769–70 and 1771–72, profits averaged f.4,849. Then came the disasters of the Fourth Anglo-Dutch War. The balance for 30 June 1781 turned in a huge underwriting loss of f.82,350. The Maatschappij had paid out f.84,285 in claims – adjusted at 65.5 percent. The next five years saw spasmodic losses, so that the average net annual loss in the underwriting accounts for June 1780 to June 1784 which covered the war was f.17,553. However, in general trading, the affairs of the Maatschappij picked up from the results of 1780–81, the worst slump in the century and a quarter from 1744 to 1873.[137] Business did not pass the 1750–51 peak until the first decade of the nineteenth century and reached a high in 1819–20, which it touched again in 1846–47.

Did Amsterdam share the experience of Rotterdam? There is little to settle such curiosity. But we should not leave the question in the air without looking at some of the long-term movements in insurance on the Amsterdam Bourse.

THE SECULAR TREND IN AMSTERDAM INSURANCE

The guise of stability and equipoise which clothed much of the closing phase of the *ancien régime* appears at odds with the progressive shift towards industrialisation. At least with the hindsight of history. An upward surge in prices disrupted many accepted values on the continent; a trend in expansion brought new opportunities, new centres to the fore. What can be said about insurance rates in the years 1766–80?

Again, we must turn to the *prijscouranten*, this time for the whole of the

---

[135] *GA, Rotterdam, Maatschappij van Assurantie*, 343–363.
[136] Slechte, 'De Maatschappij van Assurantie, Discontering en Beleening der stad Rotterdam van 1720', p. 289.
[137] *GA, Rotterdam, Maatschappij van Assurantie*, 53; 360, fo. 99 ro. 30 June 1781.

seventeenth and eighteenth centuries. Bearing in mind the seasonal disparity of the material, which we shall consider later, I have selected quotations for June, the 'best' month of the year.[138] The resulting data (see Graph 4) are therefore discontinuous and in many respects unsatisfactory; but I have used them for the following four sample sets of destinations:

(a)   the eastern Mediterranean (the Archipelago and Syria)
(b)   the eastern Baltic (Reval and Riga)
(c)   the Atlantic seaboard (Morlaix, St Malo and Rouen)
(d)   the West Indies (Surinam)

Over the long two centuries, these naturally show particular characteristics and swings in amplitude. At the same time, there is some measure of consistency. During the first century and a half, the trend is downwards to a 'trough' in the late 1760s and early 1770s. Then followed a reversal, with a moderate upswing lasting for the rest of the eighteenth century. The years 1766–80 therefore appear to have been a turning-point, or at least a period of slack water at the end of a long phase.

What do the different group data show? The display in Graph 4 shows, firstly, a downward trend most marked in the case of the Archipelago and Syria. Here the rates run at 8–9 percent in the late 1630s, at 3–4 percent in the 1730s, and reach 2–2½ percent in the late 1760s. In the second group, Reval/Riga, similar results emerge: a minor shift from 2–4 percent to 1¼–2¼ percent and then to 1–1½ percent. The destination Morlaix/Rouen shows a falling trend from 3–4 percent, to 1–1½ percent and then to ¾–1 percent. And, lastly, Surinam: the first set of data in the 1640s relate to Brazil under Dutch occupation, when the rates fluctuate between 4 and 5 percent; but by the 1730s, premiums moved between 3 and 4 percent, occasionally around 5 percent. In all four cases, war proved to be a powerful disturbance, and particularly in the two decades 1690–1710. Nevertheless, with all the shortcomings, the data emphasise a secular decline in premiums, reaching a settled period in the decade 1765–74.

It would be tempting to attribute this decline to an abatement of great wars: the Thirty Years'; the manoeuvres on land and sea in the League of Augsburg and the disputes over the Spanish Succession; the Austrian Succession, in which The Netherlands became heavily involved. However, no less important was the growth and convergence of markets in Europe, that progressive integration which did so much to level out differences between regions. Over the long-term, the gaps between regional price-levels for bulky commodities (such as wheat) tended to

---

[138] See below, pp. 122–124.

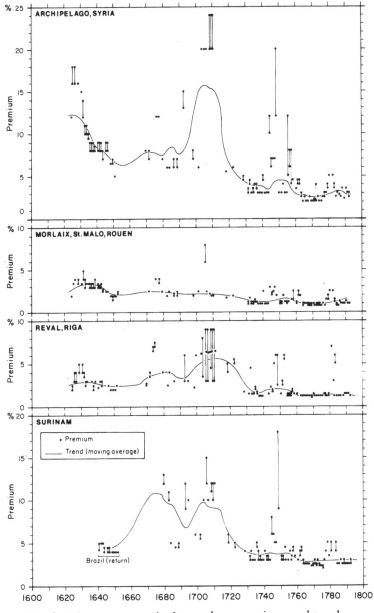

Graph 4. Insurance rates in Amsterdam: premiums and trends

close, so that by the 1730s and 1740s, when there was a run of good harvests, differentials were significantly reduced.[139] And even the markets of Poland, as Witold Kula has shown, tended to enjoy 'national' levels of prices by the end of the eighteenth century.[140] It can be inferred that marine insurance was not aloof to such structural changes which affected the profitability of trade. The establishment of insurance companies faced Amsterdam with greater competition: the Maatschappij van Assurantie of Rotterdam (1720); the developments in Hamburg, Rouen, Berlin, Copenhagen. In London, the coffee-house of Edward Lloyd developed into a prodigious success. These developments extended competition and exerted pressure for lower rates.[141] Long spells of peace, or at least of limited war, accentuated a downward trend.

The long-term fall in insurance rates may be comparable with the decline in interest rates for which the evidence for western Europe in general and for The Netherlands in particular is becoming increasingly clear. However, the indicators are not necessarily in unison. Sidney Homer is of the opinion that in The Netherlands the domestic short-term rates may have shown a slight tendency to rise, perhaps due to the influence of the higher rates offered on foreign lending.[142] Again, tendencies towards convergence in Europe would come into play. The trend of price-inflation was generally under way from the second quarter of the eighteenth century, and the price of money was not spared. However, the lag in the sector of navigation probably would not be the first – nor indeed last – occasion when the evidence spoke with many voices. A more recent case can be found before the First World War. While price inflation began again in the 1890s, freight rates in shipping under increasing competition continued to fall until about 1910. At least,

---

[139] F. Braudel and F. C. Spooner, 'The history of prices in Europe, 1450–1760', in E. E. Rich and C. H. Wilson (eds.), *The Cambridge Economic History of Europe*, IV (Cambridge, 1967), esp. pp. 470–471; B. H. Slicher van Bath, *The Agrarian History of Western Europe, AD 500–1850* (London, 1963), pp. 211–212. See also W. Achilles, 'Getreidepreise und Getreidehandelsbeziehungen europäischer Räume im 16. und 17. Jahrhundert', *Zeitschift für Agrargeschichte und Agrarsoziologie*, VII (1959).

[140] W. Kula, *An economic theory of the feudal system*, Eng. trans. (London, 1976), pp. 130–131.

[141] S. Ricard, *Traité*, I, p. 194; and see above, pp. 46–47.

[142] Ibid., II, p. 323; S. Homer, *A history of interest rates* (New Brunswick, NJ, 1963), pp. 176–178. The literature on the movement of interest rates is extensive, in particular, Buist, *At spes non fracta*, p. 28; Klein, *De zeventiende eeuw*, p. 112; Joh. de Vries, *De economische achteruitgang*, p. 63; V. Barbour, *Capitalism in Amsterdam in the seventeenth century* (Baltimore, 1949), p. 82; Davis, *The rise of the Atlantic economies*, p. 240; L. S. Pressnell, 'The rate of interest in the eighteenth century', in *Studies in the Industrial Revolution* (Oxford, 1956), pp. 211–214; Riley, *International government finance*, pp. 31–32, 73–83. For the decline in freight and insurance rates, see J. F. Shepherd and G. M. Walton, *Shipping, maritime trade, and the economic development of colonial North America* (Cambridge, 1972), pp. 60–72, 77.

that is a conclusion to be drawn from the work of Douglass North.[143] An interval of some fifteen years passed before they joined the upward spiral in prices in unison. However, such comparisons must be treated with caution. History, to be sure, does not readily approve of repetitions.

The sequence of premiums suffers from a defect common to price history: there are prices but not volumes of insurance business transacted on the Dam. To compensate, at least in some measure, for this shortcoming, we can turn to the settlements in the Kamer van Assurantie, where claims were considered and losses adjusted. If we are ready to accept that marine insurance was protection against economic loss rather than a substitute for gambling; and that the perils of the sea – leaving aside special cases of war-risks – were reasonably consistent in the long-term trend of the eighteenth century, then the *vonnissen* of the Kamer may have had a predictable relationship to the aggregate insurance taken out. Ivo Schöffer has carefully listed these *vonnissen*,[144] and the resulting series of cases can be seen in Graph 5. The changes are reasonably clear over the eighteenth century as a whole: the trend fell to 1730–34 (34.2 cases, for four years – 1730 is the only gap in the series from 1700 to 1799). After a surge of claims in the War of the Austrian Succession (1740–48), the activity of the Kamer rose through the 1760s and 1770s to a peak in 1785 (212 cases). Even when this exceptional period is omitted the century closed on an average of 136.6 cases (for the five years 1794–99), well above anything in the previous eight decades, come peace, come war.

If the level of real risk – structural uncertainties – had increased to account for this rising trend of claims, it could be expected that underwriters would have accordingly raised their premiums. As it turned out, the secular fall in premiums to the late 1760s/early 1770s, and the small subsequent rise, give adequate grounds for assuming that in fact the rise in the number of cases before the Kamer coincided with a growing volume of insurance business, during time of peace. At least, that is one possible conclusion.

This volume of business remains one aspect of the market of Amsterdam. The propensity of underwriters to accept risks responded to the flow of business, for all too often the names of insurers appeared also as shippers of parcels of cargo. Credit, freight and insurance merged. At the same time, the net risk capital – the flows of premiums – belonged to the short-term end of the investment market. In brief, insurance business was also concerned with the level of liquidity in the 1760s and 1770s.

---

[143] D. North, *The rôle of transportation in the economic development of North America*, in *Les grandes voies maritimes dans le monde XVe.–XIXe. siècles* (Paris, 1965).

[144] I. Schöffer, 'De vonnissen in averij grosse van de Kamer van Assurantie en Avarij te Amsterdam', *EHJ*, XXVI (1956); and KVA, I, *Toelichting bij de registers op de vonnissen*.

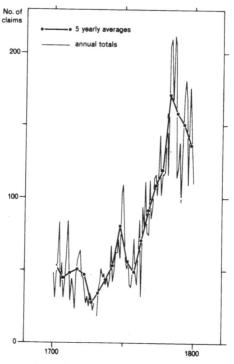

Graph 5. Amsterdam: claims in the Kamer van Assurantie en Avarij

FLOWS OF INVESTMENT IN AMSTERDAM

The mechanisms of the trade and the characteristic style of business encouraged a large measure of flexibility between different sectors of the market. Alongside commitments to domestic debt, finance in Amsterdam belonged to a wider realm beyond the confines of the Dam, predominantly, although not exclusively, in Europe. Economic growth and convergence in the eighteenth century brought funds in search of investment. Corporations had legal personalities to issue shares and accumulate debts; cities and governments could obtain loans secured on flows of income – taxes, royalties, revenues of all kinds. It is possible that these funds had preferences rather akin to those of migrants and Ravenstein's law of migration that numbers and distances were inversely correlated.[145] The long–distance, international trajectories were for the adventurous few; while the majority aimed for opportunities closer to home.

[145] E. G. Ravenstein, 'The laws of migration', *Journal of the Statistical Society*, XLVIII (1885), 198–199.

At another level, the complex nature of the market for investment emerges from the merchants and partnerships involved. Some linkages were apparent; we have only to compare the entries in the Sligtenhorst list of 1768 with the issuing houses for loans in Europe and the West Indies. A few telling names are common to both. We have already cited Frederik Dibbetz en Zoon directly concerned in the loan to the Welbedagt plantation in Surinam of f.40,000 at 5 percent. Abraham ter Borch arranged issues for the Danish Islands, but this firm was fatally mauled in the crisis of 1772–73. The house of Van Vollenhoven organised loans for Danzig; that of Raymond de Smeth for Russia; 'Tullek y Vos' (most probably Ambrosius Tulleken and Scheyderuyt de Vos, van Nieuwvliet) for Essequibo and Demerara (the latter a separate colony in 1773 but linked with Essequibo in 1789). As for Rotterdam, the noteworthy firm of merchant bankers, Joan Ozy en Zoonen, had financial interests in the southern Netherlands.[146] These names and their connections do not settle the issue, but they already indicate part of the possible financial linkages on the Bourse. When we find the same names appearing time and time again as shippers of the cargoes before the Kamer van Assurantie, the diversity of finance, investment and insurance is that much more evident.

Before turning to a few details of such flows of funds, however, three points must be made. Firstly, the different markets in Europe had evolved and in aggregate endowed operations with a distinct international character. Economies with access to fortunes and endowed with stable, or relatively stable, monetary systems offered attractive opportunities for placing money at interest. There was an undeniable market for fixed-return assets. As early as 1618, the Serenissima in Genoa was outraged on finding that citizens had sent money to Venice for investment in annuities at 12 percent.[147] Later, as Giuseppe Felloni has admirably shown, the Genoese continued to invest abroad – in Naples, Spain, France, Austria, Russia. Assets thus placed in high hopes often met with dismal returns, even downright loss.[148] The experiences on the Dam were much in the same vein as other centres of Europe.

However, Amsterdam developed range and expertise. Financial houses thrived on putting out prospectuses, issuing bonds, receiving

---

[146] *ARA, Archief van Pieter Steyn*, 332a, and above, p. 73. J. P. van de Voort, *De Westindische plantages van 1720 tot 1795: financiën en handel* (Eindhoven, 1973), p. 10, indicates the serious losses in these loans to Surinam; for Frederik Dibbetz, see ibid., p. 283.

[147] *Simancas, Estado, Genova*, Leg. 1934, fos. 61, 67, 72, 202, letters, Vivas de Canamás to Philip III, Genoa, 2, 9 and 25 September 1618, 23 April 1619; AS, Milan, *Potenze Estere, Genova*, 29, 16 February 1636. For the finances of the Republic of Venice, *Bilanci Generali*, vol. I, tom. 1 (Venice, 1912), pp. 550–553.

[148] G. Felloni, *Gli investimenti finanzari genovesi in Europa tra il seicento e la restaurazione* (Milan, 1971), esp. pp. 301, 344–360.

cash, distributing dividends, buying and selling certificates, now for clients, now on their own account. Brokers, jobbers, agents rubbed shoulders on the Bourse, meeting at the customary pillars in the courtyard, ready to speculate, but creating at the same time those weaknesses which surfaced, for example in the bankruptcies of 1772–73. Scholars have provided a great deal of information on these activities. Charles Wilson has charted the flows between The Netherlands and Britain. Marten Buist has made crystal clear how the house of Hope and Company operated, particularly in the loans to Russia.[149] James Riley has assessed the panorama of governments and their debts.[150] The dealings were extremely diverse, and the market did not always 'clear'. It sometimes needed dedicated acumen if not sleight of hand to mobilise hesitant, latent wealth, to pass off the paper of Europe. The nature of the situation can be seen in the negotiations to raise supplementary capital for the Imperial Canal of Aragon in Spain: the firm of Adolf Johann Heshuysen in Haarlem in association with Simeon Boas in The Hague, acted as agents for Badin y Compañia in Madrid. In the supplementary loan of 1776, they sent some of the bonds for sale in Switzerland, and in the fairs of Frankfurt-am-Main and Leipzig,[151] where the trading connections gave access to an international clientele. It was much the same elsewhere. K. N. Chaudhuri has commented how the shares of the East India Company in London soon found buyers abroad, for example, in The Netherlands, in Antwerp, and in Geneva. But then the capital of the company was virtually part of the British national debt,[152] and received implicitly the guarantee of Parliament.

A second aspect which presents a serious obstacle to making quantitative estimates is the matter of confidentiality. Governments pursued their worthy citizens with tax demands, and bondholders were not slow in exercising the human propensity of discretion. Dutch investors were no exception to this time-honoured conduct. Charles Wilson has shown the increasing use of attorneys in the dealings between The Netherlands and London, particularly in the crisis of 1772–73.[153] On the one hand, bondholders preferred anonymity, and on the other hand, financiers in a Europe of slow communications found it easier to deal with bearer bonds, which were readily negotiable in arbitrage. It was no secret that such business was fair game for forged certificates and coupons. At the

---

[149] M. Buist, *At spes non fracta* (The Hague, 1974), pp. 93–94; see also Wilson, *Anglo-Dutch Commerce*, pp. 65–70.

[150] Riley, *International government finance*, esp. Chapters 6 and 7.

[151] *Simancas, Estado. Holanda*, Leg. 6368, letter, Herreria to Grimaldi, The Hague, 30 April 1776.

[152] K. N. Chaudhuri, *The Trading World of Asia and the English East India Company, 1660–1760* (Cambridge, 1978), pp. 417–418, 434–436.

[153] Wilson, *Anglo-Dutch Commerce*, pp. 95–102.

outcome of the Seven Years' War, the French government found it necessary to bring some control to the issue of bonds. The reform of December 1764 included a provision to return bearer bonds to Paris for registration before designated notaries. At once a wave of lively protest came from bondholders in The Netherlands. Their *mémoire* (January 1765) left little doubt about their predilection for negotiable paper.[154] At the same time, the use of names of convenience was just another way to move funds with little trace. When the Jesuit Society was asked to leave Spain, for example, the authorities were astounded at the way their assets seemed to disappear into thin air. But what could be more simple in a Europe where funds were already accustomed to cross frontiers with discreet and slippered ease?

A third consideration, and perhaps the most complex, was the difference between funded debt and floating debt. The latter meant a rolling programme of borrowing taken out for ten or twenty years, and often renewed with fresh loans. Sometimes, estimates of current debt are grossed up, giving the total *raised* over a period, rather than the effective debt outstanding. Floating debt, refunding, and settlements, could involve a lively market in short-term paper. The flow of net risk capital from insurance premiums was directly concerned in this section of the market. It may explain in part why alternations of liquidity on the Amsterdam market in the short run sometimes seemed to run counter to the main course of events, to the long-term trend.

In sum, the points at issue settle about the opportunities for investment and profit. On the one hand, openings at home were not necessarily available to absorb the flow of savings. The domestic debt was increasing only slowly in the eighteenth century.[155] For the province of Holland, the growth of the debt divided into three phases: in the first three-quarters of a century of the Republic – the golden age virtually – it rose a hundredfold; by the time of the Treaty of Utrecht (1713), it had again trebled; by the fall of the Republic, a further quarter was added. In such circumstances, opportunities to invest in foreign loans were more than an alternative in the eighteenth century. The repayments on domestic debt, moreover, created a generous supply of funds. After the crisis of 1763, recovery was slow; but by 1766, the beginning of this study, market operations were again substantial. Certainly, in 1767, ample

---

[154] *AAE, CP, Hollande,* 516, *Mémoire de M. de l'Averdy* (January) 1765; ibid., fo. 9 ro.-vo., letter, D'Havrincour to Praslin, The Hague; ibid., fos. 17 vo.–18 vo., note from D'Havrincour, 10 January 1765; *Edit du Roi, concernant la libération des Dettes de l'Etat* (December 1764), and *Arrest du Conseil d'Etat du Roi, qui nomme les personnes chargées de la signature des Effets au Porteur, qui seront représentés en execution de l'Edit de Décembre 1764 (3 February 1765),* Paris, 1765.

[155] See W. M. Keuchenius, *De inkomsten en uitgaven der Bataafsche Republiek voorgesteld in eene national balans* (Amsterdam, 1803), pp. 2–3.

funds seemed to be on offer: 'The sums reimbursed by their Highnesses each year', reported the Marqués de Puentefuerte to Madrid on 14 April, 'are considerable . . . and as the rich capitalists here do not know where to put their wealth, they roundly welcome any slightly higher returns put to them . . .'[156] No doubt, he had his eyes on possible loans for canal-building in Spain; but the age favoured the growth of capital markets, aided by a trend of falling interest rates, conditions of abated risk, and declining insurance premiums.[157] Indeed, the interdependence of these sections of the market may have been significant in creating conditions favourable to lending abroad. The caveats already mentioned point to some of the difficulties in assessing the precise nature of the problem. At least, they set the stage for the discussion.

*

The declared size of domestic public debt in The Netherlands mesmerised observers at the time, and their comments focused on two aspects: the huge debt at home, and the flow of loans abroad. What were some of these contemporary estimates?

In a report of 19 November 1772 to the Marqués de Grimaldi, the Spanish ambassador in The Hague, the Vizconde de la Herreria, included an estimate (dated 5 July 1771) of debts outstanding in The Netherlands.[158] For Zeeland, the total was some 40 million guilders, serviced from a provincial revenue of 2.2 millions. At the end of the War of Austrian Succession (1748), Holland had ten times that amount – some 400 millions – but since that time some 18 millions had been repaid. The rates of interest ranged between 2, 2½, and 3 percent. Another estimate sent to Paris in 1775 by the French ambassador, the Abbé Desnoyers, put the total for Holland at 350 millions and for the whole Netherlands at some 513–560 millions.[159] A further set of estimates, covering the period 1760–80, proposed a total of 509.7 millions,[160] with interest charges of about 12.8 millions or a third of public revenue. The figures of Desnoyers for 1775 could have represented between two and two-and-a-

---

[156] *Simancas, Estado, Holanda*, Leg. 6327, letter, Puentefuerte to Grimaldi, The Hague, 14 April 1767: the implication, higher than the domestic rates of 2 to 3 percent; see Wilson, *Anglo-Dutch Commerce*, p. 25.

[157] See above, note 142.

[158] *Simancas, Estado, Holanda*, Leg. 6364, letter and enclosure, Herreria to Grimaldi, The Hague, 19 November 1772. I hope to publish a fuller account of these estimates, some of the items of which have been difficult to verify. The entry of f. 1 million for the Bank of Scotland does not appear in the ledgers of either the Royal Bank of Scotland or the Bank of Scotland, and I am indebted for this information to Miss C. H. Robertson and Dr C. W. Mann. For the early development of both banks, see S. G. Checkland, *Scottish banking: a history 1695–1973* (Glasgow, 1975), pp. 24–30, 59–62.

[159] *AAE, CP, Hollande*, 528, fo. 133 vo., letter, Desnoyers to Vergennes, The Hague, 8 December 1775.

[160] *AAE, MD, Hollande*, 137, fo. 10; Riley, *International government finance*, p. 77.

64

quarter years' national income. This is huge but, of course, very approximate.

The magnitudes of domestic public debt can be compared with contemporary estimates of loans raised in Amsterdam either on behalf of foreign governments, or invested in the colonies. With public funds in The Netherlands paying between 2 and 3 percent, such transfers looked attractive with returns from 4 to 6 percent, depending on the risks entailed. Again, the report from Herreria (19 November 1772) is worth more than a passing glance.[161] After numerous enquiries, he produced a total of f.250.8 millions for loans raised in Amsterdam on behalf of various governments during a period of almost a century. As he observed, most had been raised in the preceding thirty years, virtually the generation since the War of Austrian Succession. James Riley proposes the same figure for debt outstanding in 1770: f.250 millions.[162] The amounts grouped by countries and in order of size, from the list of Herreria are given in Table 3.

This list, admittedly approximate, is deceptive. For one thing, the dates mark initial loans: subsequent buying and selling, transfers of funds through arbitrage transformed the total capital of credits outstanding. Governments took out further loans, sometimes to refund the original, either in total or in part. And the device of watering the stock was not necessarily an invention of the bourses of the nineteenth century: dealers on the Dam had long since become accustomed to market paper with skill and were adept, if not at deception, at least at glossing the hard realities of insecure assets. Even the best houses such as Hope and Company were not averse to persuading clients, through agents, to digest unpalatable investments on offer.[163] And in the Amsterdam market, as elsewhere, then as now, the small investor was all too often his own worst enemy.

The totals, of course, include and conceal different types of investments. Some loans to governments carried the security of anticipated revenues – the Sound tolls, for example; or the mines in the Austrian empire. There were the loans on property in pawn, as in the case of the jewels from Saxony. Then there were the loans to planters in the Dutch West Indies, or credit of the same type extended via Copenhagen. The loans, valued on the capital assets of the plantation, attracted a rate of interest tied to the product of the cultivation. And there were, in the margin of the Herreria schedule, the significant transfers between markets through the discreet hands of attorneys in London, Paris, Geneva, Genoa. Few can doubt that official loans floated on the Dam, or

[161] See above, note 158.
[162] Riley, *International government finance*, p. 84.
[163] Ibid., pp. 44–50, and note 66.

Table 3. *Amsterdam: estimates of foreign loans*

	millions guilders		%	
France (1720)	90.0		35.9	
England (1688) and Scotland (1750)	41.0		16.3	
Germany and Danzig (1730–71)	30.5		12.4	
Austria (1763–69)	25.0		10.0	
Sweden and Denmark (1763–69)	17.0		6.8	
Russia (1768–70)	4.3		1.7	
Spain (1769)	1.3		0.5	
Sub-total (Europe)		209.8		83.6
Surinam and other Netherlands				
West Indies	34.0		13.6	
Danish West Indies	7.0		2.3	
Sub-total (West Indies)		41.0		16.4
Total		250.8		100.0

Haarlem, or Rotterdam, or The Hague were only part of an iceberg of assets melting through the channels of finance.

A more serious cause for concern about Herreria's estimates are the entries for France (f.90 millions), England (f.40 millions), and Scotland (f.1 million).[164] These seem to run counter to the received opinion of scholars. Peter Dickson and James Riley have few doubts about the magnitudes of The Netherlands commitment to Britain: a total of f.205 millions in 1770, leaving only f.45 millions for the rest of Europe, and the West Indies.[165] The heavy transfer out of British funds into the opportunities in France in the years after the outbreak of the Fourth Anglo-Dutch War (1780) is part of the long-accepted judgement of scholars. This sudden movement may be, in part at least, the shift from simple bearer bonds to those registered before notaries in Paris: a function of archives rather than the reality of the market. The stated absence of heavy investment in France before 1780 does little to explain the marked francophile partiality of Amsterdam in the political man-oeuvres before that war. It seems difficult to attribute this merely to merchandise trading. At the same time, the money markets of The Netherlands required silver, and France in the second half of the

---

[164] See above, note 158.
[165] P. G. M. Dickson, *The Financial Revolution in England: a study in the development of public credit, 1688–1756* (London, 1967), esp. pp. 322–328; Riley, *International government finance*, Chapter 6.

eighteenth century was a major manufacturer of this currency in Europe.[166]

Two instances come at the bottom of the list – the loans to Spain and to the Danish West Indies. These merit special comment. The first was a project for economic development to build the Imperial Aragon canal in the Ebro valley, outlined in Spain in the letters patent of 28 February 1768. A further plan to extend this north of the Ebro led to the Canal Real de Tauste irrigation canal.[167] The engineers came from The Netherlands, in particular, Cornelis Johannes Kraijenhof, whose plan was approved (6 September 1770). Badin y Compañia of Madrid handled the finance, as indicated in their letter of instructions of 15 February 1770; and in the letters patent of 16 December 1772 they received a forty-year concession on the revenues from the olive-oil and wine produced on the resulting estates – about 29,410 hectares – anticipated at f.873,600 annually.[168] It should not pass without notice that ships returning to Amsterdam from Barcelona and other ports with access to this hinterland in the Ebro valley were accustomed to load with wine, brandy, oil – the fruits of the South.

In The Netherlands, the sale of bonds was in the hands of Adolf Johann Heshuysen of Haarlem and Amsterdam in association with Abraham and Simeon Boas of The Hague. In that order, so it seems, for the maps and documents were deposited with the first, with only copies to the latter.[169] According to a letter of 27 July 1772, transfers by bill from Madrid were made through Jean de Neufville in Amsterdam. The original plan dated 1 March 1773 to sell 1,300 bonds of f.1,000 each. Further agreements of 11 October 1772 and 29 January 1773 envisaged 2,400 bonds dated 1 March 1773 also at f.1,000 each,[170] for twelve years plus a further five years' coupons at 6 percent making seventeen and these carried another ten coupons as bonus to promote the issue. The demand for cash remained apparently satisfied, for a third proposal in August 1775 involved raising another f.2.4 millions. A fourth proposal followed (Real Cédula of 12 February 1778) for f.2 millions at 3½

[166] This will be considered further in my forthcoming study on money in France in the eighteenth century.
[167] GA, Amsterdam, Familie-Papieren, Archief Heshuysen, 172, Bericht, p. 1; Simancas, Estado, Holanda, Leg. 6329, letter, Puentefuerte to Grimaldi, The Hague, 24 October 1769; J. Vicens Vives, An economic history of Spain, Eng. trans. (Princeton, 1969), pp. 515, 586; Buist, At spes non fracta, pp. 280–281.
[168] GA, Amsterdam, Familie-Papieren, Archief Heshuysen, 172, Bericht, p. 1; Simancas, Estado, Holanda, Leg. 6328, letter from Miguel Joachim de Lorieri et al., Madrid, 25 May 1776; ibid., 6328, Herreria to Grimaldi, The Hague, 30 April 1776, enclosure; ibid., Leg. 6330, letter, Puentefuerte to Grimaldi, The Hague, 21 June 1770.
[169] GA, Amsterdam, Familie-Papieren, Archief Heshuysen, 172, Bericht, p. 1.
[170] Ibid., 172, letter, Baptiste Condom to Adolf Heshuysen, Madrid, 8 July 1772.

percent;[171] and a fifth for another f.2 millions (probably in December 1778). The latter called for half in cash and half in old bonds. And there were further proposals for other canals – the project for the Murcia canal (1774) ran into serious resistance to selling the annuities.[172]

The second set of entries in the Herreria schedule concerns loans to the West Indies: Dutch, Danish, and British (the last for Grenada, under negotiation by Hope and Company at 5 percent).[173] The total in this list raised for The Netherlands settlements is given as f.34 millions. Joh. Petrus van der Voort shows that between 1753 and 1771 the total was f.41,175,178;[174] and for 1766–75 this reached f.57,845,657, 81 percent being issued in Amsterdam.

The loans to the Danish West Indies were listed for f.7 millions and carried a date of 1763. Marten Buist comments on the issues by Lever and De Bruine in 1768 – 'A' bonds for the planters of St Croix, St Thomas and St John; and 'B' bonds for St Croix only. Abraham ter Borch also apparently had a hand, until bankruptcy carried him off in 1773. Later, some at least of the bonds passed to Hope and Company.[175] The tentacles of credit, colonial products, cargoes and navigation remain complex. For an example, we have only to turn to the loan to the planters of Essequibo and Demerara organised in Middelburg in 1772 by Cornelis van den Helm Boddaert through the hands of Adolf Heshuysen of Haarlem and Amsterdam. Jacob Frederick Landsheer was a valuer and Johannes Loenen broker, both associated with the insurance policies of the *Haast U Langzaam*. The series of loans – f.1 million in ten 'classes' – envisaged credit transfers of five-eighths of the value of the property on mortgage and of three-quarters of the value of estimated production. The interest

---

[171] Ibid., 172, *Bericht*, p. 2; *Archivo Nacional, Madrid, Consejo*, 1523, Real Provisión, 7 April 1777; ibid., 1524, Real Cédula, 12 February 1778; ibid., *Cédulas*, 479, Real Cédula, 21 June 1778; *Simancas, Estado, Holanda*, Leg. 6369, letter, Herreria to Floridablanca, The Hague, 5 June 1777, and ibid., Leg. 6371, same correspondents, The Hague, 31 December 1778; *AAE, CP, Hollande*, 530, fo. 109 vo., letter, La Vauguyon to Vergennes, The Hague, 2 May 1777.

[172] *AAE, CP, Hollande*, 528, fo. 165 ro., letter, Desnoyers to Vergennes, The Hague, 2 January 1776; ibid., fo. 187 vo., same correspondents, 23 January 1776; ibid., fos. 195 ro.–200 vo., *Aanmerkingen over zekere Negotiatie in Lyfrenten* . . . Amsterdam, 5 December 1775; ibid., fos. 210 ro.–211 vo., *Réfutation aux Critiques faites contre la Négociation du Canal de Murcie*, The Hague, 1776; *Archivo Nacional, Madrid, Códices*, 1272B, Real Cédula, 1 September 1774; *Simancas, Estado, Holanda*, 6368, letter, Herreria to Grimaldi, The Hague, 30 April 1776; ibid., *Estado*, Leg. 4599, fo. 65, letter, Vergennes to Aranda, Versailles, 25 August 1775; and fo. 179, letter, Aranda to Grimaldi, Paris, 13 December 1775; Riley, *International government finance*, pp. 165–166.

[173] *ARA, Archief van Pieter Steyn*, 332a; see above, note 158.

[174] The conclusion of J. P. van der Voort in *De Westindische plantages van 1720 tot 1795: financiën en handel* (Eindhoven, 1973); see also P. C. Emmer, 'De vaart buiten Europa: het Atlantisch gebied', in G. Asaert et al., *Maritieme geschiedenis der Nederlanden*, III, pp. 310–311.

[175] Buist, *At spes non fracta*, p. 20.

on the loans came to 12 percent of the annual produce. With extensions the coupons on class 7 of the loan were apparently still active in 1848.[176] The interaction of capital and navigation was, therefore, subtle and complex. And passed at the highest level. When ships returning from the West Indies were captured in the summer of 1778, one from St Eustatius had her cargo returned, the greater part under consignment for Hope and Company of Amsterdam.[177] In the same vein, there was the Grenada loan which Hope and Company negotiated in 1771 for f.220,000 at 5 percent. The share-cropping gives little surprise when we find the ship *Vrijheyd*[178] sailing from the island on 2 December 1780 bound for Amsterdam with a cargo of sugar and coffee. The sugar was valued at f.57,500, and 93½ percent of it for Hope and Company. In effect, it is not excessive to see that the plantation loans promoted the assembly of return cargoes, and in turn possible demand for insurance.

The linkages between loans, cargoes and insurance were thus highly diversified. Some of the great names in finance were implicated: Ferrand Whaley Hudig of Rotterdam, and Adolf (Jan) Heshuysen, shippers from Surinam in the *Vigilantie* on 23 September 1774;[179] or Harman van de Poll and Dirk Luden, shippers from Surinam in the *Petrus Alexander* a week later on 30 September 1774,[180] both signing lines in the cargo policies of the *Haast U Langzaam* in 1777. A few names plucked from the long lists of shippers in the manifests from the West Indies serve to put the loans to planters in a matrix of plantation agriculture, trade, finance and insurance. Profits were anticipated from the cargoes prepared by the stevedores, and, if we follow the intrusive studies of Joh. Petrus van der Voort, materialised well below expectations. To be sure, the value system was hardly a reliable accomplice. With the commercial world turning to flows of American silver, those profits and price differentials between the colonies and Europe were not easy to maintain. Little wonder at the fierce protests among the planters against the unfavourable exchange rates with Europe, not least when it came to the valuation of commodities fixed in the hard currency of The Netherlands. The Commercie Compagnie considered the problem *in extenso* in 1774, and it was critical as much for the plantations in Essequibo and Demerara as in Surinam.[181]

---

[176] *GA, Amsterdam, Familie-Papieren, Archief Heshuysen*, 171, *Conditiën van eene Negotiatie ten lasten van eenige Planters in de Colonie van Essequebo en Demerary*, Middelburg, 1 July 1772.

[177] *Simancas, Estado, Holanda*, Leg. 6370, letter, Herreria to Floridablanca, The Hague, 28 July 1778.

[178] Ibid., Leg. 6364, same correspondents, The Hague, 19 November 1772 and enclosure dated 5 July 1771; *ARA, Archief van Pieter Steyn*, 332a; *KVA*, XXI, 1456; and see below, p. 114.

[179] *KVA*, XVIII, 610; see also J. Hudig, *De West-Indische Zaken van Ferrand Whaley Hudig, 1759–1797* (Amsterdam, 1922).

[180] *KVA*, XVIII, 596.   [181] *RAZ, MCC*, 1577.

In effect, the late 1760s and early 1770s saw the market briskly active in loans, in the prelude to the bankruptcies of December 1772 to January 1773. That crisis apparently did not deter investors too long, for promoters returned to the charge. The investment-trust schemes of Abraham van Ketwich in the 1770s showed both the inventiveness and fragility of the market.[182] After the date of Herreria's list (19 November 1772), important loans were either negotiated or in the air. There was the proposed sale for France of 30 million *livres* of annuities at 8 percent on one life and 7 percent on two, paid half in cash and half in bonds. The contract set the exchange rate for the *livre tournois* at 0.475 guilders while the commercial rate moved to about 0.452–0.456. This put the effective loan at f.14.25 millions, if all found buyers.[183] In 1772, the pressure for loans increased as government agents from all sides took the road to Amsterdam, hands outstretched. In March, Russia wanted f.3 millions and offered interest at 5 percent;[184] Sweden looked for f.2.5 millions but managed with 2 millions.[185] The ailing Elector of Bavaria negotiated a million at 4 percent, secured on revenues from the feudal demesne.[186] From the North in October, Denmark asked for f.4 millions at 4 percent, secured on the Sound tolls; but the deal included clauses relating to Altona and garrisons, which found little favour in either Hanover or Hamburg.[187]

In April 1774, the firm of Dull arranged f.2 millions at 5 percent for Denmark; in October 1774, Denmark continued in the market for another f.2 millions, again secured on the Sound tolls. In March 1775, Prince Henry, the estranged brother of Frederick the Great, offered 5 percent for a loan of f.900,000. In July and September, Sweden raised two loans totalling 3 millions at 4 percent, Hope and Company acting as agents.[188] By the end of 1775, the outstanding commitments of three big borrowers were as shown in Table 4.

The growing climate of conflict in 1776 raised the pressure on liquidity, and rates rose accordingly. At first, most loans called for interest at 4 percent. When Britain, at war with North America and uneasy at the state of Europe, looked in December that year for £6

---

[182] W. H. Berghuis, *Ontstaan en ontwikkeling van de Nederlandse beleggingsfondsen tot 1914* (Assen, 1967), pp. 51–74.

[183] *Simancas, Estado*, Leg. 4579, letter, Fuentes to Grimaldi, Paris, 3 August 1771.

[184] *Simancas, Estado, Holanda*, Leg. 6364, letter, Herreria to Grimaldi, The Hague, 19 March 1772.

[185] Ibid., Leg. 6364, same correspondents, The Hague, 27 October 1772.

[186] Ibid., Leg. 6364, same correspondents, The Hague, 31 March 1772.

[187] Ibid., Leg. 6364, same correspondents, The Hague, 27 October 1772.

[188] Ibid., Leg. 6367, same correspondents, The Hague, 21 March 1775; *AAE, CP, Hollande*, 525, fo. 291 ro., letter De Noailles to D'Aiguillon, The Hague, 1 March 1774; ibid., 526, fos. 219 vo.–220 ro., letter, Desnoyers to Vergennes, The Hague, 11 October 1774.

Table 4. Current loans to Austria, Denmark, and Russia[a]

		Total in millions of guilders
Austria, secured on the		
(a) Revenues of Bohemia:	1.17	
(b) Bank of Vienna:	11.50	
(c) Mercury mines, 1765–73:	10.00	22.67
Denmark, secured on the Sound tolls:		10.00
Russia, in three loans in		
(a) 1769:	4.00	
(b) 1770:	3.00	
(c) 1773:	2.00	9.00

[a] *AAE, CP, Hollande*, 525, fo. 301 ro.–vo., letter, De Noailles to D'Aiguillon, The Hague, 15 March 1774; ibid., 528, fo. 132 ro.–vo., letter, Desnoyers to Vergennes, The Hague, 8 December 1775; Riley, *International government finance*, p. 157; he estimates the Austrian loans at f.21.5 millions (deducting the Silesian loan of 1730) and the Russian loans at f.10 millions.

millions sterling at 4 percent – about f.65 millions at the going rate of exchange – Hope and Company undertook to unload some of the bonds in The Netherlands. At the time, Lord North put the stake of The Netherlands in the National Debt at £59 millions, but Alice Carter estimates the reality to have been more likely a half or less than that amount.[189] Other governments showed appetites for loans just as sharp. Denmark negotiated for f.2 millions at 4 percent. Poland looked for half a million at the same rate, made more attractive by a guarantee from Russia. As for France, Turgot struggled to inject some order into the royal finances, and a part of that scheme, outlined in the letters patent of 18 December 1774 and the *arrêt* of the Conseil d'Etat of 2 March 1776, included special arrangements for paying Dutch bondholders. The coupons were to be settled by six-monthly bills of exchange drawn by Grand et Compagnie in Paris on Horneca, Fizeaux et Compagnie in Amsterdam.[190] However, the clouds of war paradoxically made for

[189] *Simancas, Estado, Holanda*, Leg. 6369, letter, Herreria to Grimaldi, The Hague, 3 December 1776. There has, of course, been considerable speculation – and debate – about the level of Dutch investment abroad. For the transfers into the English National Debt, see C. H. Wilson, 'Dutch investment in eighteenth-century England: a note on yardsticks', *EcHR*, 2nd ser., XII (1960), esp. 434, and Alice Carter, 'Note on a note on yardsticks', ibid. Alice Carter casts doubt on the figure of £59 millions proposed by Lord North and suggests a more likely figure of half or less that amount, £25–30 millions: see 'The Dutch and the English Public Debt in 1777', *Economica*, XX (1953). Even this, hovering around a year's national income in The Netherlands, seems somewhat generous.

[190] *AAE, CP, Hollande*, 529, fo. 52 ro.–vo., letter, Clugny to Messrs Horneca, Fizeaux et Compagnie (Amsterdam), Versailles, 24 August 1776; ibid., 529, fo. 240 ro., letter, La Vauguyon to Vergennes, The Hague, 21 January 1777; *Simancas, Estado, Holanda*, Leg. 6368, letter, Herreria to Grimaldi, The Hague, 10 December 1776.

greater liquidity in Amsterdam, as anxious bondholders repatriated their assets from countries at risk. A loan of f.2.5 millions to Denmark in May 1777 at 4 percent was so heavily oversubscribed that it was necessary to send back half the cash. In passing, it should be noted that the Sound tolls were raised in 1776. As for Poland, the loan of February 1777 issued through Hope and Company was quickly taken up.[191]

Open war in 1778 furthered this movement of cutting down some areas of lending, while making others more attractive. A loan to Russia in 1778 of f.1.5 millions, was finally negotiated at 4 percent, secured on the revenues of Livonia (a separate Russian government in 1783).[192] At the other end of the spectrum, American agents asking for a million with little to offer as security, found the market both prudent and negative.[193] They met with a similar rebuff in Genoa, but this time they had powerful friends at court: France offered to guarantee both the capital and interest of those private investors who subscribed to the loans.[194]

The treaty signed between Austria and Prussia again sent swirls and eddies through the dealings of Amsterdam, for the Empire lost no time in raising new finance. With two million guilders already raised, a further loan of f.5 millions was floated in Amsterdam in February 1779 and f.7.5 millions in The Hague, both at 4½ percent. The first, for ten years, by the house of Goll went better than the second which the house of Boas offered for only five.[195] If anything the difference showed a preference for steady income, rather than security. In four years, the interest had risen one percentage point. But the debts of the Empire were mounting, and created a flow of bonds for sale. In 1767, the total had been 156 millions of florins; by 1788 they had risen to 342, with service charges taking a third of the public revenue.[196] Between 1765 and 1799, Austria managed on average to raise at least one loan a year in Amsterdam.[197]

On all sides, governments faced shortfalls in revenue: Russia, Poland,

[191] *AAE, CP, Hollande,* 529, fo. 283 vo., letter, La Vauguyon to Vergennes, The Hague, 14 February 1777; ibid., 530, fo. 118 vo., same correspondents, The Hague, 6 May 1777; Buist, *At spes non fracta,* p. 112.

[192] *AAE, CP, Hollande,* 532, fo. 104 ro., letter, Berenger to Vergennes, The Hague, 17 February 1778; *Simancas, Estado, Holanda,* Leg. 6370, letter, Herreria to Floridablanca, The Hague, 8 October 1778.

[193] *Simancas, Estado, Holanda,* Leg. 6370, letter, Herreria to Floridablanca, The Hague, 22 October 1778.

[194] *AS, Genoa,* AS.2294, letter, Ageno to Serenissima, London, 1 October 1779.

[195] *Simancas, Estado, Holanda,* Leg. 6371, letter, Herreria to Floridablanca, The Hague, 9 February 1779; *AS, Genoa,* AS.2658, letters, Massardo to Serenissima, The Hague, 12 February and 2 April 1779.

[196] F. Baltzarek, *Die Geschichte der Wiener Börse* (Vienna, 1973), pp. 20–33; see also E. Klein, *Geschichte der öffentlichen Finanzen in Deutschland (1500–1870)* (Wiesbaden, 1974), pp. 26, 36.

[197] Riley, *International government finance,* pp. 129–131.

Table 5. *Amsterdam: market rates and effective returns on loans* (July 1771)

Loan	Interest percent	Market price: par = 100	Effective return %
Austria	4	100–106	3.77–4.00
Denmark: secured on			
Customs	5	103	4.85
Asiatic Company	4	100	4.00
Sweden	5	94–100	5.00–5.32
Danzig	5	103	4.85
Russia	5	98.5	5.08
Germany:			
Leipzig	4	94–95	4.21–4.26
Brunswick–Lüneburg	5	98.5–99	5.05–5.08
Mecklemburg	5	99–100	5.00–5.05
Oldenburg	5	100	5.00
Saxony	4	100–101	3.96–4.00
Spain	6	98.5–99.5	6.03–6.09
West Indies:			
Essequibo/Demerara	5	100	5.00
Essequibo/Demerara	6	99.5–100	6.00–6.03
Surinam	5	97–107	4.67–5.15
Surinam	6	95–100	6.00–6.32
Danish Islands	6	91–98	6.12–6.59
Grenada	5	103	4.85

Sweden, Denmark, Britain, France – all were in line for loans. An escape from this overspending lay in deficit finance: an increase in the circulation of paper currency in the domestic economy loans from capital markets abroad. At one level, the expansion of paper obligations reduced the necessity for flows of specie; at another level, the market adjusted the price to accord with expected returns and risks. In his report to the Marqués de Grimaldi of 19 November 1772,[198] Herreria included a list dated 5 July 1771 in which he gave the current market prices in Amsterdam of some of these foreign loans (see Table 5). It will be seen at once that they too belonged to the network of Netherlands trade.

A summary glance at the list shows three types of loans trading at a premium: Austria, a preferred debtor in the 1770s, offered access not only to the Empire but also to the southern Netherlands, already in a phase of remarkable resurgence; Denmark (for the Sound tolls); and Danzig – the great grain outlet, but on the threshold of impending partition. In contrast, there were discounts for the West Indies, and these clearly presented uncertainties.

[198] See above, note 158.

The decade from the mid-1760s so favourable to investors in international finance came to a term as war erupted first in North America and then in Europe. As the conflicts spread and deepened, the liquidity of the market began to tighten. Speculators were more inclined to put their money into commodities and wait for the inflation of war. This, too, curtailed the funds available. In 1778, the outbreak of war in Europe circumscribed the horizons of finance, and interest rates tended to rise to 5 percent. The courts of Vienna and St Petersburg found they had to countenance this rate 'in the circumstances in which business found itself', the Spanish ambassador wrote back to Madrid, for spare money preferred to find a place in the growing stockpiles of goods of general consumption.[199] But goods had to be shipped, or placed in warehouses; and whether in transit contending with the perils of the sea or in store with the hazards of theft, spoilage, and fire, they still remained clients for protection and insurance.

Risks in navigation, risks in the short-term investment of premiums, risks in long-term government debts and loans abroad – were the various sections of the market linked and inter-dependent? It would be difficult to hazard a certain reply but no doubt differentials in rates of return must have their say. In The Netherlands, public loans paid from 2 to 3 percent. Abroad the rate ranged from 4 percent (for borrowers in Europe) to 6 (for loans to planters in the West Indies): the differential then could have been between 2 to 3 percent. In the best summer months, 3 percent covered insurance for a ship to the Baltic or the Mediterranean.[200] At the same time, the degree of security offered could affect the outcome: there were loans attached to customs tolls as in the Sound; or to revenues as in Livonia; or to the anticipated revenues from royalties of the mines of Austria and Bohemia. There were even jewels to put in pawn. And above all the imprimatur of government: in 1767, when the Duke of Brunswick won a loan for two years, he paid 5 percent; but in 1768 a further loan with guarantee from the States General, called for only 4: a government guarantee was apparently worth a percentage point. Certainly, institutional factors had a part to play, and canted the balance of investment towards national debts. Political stability and a steady monetary system were powerful inducements, when the specialist 'entrepreneurs', as the underwriters were called in the transactions of Hope and Company,[201] came to unload paper on the market. The small investor in the eighteenth century did not seem all that

---

[199] *Simancas, Estado, Holanda,* Leg. 6370, letters, Herreria to Floridablanca, The Hague, 29 January and 13 August 1778.
[200] See below, Table 5, p. 73 and Graph 9, p. 149.
[201] Buist, *At spes non fracta,* pp. 24–27.

different from his modern counterpart in asking for high returns with little heed to insecurity and the tribulations of the morrow.

As was often the case under the *ancien régime*, revenues were raised through syndicates of financiers so that private and public interests mingled and fused. Did trade follow the flag? Respect for the flag was one of the issues of neutrality, and loans to mercantilist states were not necessarily a sector set apart, but could on the contrary promote business under government protection. Such lending was associated with wider economic considerations. Taxes which paid interest on such loans could affect flows of goods to markets in which The Netherlands had a customary stake. High-risk credits to the West Indian islands could lubricate the return of cargoes, especially when the interest payments were stipulated in kind. In comparing the markets for insurance and for government and colonial loans, the association should not be overlooked that the groups of destinations quoted in the *prijscouranten*[202] relate to the countries of loans listed in Table 3 – with a few exceptions. Some of the princes of Germany were not immediately recognisable. And at first sight, the Austrian empire seemed remote – until on closer inspection we recall the arrival in Amsterdam and Rotterdam of the insurance agencies from Antwerp, Brussels, Bruges, Ghent, and still further afield, from Trieste.[203] Far from being remote, they became very close and with mutual interests. Indeed, some of the similarities were more striking than the differences. And the point carried weight when The Netherlands had a decided penchant for trading along the coasts of the continent.

★

In closing, there remains the question of the returns on public loans at home as compared with 'invisible' earnings abroad. One estimate for 1760–80 put the domestic debt charge in The Netherlands at f.12.79 millions and the capital at f.507.7 millions. An estimate for 1775 put the latter at about f.513–560 millions.[204] Investments abroad, at 4 percent in Europe and 6 in the West Indies could have produced a return of about f.10.85 millions. The difference is not all that great, although, clearly, the issues were far more complex. Taxation which appeared so heavy in The Netherlands and necessary to service domestic debt, was balanced in part by these invisibles from overseas lending. However, the heavy reliance on excise levies created a problem of social distribution, raised the cost of living and in turn that of labour. It was not the least of problems faced by the Republic. On occasion the returns from abroad could have been even higher. For example, the bonds were issued in London (1778) for £10 millions at 5 percent, carried special inducements. When these were taken into account, the bonds offered an effective return for the first year

---

[202] See below, Chapter 5 and p. 165.   [203] See above, p. 46.
[204] See above, pp. 64–65 and notes 158–160.

of 11 percent. It was rumoured that Hope and Company subscribed for f.2.5 millions.[205]

Against these invisible returns, what estimates can be made of the contribution of marine insurance? At a net rate of return of, say, $3\frac{1}{4}$ percent, the underwriting account could have added a share comparable to the dividends distributed – fictive to be sure – by the VOC, already in debt and borrowing more. In 1769–70, the latter averaged some f.1.19 millions, or an effective share-out of $3\frac{1}{2}$ percent. But that was for all six chambers of the VOC. However, underwriting was spread in the provinces, not necessarily in Amsterdam; fire and life insurance, as the emergence of companies indicated, was a fast-growing sector. And in any case, the substantive documentary evidence is lacking to give a positive answer. If later developments were any sure indication, the insurance presence was certainly not negligible.

[205] *Simancas, Estado,* Leg. 7000 (41, 42), letters, Escarano to Floridablanca, London, 3 and 10 March 1778; ibid., *Estado, Holanda,* Leg. 6370, letters, Herreria to Floridablanca, London, 10 and 12 March 1778. The new loan opened in London on 4 March 1778 for £10 millions sterling at 5 percent; but with the market price of the bonds and the discount allowed before 17 November, the effective return for the first year approached 11 percent. Hope and Company took a sizeable share for sale in The Netherlands.

Three event uncertainties: 1763, 1772–73, and war in 1780

By the eighteenth century, the market of Amsterdam retained an assured presence among the financial centres of Europe. Such recognition points to structures which were patently complex, often staid, yet at the same time capable of remarkable innovations as the projects of Abraham van Ketwich amply demonstrated. This vitality had no little import for risk-spreading since insurance was not set in a market apart. The same names bobbed up as occasion offered under the guise of underwriters, shippers, bill-brokers, warehouse-agents, entrepreneurs for loans both at home and abroad – in short, of dealers in the market. But as net risk capital looked more to short-term investment, many of these opportunities advanced together and so responded to changes both specialised and versatile. Rises and falls – as in other financial centres, more often in close conjunction with them – conformed to the modulation of economic environment. As a world market Amsterdam received the imprint of wide and intricate pressures, shocks both domestic and international, which touched all levels of its activity and disrupted its functions. Our purpose here is to consider some of these random elements in the sense that they came outside the immediate scope of insurance, and belonged implicitly as much to the uncertainties in good years as those in bad times.

In the 1760s and 1770s, three major event uncertainties interrupted that commercial and financial rhythm: the crisis of 1763, which still left scars in 1766; the string of bankruptcies in 1772–73, of shorter duration but still disastrous for premier houses on the Dam; and the slide towards armed neutrality and war, from which in the end The Netherlands was unable to remain aloof. These disturbances to the flow of funds varied greatly from bankruptcy to war: each was intrinsically different the one from the other. For instance, the first affected the writing of policies, the spread of finance, the meeting of commitments and settling claims of the sort which came before the Kamer van Assurantie. However, the second aggravated the perils of navigation and changed the scalars of risk at sea.

As naval search parties boarded ships and confiscated cargoes, hopes of peace wavered and waned. The insurers of Amsterdam protested, sometimes withdrew from business, but sometimes also gambled on the high premiums which war-risks demanded. War became a major disruption, redirecting flows of goods and changing horizons of invest-ment. On the one hand, the supply side of insurance received severe blows for, if anything, the turnover of underwriters in the market accelerated; on the other hand insecurity drove up the demand for more protection, and the willingness to pay for it. Both aspects were vital to the insurance business of Amsterdam and combined into the perform-ance of the market. How did these three event uncertainties emerge and develop?

CRISIS IN 1763 AND RECOVERY

The crisis of 1763 found immediate roots in the disruptions of the Seven Years' War, and battles more sharp and bloody than often imagined.[1] In the longer perspective, the deep structural problems which appeared at the heart of the armed conflict were not settled by the crisis. The financial aspects of both these – the immediate and the structural – have long preoccupied observers and generated considerable debate. In the discus-sion between W. M. F. Mansvelt and J. G. van Dillen,[2] the problem

[1] T. H. Bliss, 'Important elements in modern land conflicts', *American Academy of Political and Social Science Annals*, XXVI (1905), p. 107 et seq. The ten important battles returned an hourly loss of 6.05 percent, higher than any in the century and a half to follow.

[2] The crises of 1763 and 1772–73 have received extensive coverage, both at the level of the market and in the wider context of the growth of The Netherlands; for particular attention, W. P. Sautijn Kluit, *De Amsterdamsche Beurs in 1763 en 1773: eene bijdrage tot de geschiedenis van den handel* (Amsterdam, 1865); E. E. de Jong-Keesing, *De economische crisis van 1763 te Amsterdam* (Amsterdam, 1939); C. H. Wilson, *Anglo-Dutch commerce and finance in the eighteenth century* (Cambridge, 1941, repr. 1966); more recently, F. Braudel, *Civilisation matérielle, économie et capitalisme, XVe.–XVIIIe. siècle* (3 vols., Paris, 1979), III, pp. 226–234. For the structures of credit in Amsterdam, J. G. van Dillen, 'De Beurscrisis te Amsterdam in 1763', *TVG*, XXXVII (1922) and with W. M. F. Mansvelt, 'De crisis van 1763 en de economische achteruitgang van Amsterdam: een discussie', ibid., taking up their correspondence in the *Algemeen Handelsblad* of 25 October and 2 November 1922 (copies in *GA, Amsterdam*). S. Skalweit, *Die Berliner Wirtschaftskrise von 1763 und ihre Hintergründe* (Stuttgart–Berlin, 1937). For the long-term trends in bankruptcies in Amsterdam, W. F. H. Oldewelt, 'Twee eeuwen Amsterdamse faillissementen en het verloop van de conjunctuur (1636 tot 1838)', *TVG*, LXXV (1962). For the problems facing the Maatschappij van Assurantie in Rotterdam, C. H. Slechte, 'De Maatschappij van Assurantie, Discontering en Beleen-ing der stad Rotterdam van 1720, bekeken naar haar productie-factoren over de periode 1720–1874', *Rotterdams Jaarboekje*, 7e. R., VIII (1970), esp. p. 271. For contemporary assessments see *AAE, CP, Hollande*, 513, fos. 64 ro.–67 vo., *Lettre d'un Monsieur de Haarlem à son ami concernant les faillites des frères Neuville* (enclosed in letter dated 23 September 1763, and hereafter cited as *Lettre d'un Monsieur de Haarlem*); ibid., *Hambourg*, 88, fos. 241 ro.–244 vo. *Mémoire*, 12 August 1763 (hereafter cited as *Mémoire, 1763*).

made for a sharp exchange of views, focusing on the one hand on the structure of the market, on the other hand on the exorbitant inflation of credit. Each aimed to expose the weaknesses of the other's argument; but in hindsight, both had sound claims to be right.

Although the crisis had this double complexity, the conclusion of peace seemed both simple and direct. It contrasted with the bitter encounters which preceded it. On 10 February 1763 in the depth of a Paris winter, the plenipotentiaries of France, Spain, and Britain put seal to a settlement; and five days later, on 15 February, those of Prussia, Austria and Saxony likewise came to terms in the castle of Hubertusburg. As ink dried on the treaties and troops settled more contentedly into their winter quarters, the time had at last come for bells to peal and bonfires burn. There was an end to carnage and soon spring would cloak the scars in green. But ministers all too glumly counted the costs of war, and looked for ways to ward off the pressing demands of financiers. For them six months of peace brought little relief, only economic havoc.

★

Perhaps like other great crises before and since, it stemmed from changes in the economic balance of Europe. The difficulties of some Baltic ports – in Poland and Sweden – found compensation in the swelling prosperity of others: for example, Gothenburg, St Petersburg, Viborg. To the south, long caravans of merchants from Rzeczpospolita (Poland–Lithuania) made their way to the Leipzig fairs or organised consignments overland between east and west, complementing the Baltic navigation.[3] The expansion in the trade of Silesia to Italy, in the transfers on the Oder–Elbe waterways and canals to Hamburg were further signs of economic growth in Germany.[4]

All this implicated the merchant financiers of Amsterdam but the developments came to a head in the hothouse of war. Swelling shipments of goods to the theatres of war brought expanded settlements by bill of exchange. An observer 'from Haarlem' noted the long-rising trend in this business in the last half-century and that, with the crisis of 1763, the volume of paper could have reached fifteen times the currency circulating in The Netherlands. A dangerously low reserve-ratio indeed if correct, but one which reflected at least extended credits to purchase the

---

[3] S. Ricard, *Traité*, I, p. 283; III, pp. 54–55; J. A. Faber, 'De achttiende eeuw', in J. H. van Stuijvenberg (ed.), *De Economische-geschiedenis van Nederland* (Groningen, 1977), pp. 133–135; S. Högeberg, *Utrikeshandel och sjöfart på 1700-talet: Stapelvaror i svensk export och import 1738–1808* (Stockholm, 1967), pp. 238–242; R. Davis, *The rise of the Atlantic economies* (London, 1967), pp. 190–191; G. E. Munro, *The development of St. Petersburg as an urban center during the reign of Catharine II (1762–1796)* (Ann Arbor, 1974), pp. 209, 218.

[4] J. J. Oddy, *European Commerce, shewing New and Secure Channels of Trade with the Continent of Europe* (2 vols., Philadelphia, 1807), pp. 215–218.

merchandise of war and the inevitable rise in debt of the belligerent states. And, he went on, there were in particular the debts of Germany, and the subsidies from Britain. These rising flows of cash and credit created an attractive discount market in short-term paper – a serious weakness for insurance dealings in the same section of the market.[5] Indeed, the situation had the classic performers of so many financial panics: merchants with too many assets tied up in long-term commitments but short on liquidity.

In Hamburg,[6] also, observers' eyes were sharply focused on the build-up of instability: the swelling flow of tampered currencies; and paper obligations. The subsidies to Frederick of Prussia were naturally in the forefront of concerns; so too were the commitments to the King of Denmark and the merchants of Copenhagen. And then there was the shortfall from Sweden. Little wonder that the directors of prestigious public banks as much in Amsterdam as in Hamburg forecast doom and raised their interest rates to hedge disaster.[7]

Indeed, much of the paper circulation sprang from trade financed by subsidies for military operations. Britain had been a paymaster to Prussia but at the cost of increased deficit: the National Debt doubled during the war from some £78 millions sterling (1757) to £132 millions (1763).[8] Credits accelerated the flow of materials to the war in the east; and they created an enlarged market for investment in public funds.[9] Amsterdam house helped to unload that English debt, above all the firm of Hope and Company which found its metier and soared ahead in the early years of the war.[10] The surge of business to service the pay-days of battalions and the deliveries of munitions could not easily be stemmed once the fighting had ended.

The imbalance in cash-flows was not confined to Europe: it also surfaced in colonial trade. The VOC had diversified in trading activities to develop its credit and banking potential. After the 1720s, exchange arbitrage had offered promising opportunities,[11] and the transfers or *assignatiën* initially made for servants of the company from Batavia to The Netherlands, now moved to a further extension in exchange dealings or *wissels* of wider and more complex nature. Both operations

---

[5] *Lettre d'un Monsieur de Haarlem.*

[6] *Mémoire, 1763,* fos. 241 ro.–242 ro.

[7] PRO, SP, 82.80, fo. 89 ro., letter, Woodford to Halifax, Hamburg, 16 August 1763; Sautijn Kluit, *De Amsterdamsche Beurs,* pp. 2–5.

[8] Ibid.; E. L. Hargreaves, *The National Debt* (London, 1930), pp. 60–65, 291.

[9] Wilson, *Anglo-Dutch Commerce,* pp. 137 et seq.

[10] Ibid., pp. 66, 166; E. E. de Jong-Keesing, *De economische crisis,* p. 70; M. Buist, *At spes non fracta: Hope & Co. 1770–1815, merchant bankers and diplomats at work* (The Hague, 1974), pp. 12–13.

[11] F. S. Glaastra, 'De Verenigde Oost-Indische Compagnie in de zeventiende en achttiende eeuw: de groei van een bedrijf', *BMG,* XCI (1976).

grew rapidly in the eighteenth century,[12] but war in Europe disrupted colonial trade. The maladjustment of cash flows between Asia and the VOC chambers in The Netherlands tied up idle balances in the East and impaired liquidity in The Netherlands.

As the merchants and financiers took stock of the situation in Europe at the opening of a new season of trade, three weak spots emerged. There was Denmark: the cash situation in Copenhagen hardly seemed promising when Baron Schimmelmann turned up in Hamburg to draw some 4 millions Mark banco from the Giro-Bank. Added to this there were other commitments to merchants in Copenhagen, so that the total shortfall reached some 11.5 millions Mark banco.

Then there was Sweden, where the increased circulation of bank-notes reduced the facility of payments abroad, not least when the state had put an embargo on the export of copper, one of its strongest assets.[13]

And there was Prussia, which proved to be the weakest spot of all, at two levels. Firstly, currency. Those remarkable speculators, Veitel Heine Ephraim and Daniel Itzig, had farmed the mints and brought from the coinage a harvest of quick if not lasting profits. The earlier reforms of Johan Philipp Graumann (1750), important enough to be known widely as the *Graumannsche Münzfuss*, were quickly set aside. Serious debasement was the order of the day, soon at well over a quarter. The coins filtered into Paris in 1759 and were found to have only 28¾ percent of the intrinsic value of the pre-war gold *Friedrich*.[14] The currency deterioration touched all levels of society. Frederick did not even stop at paying his beloved troops with monetary rubbish: by the end of the war a soldier's pay in real terms had shrunken to a third.[15] Little wonder at the derisive jingle for the coins in circulation:

> von aussen schön
> von innen schlimm
> von aussen Friedrich
> von innen Ephraim.[16]

---

[12] This will be examined in my forthcoming study of cash-flows in Asia in the eighteenth century.

[13] *AAE, CP, Hambourg*, 88, fos. 241 ro.–245 ro., *Mémoire du comte de Modène*, 12 August 1763.

[14] *Hôtel des Monnaies, Paris, Louis XV*, Carton 14, *Arrêt de la Cour des Monnaies*, 28 April 1759; R. Koser, 'Die preussischen Finanzen im Siebenjährigen Kriege', *Forschungen zur brand. und preuss. Geschichte*, XIII (1900).

[15] *PRO, SP*, 90.82, fo. 196 vo., letter, Mitchell to Halifax, Berlin, 26 April 1763. For the potential market for debased coins, see the study of F. Redlich on the War of the Austrian Succession, 'The eighteenth-century trade in "light ducats"', *Economy and History*, XVI (1973), esp. p. 12.

[16] Often quoted, as for example in G. Meinhardt, *Münz- und Geldgeschichte der Stadt Göttingen von den Anfängen bis zur Gegenwart* (Göttingen, 1961), p. 113.

Secondly, there was the unsupported expansion of financial obligations, the financial back-log of war. When peace pulled the purse-strings
tight, trade continued in the same vein: war-credits drifted eastwards
with returns hard to find. The imbalance in cash-flows was clear: one
report put the unpaid accounts in Germany and the northern provinces at
three times the returns.[17] In Prussia the main agent was Johann Ernst
Gotzkowsky, an entrepreneur of talent gifted for speculation. He had
made himself useful to Frederick in many ways, not least during the
Russian occupation of Berlin. When Frederick squeezed Saxony for
levies, he was there to offer credit and accept the bills but as the war
ended was left with a portfolio of unsettled bonds. The treaty of
Hubertusburg (15 February 1763) closed with an unusual secret clause
stipulating payment of sums due. A total of 1,880,612 Reichstaler, or
almost four-fifths of the total, was owing to Gotzkowsky from
Leipzig.[18]

Although Berlin was the trouble centre, the weak links in the chain
were to be found among the merchants in Amsterdam. The chief
delinquents were those *arrivistes*, the brothers De Neufville. Wide-
ranging in their business, hungry for success, they had found too many
opportunities for speculation in war and its aftermath. Bullion refining
for the Berlin mint was one line of profit; another was credit for the
Brunswick army.[19] According to Gotzkowsky, 2 million Reichstaler laid
out in Saxony remained circulating on bills of exchange and after five
months of peace, the De Neufvilles continued to have on hand much of
the paper outstanding.[20] When Frederick turned to restore the Prussian
currency, a fat contract to the tune of millions, envisaged a return of 5
percent, and a float of bullion under contract from Amsterdam and
London. In April, the elder brother was in Berlin, cap in hand. But early
in July, the matter was settled not to the De Neufvilles, but to a syndicate
of *Münzjuden*.[21] It needed only such a jolt to set off the avalanche.

When the doors of the Wisselbank closed in mid-July for the biannual
count, the surface of business in Amsterdam still looked confident. But

---

[17] See above, p. 80, note 5; Joh. de Vries, *De economische achteruitgang der Republiek in de
achttiende eeuw*, 2nd edn (Leiden, 1968), pp. 75–77.

[18] *Bayerisches HSA, Gesandschaft, Berlin*, 141, p. 17.

[19] PRO, SP, 90.82, fo. 194 vo., letter, Mitchell to Halifax, Berlin, 23 April 1763; *AAE,
CP, Prusse*, 186, fo. 225 ro.–vo., *Extrait d'une lettre de M. de Verelst*, Berlin, 9 August
1763.

[20] *AAE, CP, Hollande*, 513, fo. 10 ro.–vo., letter, Prévost to Praslin, The Hague, 2
August 1763; J. E. Gotzkowsky, *Geschichte eines Patriotischen Kaufmanns* (Hamburg,
1768–69), reprinted in *Verein für die Geschichte Berlins*, VIII (1865), p. 90; S. Skalweit,
Die Berliner Wirtschaftskrise von 1763 und ihre Hintergründe (Stuttgart–Berlin, 1937), p.
41.

[21] *AAE, CP, Hollande*, 512, fo. 374 ro.–vo., letter, Prévost to Praslin, The Hague, 26 July
1763.

when those doors opened again two weeks later, the shutters went up on Arend Joseph and another Jewish banker, both deep in the bullion deals. They left a gap of several million guilders[22] and unleashed the break-up on Monday 25 July of the De Neufvilles. This major firm dragged down other merchants, and the crisis, gathering momentum, sharpened the demand for hard cash. On Saturday 6 August, the premium for bank money passed – *mirabile dictu* – to a discount of a $\frac{1}{2}$ percent.[23] By the following Tuesday, seventeen Amsterdam houses stopped payment.[24] Discounting bills of exchange was at a standstill. One rescue plan proposed a moratorium by settling bills a third at a time from four to ten months.[25] And insurance business was not spared: the failure of the De Neufvilles affected the important claims for the loss in 1762 of three grain ships sailing in the fleet from Königsberg, Memel, Libau and Riga. These were still not settled in August 1763 when bankruptcy came.[26]

The disaster left the market uncertain and divided. Some firms were not sorry to see the De Neufvilles go to the wall. As interlopers, they had broken into the charmed circle of big business on the Dam with scant respect for the establishment and the old guard simmered with resentment at their success.[27] Not least when negotiating in Berlin, they had even offered to help Frederick to promote his Emden company. The mere thought had left the Dutch minister speechless,[28] and it still rankled in many minds. When it came to set up a rescue fund, the response was patchy. Hope and Company offered half a million and others added their stint; but the wealthy Andries Pels remained aloof,[29] leaving the rough justice of the market to clear the board. Soon afterwards, he settled the Danish loan without too many rivals.[30] As for Hope and Company, they emerged from the crisis confirmed in financial ascendency. Few doubted that they were the major banking house in The Netherlands, indeed in Europe.[31] They acted virtually as a banker's banker, and a force for stability.

---

[22] Ibid., same correspondents, 2 August 1763; de Jong-Keesing, *De economische crisis*, p. 138.

[23] Sautijn Kluit, *De Amsterdamsche Beurs*, p. 15; de Jong-Keesing, *De economische crisis*, p. 165.

[24] *AAE, CP, Hollande*, 513, fo. 15 ro., letter, Prévost to Praslin, The Hague, 9 August 1763.

[25] Ibid., fos. 33 ro.–34 vo., *Projet pour rétablir le Crédit Publique* (22 August 1763).

[26] Sautijn Kluit, *De Amsterdamsche Beurs*, pp. 34–35.

[27] *AAE, CP, Hollande*, 513, fo. 10 ro.–vo., letter, Prévost to Praslin, The Hague, 2 August 1763; Buist, *At spes non fracta*, p. 13; Skalweit, *Die Berliner Wirtschaftskrise von 1763*, p. 100; de Jong-Keesing, *De economische crisis*, p. 98.

[28] *PRO, SP*, 90.82, fo. 194 vo., letter, Mitchell to Halifax, Berlin, 23 April 1763.

[29] *AAE, CP, Hollande*, 513, fo. 10 ro.–vo., letter, Prévost to Praslin, The Hague, 2 August 1763.

[30] Ibid., same correspondents, 9 September 1763; Buist, *At spes non fracta*, p. 13.

[31] de Jong-Keesing, *De economische crisis*, p. 70; Wilson, *Anglo-Dutch Commerce*, p. 66.

As merchants on the Dam grappled with the upheaval, the shocks spread out to Europe. In Hamburg, at eleven in the morning of Thursday 4 August, the merchants were in assembly considering the gloomy days – probably in the *Commerzdeputation*, for Senate did not meet that day – when a courier arrived with the fateful news of the De Neufville's bankruptcy.[32] Panic ensued as bankruptcies took the hindmost. Within a week, the shortfall in funds was said to reach some 6 million Mark banco. By 23 August, 42 houses were reported suspended; by 26th the number was 47.[33] A part of the dispute appeared to be that funds sent to Hamburg and used there, were in effect transfers from the Treasury in Berlin.[34] However, such difficulties were largely concerned with over-extended credit, for observers noted that merchants dealing in commodities remained largely unscathed. Senate set up a reserve fund to tide over the troubles, with loans to be secured on commodities (but not grain, a fluctuating asset), and provided with insurance. A prosperous merchant, Bernard Roosen, flush with profits from many years of substantial trade and successful whaling, was ready to underwrite the bills of Arend Joseph.[35] Even so, the crisis was without precedent for the Imperial city of the Elbe and one for merchants long to remember.

In Berlin, the news arrived in the evening of 7 August. Gotzkowsky and his associates tottered on the brink of collapse, protected for a while by Frederick who remembered the subtle help when the Russians occupied his capital. But even this had limits. After three weeks of uncertainty, the axe fell: Gotzkowsky and some five or six others were cast adrift into bankruptcy.[36]

Elsewhere, the storm rattled the cash-boxes. In Magdeburg on the Elbe; in Copenhagen and Danish Altona; in Leipzig, Frankfurt, Vienna, Stockholm, Danzig – all suffered in varying degrees. The London houses appeared safe, with some exceptions: La Fontaine for example, which

---

[32] *AAE, CP, Hollande,* 513, fo. 12 ro.–vo., *Copie missive des Banquiers d'Hambourg aux Banquiers d'Amsterdam,* printed, Hambourg, 4 August 1763. For the discussion in the Hamburg Senate, see *SA, Hamburg, Senatus,* C1. VIII, Nr. X (1763), fos. 334–368.

[33] *AAE, CP, Hambourg,* 88, fo. 255 vo., letter, Modène to Praslin, Hamburg, 26 August 1763; *SA, Hamburg, Senatus,* C1. VIII, Nr. X (1763), fo. 404 ro., 31 August 1763.

[34] *PRO, SP,* 82.80, fo. 100 ro.–vo., letter, Woodford to Halifax, Hamburg, 30 August 1763; *SA, Hamburg, Senatus,* C1. VIII, Nr. X, fo. 416 ro., 9 September 1763, and fo. 560 ro., 21 December 1763.

[35] *SA, Hamburg, Senatus,* C1. VIII, Nr. X (1763), fo. 402 vo., 29 August 1763; see also fos. 456 vo.–457 ro., 12 October 1763, and W. Oesau, *Hamburgs Grönlandfahrt auf Walfischfang und Robbenschlag von 17–19 Jahrhundert,* Glückstadt–Hamburg. Between 1736 and 1788, Bernard Roosen organised 215 of the 283 expeditions to Greenland.

[36] *AAE, CP, Hambourg,* 88, fo. 225, letter, Modène to Praslin, Hamburg, 12 August 1763; *PRO, SP,* 90.82, fo. 291 vo., letter, Burnet to Weston, Berlin, 20 August 1763, and fo. 293 vo., same correspondents, 27 August 1763; Skalweit, *Die Berliner Wirtschaftskrise,* pp. 53–55; K. Cauer, *Oberhofbankier und Hofbaurat* (Frankfurt am Main, n.d.), p. 16.

had connections in Hamburg; and Wildman Page and Company, which traded with Portugal and Spain, and a few others.[37] But such upsets were rare, and London escaped on this occasion. Indeed, it was even able to provide help, for a flow of gold went to The Netherlands. To such an extent that at the end of August the Bank of England put a stop on paying out new gold guineas (coined under George II and George III). In September 1763, an estimate put these transfers at a million pounds sterling for the preceding half-year.[38]

After the crash, the slowly measured recovery served only to emphasise the extent to which the upheaval derived from structural changes. The signs of returning strength pointed to new perspectives in trade and income. Silver flowing in from America was one. Germany and the Baltic gave further promise of fresh initiatives. Amsterdam found a banker's banker in Hope and Company who commanded astonishingly ample cash reserves in the Wisselbank. As for Hamburg, the city looked to a promising and widening future. And in Berlin it was the time for radical reforms. The mints were to be run by the State: Frederick set up a string of companies, including the Bank of Berlin (July 1765), on the lines of the Bank of England, with deposits, note issues, credit facilities, and, soon, branches across Prussia and Silesia. The crisis came formally to an end when the accounts with Gotzkowsky were settled on 2 April 1764; but he put his own *coda* to the rough music. Abandoned by Frederick, angry at the way the De Neufvilles had sold him short, he closed his memoirs on a note of chagrin and bitter resignation: 'So lohnet die Welt',[39] but it was a world facing the direction of rapid economic change.

★

To many, however, the slowness of the recovery was the most striking feature. It was probably not until 1765–67 that some measure of stability had returned to the commodity trade.[40] The conversion of loans to foreign governments went ahead without too much difficulty: at the time, observers could hardly believe their ears when they heard of the loan to Denmark by Andries Pels and Clifford and Sons,[41] but it proved

---

[37] *PRO, SP,* 101.93, fo. 153 ro., *Newsletter,* Stockholm, 26 August 1763; *AAE, CP, Hollande,* 513, fo. 30 vo., *Précis,* August 1763; and letter, Havrincour to Praslin, The Hague, 1 November 1763; de Jong-Keesing, *De economische crisis,* p. 197; Sautijn Kluit, *De Amsterdamsche Beurs,* pp. 22–23; Joh. de Vries, *De economische achteruitgang,* p. 76.

[38] Sir John Clapham, *The Bank of England* (2 vols., Cambridge, 1944), I, pp. 239–241, 247–249.

[39] M. v. Niebuhr, *Geschichte der Kgl. Bank in Berlin, 1765–1845* (Berlin, 1854), p. 24 and note; Skalweit, *Die Berliner Wirtschaftskrise,* pp. 49, 88; Cauer, *Oberhofbankier und Hofbaurat,* p. 16; Gotzkowsky, *Geschichte eines Patriotischen Kaufmanns,* finis.

[40] Joh. de Vries, *De economische achteruitgang,* p. 76.

[41] *AAE, CP, Hollande,* 513, fos. 46 vo.–47 ro., letter, Prévost to Praslin, The Hague, 9 September 1763.

to be typical of lending in the late 1760s and early 1770s. In the end, peace and crisis in 1763 closed one chapter and opened another. But black memories were slow to fade, for within a decade they revived in earnest.

THE BANKRUPTCIES OF 1772–73

Observers at the time, unaware of a new industrial future for Europe, remained convinced of repetition. For them, the scenario of financial collapse in 1772–73 seemed ominously similar to the stormy days of July–August 1763: the political posture of Prussia; the bloated circulation of paper and credit instruments; the rupture of a major financial house, this time Clifford and Sons, which cut a sturdy branch from Amsterdam finance. This mood of *déjà vu* carried ominous conviction. And yet in a decade of short memories was it really justified?

With the wisdom of hindsight, the salient features of the 1772–73 crisis point out the fresh character of the upheaval. While the events of 1763 moved on an axis from Amsterdam to Berlin, those of 1772–73 turned half-circle to the main stream with London.[42] In some measure the shift was temporarily encouraged by a change in fiscal policy in France. In February 1770, the new Contrôleur-Général faced the yawning deficit by suspending the payments of the famous *billets des fermes* and the *rescriptions*. With interest at 4 percent, the payments to bondholders in The Netherlands were cast in jeopardy, but the government attemped to hold the credit, even with the failure of the agent, De la Balue, and other important bankruptcies.[43] The run on gold carried into the following year,[44] and may have led to a transfer of funds from Paris to London. Certainly, in the next months, financial pressures in Britain increased. An exceptional year of trading in 1771 was followed by a renewed downturn in the gross barter terms of trade, in evidence since the mid-century.[45] Then in June 1772, a point of stress emerged in Scotland; later in London where the East India Company was unable to contain the problems of India; and in the end, crisis cast up a dismal balance sheet with the disappearance of firms of repute and enterprise. It condemned the market to nine months at least of disruption and uncertainty.

★

[42] Joh. de Vries, *De economische achteruitgang*, p. 77.

[43] *Simancas, Estado*, Leg. 4572, letters, Fuentes to Grimaldi, Paris, 22 February and 19 March 1770; 4574, same correspondents, 19 November 1770. For the complex administrative arrangements, see J. F. Bosher, *French Finances 1770–1795* (Cambridge, 1970), esp. Chapter 5.

[44] *Simancas, Estado*, Leg. 4579, letter, Fuentes to Grimaldi, Paris, 3 August 1771.

[45] P. Deane and W. A. Cole, *British economic growth 1688–1959*, 2nd edn (Cambridge, 1967), Appendix I. See also the precocious chart in W. Playfair, *A Real Statement of the Finances and Resources of Great Britain* (London, 1796).

A part of the trouble of the crisis of 1772–73 lay in the agricultural sector. Naturally enough, in a Europe still predominantly agrarian, and in The Netherlands where the rural sector retained a characteristic prosperity. Prices of wheat and other cereals soared on the *Korenbeurs* of Amsterdam – the new exchange had recently opened (1768) with a special celebration by the Directie van de Oostersche andel en Rederijen.[46] This was in part no doubt due to a serious shortfall in the harvest, and in part also to market failure from the obstacles to the grain trade in Danzig, the major outlet from the estates of Poland, following Partition. In October 1772, the Amsterdam market quoted Polish wheat at almost f.290 the *last* – the highest for half a century. Reports from Zeeland were much the same for the highly prized *Zeeuwse tarwe*.[47] Elsewhere in Europe, granaries were short. According to Ernest Labrousse, high prices and dearth in France marked a turning-point to recession, an *intercycle* lasting through 1771–1778–1787, the eye of the Revolution. That profound movement was all too apparent in the food riots of 1774 and 1775.[48] As for Britain, the data assembled by Lord Beveridge for Greenwich and Winchester also show prices at a high in 1772–74.[49] The Genoese ambassador from London on 4 December 1772 reported on 'the shortage of grain' and, he continued 'the impending dearth which threatens this country'.[50] This widespread increase tended to shift liquidity to the rural sector, by absorbing money into storage costs and settlements to dealers and farmers, and encouraging speculation in a rising market.

A second set of factors derived from the endemic power struggle in the Baltic, and directly affected a major line of Netherlands navigation. Peace in 1763 brought little respite in Prussian expansion and the pressures re-emerged sharply in the Partition of Poland (5 August 1772). Austria, Russia, and Prussia then helped themselves to generous portions of the sprawling kingdom of Stanislas Poniatowski. Frederick managed to join his lands in West Prussia to those in the east; and in turn encircled Danzig. On the Vistula, this new ring-fence cut the flow of trade, for the

---

[46] *GA, Amsterdam, Directie van de Oostersche Handel en Rederijen*, 195, 8 September 1768.
[47] N. W. Posthumus, *Inquiry into the History of Prices in Holland* (2 vols., Leiden, 1946–64), I, pp. 1–14, and there is similar evidence of high prices in 1772 from the grain market in Dordrecht, *GA, Dordrecht*, 2237 g, *Graanmarkt, 1693–1909*; D. Macpherson, *Annals of Commerce* (4 vols., London, 1805), III, p. 519; W. Kresse, *Materialien zur Entwicklungsgeschichte der Hamburger Handelsflotte, 1765–1823* (Hamburg, 1966), p. 30.
[48] C.-E. Labrousse, *La crise de l'économie française à la fin de l'Ancien Régime et au début de la Révolution* (Paris, 1944), p. xi. See also the revealing letters of Christoforo Vicenzo Spinola, the Genoese ambassador in Paris, *AS, Genoa, AS*, 2256, 28 February 1774, 24 April, 8 May, 19 June, 20 November 1775.
[49] Sir William Beveridge, *Prices and Wages in England*, vol. 1 (London, 1939), pp. 84, 291, and passim.
[50] *AS, Genoa, AS*, 2292, letter, Ageno to Serenissima, London, 4 December 1772.

rival Elbing was made the staple for goods in transit. Danzig was blockaded from the sea[51] and the island of Holm with its key granaries immobilised. The trade in salt was also crucial. In the Partition Austria carried off the famous mines of Wieliczka; but Prussia at once aimed to control salt arriving by sea. The *Seehandlungsgesellschaft* (4 October 1772) – Frederick was the principal shareholder with seven-eighths of the capital – soon received the monopoly of importing and distributing salt. Traders were ordered to deliver their consignments by way of Königsberg.[52] For The Netherlands, the significance of this was at once clear and tied up fleets as the winter ice drew near. It was reported that 40 Dutch and English ships idled at anchor waiting to load cargoes.[53] With these unexpected shortfalls in the grain and salt trade, funds in Amsterdam were understandably short to meet the payments due.

The whole region of the North and East appeared in ferment. In Denmark – an important debtor to the Amsterdam market – affairs were uncertain, with the arrest of Struensee (17 January 1772); in Sweden, a *coup d'état* on 19 August 1772 carried the Hats to power with new economic policies to improve the balance of trade. But it was no simple matter to decide the long debate on the exchange rate when mining interests directly opposed those of farming.[54] In Russia, wars with the Turks (1768–74) and disputes with the Cossacks leading to the bitter revolt and suppression of Pugachev (1773–75) brought further appeals to Amsterdam for substantial loans.

However, the disruptions and train of events had unusual results. In spite of the disappearance of epidemics in the Vital Revolution, plague raised its head in eastern Europe. Alarm spread through the continent, threatening transit-points, delaying cargoes, disrupting trade and the settlement of accounts. Through October 1770, the reports from Danzig brought apprehension.[55] Quarantine stations were set up on Vlieland for Baltic ships, and near Dordrecht for the traffic coming down the Rhine. Another was established at Cuxhaven for Hamburg in November 1772.[56] In February 1771, panic prevailed in Moscow when soldiers

---

[51] *AAE, CP, Hambourg*, 98, fo. 43 ro., letter, De la Houze to D'Aiguillon, Hambourg, 29 June 1772.

[52] G. Buss, *Berliner Boerse von 1685–1913* (Berlin, 1913), p. 66; S. Ricard, *Traité*, I, pp. 366–368; P. Schubert, *Zur Geschichte der Kgl. Preuss. Seehandlung* (Berlin, 1904); H. Schleutker, *Die volkswirtschaftliche Bedeutung der Königlichen Seehandlung von 1772–1820* (Paderborn, 1920), pp. 4–8.

[53] *Simancas, Estado, Holanda*, Leg. 6364, letters, Herreria to Grimaldi, The Hague, 7, 13, and 15 October 1772.

[54] R. Svenström and C. F. Palmstierna, *A short history of Sweden* (Oxford, 1934), pp. 254 et seq.; *AAE, CP, Hollande*, 521, fos. 59 ro.–61 vo., letter, Breteuil to Louis XV, The Hague, 14 August 1769.

[55] *Simancas, Estado, Holanda*, Leg. 6330, letter, Renovales to Grimaldi, The Hague, 11 October 1770.

[56] Ibid., same correspondents, letters, 11 and 16 October 1770 and 12 February 1771.

returned from the campaigns to die in hospital. By the autumn of 1771, deaths there were running at some 700 or 800 a day.[57] And the Mediterranean, always vulnerable, was not spared. Balthazar-Marie Emerigon recounts the drama which struck *La Vierge de Grâce* when she arrived at Satalie/Antalya in 1772 to take on board a cargo of wool for Marseilles. Some of the hands fell ill and then the captain died of plague. The crew at once refused to load the cargo and the ship sailed with the mate in command for Rhodes. Refused entry there, she sailed again for the island of Stanchio/Kos, but hearing that the epidemic had abated at Anatalya, returned there to take on the rest of the cargo. It had all the makings of another crisis of 1720 for Marseilles. Such fears remained even in 1774,[58] when *De jonge Jacob* sailed from Venice on 18 August via Zante for Amsterdam with a mixed cargo of rice, wine, currants, garnets, coral, and drugs. On arrival at Texel she was put in quarantine. Thus through long and anxious months in 1771 and following years, quarantine precautions mingled with alarm through the ports of western Europe.

A third set of pressures arose from colonial trade in America and the Far East. In Surinam, Dutch planters faced revolts among the slave populations,[59] and contended with difficulties in finding outlets for their produce. The unsatisfactory trading conditions turned to disaster when, on 31 August 1772, a hurricane hit the Windward Islands. High winds and tidal waves brought destructive violence across the settlements, levelling crops and ruining plantations, demolishing sugar-mills and buildings, sinking ships waiting for their return cargoes. On the Dutch island of St Eustatius, it was reported, 400 houses disappeared. On the Danish islands, the losses were also heavy: a 70-foot wave hit St Croix leaving some 250 dead among the devastated plantations; from St Thomas came similar reports of considerable destruction. Saba lost 180 houses; in Dominica 18 ships sank. No crops were expected for the following year.[60] And these were islands where some five years earlier planters had raised large loans on the Amsterdam market.[61] The interest, more often than not at 6 percent, came from the share-cropping deliveries of colonial produce. In the autumn of 1772, the anxious

---

[57] *SA, Hamburg, Senatus*, C1. VIII, Nr. X (1772), fo. 321 ro., 4 November 1772: through the year letters arrived in the city from a series of ports stretching from St Petersburg to Lisbon.

[58] *Simancas, Estado*, Leg. 4580, Extraits des nouvelles de Petersbourg, 27 September, 4 October 1771; B.-M. Emerigon, *Traité des Assurances*, I, pp. 631–632.

[59] Joh. de Vries, *De economische achteruitgang*, p. 77.

[60] Macpherson, *Annals of commerce*, III, pp. 526–527; see also Wilson, *Anglo-Dutch Commerce*, pp. 182–184.

[61] See above, Chapter 2, pp. 68–69; Buist, *At spes non fracta*, p. 20.

bondholders, ready with their coupons, could look bleakly on an empty prospect.

In the Far East, too, the VOC watched the mounting pressure on liquidity. The cash-flow problem was perhaps not as serious as in 1763, but exchange dealings were subject to speculation, and there was less confidence about the profitability of VOC operations, increasingly in debt. So much so that proposals came up in 1769 to cartelise the international companies and divide up the markets of Asia. Merchants in The Netherlands were often heavily committed individually in this trade and so to these exchange transactions between Asia and Europe. Delays meant extended time settlements, and imbalance at the short-term end of the market. For example, in October 1771, the VOC recorded that four bills of exchange negotiated by Clifford and Sons totalling 200,000 *sicca* rupees (estimated at 270,000 guilders and sent to Bengal) were protested.[62] And Cliffords emerged as the arch-villains of the crisis. However, the VOC was not alone in difficulty. The English East India Company after a decade of the take-over in Bengal had not managed to dominate its problems. As it turned out, these set fire to the powder-train of bankruptcy.[63]

In sum, uncertainty crowded on uncertainty, and liquidity tightened in the Amsterdam market. Troubles with the flow of crops; with trade along the coasts of Europe; with balances in the colonies: they faced merchants to their chagrin with a bear market.

★

The early summer of 1772 brought a first wave of financial trouble. This saw serious disruptions in Scotland, and then England. The linen trade of the former had expanded since the 1720s but began to face less prosperous days in the 1760s. And in the bankruptcies of 1772, the Italian silk merchants were very heavy losers.[64] Again, at the heart of the trouble: the inflation of paper. The Scots, so innovative in banking and annuities, found the situation increasingly out of hand. In May 1772, the Bank of England announced that from 24 June it would no longer discount bills under 5 percent. As cash became short, the Bank of Ayr – a syndicate of progressive landowners – foundered. On 8 June, the London–Scottish house of Neale, James, Fordyce, and Downe with which it had large dealings, collapsed. On 9 June, one of the directors, Alexander Fordyce of Aberdeen, connected with Grand et Compagnie, bolted

---

[62] *ARA, KA*, 217, 9 October 1771.
[63] Buist, *At spes non fracta*, pp. 21–22.
[64] The linen trade of Scotland had grown six times in half a century from the 1720s to 1765–75, and stabilised at some 13.5 million yards, H. Arnot, *The history of Edinburgh* (Edinburgh, 1816), p. 593; see also R. H. Campbell (ed.), *States of the Annual Progress of the Linen Manufacture, 1727–1754* (Edinburgh, 1964); *Simancas, Estado*, Leg. 6984 (2267), letter, Mazerano to Grimaldi, London, 23 June 1772.

for France.[65] In London, Sir George Colebrookdale, a director of the East India Company and with fingers in many pies, not least in loans in the loss-making West Indies, grappled with a run on funds in his bank, paid out half a million, and was saved only with a timely loan of another £200,000.[66] In France, Lavocat et Compagnie under contract to transfer bullion from London to the mints of Lille, Strasburg and Perpignan, also failed at the beginning of June. On 4 September the news of a major bankruptcy in Cádiz shook the London market.[67] According to Chalmers, the insolvencies registered in Britain in 1772 reached the astonishing total of some 550.[68]

A second wave of trouble came from the affairs of the English East India Company. Clive in triumph at Plassey (1757) seemed to open the gates of Bengal to golden fortune, and hopes soared when dividends of $12\frac{1}{2}$ percent were paid. But the eldorado of territorial power proved no easy heritage. Speculation and high running costs in the new possessions, coupled with a difficult market in Europe for Indian cloths, soon sapped expectations: '. . . we must from the nature of things be continually involved in war after war, and expense upon expense', wrote Thomas Whately (1771).[69] By 1772, a system of commercial success at public expense faced a moment of truth. The returning fleets brought thin hopes for the autumn auctions, and the inevitable followed: the company's shares began to tumble on the market. At the beginning of August they passed at $210\frac{3}{4}$; in September they hovered at 180. When the Directors met on 22 December and decided to reduce the dividend from $12\frac{1}{2}$ to 6 percent, the break came. On 24 December, the shares were down to 167 – a drop of a quarter in five months. At the end of the day, an estimate put the gap in Spain and Britain at f.70 millions, and the drop in the book value of funds in London of f.30 millions, bringing the total shortfall to f.100 millions. Sir George Colebrookdale, at three levels – at the head of those directors, of his private Bank of Ireland, and of correspondents in The Netherlands – was chief culprit. A syndicate of

---

[65] D. Macpherson, *Annals of Commerce*, III, pp. 524–525, 538; Wilson, *Anglo-Dutch Commerce*, pp. 170–172; *AAE, CP, Angleterre*, 500, fo. 40 ro., letter, De Guines to d'Aiguillon, London, 26 June 1772; *ARA, Staten Generaal*, 5985, II, letter from Van Welderen, London, 7 August 1772; *AS, Genoa*, AS. 2292, letters from Ageno, 26 June, 3 and 10 July 1772. According to the exaggerated reports, it was necessary to withdraw £600 millions from circulation: the figure serves the gravity of the situation in the minds of the public, since this figure was four times the estimated national product of England and Wales, Deane and Cole, *British economic growth*, p. 156.

[66] *ARA, Staten Generaal*, 5905, II, letter from Van Welderen, London, 12 June 1772.

[67] *AAE, CP, Angleterre*, 500, fos. 11 ro.–14 vo., letter and enclosures, Dutens to Garnier, 5 June 1772; *ARA, Staten Generaal*, 5985, II, letter from Collard, London, 4 September 1772.

[68] Macpherson, *Annals of Commerce*, III, p. 524.

[69] T. Whately, *Thoughts on our acquisitions in the East Indies, particularly respecting Bengal* (London, 1771), p. 44.

twenty backed by the Bank of England kept him in business with a rescue fund of promissory notes but the day of reckoning was not far off. On 31 March 1773 his financial world finally crumbled into dust.[70]

For Amsterdam these upheavals had serious repercussions. The capital of the EIC was an important though declining part of England's National Debt and attracted investment from The Netherlands. Charles Wilson put the Dutch commitment at f.40 million;[71] and the finance houses of the Dam with powers of attorney were active as agents. However, the time interval in dealings made arbitrage vulnerable to sharp changes in the market. The fall in shares in late 1772 proved too rapid for any successful move to cover and led to disaster. The directors of the EIC had met on 22 December to halve the dividend; a week later the crash broke in Amsterdam, this time before the Wisselbank closed.

The house of Clifford and Sons was the chief victim. They had weathered the 1763 crisis; joined in the 1765 Denmark loan (f.600,000 at 5 percent, secured on customs revenues); and appeared as a pillar of the market. Their dealings in foreign bonds were wide, but apparently sound: in July 1771 the Denmark bonds had been quoted at 3 percent over par. Cliffords also serviced another important loan to Austria, a preferred area of investment in the 1770s, this at 4 percent and secured on the revenues of mercury and copper mines.[72] However, in the second half of 1772 the firm began to face serious cash-flow problems. Their balance in the Wisselbank in the July–September quarter averaged f.393,475 banco; but by 22 December, this was down to f.82,874.[73] The arbitrage operations in English East India stock tipped the balance. The panic swallowed up the transfer of f.457,626 from Copenhagen to make the New Year payment to bondholders – but this was not enough to ward off bankruptcy on 27–28 December.[74] Other firms soon went to

---

[70] The *Course of the Exchange*, London, quoted the shares on 1 October 1772 at 190½–187½, on 1 January at 159–160½, on 3 January 1774 at 140¾, and on 2 January 1775 at 154. The shift in market prices was amply discussed at the time and since, see *AAE, CP, Hollande*, 524, fos. 330 ro.–332 vo., letter, De Noailles to D'Aiguillon, The Hague, 5 January 1773; *ARA, Staten Generaal*, 5986, I, letter from Van Welderen, London, 2 April 1773, *AS, Genoa*, As. 2292, letter, Ageno to Serenissima, London, 15 January 1773; Macpherson, *Annals of Commerce*, III, pp. 503, 529; Sautijn Kluit, *De Amsterdamsche Beurs*, pp. 66–67, 72; Wilson, *Anglo-Dutch Commerce*, pp. 173–174; Buist, *At spes non fracta*, p. 20; J. G. van Dillen, 'Effectenkoersen op de Amsterdamsche Beurs', *EHJ*, XVII (1931), 37–38.

[71] Wilson, *Anglo-Dutch Commerce*, p. 173, indicating the large volume of the business by Cliffords. Macpherson puts the total holdings of shares above £500 at £2,594,026, of which 36.3 percent were in foreign names, *Annals of Commerce*, III, p. 541.

[72] *Simancas, Estado, Holanda*, Leg. 6365, letter, Herreria to Grimaldi, The Hague, 31 December 1772; Wilson, *Anglo-Dutch Commerce*, p. 69.

[73] *GA, Amsterdam, Wisselbank*, 261 (1), 262 (1).

[74] *PRO, SP*, 84, fo. 538, *Mémoire de M. d'Ahlefeldt*, 15 January 1773; Sautijn Kluit, *De Amsterdamsche Beurs*, p. 96; *ARA, Staten Generaal*, 6518, letter from Hop, Hamburg, 19 January 1773.

the wall. 'The Jewish nation is destroyed' wrote the French ambassador, 'all bills at the moment are useless in Amsterdam.' And a month later, 'This market is exhausted of cash, credit and resources,' Adrian Hope, Jan van de Poll and Jacques Teysset were appointed as receivers. The second of these, it should be noted, featured in the Sligtenhorst lists throughout the period. But the 131 creditors found little comfort in the assets assembled. W. P. Sautijn Kluit puts the total claims outstanding at f.4.64 million, 62 percent due from Herman and Johann van Seppenwolde.[75] In April 1773 the creditors were offered a settlement at some 25 percent. Why, the angry cry went up, was a thief recently caught and sent to the gallows yet rich brokers could be allowed to escape scot-free?[76]

Cliffords carried other firms into the abyss. Some managed to struggle and survive. Blaauw and Company, for example: after six months they were back in funds.[77] Horneca, Hogguer and Company had been active in the 1770 Swedish loan at 5 percent with substantial connections in France. They stopped payments but did not go bankrupt. Help poured in, partly from a fund of f.140,000 in Amsterdam,[78] to which Hope contributed f.50,000, Marselis f.20,000, Hasselaer f.20,000 and Clifford and Schmid f.20,000; and partly from credits from Paris, for France was anxious to keep the Swedish connection.[79] Prussia, Sweden, Sardinia, and Tuscany also placed important orders for guns and munitions, so that in the end the firm managed to recover a stable trading position. But the organisation changed. In 1773 Horneca established a new partnership of Hogguer, Fizeaux and Company, to which the capital was transferred.[80]

Other firms were less fortunate. Cesar Sardi and Company had been active in foreign deals: the loans to Austria in 1766, 1768, and 1769 at 4 percent; to Leipzig in 1768 at 4 percent; and to Saxony at 3.5 percent (on the special security of the ducal regalia).[81] When faced with bankruptcy,

---

[75] *AAE, CP, Hollande*, 524, fos. 333 ro., 366 vo., letters, De Noailles to D'Aiguillon, The Hague, 8 January and 12 February 1773; Sautijn Kluit, *De Amsterdamsche Beurs*, pp. 98–99.

[76] *PRO, SP*, 84, fo. 538, letter, Yorke to Suffolk, The Hague, 6 April 1773.

[77] *GA, Amsterdam, Wisselbank*, 263 (1), 265 (1); Sautijn Kluit, *De Amsterdamsche Beurs*, p. 99.

[78] *Simancas, Estado, Holanda*, Leg. 6365, letter, Herreria to Grimaldi, The Hague, 5 January 1773; *AAE, CP, Hollande*, 524, fo. 337 ro., letter, De Noailles to D'Aiguillon, The Hague, 12 January 1773.

[79] *AAE, CP, Hollande*, 524, fos. 330 ro.–332 vo., 350 vo., letters, De Noailles to D'Aiguillon, 5 and 26 January 1773.

[80] *GA, Amsterdam, Wisselbank*, 264 (III), fo. 2422; *AAE, CP, Hollande*, 524, p. 337 ro., letter, De Noailles to D'Aiguillon, The Hague, 12 January 1773; Buist, *At spes non fracta*, p. 76, note 2.

[81] See above, Chapter 2, note 158; Riley, *International government finance*, p. 282, note 10.

the firm had a bridging loan of f.60,000 in cash from Bolongaro;[82] but it was not enough. By July 1774, their account had disappeared from the ledgers of the Wisselbank.[83]

Another victim was the firm of Abraham ter Borch and Sons. In 1767 and 1769 they had issued the 6 percent loans to the Danish planters of St Croix, St Thomas and St John, badly hit by the hurricane of 1772. In November the bonds were selling at a discount of some 2 and 9 percent (making an effective rate of interest of 6.1–6.8 percent).[84] By July 1774, their account had also disappeared from the Wisselbank.[85] Abraham ter Borch Jnr featured in the Sligtenhorst lists from 1767 to 1771, but subsequently vanished.

A third important failure was the firm of Herman and Johann van Seppenwolde. They too were caught in the bear market along with London associates: Craven, and also Dryer.[86] All belonged to that network of credit of the early 1770s made unstable, as the Genoese ambassador had forecast at the time of the summer bankruptcies in Scotland,[87] by the rapid expansion of paper in circulation. And there were other victims. The rupture of one vector put the matrix in jeopardy. An initial estimate of the book value of the market written off, was sent in the report by De Noailles to Paris on 5 January. It was of the order of 70 million guilders,[88] exaggerated no doubt, but indicative of the sense of disaster at the opening of the new year. Bills of exchange and paper credit had little value on the Dam.

In no time at all, the shock-waves spread. In Sweden, Grill and Company faced trouble. They had joined in the 1769 loan at 5 percent (secured on the iron mines); these bonds had been selling at 2 percent discount in July 1771. The 1770 loan at 5 percent (secured on alum and iron) was selling at 6 percent under par.[89] Elsewhere the news even if disquieting, was remote. From Genoa it was reported that the firm of Varese and Company had failed, but it was thought, with some relief, that it hardly ruffled the surface in Amsterdam: it concerned only business in Italy and Spain.[90]

---

[82] *Simancas, Estado, Holanda*, Leg. 6365, letter, Herreria to Grimaldi, The Hague, 5 January 1773.

[83] *GA, Amsterdam, Wisselbank*, 265 (1).

[84] See above, Chapter 2, note 158. Buist refers to the loans issued by Lever and De Bruine in 1768, *At spes non fracta*, p. 20.

[85] *GA, Amsterdam, Wisselbank*, 265 (1).

[86] *ARA, Staten Generaal*, 5986, I, letter from Van Welderen, London, 5 January 1773.

[87] See above, note 65; Wilson, *Anglo-Dutch Commerce*, p. 176.

[88] *AAE, CP, Hollande*, 524, fos. 330 ro.–332 vo., letter, De Noailles to D'Aiguillon, The Hague, 5 January 1773.

[89] Ibid., and see above, p. 73 and Table 5.

[90] *AAE, CP, Hollande*, 524, fo. 366 ro., letter, De Noailles to D'Aiguillon, The Hague, 12 February 1773

After the initial break, the recovery in Amsterdam was relatively rapid, at least by comparison with 1763.[91] Perhaps the latter may already have prepared the requisite lines of escape. Certainly in Amsterdam in January 1773, the City fathers were ready with a fund of f.2 million under strict conditions, on security, and at 3½ percent.[92] A private plan for a fund of f.6 million was also in the air.[93] Cash poured in from abroad: gold specie and Spanish pieces of eight from London;[94] 150,000 riksdalers in gold from Denmark, sent via Hamburg.[95] Another transfer of gold ducats brought by the courier of 27 January, from the Riksens ständers bank in Stockholm and another 10,000 from the King's own privy purse.[96] The situation nevertheless improved as 1773 wore on. Hope and Company emerged safely, even though their business hesitated for a time but their cash base remained remarkably substantial.[97] This, too, gave assurance to the market.

Beyond Amsterdam, other markets managed to weather the storm. In Hamburg, the air was tense when the Giro-Bank opened its doors on 12 January 1773, but the City and the Admiralty had prudently arranged for a fund of a million Reichstaler banco to provide loans on security of goods other than grain.[98]

Yet, although the repercussions of the break were severe, the situation stabilised and recovery proceeded. When the Wisselbank reopened on 29 January 1773, no further bankruptcies emerged. And as the year went on, business improved so that the season closed on a brighter note. De Noailles forecast to Paris that in the New Year 1774 the opening of the Wisselbank would be 'as brilliant as it was gloomy last year'. This proved to be correct for 'the expectations one had' he reported again on 1 February (the Bank had opened on 28 January), 'have been realised. The abundance of money is very great in the market and in general in the whole country. A fear of the private capitalists is that the State will not pay off the eighteen millions already announced.' In the Wisselbank, the

---

[91] Ibid., 524, fo. 366 vo.; Buist, *At spes non fracta*, p. 22; Wilson, *Anglo-Dutch Commerce*, pp. 182, 187.

[92] *AAE, CP, Hollande*, 524, fo. 337 vo., letter, De Noailles to D'Aiguillon, The Hague, 12 January 1773. Upper-level rates on domestic government debt carried 3 percent.

[93] Wilson, *Anglo-Dutch Commerce*, p. 187.

[94] Ibid., p. 176; *AAE, CP, Hollande*, 524, fo. 333 ro., letter, De Noailles to D'Aiguillon, The Hague, 8 January 1773.

[95] *ARA, Staten Generaal*, 6518, letter from Hop, Hamburg, 19 January 1773; Sautijn Kluit, *De Amsterdamsche Beurs*, p. 96.

[96] *AAE, CP, Hollande*, 524, fo. 366 vo.–367 ro., letter, De Noailles to D'Aiguillon, The Hague, 12 February 1773.

[97] Ibid., 525, fo. 272 ro.–vo., same correspondents, 1 February 1774. In January 1772, for example, Hope and Company had a balance of f.1,160,623-14-0, *GA, Amsterdam, Wisselbank*, 262 (III), and see Buist, *At spes non fracta*, pp. 21–22.

[98] *ARA, Staten Generaal*, 6518, letters from Hop, Hamburg, 19 and 26 January 1773.

reserves in gold rose, reaching 30 percent in the last half of the decade.[99] All seemed set fair. And in April, he could comment that 'the trade of the Republic is still flourishing'. Admittedly some firms had retired – Pels and Sons had gone into voluntary retirement – but 'there remained the House of Hope' and many others, but the former 'had reached such a point of credit and wealth that there is no business of importance in Holland without them'. If trade had weakened, it was probably in the Mediterranean and Levant. Elsewhere, in spite of alarms and anxiety, he observed, business remained profitable – with the Far East, Britain, Spain, and even after the troubles, with Surinam. A year later he remained of the same opinion '. . . business recovers there more than ever', he wrote from The Hague on 21 March 1775.[100] Nevertheless the hiatus in the crisis gave other markets opportunities – not least in London. The interregnum left the market vulnerable, and there were more blows to follow.

THE ROAD TO WAR (1775–80)

A third great event uncertainty came to dominate the Amsterdam market in the late 1770s. This was the cycle of hostilities between Britain and the settlements in North America, and then with other powers in Europe. It proved to be the first major break from colonial dependence, and the repercussions touched all levels of the trading world at a time of potential economic growth. After hardly more than a decade from the end to the Seven Years' War, it was clear that few of the basic issues had been settled. The second *pacte de famille* (15 August 1761) between Versailles and Madrid still lingered on, hankering after ceded territories and restored prestige. The *pacte* did not work too well in the crisis over the Falkland Islands (1770–71), but it was not far below the surface. In middle Europe, a succession dispute broke in Bavaria over claims from Austria, Prussia and Saxony. Emerging Russia pressed in the East, in the Black Sea, and along the length of her western frontiers in the Baltic. And then came a remote dispute in North America, enough, as it turned out, to stir up the international mill-pond in which all could fish to advantage. In March 1778, as the prospect of war threatened in Europe, the perceptive Spanish ambassador in The Hague had few illusions: 'the

---

[99] *AAE, CP, Hollande*, 524, fo. 357 ro.–vo., 525, fos. 263 vo., 272 ro.–vo., letters, De Noailles to D'Aiguillon, The Hague, 2 February 1773, 21 January and 1 February 1774; J. G. van Dillen, *Bronnen tot de geschiedenis der Wisselbanken* (2 vols., The Hague, 1925), pp. 909–921.

[100] *AAE, CP, Hollande*, 525, fo. 325 vo.–326 ro., letter, De Noailles to D'Aiguillon, The Hague, 26 April 1774; 527, fos. 195 vo.–196 ro., same correspondent to Vergennes, 21 March 1775.

[101] Samuel Johnson eloquently set out the salient considerations in Britain's position in *Thoughts on the Late Transactions respecting Falkland's Islands* (London, 1771); Simancas,

storm cloud', he noted, 'which stretches from Azov to Boston . . .'[101] The growing tension spread over half the world and left the other half with few claims to be exempt.

The Seven Years' War indeed left a heavy legacy in debt. As the peace treaties quietly gathered dust, old rancours smouldered, ready to burst into flames when it came to foot the lengthy bills of fighting. They engrossed the thoughts of ministers as much in Paris or out at Versailles, as in London. There, one estimate put the cost of war at £82.6 millions. In the first year of peace, public income there passed the £10 million mark for the first time, and that with a continuing deficit of £700,000.[102] With 46 percent of income already earmarked to pay interest on debt, the word went out to tax. No easy solution in the eighteenth century, when the hand of the tax receiver seemed harshest in levies of excise duties. These touched consumption at all levels of society, and soon many voices rose in aggrieved, aggressive dissent.

None were more forthright than the settlers in North America, where taxes grated sharply on a balance of trade heavily weighted in Britain's favour.[103] The long years of the 1760s saw abrasive discontent with the Sugar Act (1764), the Stamp Act (1765) and the Declaratory Act (1766). The 1770s accelerated into conflict and bloodshed: the Boston Massacre (March 1770); the Gaspée Affair (June 1772); the Boston Tea Party (December 1773); the Declaration of Rights (September 1774). The Spanish ambassador in Paris remarked, as the year drew to its close, that there was peace with the Turk, but conflict in store for Spain, Portugal and Morocco; and not least a confrontation between English and English. 'In three or four months', he opined, 'we should settle our curiosity.'[104] The musket shots at Concord (April 1775) proved him all too correct. In no time, independence was declared (July 1776). Although the long-term prospects of secessions in colonies sank slowly into the mentalities of their governors in Europe, some were more sanguine about the outcome. The Abbé Desnoyers in The Hague could cast a sharp eye on the scene, not least in the recollection that The Netherlands had turned early insurgence against Spain into close and interested amity. 'And so the confrontation between England and her colonies is not the most interesting in the present situation in Europe. It

---

Estado, Holanda, Leg. 6370, letter, Herreria to Floridablanca, The Hague, 25 March 1778.
[102] A. J. Wilson, *The National Budget: the National Debt, Taxes and Rates* (London, 1882), p. 34.
[103] B. R. Mitchell and P. Deane, *Abstract of British Historical Statistics* (Cambridge, 1962), pp. 309–311; J. F. Shepherd and G. M. Walton, *Shipping, maritime trade, and the economic development of colonial North America* (Cambridge, 1972), pp. 160–162.
[104] *Simancas, Estado*, Leg. 4595 (118, II), letter, Aranda to Grimaldi, Paris, 23 December 1774.

is a nation being born . . .' And with all the problems. It was not as if a people of pioneers and settlers were the same as a great power of Europe.[105] However, another seven years of war were to pass before the plenipotentiaries were on the road again to Paris, with quills in hand, ready to ratify, willingly or unwillingly, the 1783 claims of a new republic.

For insurance, the impact of these conflicts was both direct and serious. The crises of 1763 and 1772–73 had temporarily curtailed the market, impaired financial reputations, and restricted the flow of funds; but war progressively transformed the spectrum of risks in navigation. Ships could not sail with impunity on their customary routes. Cargoes were suspect and subject to search; confiscated ships languished in port, often to be sold off at derisory prices. And above all, the costs of protection soared, in finding seamen, arming ships, organising convoys. As conditions deteriorated insurers raised their rates. In February 1777, insurance premiums for ships returning from Jamaica in some cases reached 25 percent, whereas in the Seven Years' War only 7 percent had been asked.[106] There were wars and wars.

In a larger perspective, the experience of 1756–63 had shown that discretion was the better part of profit. Initially, The Netherlands leaned towards neutrality, reflecting the balance of political lobbies at home and wide interests abroad. Some favoured France, where Dutch savings had gone in search of investment; and others looked to Britain, also a haven for investors in public funds. The commitment of The Netherlands in general and Amsterdam in particular to inter-regional trade in Europe created sensitive areas and divided loyalties. Neutrality was one way of expressing that over-riding compromise. Yet, it was far from easy to maintain when caught in the cross-fire of warring nations. Protection in the market through insurance premiums appeared at pains to encompass the troubles at sea, on the routes to the Baltic and around the North Cape, to the Levant, across to the West Indies.

★

One line of trade became a lode-stone of tension and risk: the sales of munitions. In the darkening outlook, governments hastened to stockpile the tools of war: naval stores and munitions, guns and explosives. There were merchants on hand to supply these needs: in Sweden and the southern Netherlands, in Hamburg, Barcelona, Glasgow, London, and naturally in Amsterdam. International loans no doubt smoothed the purchases. In 1773, Vienna bought fire-arms in Namur for delivery via

[105] *AAE, CP, Hollande*, 526, fos. 221 vo.–222 ro., letter, Desnoyers to Vergennes, The Hague, 11 October 1774.

[106] Ibid., 529, fo. 283 vo., letter, La Vauguyon to Vergennes, The Hague, 14 February 1777.

Rotterdam and the Rhine.[107] In the Falkland Islands dispute the need had risen in Spain: although that trouble was settled for the time-being, the supplies continued to pour in. An order in April 1776 for 449 cannon from the Carron Iron-works in Scotland for the naval dockyard at El Ferrol pointed to the scale of operations.[108] Guns from Birmingham were imported into Barcelona,[109] with Americans already in the port to buy up guns and powder. And when this source dried up, France was persuaded to refurbish the *pacte familiale* with guns and bayonets from St Etienne, and supplies from the depot in Douai, shipped via Dunkirk in Dutch vessels but insured in Spain.[110]

The strategic trade in explosives was the key to the situation, but it was above all, highly selective. Some industries had the knack of producing the best-grained powder – effective and sure to fire. Rising demand saw new mills established in West Friesland and Zeeland. Philipp Nemnich on his travels in The Netherlands counted, as the century drew to its close, seven in Holland, five in Zeeland and one in Utrecht.[111] In Amsterdam, in 1775, such mills turned with busy purpose, but often, too, with less heed for safety. It was a widespread danger. The London works on Hounslow Heath were shattered with an explosion in 1772 – at first, the locals thought it was an earthquake – and again in 1774.[112] In The Netherlands, merchants were ready with supplies when orders were backed with cash freely available. Spain was a big spender, partly for military purposes, but also for mining operations. In the four years 1771–74, some 636 metric tonnes found a way to the Peninsula, enough musket shots, the Abbé Desnoyers dryly remarked, to kill a third of Europe's population.[113] In 1775 and the following years, further large consignments continued through the hands of the Portuguese consul in Amsterdam, Gildemeester (sometimes appearing in the contracts as the firm of Jean Gil de Meester et Fils), en route for Lisbon. On 11 March 1777, the *Concordia*, registered in Rotterdam, sailed from

---

[107] *Simancas, Estado, Holanda*, Leg. 6365, letter, Herreria to Grimaldi, The Hague, 1 June 1773; J. Hartog, *Geschiedenis van de Nederlandse Antillen* (4 vols., Aruba, etc., 1953–), *De Bovenwindse Eilanden*, III (1964), p. 177.

[108] *Simancas, Estado*, Leg. 6994 (21), letter, Mazerano to Grimaldi, London, 31 May 1776.

[109] Ibid., Leg. 6994 (32), same correspondents, 21 June 1776.

[110] Ibid., Leg. 4611 (64–65), letters, Aranda to Floridablanca, Paris, 20 July and 26 November 1777, Minute of 31 July 1777. For the cost of gunpowder supplied to Spain (1762–74), see ibid., Leg. 4594, *Mémoire (1774)*, and Leg. 4616 (5), *Proposition (1777)*.

[111] P. A. Nemnich, *Original-Beiträge zur eigentlichen Kenntniss von Holland* (Tübingen, 1809), p. 283.

[112] *Simancas, Estado*, Leg. 6984 (^{0}/2262), letter, Mazerano to Grimaldi, London, 7 January 1772; *ARA, Staten Generaal*, 5986 (II), letter from Van Welderen, London, 26 April 1774.

[113] *AAE, CP, Hollande*, 526, fos. 60 vo., 67 vo.–68 ro., letters, Desnoyers to Bertin, The Hague, 21 and 28 June 1774. The cost of freight and insurance came to about 10 percent.

Amsterdam bound for Lisbon with 1,500 barrels of powder, each weighing 100 lb, for transhipment to Seville. English warships stopped her in the Channel on suspicion that she was bound for North America. The intervention of diplomats secured her release. Few in the trade were in any doubt about the intricacy of the transactions. But then the promise of profits was high: in 1776 the price of gunpowder rose by a quarter. The market in saltpetre which had dragged for more than a decade had by the late 1770s revived in earnest. And that in itself was a barometer of uncertainty.[114]

At first, there were few obstacles to direct deliveries to the dedicated Minutemen of North America, who soon found their critical shortage to be gunpowder. Their home product was unsatisfactory, probably from the inferior charcoal used. In the later fighting, deliveries in quantity from France virtually saved American independence.[115] However, Dutch powder, considered by some to be more powerful than that of Sweden or France, was in great demand.[116] And this branch of the arms trade in The Netherlands flourished accordingly. Ships from Dutch ports arrived directly in Boston. The English ambassador protested in October 1774[117] but shipments continued through 1775. As the conflict worsened and loyalties divided, so direct sailing became more difficult. Dealers turned to other ways – sales through France and Spain; and smuggling. These changes reshaped the areas of risk, focusing in Europe on the Channel, and across the Atlantic on the West Indies.

The Caribbean emerged as the chief point of relay. Two Dutch islands came to the forefront of this activity: Curaçao and St Eustatius. The merchants of Curaçao were deft hands at smuggling, always ready to slip under the net of Spanish monopoly in a 'clandestino florido commercio'.[118] They ran a thriving traffic with local tradesmen and Indian pedlars often using, as in 1778, forged Caracas licences.[119] For

---

[114] Ibid., 528, fo. 342 ro., letter, Desnoyers to Vergennes, The Hague, 14 May 1776; 536, fos. 320 vo.–321 ro., letter, Grand to Vergennes, Amsterdam, 17 June 1779; *Simancas, Estado, Holanda*, 6367, 6368, 6369, letters, Herreria to Grimaldi, The Hague, 16 May, 17 June 1775, 30 July, 26 December 1776, and to Floridablanca, The Hague, 8 April 1777 and enclosure from Jean Gil de Meester et Fils d'Amsterdam, 2 April 1777.

[115] R. G. Albion and J. B. Pope, *Sea lanes in wartime: the American experience 1775–1942* (New York, 1942), p. 43.

[116] *AAE, CP, Hollande*, 526, fo. 68 vo., letter, Desnoyers to Bertin, The Hague, 28 June 1774.

[117] *Simancas, Estado, Holanda*, Leg. 6366, letter, Herreria to Grimaldi, The Hague, 25 October 1774.

[118] For an earlier example, see *Simancas, Estado, Holanda*, Leg. 6347, letter, Rodriguez to Villarias, Amsterdam, 29 August 1743; and for smuggling generally in the Spanish colonies, Dolores Bonet de Sotillo, *El tráfico ilegal en las colonias españolas* (Caracas, 1955).

[119] *Simancas, Estado, Holanda*, Leg. 6370, letter, Galvez to Floridablanca, El Pardo, 22 March 1778.

long years, trickles of gold and silver, cacao and other goods, made their way through this route to Europe. Thus, on 31 March 1772, the *Standvastigheyd*[120] sailed for Amsterdam with consignments of timber, cacao, hides, coffee, sugar, and 23 lots of specie. However, war in North America brought new and exciting opportunities. As the sharpshooting grew apace, smugglers turned to cater for the new demand. Little surprise to find that the *Concordia*[121] consigned to Lisbon with gunpowder in 1777 had already been on the route to the islands. She had sailed for St Eustatius in 1773 with a mixed cargo liberally laced with spirits. The Windward Islands, supplied with Dutch materials, seemed to offer a better route of access to the North.

St Eustatius, with few resources of its own to offer, came into favour as a lair for smugglers.[122] In the early 1770s, some 30 to 40 Dutch ships had usually sailed from the island laden with colonial goods such as sugar, coffee, tobacco, dyestuffs.[123] But the growing tension changed the scale of operations. In January 1775 already there were daily consignments from the ports of The Netherlands by way of St Eustatius – cargoes of gunpowder and other munitions, tea and liquor. In March, after protests from London, bailiffs stopped a ship sailing with saltpetre and sulphur. But the attraction of the trade proved greater than regulations. In July 1776, with declared independence in North America already on the cards, the Dam buzzed with the news that a ship from Flushing had arrived and sold its cargo of munitions at a profit of 150 percent.[124] Fat pickings indeed, and merchants lost little time in setting their stevedores to scoop the trade. They converged on the island from all sides. In the fourteen months from 25 January 1778 to 25 March 1779, 3,182 ships left St Eustatius, including 63 under Netherlands flag, and 219 under American.[125] As can be inferred, flying a particular flag did not always indicate the attachment of the ship. In 1779 the island managed a hundred sailings a day on average. By 1780, the St Eustatius shuttle claimed two-thirds of the trade of Baltimore.[126]

In return, the northern plantations disgorged their produce: tobacco from Virginia and some cotton; the islands of France and other nations found a lucrative outlet for important consignments of sugar, coffee, and

---

[120] *KVA*, XVIII, 541.

[121] *KVA*, XVIII, 488.

[122] *AAE, MD, Hollande*, 137, fo. 52, *Remarques sur le commerce de St. Eustache (1779)*.

[123] Ibid., fo. 54.

[124] *Simancas, Estado, Holanda*, Leg. 6367, letter, Herreria to Grimaldi, The Hague, 17 January 1775; *AAE, CP, Hollande*, 527, fo. 192 vo., 529, fo. 8 ro., letters, Desnoyers to Vergennes, The Hague, 14 March 1775 and 9 July 1776.

[125] *AAE, MD, Hollande*, 137, fo. 152, *Remarques sur le commerce de St. Eustache (1779)*, fo. 54.

[126] Hartog, *De Bovenwindse Eilanden*, III, p. 185; Albion and Pope, *Sea lanes in wartime*, p. 55.

cacao. In these bonanza days, St Eustatius bulged with the merchandise of war.[127] Cornelis de Jong travelling the Caribbean in 1780 found the tangible signs of its hey-day – crowded warehouses thrown up from rough boards, often two stories high and joined with bridges across the streets. They were so stuffed with colonial merchandise that dealers sometimes could get at coffee beans only by breaking a hole through the ceiling.[128] The Council of State in St Eustatius referred to itself demurely as a general staple; others adopted the more flamboyant but well-merited name of the *Golden Rock* or sometimes even the *Diamond Rock*. And what could be better deserved when everyone from the Governor down dabbled in the trade? It had been all too easy on the change of governors for Abraham van Bibber, the Maryland agent, to grease the way: 'we are as well fixed with him' he wrote in 1775, 'as we were with the former'.[129] However, the situation quickly deteriorated when in November 1776 the American brigantine *Andrea Doria* sailed into the roads, flying the colours of the Continental Congress and receiving a return salute from the guns on shore – as a merchantman, it was said at the time, but claimed later to be the first formal recognition of the young Republic. And she lost no time in taking on board a cargo of guns, powder and munitions.[130] In the following summer *De Hoop* also sailing from St Eustatius was captured by the Royal Navy and taken to Antigua. On board was colonial produce and 1,750 barrels of gunpowder.[131] The tensions led to the recall of De Graaf to The Netherlands; but his *Deductie*[132] was a spirited defence of his actions and he was allowed to return to his post. High profits also meant high risks, for soon the naval squadrons appeared offshore to tighten the fist of war. Already in the autumn of 1780, business was tottering, turning to favour the Spanish and Danish islands. And within months, on 3 February 1781, Admiral Sir Samuel Hood hove in sight, quickly followed by Admiral Sir George Rodney and the capture of the island.[133] The card had been played.

The second zone of growing tension was the Channel. Here was the

127 *AAE, CP, Hollande*, 535, fo. 74 ro., letters, La Vauguyon to Vergennes, The Hague, 14 January 1779; ibid., fo. 203 ro., Grand to Vergennes, Amsterdam, 8 February 1779; ibid., 307 ro., *Extrait d'une lettre de St. Eustache*, 6 March 1779.
128 Hartog, *De Bovenwindse Eilanden*, III, pp. 174–175, 185–186, and citing C. de Jong, *Reize naar de Caribische eilanden in de jaren 1780 en 1781* (Haarlem, 1807).
129 Ibid., p. 178; *ARA, WIC*, 639, fo. 329.
130 *ARA, WIC*, 639, fo. 205, letter, Greathead to De Graaf, St Christopher, 17 December 1776; ibid., statement by Abraham Ravene, St Eustatius, 1 July 1777; W. R. Menkman, *De geschiedenis van de West-Indische Compagnie* (Amsterdam, 1947), p. 168.
131 *ARA, WIC*, 639, fo. 313.
132 Ibid., 639, fos. 1–202, J. de Graaf, *Deductie mitsgaders Memorie van Informatiën* (23 February 1779), esp. fo. 9.
133 *AAE, CP, Hollande*, 535, fo. 307 ro., *Extrait d'une lettre de St. Eustache*, 6 March 1779; 542, fo. 86 ro., letter, Grand to Vergennes, Amsterdam, 18 September 1780; C. C. Crittenden, *The commerce of North Carolina, 1763–1789* (New Haven, 1936), p. 127.

bottleneck for strategic naval stores en route from the Baltic to France. Anglo-French relations deteriorated rapidly after American independence (4 July 1776), and already in June 1777, Vergennes was quietly accepting the prospect of war. By early March 1778, France had a secret alliance with the young Republic. The news soon leaked out, and on 13 March, the French ambassador in London, the Marquis de Noailles, gave it formal acknowledgement. The outcome was predictable. George III recalled his ambassador from Versailles and the fight was on.[134]

In the first important naval engagement of the war (27 July 1778), the match was drawn. The French navy, carefully reformed by Choiseul, Sartine, and Castries, carried itself with so much distinction that the young Louis XVI at once dashed off a letter of congratulation to the admiral.[135] The struggle to control the high seas, however, turned to attrition. Navies required maintenance; the best naval stores came from the Baltic; and the delivery of these supplies called on the ready services and commercial competence of merchants, not least in Amsterdam. However, the trade in war materials set a dilemma of political conscience for The Netherlands: was it to support one of the belligerents, or remain an honest broker?

Neutrality had been effective and rewarding in the Seven Years' War; now the stakes were higher. Most still favoured neutrality, but as the dispute spread, the gravamen touched all levels of activity in The Netherlands. Some favoured France, others followed an open line for Britain. Eddies and currents of interests carried opinions, swayed assemblies. Merchants with business to pursue; bondholders with commitments to swelling public debts, aristocrats with family connections – these militated for divided loyalties. And the lobbies became both powerful and vocal. The news of the Franco–American alliance (March 1778) was enough to push up the blood-pressure of the anglophile Fagel, greffier of the Republic,[136] for the Stadhouder and his party stood for Britain. In Amsterdam, the merchants lost no time in joining a wave of speculation in commodities, especially those of colonial America.[137] The city favoured France. According to the grand pensionary van Berckel in a *Memorie* to push the case to the States of Holland and West Friesland (16 December 1778), the trade with France was seventeen times that with Britain; and it sustained a major part of the deliveries to Germany and the

---

[134] *Simancas, Estado*, Leg. 4611 (5, II), letter, Aranda to Floridablanca, Paris, 22 June 1777; ibid., Leg. 7000 (55), copy of Address to Parliament (15 March 1778).
[135] *Simancas, Estado*, Leg. 4617, fo. 70, and fo. 75, for an hour-by-hour plan of the battle.
[136] *AAE, CP, Hollande*, 532, fos. 216 ro.–218 ro., letter, Berenger to Vergennes, The Hague, 20 March 1778.
[137] Ibid., 532, fo. 362 ro., letter, La Vauguyon to Vergennes, 24 April 1778; *Simancas, Estado*, Leg. 7000, fos. 49–55, letter and enclosures, Escarano to Floridablanca, London, 15 March 1778.

Rhineland.[138] As the pressures grew, the ambassadors of both England and France sapped and countersapped the system, conniving to bring The Netherlands to declare her interest. Share-pushing was licit: at times it seemed as if the conflict could have been settled on the floor of the Bourse rather than in the sessions of the States General. As the conflict sharpened, it was even suggested in August 1779 that the firm of Hope and Company was in the market to buy 200 millions in British funds on French account.[139] Exaggerated perhaps, but such were the political ramifications of quoting public funds.

The issues of neutrality focused on an old debate: what constituted a munition of war? Was it strictly guns and powder? Or did it extend to cover naval stores, the materials for ship-building and ship-repair? And a secondary debate surfaced over the measure of protection which The Netherlands should provide for its own shipping. Both issues proved to be critical, and in the end altered the format of neutrality.

The question of contraband was enshrined in treaty obligations, but *casus foederis* was a doubtful card to play. The Anglo-Dutch treaty of 1674, Article III, defined munitions; but Article IV excluded rope, sails, anchors, masts, planks, beams.[140] Britain now took the stand that the treaty clause did not give explicit exemption,[141] and so ordered her navy to stop contraband timber on the way to France. Similar points of dispute emerged from the Anglo-Swedish treaty (1661) and the Anglo-Danish treaty (1670). Zealous naval commanders followed their instructions to the letter, ordered away boarding parties and made seizures with impunity. Four-fifths of ships sailing, according to one estimate, made port in safety.[142] But it was the loss of the other fifth which rankled. By September 1778, at least 59 ships were taken prize – 8 Danish, 16 Swedish and 35 Dutch, not mentioning others from Prussia.[143] Protests were loud. They served to enlarge the concept of *vrij van molest* in the last quarter of the eighteenth century. But, understandably, ships disappeared into the registers of neutral ports such as Emden, Hamburg, Bremen, Ostend. The Sø–Assurance Kompagni of Copenhagen, for

---

[138] *AAE, CP, Hollande*, 532, fo. 216 ro., letter, Berenger to Vergennes, The Hague, 20 March 1778; *Simancas, Estado, Holanda*, Leg. 6371, letter and enclosure, Herreria to Floridablanca, 12 January 1779; and see also Leg. 6370, same correspondents, The Hague, 19 November 1778.

[139] *AAE, CP, Hollande*, 537, fo. 257 vo., letter, Grand to Vergennes, Amsterdam, 19 August 1779.

[140] N. Magens, *An Essay on Insurances* (2 vols., London, 1755), I, p. 459; see also A. Kluit, *Jets over den laatsten Engelschen oorlog met de Republiek* (Amsterdam, 1794), pp. 12–13.

[141] Article in *The Sun*, London, 2 September 1801; Joh. de Vries, *De economische achteruitgang*, p. 69.

[142] Albion and Pope, *Sea lanes in wartime*, p. 35.

[143] *AS, Genoa*, AS. 2293, letter, Ageno to Serenissima, London, 29 September 1778; for the protest of the Prussian ambassador, see ibid., 28 October 1778.

example, enjoyed bonanza days from 1778.[144] However, for those proud to fly the Dutch flag, the discussions turned to argue from strength, and that meant convoy protection for merchantmen.

The rôle of convoys was a well-accepted routine: for the West Indian consignments; for the winter fleets sent to Spain and Portugal; for the returning East Indiamen; and above all, for the trade to the Mediterranean, which flourished to the third quarter of the eighteenth century.[145] Protection for ships going to the Inland Sea was a continuing commitment to contain the 'piratical states of Barbary', with their *métier* to prey on shipping, confiscate cargoes, ransom crews. The cry to surrender as pirates came alongside – 'Roppi, roppi, Christiana'[146] – recalled in many a sailor's yarn, struck fear. While ships themselves on the way to slave on the coasts of Guinea or Angola took care to avoid capture by Moroccan pirates with a course well out into the Atlantic.[147] There were other precautions to provide for ransoms – private insurance and friendly societies such as the famous *Slavenkas* of Zierikzee.[148] And not least the aid of the State, for the States General set out once more complex arrangements in the Generaal-Plakaat of 31 July 1725 on convoys and licences.[149] In effect, a squadron was maintained to cruise off Morocco and Algiers. Five frigates were on station in 1771, six in 1772.[150] The cost of this protection was covered by dues paid to the different admiralties, and their incomes reflected the changing climate of risk. In the case of Amsterdam, this revenue declined after the Seven Years' War, but from

---

[144] Joh. de Vries, *De economische achteruitgang*, p. 69; see also P. J. Prinsen Geerlings, *De zeeverzekering tegen molest en vrij van molest* (Amsterdam, 1916); Albion, *Forests and Sea-power*, p. 193; C. Thorsen, *Det Kongelig Oktroierede Sø-Assurance Kompagni, 1726–1926* (Copenhagen, 1926), p. 234; W. Kresse, *Materialien zur Entwicklungsgeschichte der Hamburger Handelsflotte 1765–1823* (Hamburg, 1966), p. 22.

[145] For the three or four annual convoys in the seventeenth century see the classic study of J. R. Bruijn, *De admiraliteit van Amsterdam in de rustige tijd* (Amsterdam, 1970), and his 'De vaart in Europa', in G. Asaert et al., *Maritieme geschiedenis der Nederlanden*, II, p. 237; and for the expansion in the third quarter of the eighteenth century and subsequent decline from the mid-1770s of the Levant trade, see J. V. Th. Knoppers, 'De vaart in Europa', ibid., III, p. 259.

[146] *PRO, SP*, 84, 502, letter, Yorke to Halifax, The Hague, 27 September 1763. The problems faced by Hamburg are studied in E. Baasch, *Die Hansastädte und die Barbaresken* (Cassel, 1897). See also H. Hardenberg, *Tussen zeerovers en Christenslaven* (Leiden, 1950), p. 153.

[147] Sailing orders in *RAZ, MCC*, 509.

[148] J. Schot, BWzn., 'De "Slavenkas" te Zierikzee: een uit 1735 daterend verzekeringsfonds', *Zeeuws Tijdschrift*, XXI (1971), 19–20.

[149] J. L. F. Engelhard, *Het Generaal-Plakkaat van 31 juli 1725 op de convooien en licenten en het lastgeld op de schepen* (Assen, 1970), esp. pp. 326–328.

[150] See, for examples, *Simancas, Estado, Holanda*, Leg. 6327, letter, Puentefuerte to Grimaldi, The Hague, 15 September 1767; ibid., Leg. 6364, letters of 14 January 1771 and 14 April 1772; Leg. 6367, letter of 22 September 1775; Leg. 6369, letter of 18 February 1777, Herreria to Grimaldi.

1773 the trend changed, rising to almost a million guilders in 1778, the highest for more than a decade.[151]

The advent of war enlarged the dimensions of convoying, then as now. In the late 1770s, as the reality of peace waned, the need grew to protect the passage of ships through the Channel and the sea-lanes to the Atlantic. A *resolutie* of the States of Holland (29 October 1777) acceded to the requests of the West Indian interests: outward convoy would be only for Dutch ships; their powder and shot were to be limited; but, ominously, cargoes of munitions were to be marked on the manifest as 'not known'.[152] This high-cost protection nevertheless did not satisfy everyone. When forty ships sailed from Texel in January 1778 without convoy, it was clear that some shippers preferred to carry contraband at their own risk than submit to the restrictions of convoy.[153]

The question of convoy eventually set the scenario for war. With open conflict between France and Britain (March 1778), the market of Amsterdam, built around the dealings of private insurers, either could not or would not handle the rising risks of navigating the Channel. In April, business dragged with insurers willing to sign policies only at war premiums. By September a supplement of 3 percent was levied on shipments of silver *reales* from Cádiz, where previously only ¾ or 1 percent had been asked.[154] In November, insurance for either ships or cargoes was not to be had on the Bourse at any price.[155] As for London, the situation was much the same and insurance premiums soared: already in February 1778, ships bound for the Caribbean in convoy were insured at 5 guineas (officially at £1.05) per £100; without convoy at 15.[156] And on claims submitted for French ships insured in the City, no settlements were to be had after the outbreak of war. But in France, ministers kept a watchful eye on this tell-tale barometer: from September, copies of Lloyd's List were meticulously sent to Paris by way of Amsterdam and the complaisant hands of Grand et Compagnie.[157]

---

[151] Ibid., Leg. 6370, letter, Herreria to Floridablanca, The Hague, 3 December 1778; Joh. de Vries, *De economische achteruitgang*, p. 41, 189–190.

[152] ARA, *Staten Holland* (1572–1795), 1777, p. 1464; see also the commentary in *Simancas, Estado, Holanda*, Leg. 6369, letter, Herreria to Floridablanca, The Hague, 25 November 1777; Kluit, *Jets over den laatsten Engelschen oorlog*, pp. 12–13.

[153] *Simancas, Estado, Holanda*, Leg. 6370, letter, Herreria to Floridablanca, The Hague, 10 January 1778.

[154] AAE, CP, *Hollande*, 532, fo. 279 ro., 533, 283 vo., letters, Grand to Vergennes, Amsterdam, 3 April and 3 September 1778.

[155] *Simancas, Estado, Holanda*, Leg. 6370, letters, Herreria to Floridablanca, 5, 19, and 24 November 1778. Even so, the first of these indicated a fleet of merchantmen planning to leave Rotterdam on 10 November under convoy of two frigates, destined for France.

[156] *Simancas, Estado*, Leg. 7000 (25), letter, Escarano to Floridablanca, London, 10 February 1778, and ibid., Leg. 7000 (⁰/145), same correspondents, 24 April 1778.

[157] AAE, CP, *Hollande*, 533, fo. 283 vo., letter, Grand to Vergennes, Amsterdam, 3 September 1778; *Simancas, Estado, Holanda*, Leg. 6370, letter, Herreria to Floridablanca, The Hague, 17 November 1778.

As the seizure of ships became frequent and offensive, the Amsterdam merchants vented their anger. In September, the 'merchants, charterers and underwriters of the Bourse of the City of Amsterdam' put their grievances to the States General; and again in October.[158] In London, the Dutch ambassador received special assurance that the seizures were only to stop cargoes for France.[159] This failed to convince those with large interests at stake. In November, the city of Amsterdam and the merchants joined in making their views known: the 1778 revenue from freight to French ports, they declared, alone amounted to f.1,600,000.[160] With underwriters holding back, and tempers rising, the anglophile Stadhouder's party still managed to hold sway. Then followed the debate of 19 November 1778, virtually an altercation by Amsterdam: by *resolutie*, the States General provisionally adopted a ruling to exclude naval timber from the list of goods qualifying for convoy.[161]

And so the business of marine insurance, under the rising pressure of belligerence, found itself driven from the consortium of the market into the arena of both domestic and international politics. The weaknesses of the federal system became at once apparent: there was no clear arbiter to regulate disputes of such scale. What was decided in the powerful States of Holland under the impulse of Amsterdam found rebuttal in the States General with the intricate deployment of political *savoir-faire* by the Stadhouder and his party. The war-makers in France and England lost no time in manoeuvring the debate. To soften the rising altercation over confiscations at sea, the Admiralty Court in London showed marked partiality in December by deciding cases in favour of Dutch ships. These were gestures with a limited future. When an Amsterdam ship en route from Cádiz to Le Havre in August 1779 with 300,000 silver *reales* on board was captured and taken to Portsmouth, merchants on the Bourse were offered an insurance policy that she would be freed–but at a premium of 22 percent.[162]

The attack from France was directed to Dutch trade. A series of orders turned the screw on the lucrative business in the western ports. An *arrêt* of the Conseil d'Etat (14 January 1779) revoked from 29 January the exemption of Dutch ships from paying *droit de frêt* or *vatgeld* in French ports. And then to split the opposition in The Netherlands, the exemp-

[158] *Simancas, Estado, Holanda*, Leg. 6370, letter, Herreria to Floridablanca, The Hague, 22 September 1778; *AAE, CP, Hollande*, 534, fos. 94 ro.–97 ro., document of 23 October 1778.

[159] *AS, Genoa, AS.* 2293, letter, Ageno to Serenissima, London, 13 November 1778.

[160] *Simancas, Estado, Holanda*, Leg. 6370, letter, Herreria to Floridablanca, The Hague, 19 November 1778.

[161] Kluit, *Jets over den laatsten Engelschen oorlog*, p. 78.

[162] *AS, Genoa, AS.* 2293, letter, Ageno to Serenissima, London, 25 December 1778; *AAE, CP, Hollande*, 537, fo. 331 ro., letter, Grand to Vergennes, Amsterdam, 10 September 1779.

tion was continued for both Amsterdam and Haarlem.[163] In spite of this pressure, the Stadhouder's party would not give way: the States General (21 January) held to its course against convoys for naval timber. But interests diverged. The ports of the Meuse were seriously affected. On 26 February, the 'Kooplieden, Rheeders en Assuradeurs van Scheepen te Rotterdam' put their case to the States General, setting out the damage they incurred. On 5 March, came a similar statement from the interested parties in Dordrecht.[164] These widening divisions at the level of public debate created reverberations within the market for insurance and upheavals among the cohorts of underwriters on the Dam. As we have already seen,[165] the entry to war (1778–79) proved a time of rapid turnover in the entries in the Sligtenhorst lists: both an accelerated loss of existing practitioners and the arrival of new listings in the directories. In sum, the uncertainties at the level of public affairs proved to have the most serious repercussions in the years under study, 1766–80.

The issues came to a head in the March sessions of the States of Holland. The Stadhouder countered the demands for unlimited convoys with a speech to the States of Holland on 10 March, demanding an increase in the size of the army.[166] When it came to a vote, the sides were evenly divided. The trading ports sided with Amsterdam and came out for unlimited convoys; the decaying towns in the Noorderkwartier (with the exception of Alkmaar) were against. As for the nobles, they were equally divided, a state of affairs unknown in living memory, but here the College was finally carried by the casting vote of the Stadhouder: the defeated minority minuted a protest for posterity to remember. In the last count, Gouda changed sides, Gorinchem declared for the majority, so that, eleven votes against eight, Holland decided to give convoy protection to naval timber en route to France.[167] The outcome, nevertheless, was not as clear as it first appeared. Decision by Holland was one thing, execution by the States General another.

The powers abroad increased the pressure. In Britain, George III replied by giving orders for all neutral ships with timber and munitions to be stopped but without violence.[168] In France, the Conseil d'Etat replied with a series of *arrêts*: on 27 April with an extra duty of 15 percent

[163] *AAE, CP, Hollande,* 535, fos. 78 ro.–80 vo., Arrêt du Conseil d'Etat (14 January 1779).

[164] Ibid., 535, fos. 159 ro.–160 vo., 312 ro., 360 ro., documents of 21 January, 9 and 15 March 1779; *ARA, Staten Generaal,* 3834, pp. 130 et seq.; *Simancas, Estado, Holanda,* Leg. 6371, letter, Herreria to Floridablanca, The Hague, 9 February 1779.

[165] See above, Chapter 2, pp. 29–33 and Graph 1.

[166] J. S. Bartstra, *Vlootherstel en Legeraugmentie, 1770–1780* (Assen, 1952), esp. pp. 196–226, 239–263.

[167] *Simancas, Estado, Holanda,* Leg. 6371, letters, Herreria to Floridablanca, The Hague, 18 and 30 March 1779; *AS, Genoa, AS.* 2658, letter, Massardo to Serenissima, The Hague, 2 April 1779; Kluit, *Jets over den laatsten Engelschen oorlog,* p. 98.

[168] *AS, Genoa, AS.* 2658, letter, Massardo to Serenissima, The Hague, 23 April 1779.

on imports (excluding dyestuffs, raw wool, hemp and naval stores) from
The Netherlands, but once more giving Amsterdam and Haarlem
exemption;[169] on 5 June, exempting timber and naval stores from the
new levies;[170] on 3 July suspending the levies, but only for the province
of Holland;[171] and on 18 September an attack on the towns of the
Noorderkwartier, prohibiting the import of Dutch cheese into France.[172]
For the depressed towns of West Friesland, the substantial trade in dairy
products carried weight.[173] The declining payments for convoys and
licences from Enkhuizen and Hoorn were signs of their plight in the
eighteenth century.[174] As the conflict worsened, the Stadhouder tried to
maintain the balance in neutrality, mollifying France on the one hand
over convoys, but on the other hand offering Britain proposals of aid.
The balancing act can be understood and forgiven when it is recalled that
defence expenditures in The Netherlands had fallen by half between 1749
and 1779. The rôle of honest broker carried a price, for with the absence
of firm protection, marine insurance premiums pressed upwards. In
August, the uncertainties made themselves felt on the Bourse. But
honest brokerage was not all on the debit side. It even facilitated an
exchange of French and British prisoners at Texel: an agreement was
signed by the ambassadors in The Hague on Christmas Day, a festive
moment of fraternisation.[175] And that in the climate of *Machtpolitik* was
no mean achievement.

A few days later, however, fate took a hand. On 27 December a
convoy of merchantmen also set sail from Texel for France and the
Mediterranean under convoy commanded by Lodewijk graaf van
Bylandt and Jhr. Jan Hendrik van Kinsbergen; they were intercepted off
the Isle of Wight and taken to Portsmouth. Nine with cargoes of iron and
hemp for France were detained.[176] In March, the Admiralty Court in
London declared them prize. And in August they were sold by

---

[169] *AAE, CP, Hollande*, 536, fos. 112 ro.–113 vo., document, 27 April 1779; *Simancas, Estado, Holanda*, Leg. 6371, letter, Herreria to Floridablanca, The Hague, 1 June 1779; Kluit, *Jets over den laatsten Engelschen oorlog*, pp. 95–98.
[170] *AAE, CP, Hollande*, 536, fos. 281 ro.–282 ro., document of 5 June 1779.
[171] Ibid., 537 fos. 13 ro.–14 ro., document of 3 July 1779.
[172] Ibid., 537, fos. 367 ro.–368 ro., document of 18 September 1779.
[173] P. N. Boekel, *De zuivelexport van Nederland tot 1813* (Utrecht, 1929), Bijlage A.
[174] P. D. J. van Iterson, 'Havens', in G. Asaert et al., *Maritieme geschiedenis der Nederlanden*, III, p. 78.
[175] *AAE, CP, Hollande*, 537, fo. 276 vo., letter, La Vauguyon to Vergennes, The Hague, 24 August 1779; ibid., 537, fo. 240 vo., letter, Grand to Vergennes, Amsterdam, 17 August 1779; *Simancas, Estado, Holanda*, Leg. 6372, letter, Herreria to Floridablanca, The Hague, 30 December 1779; *AS, Genoa*, AS. 2294, letter, Ageno to Serenissima, London, 4 January 1780.
[176] *Simancas, Estado, Holanda*, Leg. 6372, letters, Herreria to Floridablanca, The Hague, 30 December 1779, 11 and 25 January 1780; *AS, Genoa*, AS. 2294, letter, Ageno to Serenissima, London, 4 January 1780.

Table 6. *Amsterdam: claims in the Kamer van Assurantie en Avarij*
(in guilders)

Ship	Destination	Value of cargo		Total cargo	Value of ship	Total Valuation
		Hemp and iron				
		Value	Share of Jean (Jan) Texier			
Jongvrouw Levina en Jacoba Johanna	Bordeaux	32,350	31,000	32,350	9,000	41,350
Michael en Agatha	Bordeaux	33,500	33,500	33,500	10,500	44,000
De jonge Gerben Kugina	Lorient	27,500	27,500	27,500	12,000	39,500
De jonge Ymkia	Lorient	28,350	27,000	28,350	16,000	44,350
Resolutie	Lorient	26,700	26,700	26,700	3,200	29,900
De jonge Sieberg	Rochefort	22,000	22,000	25,700	6,500	32,200
Total		170,400	167,700	174,100	57,200	231,300

auction.[177] The Amsterdam Kamer van Assurantie[178] has details of some of the claims: six are given in Table 6. Two ships were freighted for Bordeaux, three for Lorient (both these ports could provide substantial return cargoes of colonial produce); and one for Rochefort (the great naval depot created by Colbert a century before). Of the total value – f.174,100 – 96.3 percent was shipped by Jean (Jan) Texier en Compagnie. He had his place in the Sligtenhorst lists. At the same time, it should be noted that he spread his cargoes – and risks – in several ships. Richard Muilman and John Berens acted as agents in London, but their reports brought little comfort. The August auctions produced derisory results. The *Jongvrouw Levina en Jacoba Johanna*, for example, valued at a total of f.41,350 went for £800 (f.8,974); the *Michael en Agatha* valued at f.44,000 for £800 (f.8,974); *De jonge Ymkia* valued at f.44,350 for £961 (f.10,780); the *Resolutie* valued at f.29,900 for £435 (f.4,880).[179] Serious losses indeed.

[177] *Simancas, Estado, Holanda*, Leg. 6372, letters, Herreria to Floridablanca, The Hague, 14 and 23 March 1780; see also *ARA, Staten Generaal*, 3825, fo. 794, *Requeste van Texier cum suis*, 19 October 1780.

[178] *KVA*, XXI, 1559, 1575, 1580, 1586, 1587, 1600.

[179] *AAE, CP, Hollande*, 540, fo. 236 ro., letter, Muilman and Berens to Texier en Compagnie, London, 7 March 1780; *Simancas, Estado, Holanda*, Leg. 6373, letter, Llano to Floridablanca, The Hague, 15 August 1780. For the exchange conversions into current money for August 1780, I have used N. W. Posthumus, *Inquiry into the History of Prices in Holland* (2 vols., Leiden, 1946–64), I, p. 608, together with bank agio at 4½ percent, ibid., p. 654.

The repercussions from the captures were profound both for the history of The Netherlands in general and for the Amsterdam insurance market in particular. The protest was, understandably, immediate and sharp. Even towns which had been reluctant to take a hard line now turned against Britain. The Stadhouder struggled to hold the landslide of opinion, calling special meetings in secret, but the wave of revulsion proved too strong.[180] Indignation carried the day and convoys were finally made unlimited. The firm of Hope sent the news to Versailles: it brought evident satisfaction for the earlier restrictions were withdrawn to recognise 'the new firmness'.[181]

The lines of conflict, now sharply drawn, clearly raised the risks of Channel navigation. A proclamation in London on 17 April added fuel to the flames. As Grand commented to Paris, the underwriters on the Bourse were in consternation and 'unwilling to write any policy at any premium and for any risk unless for shipments which were absolutely neutral'.[182] Protection moved away from the customary market so that shippers looked for other routes or for government support. On the one hand, the traffic in munitions for France found an alternative route overland; and on the other hand, the neutrality of The Netherlands sidled towards armed neutrality with the northern powers.

The first aimed to satisfy the pressing demand from France for masts and naval timber. Some supplies came from the Mediterranean – Corsica, Italy, Albania – others from the North notably through the hands of Hamburg and Dutch merchants.[183] A simple plan emerged to use the inland waterways and canals recently reorganised in the southern Netherlands. The French ambassador renewed his proposal on 28 March to send timber from The Netherlands by way of the Meuse, Charleville, the Aisne, Oise, Seine, and on to the naval dockyards of Brest. A mast floated from Amsterdam to Dordrecht cost three guilders and to Ghent a further seventeen. The route could also be used for hemp. A shorter line was found by way of Valenciennes and Cambrai. The firm of Marselis in Amsterdam was eager to join the venture.[184] When the sums were worked out, the additional costs of transport by land and river were well balanced by savings on insurance, so that what seemed at first to be a preposterous adventure turned into an acceptable enterprise.[185] By

---

[180] *AAE, CP, Hollande*, 540, fo. 72 ro., letter, Vergennes to La Vauguyon, Versailles, 21 January 1780.

[181] Ibid., 540, fo. 127 ro., letter, Hope to Vergennes (probably from Rotterdam), 4 February 1780.

[182] Ibid., 540, fo. 454 ro., letter, Grand to Vergennes, Amsterdam, 24 April 1780.

[183] P. Bamford, *Forests and French Sea Power* (Toronto, 1956), esp. Chapter 6.

[184] *AAE, CP, Hollande*, 539, fos. 277 vo.–278 ro., 282 vo.–286 ro., letters, La Vauguyon to Sartine, 28 March and 23 May 1780.

[185] *Simancas, Estado, Holanda*, Leg. 6373, letter, Llano to Floridablanca, The Hague, 22 August 1780.

August, the route through Picardy was actively developed, and it was confidently expected by Christmas to deliver some 1,500 masts of various sizes, enough to last three years. By September, some 700 great masts had made the trip. Hemp and copper were also on the way.[186] According to R. G. Albion, Riga exported a total of 3,425 masts and spars to The Netherlands in 1778–82 and another 1,968 to France – together more than half the exports from the Baltic port.[187] At the same time, the States of Holland gave Texier en Compagnie, principal losers from the convoy captured in December 1779, exemption from tolls and dues for this business, but only as a special case. Sartine could write from Versailles that the trial fleet laden with masts had arrived at Nantes on 29 November.[188]

The second development shifted The Netherlands towards armed neutrality, bringing a reversal of the position a century before in the pact of Sweden and Denmark (1691). In the winter of 1779–80 Russia was active in joining Sweden and Denmark in alliance, and discreet approaches to The Netherlands went ahead in February.[189] On 31 March, proposals arrived in The Hague from Catherine the Great, setting guide-lines for neutral ships and their cargoes similar to those already sent to Stockholm, Copenhagen and Lisbon. On 3 April, Prince Gallitzin put them to the States General.[190] The assembly heard him in courteous silence, tempered with prudence. Through the summer and autumn, however, opinions hardened. When the French fleet returning from the West Indies laden with colonial produce was captured and sold, the outlook of Dutch trade with the Atlantic ports of France darkened.[191] In September, a secret draft of a treaty (signed two years earlier in Aachen on 4 September 1778) between The Netherlands and the United

---

186 Ibid., Leg. 6372, same correspondents, 24 August and 6 September 1780; *AAE, CP, Hollande*, 539, fo. 303 ro.–vo., letter, La Vauguyon to Sartine, The Hague, 22 August 1780.

187 Albion, *Forests and Sea-Power*, p. 193.

188 *ARA, Staten Holland* (1572–1795), 1780, p. 716, 6 September 1780, p. 768, 15 September 1780; *AAE, CP, Hollande*, 539, fo. 319 ro., letter Sartine to La Vauguyon, Versailles, 10 December 1780; *Simancas, Estado, Holanda*, Leg. 6376, letters, Sanafé to Floridablanca, The Hague, 19 September and 14 December 1780.

189 *Simancas, Estado, Holanda*, Leg. 6372, decoded letter, Herreria to Floridablanca, The Hague, 29 February 1780. The bibliography on Armed Neutrality is extensive, but see J. Stephens, *War in disguise: or the frauds of the Neutral Flags* (London, 1805); C. Bergbohm, *Die bewaffnete Neutralität, 1780–3* (Berlin, 1884); F. T. Piggott and G. W. T. Ormond (eds.), *Documentary History of the Armed Neutrality of 1780 and 1800* (London, 1919); F. P. Renant, *La neutralité hollandaise pendant la guerre d'Amérique* (Paris, 1925).

190 *Simancas, Estado, Holanda*, Leg. 6372, letter, Herreria to Floridablanca, The Hague, 1 April 1780; *ARA, Staten Generaal*, 3835, p. 252, *Memorie* of Prince Dmitri Gallitzin, 3 April 1780.

191 *AS, Genoa, AS.* 2294, letter, Ageno to Serenissima, London, 3 August 1780.

States, came to light in a ship captured off Newfoundland.[192] Then, on 21 November, the news leaked out that the Dutch plenipotentiaries in St Petersburg were on the point of signing the agreement of Armed Neutrality. In Amsterdam, insurance business came once more to a standstill.[193] The situation was clear: with important interests in strategic materials at stake, the shortfall in the market itself could be compensated by the state. Neutral flags were to cover neutral cargoes; and merchant-men in convoy were to have protection from search. Yet, all to little avail. On 21 December 1780, George III forestalled armed neutrality by signing his manifesto of war on The Netherlands. Ambassadors packed their bags for home. As a softener to the immediate threat to invest-ments, the States General proposed to raise a loan of f.15 millions and the States of Holland offered a further f.30 millions, both at 3 percent, in the hope that these would mop up loose money repatriated from British 3 percent Consols.[194] More real was the threat of war in coastal waters: on the island of Zeeland heavy guns moved into position at Rammekens to protect the exposed ports of Flushing and Middelburg.[195]

★

In the foregoing survey, we have set out three sets of event uncertainties affecting the Amsterdam market – the crisis of 1763 and recovery; the bankruptcies of 1772–73; and the war gathering momentum from 1775–76 to the open declaration of 1780. Each, however, was different from the other. The 1763 crisis came in July at the reopening of the Wisselbank and at the height of the trading year. Recovery was relatively slow, since the problems of financial convalescence from a destructive war fused with profound structural changes and expanding trade in the economy of Europe. By 1766, relative stability had returned.

The second upheaval of 1772–73 appeared both shorter and sharper, more in the nature of a market readjustment. As such, the effects on insurance dealings could have been appreciably less important, although still affecting the capacity of Amsterdam to write policies and settle claims. The first flurry came in June–July 1772, but the important break in the market followed in December–January. This was on the eve of the half-yearly closure of the Wisselbank; and in the depth of winter, when navigation to the North was virtually at a standstill. In this instance, sharp swings in the shares on the stock exchange had a crucial part to

[192] *Simancas, Estado, Holanda*, Leg. 6373, letter, Sanafé to Floridablanca, The Hague, 24 October 1780; Albion and Pope, *Sea lanes in wartime*, p. 51.

[193] *Simancas, Estado, Holanda*, Leg. 6373, letters, Sanafé to Floridablanca, The Hague, 21 and 28 November 1780.

[194] *AS, Genoa*, AS. 2658, letter, Massardo to Serenissima, The Hague, 29 December 1780.

[195] *Simancas, Estado, Holanda*, Leg. 6373, letter, Sanafé to Floridablanca, The Hague, 28 December 1780.

play in the collapse, at a time when the rural sector – that sheet anchor of all pre-industrial economies – was itself facing serious shortfalls in output.

The third sequence of events leading to war in 1780 was of a different nature. While the crises of 1763 and 1772–73 affected the ability to put up funds and settle claims, war altered the spectrum of perils of the seas. Political debate on convoys reacted directly on insurance dealers, and set constraints on their willingness to stay in the market at all. The opportunities for both profit and loss changed sharply, even when Dutch ships sailed to areas – as for example to St Eustatius – where profit-margins were high. War closed links with other markets, and so moved the business of insurance away from the central tendency of competition which the eighteenth century implicitly did so much to promote. For a sample of Dutch maritime trade in conditions of naval warfare, we can look at the adventures of the *Vrijheyd*[196] returning from Grenada on 2 December 1780 with a cargo of some coffee but mainly sugar, totalling in value f.68,950. Hope and Company held a 78 percent share (in sugar) – Grenada was, after all, the location of the important plantation loan issued by them in 1771. The ship, with sickness on board, went to St Eustatius and there joined the returning convoy. Attacked and captured by the British navy she was taken to St Kitts. There set free – the interests of Hope and Company no doubt carried their weight – she was captured by the French navy but set free once more. The *Vrijheyd* finally arrived in Amsterdam on 22 August 1781, after nearly ten months of voyage, an example of commercial enterprise in time of war. And that when the indicators in the 1770s and 1780s were not always pointing to favourable balances of trade.

The crises and hostilities affected the insurers in Amsterdam in varying degrees. The underwriting accounts of the Maatschappij van Assurantie in Rotterdam seem to indicate that the Fourth Anglo-Dutch War spelled disaster, a sharp reversal from the general profitability of the 1760s and 1770s.[197] The trading year July 1780 to June 1781 handed in a stupendous loss. At the same time, the response of the Amsterdam market to crises and war was complex. The evidence appears to indicate that political rather than financial disturbance eroded the substance of operations. If the Sligtenhorst lists are an accurate record, the numbers of active underwriters increased as war first threatened and then became a reality. High premiums were ground-bait in the mill-pond of profit. Often they could be high and exceptional, as can be seen again from the risk books of the Maatschappij van Assurantie in Rotterdam. When Edward Bacon and Samuel Briggs left Amsterdam on 6 May 1782 bound for Boston,

[196] *KVA*, XXI, 1456; *ARA, Archief van Pieter Steyn*, 332a; and see above, p. 69.
[197] See above, Chapter 2, Graph 3.

the Maatschappij joined in the insurance of their ships with lines of f.1,000 on each at premiums of 30 percent.[198] This was the rate at which shippers and merchants in 1777 could not find insurance cover, in either Amsterdam or Rotterdam, for hulls and cargoes destined for The Netherlands West Indies.[199] Little wonder that speculation took hand when prudence would rather tarry a while. Certainly, the names in the Sligtenhorst lists demonstrate a heavy turnover in the cohorts of underwriters. While the crises of 1763 and 1772–73 did not seem to have altered appreciably the tenor of market renewal, the prelude and advent of war saw established underwriters decamp and their places more than filled by fresh and more speculative contingents. These transients served to high-light a striking characteristic of the social distribution of capital and commercial wealth on the Dam. It was easy to enter the market; but difficult to survive there without substantial assets.[200] The upheaval and risks of war brought such weaknesses to the surface. So, too, did the urban revolt and its demise in 1786–87. On balance, taking together the effects of financial crisis and active war, the most serious disturbance to marine underwriting in the Amsterdam market seems to have derived from political and naval acts. If anything, these altered the prognosis of risk and uncertainty. The limitations of received experience and incomplete information combined to create commercial acatalepsy among the practitioners of protection on the Dam.

[198] *GA, Rotterdam, Maatschappij van Assurantie, 246, Lopende risicos ter zee.*
[199] *Simancas, Estado, Holanda,* Leg. 6369, letter, Herreria to Floridablanca, The Hague, 25 March 1777.
[200] S. Ricard, *Traité,* I, p. 207.

CHAPTER 4

Structural risks and marine insurance: problems and case-studies

Thus far, event uncertainties have found their place mainly on the supply side: they affected the functioning of the market itself. In contrast to these, we must now consider the structural risks implicit in demand functions. They conditioned the limits to which shippers and ship-owners were prepared to go in seeking protection. In turn, the evolution of premiums made apparent the sets of predictions – either consciously or intuitively – made by underwriters. As such, the category of structural risks belongs to rationality, to the mentalities and mental furniture at the time.[1] Needless to say, it should not pass without notice that the prosperity of maritime enterprise drew on improved technical skills – more accurate map-making, for example; and more precise chronometers, which endowed navigation with greater precision and more assurance. Alongside such achievements, came the outstanding refinement of probability analysis and actuarial valuation. The publications of Edmund Halley, Abraham de Moivre, Willem Kersseboom, Nicolaas Struyck, Antoine Deparcieux, Pår Wargentin, Johannes Süssmilch have stood the tests of time; and the thinking of Kenneth Arrow,[2] Milton Friedman, Frank Knight, Oscar Morgenstern has continued to enlarge a long and remarkable bibliography.[3] The practical problems of forecasting and prediction in eighteenth-century marine insurance, however, remained in the margin of these intellectual achievements. A gap yawned between theory and practice. For the latter, adequately received intelligence derived from three centuries of ocean-sailing in the opportunities of the Atlantic furnished insurers with competence and resources, intuition and experience – enough at least to pursue their affairs with

---

[1] This implies an extension of the discussion in L. Febvre, *Le problème de l'incroyance au XVIe. siècle* (Paris, 1944), Part II.

[2] Notably the brilliant collection in K. J. Arrow, *Essays in the Theory of Risk-Bearing* (Amsterdam, 1970; repr. 1974).

[3] For the best survey of the literature, see J. Hirshleifer and J. G. Riley, 'The analytics of uncertainty and information: an expository survey', *Journal of Economic Literature*, XVII (1979).

deterministic rather than probabilistic concepts. The scalars of risks seem to have settled into patterns, adjusting to the norms of daily business. At the time, of course, such routines gathered a patina of skill and dexterity: 'there is more expertise than one would suppose in writing policies correctly in many cases', declared Jean-Pierre Ricard (1722),[4] pointing to acumen which fed on the speculation of navigation. This chapter proposes to look at some of the possible boundary limits.

Two particular packages of risks emerge from the data. On the one hand there is the seasonal movement, and on the other hand distance. These do not, of course, exclude other possible areas of discussion. However, before turning to them, I must enter a certain number of caveats about the data, about the conditions prevailing in the period 1766–80. In the first place, since we are dealing with *structural* risks, these years must find their place in the long-term movement, in a trough in the long evolution of premiums on offer in the Amsterdam market already discussed in Chapter 2. This special characteristic influences the conclusions reached since our purpose here is to seek to measure the degree of equilibrium and the boundary limits within which insurance business was carried on.

Secondly, the *prijscouranten* list the premiums by groups of destinations, giving an impression of bi-lateral navigation. This was not necessarily a valid classification. A growing feature of the Amsterdam market in the eighteenth century was the commission trade and the erosion of the established position of Amsterdam as a staple. Even so, much of the navigation still appeared to demand ships designed with a particular route in mind. The *fluit* was a notable example. There were various models. The version for the Baltic drew perhaps a foot or two less in the water in order to negotiate the difficult shoals of the Sound.[5] Its bulging cargo capacity and marked 'tumble-home' – at least until the customs reforms about 1700 – suited the demanding conditions of sailing the Baltic: entries into harbours and river estuaries, abrupt changes in course, fickle winds and currents, besides the practical constraints of meeting the customs measurers coming aboard to claim their dues. The type of *fluit* typical of the *noordvaart* for the timber of Norway was another example of a ship designed with a special run in mind. In the eighteenth century, a further version emerged in the *katschip*, a popular and efficient cargo-carrier. The North Cape run encouraged strongly built ships; the West Indies and oceans called for deeper draughts and capability to sail in the trade winds. And then there was the age and timber of the vessels: according to Samuel Ricard, ships

---

[4] J.-P. Ricard, *Le Négoce d'Amsterdam*, p. 250.
[5] J. van Beylen, 'Scheepstypen', in G. Asaert et al., *Maritieme geschiedenis der Nederlanden*, II, p. 31.

built of pine had to be specially declared in the hull insurance – otherwise the underwriters accepted only half-liability.[6] In many respects, the insurance market was far from homogeneous. Premiums quoted in the *prijscouranten* already present an approximation to a wide variety of ships and conditions of navigation.

Thirdly, the image of stability calls for further caution. Balthazar-Marie Emerigon could give the impression – largely correct – that policies and procedures were so well established that 'in most marine markets, there are printed pro-forma policies with blank spaces to be completed by hand'.[7] However, the finer points of policy construction were in the process of definition. As illustrated above (see Plates 2, 3, 4, 5, and 6), the policy forms of Amsterdam, Middelburg, and Rotterdam were not precisely the same, but for the *Haast U Langzaam* were used for precisely the same hull and cargoes. The ratio of printing to handwriting in the three policy forms showed variations. There were opportunities for ambiguities, and these had to be construed. Moreover, the question of deductibles – then, and even now if we follow the work of Hans-Peter Sterk[8] – remained an ill-defined area in determining the appropriate premium. Some aspects of these problems will be taken up in the context of the case-study discussed later in this chapter.

The Amsterdam regulations of 1598 had been adamant on the point of declaring the value of the goods carried; these received confirmation in 1744, and further elaboration in 1756 and 1775. Up to 90 percent of the value of the cargo was liable for insurance, so that the assured claimed the excess in eventual risks or losses. The same applied to hull insurance, but it should be noticed that, in this case, Rotterdam set a limit of seven-eighths and Middelburg a half. Insurance on returning cargoes, particularly trans-Atlantic, presented a particular problem. In Amsterdam, underwriters were cautious, allowing appreciation of value only on full information. The same prevailed in Rotterdam: without declaration, insurance could be allowed only at 10 percent over the value of the outward cargo. In Middelburg, however, this could be doubled.[9] And, of course, all the facts had to be known for claims to be valid.

Even so, at times, writing lines on policies seemed hardly more than gambling. The popularity of the sport in the eighteenth century was a social phenomenon, not too far away from the business of insurance. In England, it became patently clear with the insertion of 'let-on' clauses

---

[6] Ibid., II, pp. 32–34; B. E. van Bruggen, 'Schepen, ontwerp en bouw', ibid., III, p. 24; H. J. Koenen, *Voorlezingen over de geschiedenis van scheepbouw en zeevaart* (Amsterdam, 1854), pp. 160–161; S. Ricard, *Traité*, II, p. 466.

[7] B.-M. Emerigon, *Traité des Assurances*, II, p. 32.

[8] H.-P. Sterk, 'Deductibles from a risk-theoretical point of view', *The Geneva Papers on Risk and Insurance*, XVII (1980), pp. 82, 87–88.

[9] S. Ricard, *Traité*, II, pp. 466–468.

when the policy was taken as sufficient proof of interest. This loop-hole was supposedly closed by the Act of 1746, during the War of the Austrian Succession. But the popularity of playing the market was not abolished with the flourish of a quill. It can be seen in the subscriptions to a policy on the life of Louis XV, opened in London in August 1773: his survival for one year carried even chances with a premium of 50 percent. In the event, he died at 3.15 p.m. on 10 May 1774, within the year stipulated.[10] An incident apart from marine insurance, to be sure, but one which serves to underline issues remaining complex and arcane in the eighteenth century.

And finally in the packages of risks, there is the efficiency or rather the imperfection of the market. While the seasonal movement and the factor of distance shaped the profile of the demand curve for insurance, on the supply side brokers rarely provided a continuous service of insurance during the whole year. For one thing, registered brokers were often at odds with the amorphous, volatile group of free-lance dealers, the *beunhazers* or unsworn *commies*. These formed a 'market' which fluctuated during the year. Some would slip away from dealings in the third quarter, an accepted practice as much in Amsterdam as in London. At least, this appeared to be the custom if we follow the evidence put to the Parliamentary Committee of 1810:[11] more than a few underwriters were conspicuous by their absence from August to December. This alternation in insurance business gave special edge to the crises of 1763 and 1772–73 and conditioned the effective liquidity of the Amsterdam market. High premiums which followed the capricious policies of naval search may have offered the prospect of profit, but high losses also contributed to drive insurers underground. These swings may have been more specially noticeable among the free-lance dealers. In this sense, the market was not always a good detective, able to report a consistent performance.

★

In the pages which follow I propose to turn to the detail of the risks associated with navigation in the 1760s and 1770s. These can be defined for convenience in a model of the following type:

$$P = f(S, D, Z, r)$$

where P is the premium rate quoted in the market; S represents seasonal movements; D distance; and Z market structures. The residual factor r

---

[10] *AAE, CP, Hollande*, 525, fo. 103 ro., letter, Grand to Desnoyers, Amsterdam, 22 August 1773; *Simancas, Estado*, Leg. 4593, letter, Aranda to Grimaldi, Paris, 11 May 1774.

[11] *British Parliamentary Papers, Report of the Parliamentary Committee on Marine Insurance*, 1810 (226), IV, p. 247.

takes care of stochastic variables in event uncertainties. For the purposes of this study, these factors are considered in turn; but the model must assume a large measure of structural interdependence. The residual factor leaves it open in order to reconcile on the one hand empirical factors of steady state and periodicities; and on the other turbulence – or 'chaos' as mathematicians would no doubt prefer – deriving from small changes in market or political behaviour. It would require a certain topology to allow forms which have structure and continuity to accommodate with those which are 'catastrophic' and random.[12] The closing section of this chapter takes up the practical aspects of the problem in the case-study of a ship registered in Middelburg in 1764–81.

THE SEASONAL MOVEMENT

The dynamic movement in annual crop production and transfers to market penetrated to the core of agrarian Europe. The seasonal movement was the dominant cycle. It affected society from top to bottom, preoccupying the thoughts of farmers and merchants, ministers and prelates, army commanders and dons, and not least seamen and their masters. All dallied on the prospect of Michaelmas, the moment of fullness in the year, the prelude to the harshness of winter.

This annual movement imposed on the trade of Europe a preferred calendar – or rather calendars for, as Samuel Ricard was quick to point out, each commodity virtually had optimal dates for placing orders and receiving deliveries. In northern Europe, climate held sway. In winter, merchandise flowed to the ports by sledge, in summer by road or river. Consignments of grain moved best not in high summer but rather in March–April or in September–October. A great entrepôt such as Danzig provided the adjacent island of Holm with well-guarded warehouses where grain dampened during transit down the Vistula by open boat or raft could be brought back to condition. The grain was aired and dried, turned over regularly with wooden shovels, in much the same way as brewers prepare malt.[13] Thus restored, it could travel widely through Europe in bulk and without difficulty. The calendar was not always followed to the letter. For example, we find the ship *De drie Gebroeders*[14] sailing from Danzig on 8 July 1765 in the height of summer for Amsterdam with a single cargo of 56 *lasts* of wheat; and *De jonge Juffrouw Tygesen*[15] on the same trip similarly laden. In Russia and East Prussia warehouses were accustomed to assemble cargoes in good time. There was the ship *De jonge Pieter de Jong*[16] leaving Memel on 24 May 1775 for

[12] See above, Chapter 1, pp. 11–12, note 35.
[13] S. Ricard, *Traité*, I, pp. 388–390, 395; and see below, p. 121.
[14] *KVA*, XV, 3546.   [15] *KVA*, XV, 3551.   [16] *KVA*, XIX, 766.

Table 7. *Genoa: opening hours of the* Dogana

Months	Hours opened Morning	Afternoon
December–January	5	–
February–March	4	2
April	4	3
May	4	$3\frac{1}{2}$
June–July	5	$2\frac{1}{2}$
August	4	$3\frac{1}{2}$
September	4	3
October–November	4	2

Oporto with a single cargo of hemp valued at f.41,100. The departure so early in the season could have meant an 'overwinter' or shipment of the previous year's crop. In this case, there was the likelihood of insurance for consignments waiting in warehouses – such as hemp, flax, and timber, which could be done in The Netherlands, usually at $\frac{1}{2}$ to $\frac{3}{4}$ percent, for particular stores by name.[17]

Such periodicities of trade put pressure on liquidity. In St Petersburg, for example, the exchange rate in summer could on rare occasions rise to a fifth over that in winter, so that there were incentives to settle contracts in the 'dead' months. Purchases were often made in November–December, for delivery in April–June. The ships would then leave The Netherlands one or two months before the deliveries in the ports. In this way, trade enjoyed a float of credit – for the outward cargoes and the returns. And not least, there was the need to prepare for the payment of the tolls at the Sound, for which ships' masters usually carried letters of credit drawn on a merchant house in Helsingør, in the shadow of the great fortress of Kronborg.[18]

In southern Europe, the same rhythms prevailed: Fernand Braudel has shown this admirably for the life of the Mediterranean.[19] In the eighteenth century, that profile continued. In Genoa, for example, customs officers in the Dogana enjoyed a time-table for all seasons.[20] Traders from northern Europe came to join in a web of credit, as old as the hills, but made more significant with the growth of extensive maritime trade. It amounted to forward buying, commercial credit extended to the small farmers to sell their produce before the harvest, and settle for prices 'almost always considerably below what this produce

[17] S. Ricard, *Traité*, I, p. 390. [18] Ibid., I, pp. 389–393.
[19] F. Braudel, *La Méditerranée et le monde méditerranéen à l'époque de Philippe II*, 2nd edn (2 vols., Paris, 1966), I, pp. 225–245.
[20] AC, Genoa, MS. *Brignole Sale*, 108.E.5, and see Table 7; for illustration of work hours in Amsterdam in 1778, see van Bruggen, 'Schepen, ontwerp en bouw', in G. Asaert et al., *Maritieme geschiedenis der Nederlanden*, III, p. 57.

would probably fetch at the time of the harvest, even when in glut'.[21] Perhaps this two-way stretch of credit can be seen in the bankruptcy of the De Neufvilles. Caught at the re-opening of the Wisselbank (July 1763) when a spate of bills of exchange fell due for settlement, they had credits in Sweden and Germany, but at the same time sizeable debts for goods purchased in southern Europe.[22]

The signing of insurance policies spliced into this immemorial rhythm of trade. Our purpose here is to fix the movement, and the task is far from simple. As an initial essay, we can turn again to the *prijscouranten* and create a 'type-year'. A few calculations will set out the problem. For the 20 groups of destinations in Europe, I have used annual median monthly rates for the whole period 1766–80. In each simulated 'year', the June quotation is always the lowest of the monthly series. This has been taken as a base period (=100). The resulting indexes (see Graph 6) fall into two groups:

(a) northern Europe – Baltic, Scandinavia, Russia for which the quotations cover the period March–November.
(b) Atlantic and southern Europe – Hamburg–Bremen; British Isles, France, Portugal, Spain, Mediterranean, for which the quotations cover the whole year.

The first observation is the central tendency of the market during the 'best' summer months, the period most favourable for navigation and when brokers were active in the market. From the sample of the movement of ships from France, Spain, and the Mediterranean into the Baltic in 1785, the heavy months of insurance were May and June (36.75 percent of the total); and for the returns July and August (38.87 percent of the total).[23] These ship movements meant a prologue of commercial activity, signing contracts to deliver and collect, arranging for stevedores to assemble cargoes in preparation.

A second observation: outside this central base period, the series diverge. The dispersion has greater amplitude in the closing months of the year. From August the rates for the northern group rise rapidly and during the last quarter (October–December), both the rate of increase and the spread within the group are significant. The divergence from the southern group is clear. The latter, however, shows more consistency, firstly, in amplitude (the shift away from the June base (=100) shows a maximum in November of 265 against 560 for the northern group);

[21] S. Ricard, *Traité*, I, p. 612.
[22] E. E. de Jong-Keesing, *De economische crisis van 1763 te Amsterdam* (Amsterdam, 1939), p. 218.
[23] C. Johansen, *Trade and Merchant Shipping between the Baltic and Southwestern Europe in the Eighteenth Century*, communication to the International Conference of Economic History, Copenhagen, 1974, Table IV.

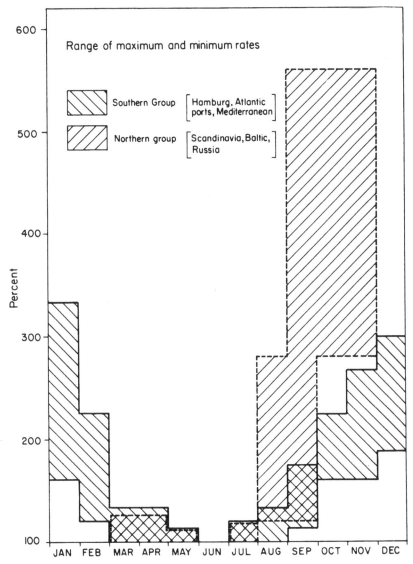

Graph 6. Type-year of Amsterdam insurance rates (outward): index of median rates 1766–80 (June = 100)

secondly, in range between the maximum and minimum rates (105 against 280 respectively); and thirdly, in continuity (the quotations for the southern group are for the whole year, while those for the north cover only the period March–November). These point to the increasing risks of winter, which tended to split the north from the south. While trade continued amiably in southern Europe, the northern winter raised levels of uncertainty. Entrepreneurs had either to face those risks or 'overwinter' until the following spring. There was the *Vrouw Anna Clasina*[24] which sailed from Archangel for Amsterdam on 13 August 1773 with a cargo of flax-seed, mats, and rye for a total value of f.29,326. After running into heavy weather, she put into Bergen for repairs and finally managed to reach Amsterdam on the 15 May following. And the case of the Rotterdam ship *Zeenimph*[25] sailing from Archangel to Barcelona. She lost her mainmast en route and was obliged to 'overwinter'. The claims in 1779 were adjusted at 75 percent on the hull and 25 percent on the cargo. In this context, it is worth recalling that in the policies for hull insurance on the *Haast U Langzaam*, Frederik Dibbetz added in handwritten wording 'vrij van Legdagen, Onkosten van Overwintering, en van Avarij, Schade en Avarij Grosse onder drie per cento'.[26]

A regional system for Europe thus emerges, dual in nature and conditioned by weather and climate. The pressing obligation to trade in the north during spring and summer raised incentives to assemble cargoes in the south during the less favourable months in order to meet the timetable of open ports in the north. It would be possible to fix this hypothesis, if we have the necessary statistics for the aggregate volumes of cargoes insured in Amsterdam. Regrettably this is not so far available, at least to the extent required. However, the registers of *Lopende risicos ter zee*, kept by the Maatschappij van Assurantie in Rotterdam[27] shed some light on the problem; but we must bear in mind that Rotterdam was not Amsterdam, either in size or in distribution of interests. The totals of insurance registered in these risk books show the following results for 1765–74 (see Graph 7). The total premiums for this period came to f.694,900, to and from the different destinations. It is evident that the insurance of the Rotterdam company looked to the south: while the North and Baltic took 11.4 percent, France–Mediterranean claimed 51.4; the British Isles 23.7. The remainder had small shares: America 7.7, Africa 3.0, Asia 2.1 (probably on private account, outside the Rotterdam chamber of the VOC) and 0.7 for whaling to Greenland and the Davis Strait. These totals, however, are one consideration; the seasonal distribution another. The alternation between the different regions during the year may reflect on the basic seasonal problem which we have been

[24] *KVA*, XVIII, 521.
[25] *GA, Rotterdam, Maatschappij van Assurantie*, 246.
[26] *RAZ, MCC*, 509, and see above, pp. 122–124.
[27] The entries in the risk books, *Lopende risicos ter zee*, give dates of registering the policy, the amount insured, the name of the assured, destination (or origin) and premium: *GA, Rotterdam, Maatschappij van Assurantie*, 245–246. Dr R. A. D. Renting has been exceptionally kind in making available this material.

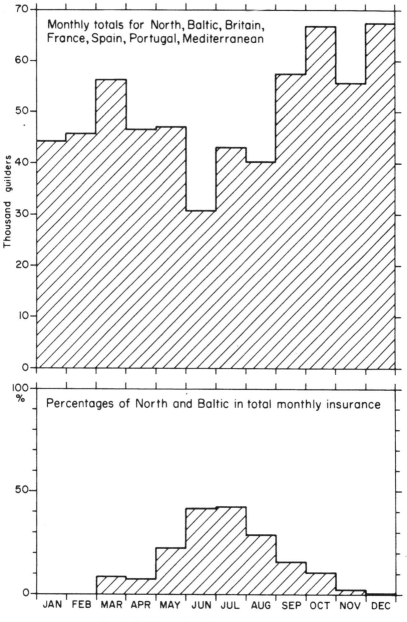

Graph 7. Rotterdam insurance (1765–74)

considering for the insurance market of Amsterdam (see Graph 6). For Europe (that is, excluding Asia, Africa, the Americas and Greenland/Davis Strait), the highest volume in the spring came in March; and in the autumn and winter in September–December. This double peak left the lowest month of all in June. The fact that the total demand for insurance was reduced during this month may have contributed to the low rates quoted for all destinations: total demand for finance on the market may then have been reduced. At the same time, the data in Amsterdam show a longer period of low rates – April to August, so that the demand for funds in June could have been only one factor influencing the market.

The data for Rotterdam reveal further aspects of the problem of regional differentiation. For France (the Atlantic ports), the highest monthly total was December; for the British Isles, January. In the case of both Spain/Portugal and the Mediterranean there were two peaks; in April–May and then in the last quarter of the year. Spain may have been a special case, having the returning American fleets with their colonial products and bullion in the autumn but requiring goods for despatch in the spring. For all these destinations, the months of June–July were apparently a relatively slack period. In contrast, the peak for the Baltic came in May–July; and for Norway/Archangel in July. The data therefore show a clear alternation between the destinations: the insurance for traffic to the south was active in the winter and spring to collect cargoes for the Baltic and northern ports during the favourable months of summer.

In a regional matrix, the hypothesis can be offered that the regions of the Baltic and the north emerge as risk-leaders. They produced the strategic materials for mercantilist Europe: food and grain; the best metals – iron and copper; and the best naval stores – timber and masts, hemp and flax, pitch and tar – which were critical in keeping warships and merchantmen afloat. Their timetable set a pattern for the market; first, in creating an alternating navigation of winter and summer; and second, in an over-riding commitment to exploit the resources of the north during the summer. The function – indeed success – of Amsterdam lay in fine-tuning this alternating trade and its insurance.

RISKS OF DISTANCE

We can now turn to the second set of factors proposed in the model, the length of the voyages undertaken. At the outset, it is worth noting that marine insurance was concerned principally with the voyage and not, as to-day, the calendar year. In many respects, it emphasises the discontinuities of agrarian Europe; and the time involved in ocean-navigation.

That is not to say that annual marine insurance did not on occasion exist. In Copenhagen, such policies were offered for China and the Far East.[28] In London, similarly, a ship (36 guns) bound for Manilla in December 1768 was insured for two years at 16 percent on £25,000.[29] Nevertheless, the concept of distance remained deeply embedded in the system of marine insurance. Medieval theologians had been prepared to accept the principle of spatial distance, but not that of the distance of time,[30] which had proved a serious impediment to the development of life insurance. In Amsterdam, the latter principle was embodied in Clause XXIV of the regulations of 1598; and confirmed in the regulations of Rotterdam in 1604 and 1621. Even the revised regulations of 1744 in Amsterdam, did not include the clause on time, but on the other hand did not expressly permit it.[31] All the same, the factors of time and distance remained closely related, and this proved to be significant in the insurance of return cargoes on long voyages. In some cases such as those from Curaçao, Surinam, and Archangel, the ships arrived home at the same time, according to J.-P. Ricard (1722), as the news that the cargoes had been put on board. In this case, information was crucial to liability.[32] For this present exercise, I propose to concentrate on the spatial factor. How did it affect the premiums?

A first task in analysing the data is to find a year of relative equilibrium. From what has already been said in this study, no particular year has an immediate claim, the sequel to 1763, the bankruptcies of 1772–73, the mounting wave of war all presented special tensions. Wherever we look, some measure of constraint and conflict was rarely absent. However, in the long-term, the years 1765–74 could perhaps offer relatively better conditions, and if a particular year were required, then 1769 would appear to have come closer than most others. The Amsterdam market then seemed to be less disturbed by major upheavals.

---

[28] C. Thorsen, *Det Kongelig Oktroierede Sø-Assurance Kompagni, 1726–1926* (Copenhagen, 1926), pp. 114, 242.

[29] *Simancas, Estado*, Leg. 6969 (⁰/1770), letter, Maserano to Grimaldi, London, 15 December 1768.

[30] B.-M. Emerigon, *Traité des Assurances*, II, p. 7: time was not merchandise; he also comments on the clauses of limited and unlimited time in the delivery of goods. In France, the *Ordonnance de la marine* (1681) forbade insurance on life on the basis that only things which had a price could be insured: R.-J. Pothier, *Traité du contrat à la grosse et du contrat d'assurance* (Paris, 1777), pp. 34–35. See also, C. F. Trenerry, *The Origin and Early History of Insurance* (London, 1926), p. 276.

[31] Vergouwen, *De geschiedenis der Makelaardij*, pp. 70–73. A century and a half later, the theological debate remained open, P. Barendregt, *Mag een christen zich assureeren?* (Brille, 1882).

[32] J.-P. Ricard, *Le Négoce d'Amsterdam*, pp. 251–252. In The Netherlands, the delay in the arrival of information in order to establish liability was calculated at one-and-a-half miles an hour – half walking speed, but such speeds varied in different countries, S. Ricard, *Traité*, II, p. 467.

A second task is to consider navigation and insurance as a system of continuities moving away from the focal market. From the premiums quoted in the *prijscouranten*, there is a *prima facie* case that risks rose in proportion to the distance from the home port. That base point was a reservoir of resources: flows of information; convenient supplies of ships' stores or victuals; a place for repairs; access to government protection; and perhaps not least, a catchment area for recruiting seamen. In the eighteenth century, manning was a major problem and, from the evidence available, cosmopolitan. In the VOC ship *Nijenborg*, the scene of the great mutiny of 1763–64, the complement consisted of seventeen nations, to which the Dutch contributed 29 percent but the Germans an extraordinary 47. All the officers, however, hailed from The Netherlands.[33]

Keeping the two conditions – equilibrium and continuity – in mind, what do the premiums of the *prijscouranten* show? Taking fourteen of the groups in Europe and one in the West Indies (Surinam), an analysis can be based on the quotations for June (summer sailings), and for December (winter sailings). Calculating the warranted distances from Amsterdam to the different destinations is far from easy,[34] for navigation in the pre-industrial period contended above all with wind and tide. In the special case of Atlantic voyages, the outward trip was almost always longer than the return. However, at the same time, certain of the routes had assumed customary patterns. Perhaps only in whaling and fishing did vessels not conform to these basic rules, since they wandered to and fro to garner the resources of the sea, here in the North Sea and Baltic for catches of herring, there in the waters of Greenland and the Davis Strait hunting hauls of seals and whales.[35] Again, the actual distances sailed varied widely, and relate to that difficult problem of navigation: the difference between distance travelled 'through water' and that 'over ground'. It was, to be sure, navigation at the behest of wind, tide, and current; and for these reasons far from accurate.

In the tests which follow the regressions use estimated distances, with the premiums in the *prijscouranten* as dependent variables. The results for June show that the quotations form a pattern (see Graph 8). The

---

[33] J. C. Mollema, *Een muiterij in de achttiende eeuw* (Haarlem, 1933), p. 17.

[34] The distances calculated include the passage of the former Zuiderzee. Of great assistance have been the service of the Havenmeester's office in Amsterdam; and reference to H. Whittingham and C. T. King (eds.), *Reed's Tables of Distances*, 10th edn (Sunderland, 1913).

[35] R. G. Albion and J. B. Pope, *Sea lanes in wartime: the American experience, 1775–1942* (New York, 1942), pp. 26–27. Although not listed in the *prijscouranten*, some policies for whaling were written in the eighteenth century, Vergouwen, *De geschiedenis der Makelaardij*, pp. 74–75; for the developments in Hamburg, see W. Oesau, *Hamburgs Grönlandfahrt auf Walfischfang und Robbenschlag vom 17–19 Jahrhundert* (Glückstadt–Hamburg, 1955).

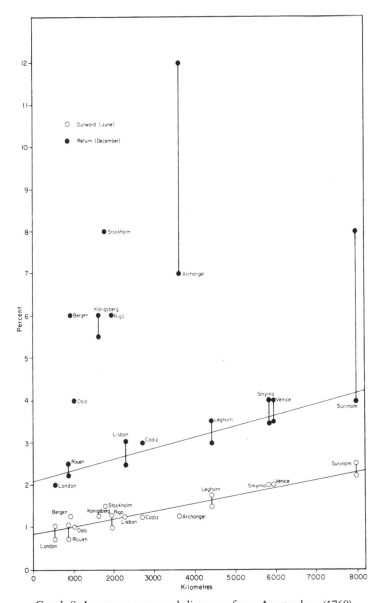

Graph 8. Insurance rates and distances from Amsterdam (1769)

correlation between premiums and distance to destinations in Europe
and Surinam is significant: the coefficient (r^2) is 0.887 and the t-ratio
9.7892.[36] In the spacious days of summer, a possible conclusion is that

[36] John Hey and Richard Morley have very kindly helped with these estimates.

navigation enjoyed a high degree of linearity. It gave insurance dealers the opportunity to live with fixed probabilities.

In mid-winter, the opposite prevailed: the return rates present an entirely different picture. The results are negative, without any fit at all: r^2 is 0.0067 and the t-ratio 0.2836. However, if we divide the premiums into two groups – firstly, the Channel ports, Portugal, Spain, and the Mediterranean; and secondly, the Baltic, Scandinavia and Archangel – the outcome is significant. The southern group shows high correlation ($r^2 = 0.9548$) similar to that for the summer months; but the northern group remains inconsistent. Nevertheless, the results in the latter case must be viewed with caution for the data have been reduced to eight pairs of observations.

The measure of consistency in the summer and winter navigation of Europe calls for further comment. The first is that the slopes of the regressions are different. These details, where x is the estimated distance in kilometres and y the premium percent, are given in Table 8. These suggest four sets of conclusions. Firstly, in the favourable conditions of summer, navigation to the different groups of destinations was consistent with distance over ground. Premiums (and presumably estimated risks) increased in proportion to the preferred route distance from Amsterdam. Although actual voyages may have diverged from this it remained at least warranted. Secondly, winter destroyed the apparent unity of the system. The harsh conditions in sailing to the north moved the market from fixed risks to conditions more affected by event uncertainties. The southern group nevertheless continued to maintain a significant unity, while taking account of winter sailing in the steeper slope of the regression. Thirdly, there is a variation on this theme in the case of convoy rates. For Surinam the convoy return rates (December) join the 'consistent' group: the premiums on the Amsterdam market were running at 4 percent with, or 8 percent without, convoy. The combination of winter gales, valuable colonial cargoes, and liability to capture, put the West Indian returns into a high-risk category, but it would seem, at least in this example, that convoy protection brought them back into the range of conventional risks.

Lastly, and perhaps most important of all, the analysis shows that the regression does not start from zero but from an intersect of the y-axis which registers premium rates. For the 1769 data, the intersections for June and December are 0.85 and 2.11 respectively. The premise of linearity of risks on the high seas thus requires closer scrutiny. We can talk of this linearity in the sense that risks increased in ratio to the distance navigated. However, this did not begin from zero, from the moment the ship cast off or raised anchor to set sail. There was a preliminary stage of hazards which I prefer to call a 'risk-trap' below

Table 8. *Premiums and distances (1769)*

June series (whole group)

x	0	7,990
y	0.85	2.33

December series (southern group only)

x	0	7,990
y	2.11	4.20

which premiums did not fall. As a working hypothesis for the June data, this can be set at about $\frac{3}{4}$ percent, which was the rate for the premiums listed for London and Rouen. One possible explanation is that the manoeuvres of entering and leaving port exposed the carrier to special risks. Certainly, in the days before organised pilotage and steam tugs, the patent difficulties in negotiating harbours and fairways, or in setting sail after leaving the hard, exercised powerful constraints and even had a marked influence on ship-design.[37] The poor maintenance of fairways, the indifferent navigational aids, and the lack of effective pilotage combined into added hazards. And this in a Europe where access to continental markets by waterways was a necessity of trade[38] and placed high demands on coastal shipping.

On the other hand, there was the linear freedom of the high seas. The slope of the least squares regression line infers that as far as marine risks were concerned the ocean offered economies of scale. The rate for Venice, for example, was not twice that for Cádiz. In brief, the problem can be set in the category of a 'turnpike theorum',[39] with an initial phase of difficulties and increased costs in leaving harbour and coastal waters, before attaining to the rapid growth potential for profit on the high seas. Once on the open sea the problems of 'in-shore soundings' gave place to those of plotting the ship's position out of sight of land. But the perils of navigation were of a different order. In the favourable year of 1769, the system could offer guarantee of indemnity on the high seas at about 0.19

---

[37] R. and R. C. Anderson, *The sailing ship* (London, 1926), esp. p. 188. The lowest fractions printed in the *prijscouranten* did not normally fall below three-quarters.

[38] A. Predöhl, *Verkehrspolitik* (Göttingen, 1958), esp. pp. 17–19, 38; D. Krafft, *Der Einfluss eines Hafens auf die Wirtschaftsstruktur und die Wirtschaftskraft seiner Hafenstadt* (Göttingen, 1966), p. 13.

[39] For the development of the turnpike theorem from the original work of John von Neumann (1936) and the impetus of Robert Dorfman, Paul Samuelson and Robert Solow (1958), see T. C. Koopmans, 'Economic growth at a maximal rate', *QJE*, LXXVIII (1964).

percent per 1,000 kilometres at the height of summer, and about 0.26 percent in the depth of winter. At least, that is one conclusion to be drawn. Given the vagaries of navigation under sail, such a matrix of premiums and distances must be regarded as an optimum objective to be attained. Closing that gap in large measure remained a target for the efficient steamship.

At the time, the type of ship and the experience of sailing in waterways of the coasts of Friesland and Holland, in the Delta system of the Rhine–Meuse–Scheldt suited the Dutch style of navigation to admiration. This had many of the requisites to handle the complexities of coastal shipping. However, were the ports of Europe equal to the occasion? Was distance on the high seas one consideration, but pilotage to enter and leave port another – and an entirely different one at that?

PROBLEMS OF SHIPS AND PORTS

The growth of mercantilist Europe made huge demands on navigation, but the prizes lay in the territorial and commercial opportunities of empire. The mastery of entry into harbours and estuaries gave access to the great river systems and their hinterlands of continental resources or colonial plantations. In consequence, cost-effective coastal shipping had to contend with a variety of conditions. All too often it was not a question of tying up to wharves and quays, but of anchoring in the fairway, or allowing the ship to settle on the beach when the tide was out. Apart from transport on land, there was often the intermediate stage of carrying the cargo to the ship, before it could be said to be laden. Little surprise then that the typical Amsterdam policy – as indeed the earlier formula of Antwerp[40] – took account of this and gave insurance on cargo from the hour and day the goods arrived on the quay.

The navigation of The Netherlands took to the task in the manner born. The golden age of the early seventeenth century showed the adoption of 'best-practice techniques' in navigation, notable innovations both in design and freight capacity. Received opinion on the evolution of the *fluit* assigns it to Pieter Jansz. Liorne of Hoorn in 1595. Its striking characteristics in design made it a work-horse of maritime trade. It had greater length (a length/beam ratio of 1 to 5 or even 1 to 6), a rounder stern, and sharp 'tumble-home' (to minimise the dues at the Sound, at least until about 1700). It had marked rubbing strakes for tying up at wharves or mooring together in fairways; and the bottom was noticeably flat, an advantage in settling on a hard or negotiating shallow waters in difficult channels. It handled well in changing weather conditions; but its blunt, rounded design was less content with the rollers of the Atlantic.

[40] B.-M. Emerigon, *Traité des Assurances*, II, pp. 11–12.

The design adapted to different routes and destinations. The 'great' *fluit*, often used far afield, even in Asian waters, could be 130 voet in length with a draught/length ratio of 1 to 9.56. Small *fluits* for Norway could be 100 voet and 1 to 9.09 respectively; while the preferred *fluit* for the Baltic could be 100 voet and 1 to 11.11.[41] The difference in the last version, no doubt to handle bulky cargoes through the difficult channels of the Sound, gave the navigation of The Netherlands a special edge in competition. The emergence of the *katschip*, a type of *fluit*, was a further facility for moving heavy cargoes.

Such innovatory drive tended to diminish after 1630, certainly after 1670.[42] The cargo-carriers of the eighteenth century reached full development with 'Atlantic' versions combining both square and fore and aft rigged, in place of the reliance on lateen sails so often employed in the Mediterranean. Naturally there were variations in size, ranging from the great East Indiamen of some 1,000–2,000 tons to the 200–300 tonner for the heavy trade of Europe, and to the smaller versions adapted for local coastal waters. The size of ship was related both to the type of trade and to ship-building costs. The rising cost of masts and naval timbers, for example, tended in the inflation of the eighteenth century to make the ship of some 200–300 tons a preferred best-practice cargo-carrier.[43]

Ocean-sailing and increased carrying capacity, then, required deeper draught and a high ratio of length to beam. This presented no few problems in entering and leaving many of the older ports of Europe. In some cases, they were no longer equal to the task, not least when they contended with the old problem of silting. It had undermined the prosperity of Bruges.[44] And other ports were not exempt. Venice found itself hampered by difficult access to the basin of San Marco: a plan of 1667 to join Malamocco to Venice dragged on, but came to life again in 1725 with a channel 15 kilometres long, some 2 metres deep, and 12 wide.[45] Genoa, too, had its problems, which the Serenissima did its best to solve. The *molo* to protect the port after the great storms of 1592, 1613, and 1636 was a notable achievement; but was constructed on the east side, to the *levante*. This breakwater hindered the disposal of debris and indeed increased silting. In consequence, the Republic, in order to maintain its maritime facilities, was saddled with elaborate and costly

[41] J. van Beylen, 'Scheepstypen', in G. Asaert et al., *Maritieme geschiedenis der Nederlanden*, II, pp. 28–32.
[42] R. W. Unger, *Dutch shipbuilding before 1800* (Assen, 1978), pp. 59, 109.
[43] Albion and Pope, *Sea lanes in wartime*, p. 18; van Beylen, 'Scheepstypen', in G. Asaert et al., *Maritieme geschiedenis der Nederlanden*, II, pp. 31–32.
[44] J. Maréchal, 'Le départ de Bruges des marchands étrangers', *Annales de la Société d'Emulation de Bruges*, LXXXVIII (1951), 43; J. Decavèle, R. de Herdt, N. Decorte, *Gent op de wateren en naar de zee* (Antwerp, 1976), p. 51.
[45] G. Luzzatto, *Introduzione* in L. Candida, *Il Porto di Venezia* (Naples, 1950), pp. 25–27.

operations to clear the Darsena: the famous manoeuvre of the 'dispaccio' using special flat-bottomed boats, cofferdams, a forest of bucket-hoists, and swarms of labourers to empty the water and dig out the accumulated refuse.[46] Such exercises continued into the eighteenth century. Further along the coast, the old port of Sète was subject to heavy silting and could admit only galleys and small boats; the province of Languedoc contributed heavily to the cost of keeping it open.[47] On the western coast of France, according to complaints in 1724, sand blocked the harbour of St Valéry, one of the privileged ports for importing into north-western France.[48] At the other end of Europe, access to St Petersburg was hindered by the silt of the Neva. Danzig found similar problems in the scour of the Vistula: to such an extent that a canal was projected in 1717 to remedy the difficulties.[49] And Hamburg was not spared. In 1775, the city faced costs of dredging the outlet to the Elbe, but the awkward question remained: who should foot the bill? The *Commerzdeputation* finally agreed to make a small contribution but only with marked reluctance.[50]

As for Amsterdam, the problem reached classic proportions. In the eighteenth century, it remained the premier port of The Netherlands – but at a price. Severe silting became a major concern in the commercial life of the Dam not only for the harbour but also for the intricate network of canals to the warehouses, lofts, and counting houses of the city. In 1778, five dredgers were at work, served by 150 barges. In the period 1778–93, f.1,598,000 was spent on improvements for depth.[51]

However, the harbour was one thing, the channels of access another. Amsterdam probably suffered more from sandbanks than Rotterdam. The channel winding through the Zuiderzee to the outports of Den Helder, Texel, and Vlieland – the *stroom* or *rivier* – had special snags and hazards. At the start of the voyage, there was *Het Pampus*, a sandbank at

---

[46] G. Faina, *Ingegneria portuale genovese nel Seicento* (Florence, 1969), pp. 2, 22, 35 et seq. Giorgio Doria admirably explained the scale of these operations. They are amply demonstrated in the paintings in the Museo Navale, Genoa, kindly made available through the kindness of Dr Laura Secchi.

[47] S. Ricard, *Traité*, I, p. 519; J. W. Konvitz, *New Port Cities of Louis XIV's France: Brest, Lorient, Rochefort and Sète, 1660–1715* (Ann Arbor, 1974), p. 254.

[48] S. Ricard, *Traité*, I, pp. 511–512; G. C. Vasseur, *Documents inédits pour servir à l'histoire maritime et commerciale de la Picardie, 1682–1792* (Abbeville, 1954), Introduction, p. 9: the silting in the harbour of St Valéry continued during the eighteenth century.

[49] J. J. Oddy, *European Commerce, shewing New and Secure Channels of Trade with the Continent of Europe* (2 vols., Philadelphia, 1807), I, p. 243.

[50] *SA, Hamburg, Senatus*, Cl. VIII, Nr. X (1775), fo. 54 ro., meeting on 27 February 1775; see also E. von Lehe and F. Böer, *1189–1939: die Geschichte von Hamburgs Hafen, Schiffahrt und Handel in 750 Jahren*, in *750 Jahre Hamburger Hafen* (Hamburg, 1939), p. 32.

[51] P. D. J. van Iterson, 'Havens', in G. Asaert et al., *Maritieme geschiedenis der Nederlanden*, III, p. 73.

the entrance to the IJ. If the prevailing south or south-westerly winds were strong, then the IJ could be dry before the city.[52] Sailing tugs were on hand to help ships over the *Pampus*. Take, for example, the plight of the ship *De vrouw Alida*.[53] She sailed from Málaga with a cargo of raisins, wine, and fruit on 4 October 1775. She managed to reach Texel on 17 November, and leave for Amsterdam, but with the ice ran aground and stuck fast on the *Pampus*, arriving at Amsterdam only at the end of December. Captains often unloaded part of the cargo to lighten the ships before negotiating the passage. And the delays encouraged passengers to tranship to smaller craft. When Gerrit Metzou arrived at Den Helder, returning after two years and seven months capture in Algiers, he disembarked into a *vaartuig* which came alongside to carry the passengers to Amsterdam.[54]

Yet, the snags of the Zuiderzee were not all on the debit side. They spelled prosperity for the repair-yards and ship-chandlers of Medemblik. There was the *Maxiliaanse Vriendschap*,[55] sailing from Málaga on 7 March 1774. She passed Den Helder on 15 November, and with a Texel pilot on board, ran into a storm in the Vlieter channel, encountered ice, and sprang a leak. And so the master put into Medemblik for repairs but was unable to sail again until 9 January 1775, to arrive at Amsterdam a week later.

As the years passed, access to the Zuiderzee became beset with difficulties and in consequence underwent changes. The deterioration of the shore at Texel proved to be the fortune of Den Helder. When Brandligt published his chart (1780, but no doubt drawn about 1776) there were two channels of access – at the north entrance to the *Nieuwe Gat Stroom* (18 feet deep); and the *Drempel*, a sandbank between the *Zuider Haaks* and *Helder* (marked 17 to 18 feet deep).[56] The latter, a preferred egress, was clearly an obstacle and the use of camels was a regular feature. Such was the case of the *Indien*, a *flute fregattée* built in Amsterdam for France, the finance being arranged through Horneca, Fizeaux en Compagnie on the Dam and Grand et Compagnie in Paris. Ready in 1778, the decision was finally taken in November to put off her

---

[52] H. Elking, *A view of the Greenland Trade and Whale Fishery, with the national and private advantages thereof* (London, 1722), p. 54; I. G. Biben, *Verhandelingen over de aanslibbing der haven van Amsterdam en de afdamming van Pampus* (Amsterdam, 1828), pp. 2, 79–80; A. Huet, *De Noordzee voor Amsterdam* (Amsterdam, 1862), p. 4; L. J. W. H. Goedkoop, *Lekko! . . . geschiedenis der sleepvaart* (Amsterdam, 1951), p. 16; S. Hart, 'De ondiepte Pampus', *Amstelodamum*, XLI (1954).

[53] *KVA*, XVIII, 672.

[54] H. Hardenberg, *Tussen zeerovers en Christenslaven* (Leiden, 1950).

[55] *KVA*, XVIII, 583.

[56] L. Brandligt, *Scylla and Charybdis* (Amsterdam, 1780), p. 194 and map; J. G. A. Veerman, 'De ontwikkeling van Den Helder als marinebasis', *West-Frieslands Oud en Nieuw*, XXX (1963), p. 95.

maiden voyage until March in view of the weather conditions. In the end, it was necessary to unload the armament to pass the sandbanks.[57] All such manoeuvres were expensive, but they were part of the cost of keeping the established market of Amsterdam in the competition of maritime trade.

Certainly, in the end, Den Helder gained. The report of 1772, the commission of enquiry of 1774, and the serious storm damage in 1775 and 1776 brought new initiatives. In two decades, f.2.5 millions worth of stone was dumped in the water to consolidate the channel and create the Nieuwediep.[58] But access to the Zuiderzee remained a hazard; and a profession. There were important series of orders concerning this pilotage by the States of Holland, for example, in 1772. The pilots of Texel and Vlieland formed a sworn guild. At Petten, in 1777, there were 66 pilots in the village and its neighbourhood. In Den Helder/Huisduinen there were 89.[59] Not always with successful results. The *Rebecka Gosvina*[60] sailed from Bordeaux on 2 February 1774 with a cargo of sugar, wine, coffee, and prunes valued at f.30,775. She left the port of Texel on 2 March but the pilot managed to strand and then refloat her, to arrive at Amsterdam two days later. Or *De Polly*,[61] sailing the same year on 15 July from New York bound for Amsterdam with a cargo of sarsaparilla, campeche wood, rice, and *reales de a ocho*: on 16 August a Texel pilot came aboard and at once stranded the ship, but she refloated and reached port two days later. Perhaps the tailpiece should be written by the fate of the famous *Lutine*. Originally a French frigate taken prize, she sailed from Yarmouth in 1799 with perhaps £1 million sterling in gold consigned to Hamburg. She was wrecked at the entrance to the Zuiderzee on the Westergronden. The no less famous bell hangs in the Underwriting Room of Lloyd's to ring out now bad, now good news, a symbol as much of the general perils of the sea as of the particular hazards in reaching Amsterdam.

What related to Amsterdam was shared by other ports in The Netherlands, particularly in the Delta with the scour from the Rhine,

---

57 *AAE, CP, Hollande*, 530, fo. 187 ro., letter, La Vauguyon to Vergennes, The Hague, 24 June 1777; 533, fos. 343 vo.–344 ro., same correspondents, 11 September 1778; 534, fo. 129 ro., letter, Sartine to La Vauguyon, Versailles, 2 November 1778. See also R. W. Unger, *Dutch shipbuilding before 1800*, p. 111.

58 F. J. A. Broeze and W. M. Jansen, 'Dan Helder en het Nieuwe Diep (1770–1822)', *Mededelingen van de Nederlandse Vereniging voor Zeegeschiedenis*, XXII (1971), 6 et seq.; I. G. Biben, *Verhandelingen over de aanslibbing der haven van Amsterdam en de afdamming van Pampus* (Amsterdam, 1828), pp. 15–16.

59 P. Dekker, 'De pilotage te Petten in de 18e. eeuw: het oude loodswezen bij de Hondsbosche', *West-Frieslands Oud en Nieuw*, XLII (1975), 36, 40–44. The Russian squadron arrived in the North Sea in August 1780 with expert Dutch pilots on board, *Simancas, Estado, Holanda*, Leg. 6373, letters, Llano to Floridablanca, The Hague, 1 and 10 August 1780.

60 *KVA*, XVIII, 495. 61 *KVA*, XVIII, 530.

Meuse, and Scheldt. The Goeree-Dordtsche Kil-Meuse access to Rotterdam became a serious problem. So much so that in 1770, a deputation of some fifty from Rotterdam went to the States of Holland with the submission that the Krabbegat had only twelve to thirteen feet of water and craft could hardly pass. The bigger ships had to unload some of their cargo at 's-Gravendeel. In spite of some remedy, another deputation made virtually the same approach to the States in 1778.[62]

Across Europe, along its coasts, ports contended with the combined problems of silt, debris and growth. The changing technology of shipping reclassified their facilities, and some admittedly were unable to cope. The bigger cargo-carriers often found themselves obliged to discharge in the estuary, with small craft making the final trip to reach the old-established city. For ports listed in the *prijscouranten* the evidence is mixed. Reval, for example, had a good port but a poor commercial performance – it was apparently the only outlet of Baltic Russia with an adverse balance of trade.[63] At Königsberg, the big ships used Pillau, from which lighters made their way to the city. For Stettin on the Oder the big ships anchored in the estuary at the out-port of Swinemünde. Stralsund, a fine city lavishly provided with five bridges, nevertheless offered harbour access only to ships drawing 10 to 11 feet of water, hardly enough for a small *fluit*; others found it safer to discharge their cargoes at the bar.[64] Rostock relied on the out-port of Warnemünde.[65] However, all was not on the debit side of the account. A new generation of ports came to the fore, with either new locations, or refurbished facilities. Some invested in important improvements, such as the canal from Ostend to Ghent: the famous *coupure*, dug by cohorts of labourers, was declared open to sea-going ships in December 1753. The first vessel, the *Concordia*, made the trip carrying a cargo of wine and chestnuts from Nantes, and received a spirited welcome from the jubilant citizens with fireworks and festivities.[66] By the eighteenth century, Hamburg, Altona, Glückstadt, Bremen, Emden, Lübeck, Memel, and Wismar, grew in activity as other older names slipped down the scale and slumbered in past achievements. So in southern France where Marseilles thrived in opposition to Sète. In Spain, the bay of Cádiz dominated Seville, hampered by the bar at Sanlúcar, a serious hazard during the dry months

---

[62] C. Wiskerke, *De Sheepvaartwegen van Rotterdam naar zee* (Rotterdam, 1948), pp. 24–26; for pilotage, see A. M. Overwater, 'Ruim 300 jaar Rotterdamse loodsdienst', *Rotterdams Jaarboekje*, VIII (1973).

[63] S. Ricard, *Traité*, I, p. 311.

[64] Ibid., I, p. 377.

[65] Ibid., I, p. 383; F. Barnewitz, *Geschichte des Havenorts Warnemünde* (Rostock, 1919), p. 87.

[66] J. Decavèle, R. de Herdt, N. Decorte, *Gent op de wateren en naar de zee* (Antwerp, 1976), p. 106.

of summer.[67] Appropriately, building of the great Customs House overlooking the bay began in 1764. In England, Liverpool succeeded against Chester; Deal and Dover against Sandwich; Hull against Boston. As for London, a capital city and focal port, it forged ahead, enjoying at the Customs House the tidal limit and virtually fresh water.[68] Every port had advantages and disadvantages but growth was selective and some prospered more than others.

Access to markets or to the great river estuaries which penetrated the continent was a prime consideration. The manoeuvre often carried a special supplement of costs and perils. Part of the outlay for protection was carried by governments avid to claim national or territorial waters. Pilotage and aids to navigation grew in favour: lighthouses appeared early at Scheveningen, Huisduinen, Vlieland, Terschelling, Urk, and in the Channel.[69] Authorities placed beacons, as for example in the estuary of the Meuse, on Schouwen, just as further north the same precautions appeared on the Elbe, at Skagen and Anholt in Denmark, at Örskär in Sweden, at North Shields and Caister in Britain. In the second half of the eighteenth century the improvements with the flat-wick and the patent lamp of Argand (1783) gave lighthouses added efficiency, but there were still fees and costs to be met.

A great deal of the navigation to the destinations around the coasts of Europe to the ports listed in the *prijscouranten* was 'in soundings' and often in sight of land. A large part of the southern section of the North Sea was at less than 50 metres deep, sometimes less than 25. The problems were summed up in the vignette on the title page of Klaas de Vries, *Schat-Kamer ofte Konst der Stierlieden* (eleven editions between 1702 and 1818) which featured the seaman with a lead and line. Jan Abrams Nanninga was clear enough on the dangers of neglecting the use of the deep-lead in heavy weather, all too often resulting in disaster at sea.[70] The hand-lead recovered from the VOC ship *Hollandia* wrecked off the Scillies in 1743 weighed twelve Amsterdam ponden (about 5.9 kg). The

---

[67] The problems of Seville, which appeared early, are explained in P. and H. Chaunu, *Séville et l'Atlantique* (8 vols., Paris, 1955–59), VIII (1), pp. 177–190.

[68] J. H. Bird, *The geography of the Port of London* (London, 1957), p. 61.

[69] J. P. Sigmond, 'Havens', in G. Asaert et al., *Maritieme geschiedenis der Nederlanden*, II, pp. 81–82; A. C. H. van Lieshout, 'Betonning, bebakening en verlichting', *Uit de Peperhuis*, I (1952), sections I and II, pp. 76–82; H. Toose, 'Over de scheepvaart op de vaderlandse kust en in de belangrijkste zeegaten', *Tijdschrift voor Geschiedenis, Landen Volkenkunde*, XVII (1902), pp. 39–44, note 1. At Cowes, on 4 November 1772, John Miller collected £13.10.0 from the captain of the *Haast U Langzaam* in dues for the upkeep of seven groups of lighthouses from the Forelands to the Scilly Isles, RAZ, MCC, 509, 4 November 1772.

[70] G. Schilder and W. F. J. Mörzer Bruyns, 'Navigatie', in G. Asaert et al., *Maritieme geschiedenis der Nederlanden*, III, p. 212; J. A. Nanninga, *De practicale Zeeman, of goede Raad aan Scheepsbevelhebbers* (Emden, 1815), pp. 49–51.

quartermaster's stores of the *Haast U Langzaam* (1764) listed one deep-lead of 24–26 ponden (about 12.8–11.8 kg), one of 16 ponden (7.9 kg), and two of 5 ponden (2.5 kg): this was the provision for a trading frigate.[71] It was *de rigueur* when sailing inshore. Not least when it is recalled that reliable maps of the coastal waters and estuaries of The Netherlands had to wait for the work of Beautemps-Beaupré and his remarkable chart of 1798–99.[72]

Few will doubt the substantial contribution made by The Netherlands to the technology of shipping and navigation. As for the cargo-carriers they were often of moderate tonnage, bulging and manoeuvrable, with small crew, few guns, and minimal draught. Such equipment was admirably suited to cope with poor port facilities, the vagaries of bad weather, and the hazards of ice. However, shallow draught was vintage technology for the oceans, especially when French and English design favoured deeper-draughted ships for the Atlantic.[73] Ship-design probably affected insurance premiums quoted in Amsterdam, although it is difficult to find accurate information on this. The Netherlands remained largely committed to Europe – the groups of destinations quoted in the *prijscouranten* were an indicator – and less to the Atlantic than some of her competitors. Overall, there remained the dichotomy of harbours and high seas. Once clear of port, it seems that risks attained to linearity, the continuity of distance, and conditions of equilibrium.

SOME PERILS OF THE SEA

For sailing ships, the perils of the sea were legion. And no survey of navigation would be complete without a few indications of this intricate scenario in the second half of the eighteenth century. There were, of course, collisions: the crowded channel of the Sound at the height of the season turned in numerous cases of actual physical contact. The *Jonkvrouw Catharina*,[74] for example, which left Arensburg for Amsterdam on 25 September 1774 with a cargo of rye: after colliding in the Sound and then battling against adverse winds, she returned to Sound and finally made her destination on 17 November. And the same year the *Vrouw Anna Catharina*,[75] sailing from Kronstadt for Barcelona this time with a

---

[71] G. Asaert et al., *Maritieme geschiedenis der Nederlanden*, II, p. 189, illustration; *RAZ*, *MCC*, 509 (1764), *Inventaris van het Schip, Stuurmans Goed* (1763).
[72] Schilder and Mörzer Bruyns, 'Navigatie', in G. Asaert et al., *Maritieme geschiedenis der Nederlanden*, III, p. 197.
[73] L. van Zwyndregt, *Verhandeling van den Hollandschen Scheepbouw raakende de Verschillende charters der oorlogschepen* (The Hague, 1759), pp. 4–6; Unger, *Dutch shipbuilding before 1800*, pp. 43–45, 59–60; R. Davis, *The rise of the Atlantic economies* (London, 1973), p. 193.
[74] *KVA*, XVIII, 572.   [75] *KVA*, XVIII, 691.

cargo of wheat: a collision in the Sound obliged her to put back to Copenhagen for repairs. She was able to sail again only on 19 April the following year having 'overwintered', and reached her destination on 11 June.

There was fire. We can look at the claim on *De 2 Gebroeders*[76] sailing from Gothenburg on 29 September 1775. Her cargo, valued at f.94,000, was composed almost entirely of tea for shippers who included Jean Fizeaux en Zoonen and Horneca, Fizeaux en Compagnie. After receiving storm damage, fire broke out on board; she arrived finally at Amsterdam on 4 November.

And a master hazarding his ship, although this delinquency emerged clearly only when he was a servant of a company. As in the case of the VOC ship *Leijmuijden* (Amsterdam Chamber)[77] sailing from the Texel on 29 December 1769 en route for Ceylon with a quarter of a million guilders in bullion and specie, mainly gold. She took the ground on 25 January 1770 and was wrecked near the island of Bonavista. Only a trifling 16 bars and 13 coins were salvaged. The master, Jan Hermanus Kinsbergen, and his navigator, Barend Wedelink, were dismissed their ship 'never again to be employed in any position in the service of the Company'.

As for stranding, a ship even under pilot was not always safe. Wreckers were waiting, apparently swarming the coasts, ready to carry out an impromptu salvage, little more than looting. The States of Holland set out the conditions of rescue in the *ordonnantie* of 12 January 1769: Article I stated that no-one could board a ship without permission from the master or crew; and Article 18 that no-one could prowl the beaches at night or during storms with axes, hammers, and saws.[78] Such legislation did not save *De Helena*[79] returning from Bordeaux on 15 November 1772 bound for Amsterdam with a cargo valued at f.27,100 (coffee for f.400 and barrels of red and white wine for f.26,700). In heavy weather in the Channel, she sprang a leak and ran ashore on the Sussex coast near Shoreham. The English locals were ready for the occasion and lost no time in going aboard to pilfer. The hull stripped of everything went for f.1,425 at a subsequent auction.

Then, since the commitment of the navigation of The Netherlands was to co-ordinate flows of trade between regions of the north and south of Europe, there remained the huge problem of ice. Sailings out of the optimal season in the Baltic, Scandinavian waters, or the White Sea were

---

[76] *KVA*, XVIII, 707.   [77] *ARA*, *KA*, 217, 1 October 1770.

[78] Van Iterson, 'Havens', in G. Asaert et al., *Maritieme geschiedenis der Nederlanden*, III, p. 68; H. Th. de Booy, *Geboorte en groei van het Nederlandsche reddingwezen* (Leiden, 1943), pp. 14 et seq.

[79] *KVA*, XVIII, 485.

at risk. The *Handelaar*[80] leaving St Petersburg late on 15 October 1773 ran into storms and returned to Kronstadt for repairs. Although ready on 5 December, she was caught in the freeze. She sailed the following year on 6 May and arrived in Amsterdam on 2 June. And *De twee Gezusters*[81] sailing from Gothenburg on 2 December 1767 with a cargo partly from the Swedish East India Company (1731) – tea, with some silk, porcelain and drugs; and partly from the hinterland – 986 bars of iron. Once out of port, normally classed as ice-free, she ran into ice and suffered heavy damage, surely a penalty for late-season navigation.

And no brief survey of damage received should pass without reference to bad or unusual weather around the coasts of Europe. The factor of event uncertainties included in the model would not be complete without some indication of such vagaries. Three particular instances arose in the 1770s: the unusual winds from July to November 1773 said to have kept some 500 vessels idling at their moorings for five months at Texel, holding up the flows of colonial goods and wines to the north, and of iron, hemp, and masts to the south, matters of concern to governments.[82] It was said at the time that the delays allowed ships from North America to steal the market. There is another example from St Petersburg: in the spring of 1777 the port suffered from persistent westerly winds meeting ice-floes coming down from Lake Ladoga. The River Neva rose more than three metres and the extensive floods were not experienced again until the nineteenth century. At that time, the evidence of winds at Deal shows an unusual 112 out of 365 daily reports were for winds from the south-west.

Then came the great gale of 13–15 November 1775, without equal in living memory, worse even, so it was said, than that of 1717. With destructive force, it lashed the dykes of the Hook of Holland, flooded warehouses in Rotterdam, put the Amsterdam–Harleem road under water, and at Delfshaven demolished the old sluice-gates built 180 years before. Many a building and warehouse lived to bear a tell-tale plaque on its walls marking the height of the flood waters. A few more inches, according to the English ambassador, would have delivered the *coup de grâce* and rendered his embassy redundant.[83] But the Dutch nation rose to the occasion: the storm turned them, the French ambassador reported, into 'a colony of beavers swarming to plug the holes'.[84] For shipping, it

---

[80] *KVA*, XVIII, 546.   [81] *KVA*, XV, 3583.

[82] *Simancas, Estado, Holanda*, Leg. 6365, letter, Herreria to Grimaldi, The Hague, 16 November 1773.

[83] *PRO, SP*, 84, 547, letter, Yorke to Eden, The Hague, 24 November 1775; P. Schotel, *Historische Overzicht van den hooge vloeden en overstroomingen tot het jaar 1868* (The Hague, 1922); C. A. A. de Graaf, 'Delfshavens sluizen in en na de stormvloeden van 1775 en 1776', *Rotterdams Jaarboekje*, 7e. R., X (1972), 263–264.

[84] *AAE, CP, Hollande*, 528, fo. 117 vo., letter, Desnoyers to Vergennes, The Hague, 28 November 1775.

nevertheless left a trail of disaster: some 145 ships, it was said, were wrecked on the coasts of Holland, left strewn with debris.[85] One of them, *De jonge Pieter*[86] sailed from Cádiz on 30 September 1775 with salt, hides, and a special cargo of 50,000 pieces of eight from Carlos III to his agent in Amsterdam for payment to Cornelia Anna van der Wall; and, it was rumoured, another 30 sacks for merchants in Amsterdam sent in contraband. She lost her masts and ran aground near Egmond. Claims later submitted to the Kamer van Assurantie proved the rumour to be correct for the cargo was salvaged. The hull and cargo were valued at f.76,075; this included 4,300 *mexicanen* for Raymond and Theodor de Smeth and five lots of specie for Hope and Company. Another ship, *De Vriendschap*,[87] sailing from Cádiz on 29 September met the storm off Dover and sprang a leak. She carried a large consignment of wool but shared the same consignment to Cornelia Anna van der Wall in the cargo value of f.252,925 and included tobacco (f.17,770) for Horneca, Fizeaux and Company; *mexicanen* for Muilman en Zoonen (f.2,525), specie for Hope and Company (f.13,150), and silver, gold, and *mexicanen* for Raymond and Theodor de Smeth (f.16,700). These were the commissioners' adjustments, reducing specie values to the conventional rates in the Wisselbank. Such salvage concealed high losses in insurance generally – in London 300 wrecks were listed – and in Amsterdam in particular. The fate of underwriting business was still pending when the New Year opened in 1776, another year of heavy floods and equinoxial gales.[88] The premiums quoted in the market showed little response; it was for the individual dealer to receive the full weight of disaster. And the Amsterdam market, as we have seen, relied heavily on the private underwriter.

SOME REMARKS ON THE LAW OF LARGE NUMBERS

The model proposed at the beginning of the chapter has a residual factor, and this should include the elasticity of 'large numbers'. The general evidence for the eighteenth century is that navigation had settled for customary routes. Jacques Heers has admirably shown the early

[85] *Simancas, Estado, Holanda*, Leg. 6367, letters, Herreria to Grimaldi, The Hague, 16 and 23 November, 7 December 1775; *AAE, CP, Hollande*, 528, fo. 105 vo., letter, Desnoyers to Vergennes, The Hague, 17 November 1775.
[86] *KVA*, XVIII, 732.
[87] *KVA*, XVIII, 726.
[88] *Simancas, Estado, Holanda*, Leg. 6367, letter, Herreria to Grimaldi, The Hague, 2 January 1776; *AAE, CP, Hollande*, 513, fo. 10 ro.-vo., letter, De Guines to Vergennes, London, 2 November 1775; ibid., 528, fo. 160 ro., letter, Desnoyers to Vergennes, The Hague, 2 January 1776.

evolution of this network of the trading world.[89] Types of ships, preferred cargoes, periodicities of trading, trade winds and tides, all these militated for a certain conventionality. The regularity of the system was enhanced by sailing in groups – fleets, flotillas or convoys, although these were disappearing in some measure in the last third of the eighteenth century – a part of old traditions as much of the Flanders galleys, as of the fleets shuttling to Asia around the Cape of Good Hope or to America across the Atlantic. In time of war or particular peril – from the pirates off the coast of North Africa or in the China Sea – merchantmen could sail under convoy with the guardian guns of a frigate or two. Unity enhanced security, but on some routes the numbers were small. And others escaped the patterns of conventional sailings. In consequence, not all the potential demand for protection came within the scope of insurance through the open market.

The great companies tended to look after their own affairs, either wholly or in part. Niels Steensgaard has shown how the VOC 'internalised' protection costs, and particularly after the fall of Hormuz (1622), a turning-point for the success of Dutch strategy in the Far East.[90] Indeed, the voyages to and from Asia were not easy to organise. Jacques Accarias de Sérionne commented on the special conditions for Far East navigation due to its 'innavigability', this another version of the definition later formulated by Robert-Joseph Pothier of a particularly important *fortune de mer*.[91] In any case, there were evident limitations to the liabilities acceptable to underwriters. The great East Indiamen were often three or four times the size of those normally plying the lanes of Europe; and the unit value was therefore high on a long haul. The ships could reach land in Europe in small groups and in unexpected places. The English East Indian fleet in 1777, for example, made land-fall off the coast of Ireland.[92] The VOC came to prefer the arrival around the north of Scotland and the Orkneys. Both institutionally and in navigation, the law of large numbers thus had uncertain application. In the early days of the Company and its adventure to the Far East, insurance was taken out. There is a surviving price-list for 1609 which quotes 25 percent both for

[89] J. Heers, 'Rivalité ou collaboration de la terre et de l'eau? Position générale des problèmes', in *Les grandes voies maritimes dans le monde, XVe.–XIXe. siècles* (Paris, 1965); J. F. Shepherd and G. M. Walton, *Shipping, maritime trade, and the economic development of colonial North America* (Cambridge, 1972), p. 156.

[90] N. Steensgaard, *The Asian Trade Revolution of the Seventeenth Century* (Chicago, 1973), p. 412.

[91] Accarias de Sérionne, *La Richesse de la Hollande*, I, p. 87; R.-J. Pothier, *Traité du contrat à la grosse et du contrat d'assurance* (Paris, 1777), pp. 433 et seq.; see also B.-M. Emerigon, *Traité des Assurances*, I, pp. 575 et seq.

[92] *AAE, CP, Hollande*, 537, fo. 350 ro., letter, Grand to Vergennes, Amsterdam, 13 September 1779.

outward and return.[93] The round trip therefore carried even chances – high insurance rates, it would seem, but not so high when the survival of ships is seen in the long-term. The balance sheet of the despatch and return of ships between Lisbon and the Portuguese factories in India for the period 1500–1635 shows that from 912 departures only 438 ships returned to the Tagus.[94] Some naturally remained in the Far East, but effective returns settled at 48 percent.

In those early days, even so, the policies were substantial. According to Pieter van Dam, the VOC in 1613 took out insurance for f.3.2 million, and a list survives for about half that amount: f.1,825,525, and under the conventions, the Amsterdam Chamber was liable for about half the operation.[95] As the Company established itself – and this meant conventional routes and timetables – the use of such insurance apparently diminished, and after 1700 the main evidence disappears.[96] Occasionally, the VOC took out insurance in special circumstances. On 12 September 1748, for instance, when the *Heeren Zeventien* were anxious to cover the transit of gold and diamonds;[97] and again in war, as with the decision on 18 April 1782, when the Company was following a policy of chartering ships.[98] However, it was adamant (2 May 1785) not to take out insurance on its own vessels.[99] And the Company was clear on the principle that protection was at fault when part of the assets was covered and part remained at risk. The meeting of 21 April 1786 in consequence agreed to limit the value of single consignments of specie – f.500,000 in a VOC ship and f.300,000 in one that was chartered.[100] In May 1793, there was even the possibility of insuring the VOC fleet on the London market.[101] In Rotterdam, the Maatschappij van Assurantie handled policies for the Far East, but these tended to be on a small scale and probably concerned with private shipments.[102] In Copenhagen, the Sø-Assurance Kompagni, cheek by jowl with the Asiatisk Kompagni, regularly quoted for the Far East. And the same apparently held good for the English East India Company.[103]

---

[93] N. W. Posthumus, *Inquiry into the history of prices in Holland* (2 vols., Leiden, 1946–64), I, esp. xviii–xxxix; see also J. Ijzerman and E. L. G. den Dooren de Jong, 'De oudst bekende Hollandsche zee-assurantiepolis (1592)', *EHJ*, XVI (1930).

[94] V. Magalhães-Godinho, *L'économie de l'empire portugais aux XVe. et XVIe. siècles* (Paris, 1969), pp. 672–673. The VOC returns in the eighteenth century were much higher.

[95] F. W. Stapel and E. L. G. den Dooren de Jong, 'De Zeeverzekering der Vereenigde Oostindische Compagnie', *Het Verzekeringsarchief*, IX (1928), 81.

[96] Ibid., p. 85.   [97] *ARA, KA*, 207, 12 September 1748.   [98] Ibid., 227, 18 April 1782.

[99] Ibid., 230, 2 May 1785.   [100] Ibid., 231, 21 April 1786.   [101] Ibid., 242, 13 May 1793.

[102] *GA, Rotterdam, Maatschappij van Assurantie*, 245–246, *Lopende risicos ter zee.*

[103] C. Thorsen, *Det Kongelig Oktroierede Sø-Assurance Kompagni, 1726–1926* (Copenhagen, 1926), pp. 114, 242; and for the English East India Company, see C. E. Fayle, 'Shipowning and marine insurance', in C. N. Parkinson (ed.), *The Trade Winds* (London, 1948), p. 40; A. H. John, 'The London Assurance Company and the marine insurance market of the eighteenth century', *Economica*, XXV (1958), 132, 138.

Another variation on the theme of large numbers was fishing and whaling. This was different in that the purpose of the voyage was to scour the seas for catches rather than to follow a sea-lane from departure to destination. For fishing off Newfoundland, insurance could be found in Amsterdam at 3½ percent. However, for whaling there were two sets of hazards. Firstly, there were the special perils of Arctic waters – the history of the Antarctic hardly goes back much before 1772[104] – pack-ice, or the ominous prospect of 'overwintering', or failing to make good in a limited season. The ships left The Netherlands for Greenland or the Davis Strait in late February or early March and hoped to return in August or September before the equinoxial gales.[105] Secondly, the great days since 1720 were beginning to fade: already in the 1770s there were signs of sharply declining incomes from the search for those monsters of blubber and bone. They supplied the oil factories in Zaanstreek, in De Rijp and Jisp. According to Accarias de Sérionne, a voyage was good when the crew managed a catch of two whales. The fleet of 69 ships returning from Greenland on 11 August 1775 in effect brought the proceeds from 94 whales.[106] In 1777, there were more disasters than usual, with ships lost in the pack-ice.[107] Indeed, the late eighteenth century saw fewer sailings – there were only 66 in 1785 when in 1750 there had been 185. It was the reverse for Britain: two and 152 ships respectively. And the falling product of Dutch whaling was apparent – about 3,000 barrels of oil when the Republic fell compared with 50,000 a century before.[108] It seems that the grounds were being fished out, especially east of Greenland. The whales caught were smaller, and the amount of oil produced was less.[109]

The resulting insurance cover for such whaling expeditions was necessarily complex. Alongside the early *rederijen*, especially in Amsterdam and Zaanstreek, operators often took shares in several vessels,

---

[104] C. M. A. Brunner, 'Nederlands blik op Antarctica', *Ons Zeewezen*, LII, 10 (1963), 14; Vergouwen, *De geschiedenis der Makelaardij*, pp. 74–75; *AAE, CP, Hollande*, 528, fo. 260 ro.–vo., letter, Desnoyers to Vergennes, The Hague, 26 March 1776; J. Le Moine de l'Espine, *Le Négoce d'Amsterdam* (Amsterdam, 1710), pp. 104–105.

[105] S. Ricard, *Traité*, I, pp. 63–64.

[106] *AAE, CP, Hollande*, 528, fo. 18 ro., letter [Desnoyers to Vergennes], The Hague, 8 September 1775; Accarias de Sérionne, *La Richesse de la Hollande*, II, p 41.

[107] C. de Jong, 'Walvisvaart', in G. Asaert et al., *Maritieme geschiedenis der Nederlanden*, III, p. 348; Finn Gad, *The History of Greenland*, Eng. trans. (4 vols., London, 1970–), II, p. 383; P. Dekker, 'De Heldense en Huisduiner bevelhebbers ter walvisvaart in de 18e. eeuw', *West-Frieslands Oud en Nieuw*, XLI (1974), pp. 143–151, and 'Ruilhandel met de Groenlanders', *ibid*., pp. 110–111.

[108] H. J. Koenen, *Voorlezingen over de geschiedenis van scheepsbouw en zeevaart* (Amsterdam, 1854), p. 164. For lists of English ships sent whaling in 1780–82, see *GA, Amsterdam*, N.20.01.64.

[109] de Jong, 'Walvisvaart', pp. 346 et seq.

sometimes with an insurance policy.[110] The contract for an association drawn up on 15 February 1746 by Pieter Leur, a notary in Zaandam, is a revealing example of the highly varied arrangements for a whaling expedition to Greenland.[111] There were 66 ships (assuming there were two named *Jonge Gerrit*). The act of association stipulated a minimum subscription of f.300 and a maximum of f.5,000 for any one ship, although it appears that the *Vrouw Catharina* had four subscriptions totalling f.5,400. The 42 subscribers put up a total of f.212,400. The lowest amount was f.300, the highest f.20,000, both by single subscribers. The average was f.5,057.14, and 64.4 percent of the total came in amounts of f.5,000 and below. A third of the ships – 22 out of the 66 – received multiple subscriptions. Insurance premiums for whaling did not feature in the *prijscouranten* of Amsterdam, but we know from the Sligtenhorst lists that underwriters were resident in Broek in Waterland, Zaandam, Oostzaan, De Rijp, Jisp and other towns in the Noorderkwartier.[112] Elsewhere, some protection was available. The Maatschappij van Assurantie in Rotterdam provided insurance but the volume was low – hardly 1 percent of the total risk capital.[113] The market of Hamburg offered quotations: the price-list of April 1736, for example, gave outward rates at 5 percent for whaling and sealing; but none for the return.[114] Up and coming markets, so it seemed, had fewer conventional constraints, but then they also had different capital structures.[115]

★

The problem remains whether we can assign weights to the two major components of the equation proposed: the factors of season and distance. The task, it will be at once appreciated, has more than a few difficulties, partly from the complexity of the commercial network, and partly from the shortcomings of the documentary evidence to assess it. One approach, among others, is to aggregate the arrivals of ships at Amsterdam. Samuel Ricard (1780) was prompt to report the totals of arrivals at the out-stations of Texel and Vlieland for 1778 and 1779, from the lists

---

[110] S. Ricard, *Traité*, I, pp. 63–64; de Jong, 'Walvisvaart', p. 309; J. R. Bruijn, 'Zeevarenden', ibid., III, p. 150; S. Lootsma, *Nederlandsche Walvischvaart* (Wormerveer, 1937), pp. 59–62.

[111] E. L. G. den Dooren de Jong, 'De Zeeverzekering der Nederlandse Walvischvangst, 1612–1803', *Het Verzekeringsarchief*, XVI (1935), 50–58.

[112] See above, pp. 27–29.

[113] *GA, Rotterdam, Maatschappij van Assurantie, 245–246, Lopende risicos ter zee.*

[114] *Preiscourant der Wahren in Partheijen*, Hamburg, 13 April 1736, reprinted in E. Achterberg, *Kleine Hamburger Bankgeschichte* (Hamburg, 1964), pp. 32–33.

[115] Faber, *De achttiende eeuw*, p. 130; A. Kluit, *Iets over den laatsten Engelschen oorlog met de Republiek, en over Nederlands koophandel, dezelfs bloei, verval en middelen van herstel* (Amsterdam, 1794), p. 282; W. Kresse, *Materialien zur Entwicklungsgeschichte der Hamburger Handelsflotte, 1765–1823* (Hamburg, 1966), p. 15; W. Oesau, *Schleswig-Holsteins Grönlandfahrt auf Walfischfang und Robbenschlag, vom 17.–19. Jahrhundert* (Glückstadt, 1937), Table XXIV.

posted in the Bourse. Frits Snapper has used the same material for different years for Holland in 1758–61, and for Texel and Vlieland in the period 1783–86; the totals average 2,600 for the former and 2,692 for the latter. W. F. H. Oldewelt has published a series for Texel in 1734–76 and for Texel and Vlieland for 1778–93.[116] All these lists in varying measure cover years of disturbance and war. For the purpose in hand, I have preferred the list for 1778 (2,582 ships), if only because this year was one stage further removed from active war (1780–84). However, the gathering hostilities in 1778 cut across the links with France and England, disrupted the trade to the Mediterranean, and soon, too, to northern Europe. The prelude to war clearly affected the returns from St Eustatius, the Golden Rock, a smugglers' paradise.[117] It was one link in the chain of munitions travelling to North America. Normally, according to Samuel Ricard, there were about 30 ships, but the figures for 1778 were 35; and in 1779 they leapt to 83. In addition, the registrations refer to return voyages and, in many cases no doubt, last ports of call. And finally, not all ships called at Amsterdam as 'staple'. Ricard was careful to note that the total number of ships engaged in entering the Baltic was about 1,500, with another 750–800 bound for Norway and Archangel: over half these left for destinations in Europe without calling at Amsterdam.[118] And even he was at a loss to put an exact figure on the registered tonnage of Amsterdam: at a guess he thought 500 ships had Amsterdam registry, but there was no certainty in the figure. Generally these data require caution.

Using the data, such as they are, I have estimated the totals of ship-kilometres[119] for the 22 groups of destinations listed for insurance in the *prijscouranten*. A second set of estimates – which further increase the margins of error – convert these into ton-kilometres. For the different regions in Europe, for example, I have used the figures proposed by Jake Knoppers.[120] What emerges from these calculations?

[116] S. Ricard, *Traité*, I, pp. 182–187; F. Snapper, 'De generale lijsten van de schepen die in de perioden 1758–1761 en 1783–86 in Holland zijn binnengelopen', *EHJ*, XLII (1979), Bijlage C; W. F. H. Oldewelt, 'De Scheepvaartstatistiek van Amsterdam in de 17e. en 18e. eeuw', *Jaarboek van het Genootschap Amstelodamum*, XLV (1953); see also H. Brugmans, *Geschiedenis van Amsterdam* (4 vols., Amsterdam, 1930–33), IV, pp. 260–261; and J. V. Th. Knoppers and F. Snapper, 'De Nederlandse scheepvaart op de Oostzee vanaf het eind van de 17e. eeuw tot het begin van de 19e. eeuw', *EHJ*, XLI (1978), esp. Table H.

[117] See above, pp. 100–102.   [118] S. Ricard, *Traité*, I, pp. 183–186.

[119] Commander F. C. van Oosten has most kindly offered information and advice on a number of points and difficult place-names at issue. For contemporary places, references can be made to B. C. Damsteegt, *Nieuwe spiegel der zeevaart. Nederlandse namen op zeekaarten uit de 16e. en 17e. eeuw* (Amsterdam, 1942); for the map key, see p. 205. I have used kilometres rather than nautical miles in order to provide comparison with land distances.

[120] J. V. Th. Knoppers, 'De vaart in Europa', in G. Asaert et al., *Maritieme geschiedenis der Nederlanden*, III, p. 227.

Table 9. *Sailings for Amsterdam (1778) in ton-kilometres: registrations at Texel and Vlieland in percentages*

	% of total
Greenland and Davis Strait	5.7
Baltic, Norway, Archangel	51.5
North Sea, Biscay, Spain, Portugal, Mediterranean	13.2
Netherlands West Indies	13.4
Other Atlantic (West Indies, North America, Africa)	1.1
Far East	15.1

The total ship-ton kilometres reaches a total of approximately 1,491 million. The regional percentages are as shown in Table 9 and Graph 9. The divisions are large enough to warrant comment. The volume of shipping to the north – just over half – underlines the importance to Dutch navigation both of consignments of bulky strategic commodities; and, at the same time, of the significance of seasonal factors.[121] If we limit these weights to the groups of destinations listed in the *prijscouranten*, three require special notice:

	% of total
Königsberg, Danzig, Pomerania, Lübeck	16.2
Trondheim, Bergen	11.6
Reval, Riga	9.3

That is, over a third of the total. At the same time Surinam/Berbice accounted for 11.9 percent of the total. This figure, however, includes the important sailings from St Eustatius (35.4 percent of the contribution of this region), on the assumption that during this period and particularly in 1778 a number of ships sailed from Surinam for The Netherlands via the island. Later, of course, St Eustatius was grouped with Curaçao; in 1788, the two were linked for insurance quoted on the Bourse.

Among the zones listed in Table 9, three do not appear in the insurance sections of the *prijscouranten*: firstly 'other' Atlantic, that is other West Indian destinations, North America and Africa; secondly, the Far East; and thirdly, Greenland/Davis Strait. The first represents a small share of the total; but the others take a fifth. The average tonnages assigned have perhaps been generous, but even allowing for a bold margin of error, they still represent categories of risk outside the conventional arrangements for insurance on the Amsterdam Bourse. They point to both the 'innavigability' of Asiatic trade, and to the special uncertainties in whaling. From its inception, the VOC required high inputs of capital, brought together through a joint-stock corporation. This in itself was a

[121] See above, pp. 120 et seq.

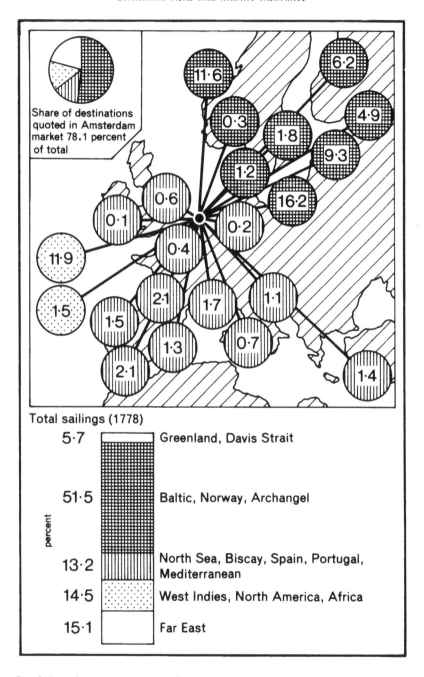

Graph 9. Sailings for Amsterdam (1778) in ton-kilometres: registrations at Texel and Vlieland in percentages

form of risk-shifting and 'internalised' protection. In turn, it required high profitability and plough-back investment. The heavy commitment in ship-ton kilometres may in some measure serve to explain the drive to establish successful monopolies in the 'wholly-owned subsidiaries' of Amboina, Banda, Ceylon; and on the other hand the ease which which it fell into borrowing and debt in the late eighteenth century in order to satisfy shareholders. As for whaling, the catches were less propitious from the 1770s and that too presented a dilemma for the risks encountered and the cover on offer.

The level of yield-ratios holds some of the answers to such questions. The mercantile activity of Amsterdam in effect presented a focal market and a matrix of trade. Each vector carried its own particular risks but also, it must be emphasised, its profits and concomitant probability distribution. The problem is similar to that tackled by E. Domar and R. A. Musgrave:[122] how to assess a system with a range of possible incomes with appropriate probabilities for risks? Those incomes represented a continuity on the high seas – once past, that is, the *risk-trap* of entering and leaving port.

★

The closing section of this chapter concentrates on the performance of a particular ship, the *Haast U Langzaam*, already mentioned above on several occasions. Like other vessels before and since, she had a career of her own, generating trade and providing a living for her crew. The hull had a life of perhaps 20 years in mind when built, and as a capital asset it depreciated over the years at sea. In commission for the first time in 1764, spick and span, and manned with a fresh complement, all was set fair for success. In time, however, the sea took its toll and each voyage completed, she came in for refit and overhaul. All this was taken in hand, ordered, paid and accounted for in the ship's ledgers, in more or less continuous expectation of profit. These accounts thus offer the advantage of continuity for a series of voyages – eight in all – during sixteen and a half years. However, it is evident at once that such a case-study belongs to an institution, a company operating at a level of risk-sharing far different from that of individual shippers. The example nevertheless sets out some of the problems involved.

THE EIGHT VOYAGES OF THE *HAAST U LANGZAAM*

The *Haast U Langzaam*, a frigate of some 200 tons, found service in the

---

[122] E. Domar and R. A. Musgrave, 'Proportional income taxation and risk-taking', *QJE*, LVIII (1944), and K. J. Arrow, 'Alternative approaches to the theory of choice in risk-taking situations', in *Essays in the Theory of Risk-Bearing* (Amsterdam, 1970; repr. 1974), esp. p. 25.

Commercie Compagnie of Middelburg (1721–1889).[123] This company engaged mainly in the nefarious triangular trade, under licence from the ailing West India Company and the *Geoctroijeerde Societeit van Surinam*:[124] of the 114 voyages effected from 1750 to 1807, 92 went to Africa to barter for slaves for subsequent sale in the West Indies.[125] The return cargoes consisted of colonial produce but often included some items brought over from Africa such as gold, ivory, malaguetta.[126] The *Haast U Langzaam* was no exception to this trading pattern.[127] She went to slave; and most of the details have survived in her accounts and papers.

In the sixteen and a half years from July 1764 when she first put to sea from Middelburg until 24 February 1781 when she was captured by privateers in the Demerara River, the *Haast U Langzaam* made eight voyages. Each followed a set routine: an outward voyage (giving a wide berth to the pirate lairs of the North African coast) to either Guinea or Angola. Several months sometimes followed while the careless task of bartering went on; then with the assembled slaves – the 'merchandise' as some insurance manuals called them[128] – on the middle passage to Surinam; and finally, the return to Middelburg. Her complement was about 40, including the captain and four officers. The latter received slave money and usually a bonus. Often the ships carried a surgeon to look after the slaves. And – almost without saying – she carried guns, sometimes 12-pounders, at other times 3-pounders, 2-pounders and one or two smaller pieces. The purpose here, however, is not so much to assess the detail of her trading, rather to set these against the costs and depreciation, in conjunction with the insurance arranged for both hull and cargo. The ship's ledgers giving most of the details were kept not on board but ashore in Middelburg. What do they show?

---

[123] W. S. Unger, *Het Archief der Middelburgsche Commercie Compagnie* (The Hague, 1951), pp. 4–6; see also A. Wisse, *De Commercie-Compagnie te Middelburg van het oprichting tot het jaar 1754* (Utrecht, 1933), pp. 13–18.

[124] J. Hudig, *De Scheepvaart op West-Afrika en West-Indië in de achttiende eeuw* (Amsterdam, 1926), p. 10.

[125] Unger, *Het Archief der Middelburgsche Commercie Compagnie*, pp. 4–6.

[126] Insurance for such items was included in the handwritten section of the Amsterdam policies, giving cover during the 'middle passage' from Africa to the West Indies, see above, p. 34.

[127] The documents used in this concluding section, unless otherwise indicated, refer to the collected papers in RAZ, MCC, 508, 509, 510.

[128] The consignment of slaves being defined as merchandise. In March 1776, a relevant case of revolt on board was decided by the Admiralty court, Marseilles: the slaves were considered to be merchandise; the insurance policy included navigation to the Guinea coast and so it was construed that the cargo should consist of slaves; and the revolt took place at sea, so that the underwriters were liable, R.-J. Pothier, *Traité du contrat à la grosse et du contrat d'assurances* (Paris, 1777), p. 37.

The company arranged for both hull and cargo insurance, and, if the documents give an accurate picture, hardly at breakneck speed but rather at a leisurely pace. In 1772, for example, the writing of policies began 14 days before sailing; on other occasions, the interval was even longer: 46 days in 1766, and an extraordinary 74 days in 1775. In the latter case, the policies were completed in both Middelburg and Amsterdam on 21–23 January 1775, but the ship finally left port on 5 April (see Table 10). There were, to be sure, delays in completing the commissioning; and the master had always to contend with capricious winds and tides. And then the year of 1775 was no doubt unusual: it closed with the great gale of 13–15 November.

The policies were for the voyage, rather than for a set period of time. One policy dealt with hull, fittings and 'consumables'; another with the cargo. The printed form in Middelburg had one large blank space for handwritten wording (see Plate 5). Hull insurance contained the particular clause for the African trade, to sail for the 'places in America' under franchise, then, if the commander considered it necessary, to other places; and finally to make for the home port of Middelburg. The policy excluded average below 3 percent. In Amsterdam there were separate forms for hull and cargo. Each policy had two blank spaces for handwritten wording. Hull insurance specified the voyage to Africa, Guinea, Angola and along the whole coast of Africa, then to 'places in America' and afterwards to Middelburg. The policies excluded 'leg-dagen, onkosten van overwintering' and average, damage and general average below 3 percent. In Rotterdam, similar to Amsterdam, there were separate forms for hull and for cargo. Each policy had one large blank space for handwritten wording. Hull insurance was valid for the voyage to Guinea and the coasts to north and south; then to Surinam, Berbice, Essequibo, Demerara, St Eustatius, St Thomas, St Croix, Curaçao and other 'free' places. The policy on this occasion – it was 1779 – ended in America, the actual date being fixed by the sale of the last slave.

The policies for the cargo were invariably for the first two sections of the voyage, to America. In the Middelburg policy for 21 June 1764, the value of each slave – that is slaves per capita rather than the notional slaves or *piezas de Indias* – was set at f.275. In the policy for 15 October 1766, the amount was increased to f.300 and this continued in subsequent policies. A 'cargo' of 400 slaves thus had a possible value for insurance of f.120,000. Some of the outward cargoes of merchandise direct from The Netherlands to the West Indies hovered around this level. In addition, there were deductibles. The Middelburg cargo policy for 24 November 1768 contained the handwritten endorsement after stating the premium at 6 percent of 'not liable for average under three percent, and on sugar, cotton or wool, slaves under ten percent, slaves dying on board shall not qualify for average'.[129]

In the Amsterdam cargo policy each slave had a valuation at f.300 current money. The policy also included insurance for gold and silver specie and bullion, some no doubt brought over from Africa; and excluded average under 3 percent. The Rotterdam policy of 19 July 1779 set a value of f.300 per slave and included a clause for revolt or riot and those lost overboard.

The cargo policies were valid until the sale of the slaves. This was done at a public auction or for cash, through the hands of Adriaan Gootenaar, the local agent. In any case, the captain's sailing orders usually gave instructions, after selling the slaves, to go to St Eustatius 'to see what cargo was going'. If prospects were unpromising, the poor slaves themselves were on occasion taken to St Eustatius, where a return cargo of colonial produce could be found without too much difficulty. On the second voyage (1766–68), the captain did not hesitate to sell 110 kegs of gunpowder on the island. For the 'third' leg of the voyage to St Eustatius, there were entries, for example in 1767, 1774, and 1776, of insurance at 3 percent. Two policies in 1778 were recorded for 31 July at 5 percent for the return voyage to Middelburg, on both hull and cargo (ivory tusks, sugar, coffee beans, cotton). In Amsterdam, the *prijscouranten* for 1778 give a July rate of 5 percent for the outward rate but no return. In that particular year, there were convoy rates for August. The problem of the return cargoes was clearly difficult since the trading profits were sometimes repatriated by bill of exchange.

The insurance on the hull covered the round trip (Middelburg – Africa – West Indies – Middelburg) and this usually lasted about 18 months. The premium was invariably 9 percent, that is roughly equivalent to an annual rate of 6. The fixed rate approximates to the premiums quoted on the Amsterdam Bourse and can no doubt be explained in part by the institutional nature of the Commercie Compagnie. However, the triangular trade was distinct from direct voyages to and from the West Indies, which proved to be a popular form of Netherlands trading in the late eighteenth century.

The insurance policies were written partly in Middelburg and partly in Amsterdam. In Middelburg, as we have seen above, groups of underwriters acted through local brokers (see Table 11). The names changed over the period, a reflection of the capital base of the local market too narrow to cover all the risks. In Amsterdam, the policies were completed

---

[129] *RAZ, MCC*, 509: the policy of 24 November 1768, for example, carried the endorsement, after the premium of 6 percent, 'not liable for average under three percent, and on sugar, cotton or wool, slaves under ten percent, slaves dying on board shall not qualify for average'.

Table 10. *Dates of sailing and policies*

Voyage	Date of sailing	Date of policy (A) Amsterdam, (M) Middelburg, (R) Rotterdam		Maximum interval in days
		Hull	Cargo	
1	(8 August 1764)	21 June 1764 (M) 26 June 1764 (A)	21 June 1764 (M)	–
2	30 November 1766	15 October 1766 (M) 24 October 1766 (A)	15 October 1766 (M)	46
3	5 January 1769	24 November 1768 (M) 3 December 1768 (A)	24 November 1768 (M) 3 December 1768 (A)	42
4	– 1770	10 October 1770 (A) 15–16 October 1770 (M)	10 October 1770 (A) 15–16 October 1770 (M)	–
5	22 October 1772	8 October 1772 (M) 16 October 1772 (A)	8 October 1772 (M) 16 October 1772 (A)	14
6	5 April 1775	21 January 1775 (A) 23 January 1775 (M)	21 January 1775 (A) 23 January 1775 (M)	74
7	6 June 1777	14 April 1777 (A) 17 April 1777 (M)	14 April 1777 (A) 3 May 1777 (A) 17 April 1777 (M)	53
	Return*	31 July 1778 (M)	31 July 1778 (M)	–
8	29 August 1779	15 July 1779 (M) 20 July 1779 (R)	15 July 1779 (M) 19 July 1779 (R)	45

* Surinam to Middelburg

Table 11. *Insurance brokers in Amsterdam, Rotterdam, and Middelburg*

Year	Amsterdam	Middelburg
1764	Frederik Dibbetz & Schorer	Adriaan van Dijk, Pieter de Swarte, Paulus Vink, Roeland Pagter
1766	Frederik Dibbetz & Schorer	Adriaan van Dijk, Paulus Vink, Roeland Pagter, C. Perduijn
1768	Frederik Dibbetz & Zoon	Adriaan van Dijk, Paulus Vink, Anth. Leliaart, Johannes Loenen
1770	Frederik Dibbetz & Zoon	Paulus Vink, Anth. Leliaart, Roeland Pagter, Willem de Bruijn
1772	Frederik Dibbetz & Zoon	Anthonij de Schoezetter, Daniel van den Berge Wz., Paulus Vink, Anth. Leliaart
1774 (?†) (return)	–	Anth. Leliaart
1775	Frederik Dibbetz & Zoon	Anthonij de Schoezetter, Daniel van den Berge Wz., Anth. Leliaart, Willem de Bruijn & Zoon
1776† (return)	–	Willem de Bruijn en Consoorte
1777	Frederik Dibbetz & Zoon	Adriaan van Dijk, Daniel van den Berge Wz., Anth. Leliaart, Johannes Sohier
1778† (return)	–	Adriaan van Dijk, Daniel van den Berge Wz., Anth. Leliaart, Johannes Sohier
1779	Jan Martveldt (Rotterdam)	Adriaan van Dijk, Anth. Leliaart, Willem de Bruijn & Zoon, Jan Cornelis van Hemert

★ Surinam to Middelburg
† Surinam to St Eustatius

155

through the firm of Frederik Dibbetz, at first in partnership with Schorer, and then with his own son.

The insurance on the hull and fittings was reasonably consistent and probably conformed to a pattern set by the Compagnie. When the *Haast U Langzaam* put to sea on her first voyage for the Compagnie – all new and shipshape – the hull and fittings had an estimated book value of f.33,000. This capital sum was depreciated after each voyage by f.3,000. For the beginning of the eighth voyage (1779–81), the book value came to f.12,000 (see Table 12). To this asset value were added the costs to put the ship into commission and make it ready for sea. As the ship grew older, these costs gradually rose – from f.15,120 in 1764 to f.22,260 in 1779. A small part of this could no doubt be attributed to inflation in the eighteenth century; and over 15 years as silver poured into Europe in general and The Netherlands in particular, this was not negligible. However, the greater part of the expenditure related in real terms to making good the deterioration of the hull and fittings. The total estimated value of the hull, fittings, and inventory declined from f.48,120 in 1764 to f.34,260 on the last voyage of 1779. As a rough average over the period, this decline approximated to f.69 per ton over 15 years. The combined insurance in Middelburg and Amsterdam declined by half from f.18,000 (for the first two voyages) to f.9,000 (for the seventh and eighth voyages: see Table 12, column 7). However, if these are related to the estimated total value of hull, fittings, and inventory, the percentage cover moved from 37.4 percent on the first voyage to 26.3 percent on the last. From the book value of the hull and fittings (see Table 12, column 1), there is again reasonable consistency: the sum insured was reduced from the fourth voyage by f.3,000 each year; in percentage terms this averaged 62.6 percent over the period. If anything, the percentage cover tended to rise from 54.4 percent for the first voyage to 75.0 percent for the last (see Graph 10). On this last voyage (1779–81), however, the supplementary insurance was raised not in Amsterdam but in Rotterdam; and the policy gave cover only as far as the West Indies. Taking the eight voyages as a whole, it appears that the Commercie Compagnie was prepared itself to carry the risk for between two-fifths and a quarter of the book value of the hull and fittings, and to this extent, 'internalised' part of the protection costs.[130]

The second section of the finance was for the cargo on the outward voyage. This consisted, firstly, of goods shipped to the Guinea coast or

---

[130] The accounts of the Commercie Compagnie were kept in *pond vlaams*, the Zeeland money of account (£1 vl. = f. 6). The hull and cargo policies used this system. However, some underwriters signed lines in guilders, converted into *pond vlaams*, and in 1777, the Assurantie Compagnie also did so. The conventional value of a slave appeared in the policies in guilders. Cf. above, p. 118.

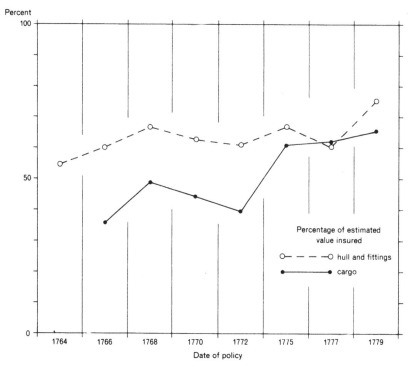

Graph 10. Insurance on the *Haast U Langzaam*: percentage of estimated value

Angola to barter for the slaves; and of products purchased on the coast; and then the transfer of the slaves, gold, ivory, malaguetta, to Surinam. The insurance policies usually combined these two stages 'tot Amerika'. The value of the cargo put on board in Middelburg fluctuated between f.50,250 (1766) and f.76,080 (1772) and averaged at f.61,365 (see Table 13). The first voyage carried insurance for f.18,000, this for Middelburg – the Amsterdam policy if it existed has disappeared. On the round trip, the first two expeditions both produced a net loss to the company. The next three voyages carried cargoes insured for f.30,000 each and for the last three voyages the insurance was raised to f.36,000. The high costs of the cargoes for the third, fourth and fifth voyages thus apparently did not show in an equivalent sum in the policies. The expenditure of f.76,080 for the fifth voyage was covered for only two-fifths of the total outlay. The increasing risks from hostilities may have accounted for the growing difficulty in obtaining insurance cover, especially after 1775. The premium was usually 6 percent; but for the last voyage (1779) the policies in both Middelburg and Rotterdam required 9 percent, for the trip as far as America. This change in the market appeared to develop

Table 12. *Hull insurance on the* Haast U Langzaam *(in guilders)*

		Costs of commissioning			
Voyage	Dates	Book value of hull and fittings	'Inventory'	Total of hull and 'inventory'	Supplementary costs of fitting out
Column		1	2	3	4
1	1764–66	33,000	15,120	48,120	10,098
2	1766–68	30,000	19,140	49,140	12,702
3	1769–70	27,000	20,430	47,430	10,308
4	1770–72	24,000	19,200	43,200	12,198
5	1772–74	21,000	19,800	40,800	10,344
6	1775–76	18,000	20,700	38,700	8,520
7	1777–78	15,000	20,640	35,640	10,200
8	1779–81	12,000	22,260	34,260	[10,800]

from the sixth voyage (1775–76) with the increased insurance on the cargo (60.9 percent; 65.4 percent for the eighth voyage in 1779). The growing tension and war may offer an explanation for this increase in insurance cover. It is also possible that there may have been munitions smuggled on board for sale in the West Indies. On the last voyage, the hull insurance reached 75 percent of the book value of hull and fittings (but 26.3 percent of the total book value of capital outlay).

In the final analysis, the effective risks must be measured against the long-term profitability of the venture. The account-books closed in Middelburg show that the first seven voyages of 1764–1778 produced an aggregate profit of f.89,718. This included losses on the first, second and fifth voyages amounting to f.21,708. The average profit was thus f.12,817 net per voyage.

The eighth voyage ended on 24 February 1781 in the Demerara River, that famous waterway lined with sugar plantations and tropical trees.[131] Privateers came aboard and took the ship as prize, but by then, the slaves had been sold and the proceeds laid out in a return cargo. Captain Kakom was made prisoner and taken to cool his heels on St Kitts. On 10 April he wrote plaintively to the Compagnie that he had been stripped of everything but the clothes he stood in. The only response in Middelburg appears to have been an endorsement on his letter that he had sold 304 of the original 373 slaves for f.147,000. Later in July, Cornelis de Jong on his travels in the Caribbean[132] found him languishing in the company of

[131] J. J. Reesse, *De suikerhandel van Amsterdam van het begin der 17de. eeuw tot 1813* (2 vols., The Hague, 1908–11), p. 217, and Plate XXIX for map of river and plantations.
[132] C. de Jong, *Reize naar de Caribische eilanden in der jaren 1780 en 1781* (Haarlem, 1807), pp. 261–262.

Table 12. *(contd.)*

Insurance cover			Premium for round voyage %	Percentage cover of total capital	Percentage cover of hull and fittings
Middelburg	Amsterdam (A) or Rotterdam (R)	Total			
5	6	7	8	9	10
3,000	15,000 (A)	18,000	9	37.4	54.5
12,000	6,000 (A)	18,000	9	36.6	60.0
6,300	11,700 (A)	18,000	9	38.0	66.7
9,000	6,000 (A)	15,000	9	34.7	62.5
6,000	6,750 (A)	12,750	9	31.3	60.7
4,800	7,200 (A)	12,000	9	31.0	66.7
3,600	5,400 (A)	9,000	6*	25.3	60.0
6,000	3,000 (R)	9,000	9*	26.3	75.0

* 'to America' only

26 other misfortunates – four from Berbice, 14 from Demerara and eight from Essequibo – all part of the flotsam of war which raised the perils of colonial navigation and furrowed the brows of underwriters and company officials in The Netherlands.

The year 1781 was, after all, a record year for underwriting losses, at least if we look at the risk books of the Maatschappij van Assurantie in Rotterdam. There, the claims settled averaged 65½ percent on a total of f.128,710 insured. Among these, the cargo insurance on the *Haast U Langzaam*, for which the Maatschappij had signed the *lead-line* for f.2,000. The policy was valid 'tot de Plaats daar de laatste Slaaf of Slavin zal worden verkogt'; the claim was settled in the annual accounts of 30 June 1781 at 98 percent and endorsed 'weete niet of is afgelopen'.[133] Was there a return cargo? Apparently, on 12 January part had been unloaded; and on 31 January, another consignment of sugar, cotton, and coffee purchased. The ledgers are silent on the outcome.

★

Although the tribulations of the *Haast U Langzaam* relate to the special case of a Company ship engaged in the triangular trade, her performance conformed to economic conditions in general, and marine risks in particular. As for insurance cover, the acid test came in the last voyage. A corporation such as the Maatschappij van Assurantie of Rotterdam could incur heavy losses and survive. However, for the private underwriters in Amsterdam, the outcome in war may have struck a more sombre, destructive note. If the Sligtenhorst lists are correct, the survival rate

[133] GA, *Rotterdam, Maatschappij van Assurantie*, 225, fo. 219, and 360, fo. 97; the account in the risk book, *Lopende risicos ter zee*, 246, fo. 123, appears incomplete.

Table 13. Cargo insurance on the Haast U Langzaam (in guilders)

| Voyage | Dates | Value of cargo outward | Insurance | | | | | Insurance as percentage of value of cargo | Net profits of round voyage (loss in brackets) |
			Middelburg	Amsterdam (A) or Rotterdam (R)	Total	Premium		
1	1764–66	62,790	18,000	?	?	6	?	(1,494)
2	1766–68	50,250	12,000	6,000 (A)	18,000	6	35.8	(12,228)
3	1769–70	61,320	18,000	12,000 (A)	30,000	6	48.9	36,240
4	1770–72	68,022	24,000	6,000 (A)	30,000	6	44.1	43,992
5	1772–74	76,080	24,000	6,000 (A)	30,000	6	39.4	(7,986)
6	1775–76	59,148	30,000	6,000 (A)	36,000	6	60.9	7,194
7	1777–78	58,200	7,200	28,800 (A)	36,000	6	61.9	24,000
8	1779–81	55,020	24,000	12,000 (R)	36,000	9	65.4	?

160

sagged substantially with the threat and onset of hostilities. On the one hand, the higher premiums in time of war initially may have attracted speculators. The second cargo policy in Amsterdam (May 1777) was signed by a mainly fresh group of underwriters (see Graph 2). On the other hand, while the cohort of 1771 sagged in 1779 but did not depart much from the loss rate of other 'pre-war' groups, the cohort of 1777 showed over a decade a progressive annual loss of 12 percent. As for the fresh group of underwriters who hastened to sign the second cargo policy in 1779 for the *Haast U Langzaam* (see Graph 2), half had been in the Sligtenhorst lists for less than a decade. Some such as Gerrit Versteegh en Zoon, Jan de Wit (De Rijp), Jurriaan Bartelse did not survive the war and the troubles of 1786–87. The case-study of the *Haast U Langzaam* has relevance in setting out the pressures of war on the market. For the last voyage the insurance was taken out not in Amsterdam, but in Rotterdam. Whether the dealers in Amsterdam refused to sign policies, or the premiums on offer were excessive – this is not clear. But their rivals – sometimes agents – in Rotterdam were willing to step in. The Maatschappij van Assurantie offered the *lead* to other underwriters, including lines written by insurers in Middelburg and Maassluis. In the final outcome, this opportunity may have been a sign-post to the future, an inflexion point for The Netherlands in general. Events seemed to be deciding the issues at stake: participation in Armed Neutrality was forestalled by war (December 1780), long in gestation, and marked by the irregular quotations of premiums after 1774–75. There was, of course, little to compare with the contemporary system operated by the War Risks Rating Committee of the Institute of London Insurers, setting war rates for designated zones. However, at the time, the shortcomings of the market made it necessary to look for alternative solutions. Some could investigate offers by less committed dealers. Others could apply to the companies. Others still hoped for the arm of State to provide convoy protection. The shield of government offered a reprieve and returned some premiums to 'equilibrium'. Yet, convoys were little match for organised violence. History with muted step was taking insurance away from an open market, for so long dominated by private underwriters.

CHAPTER 5

~~~~~~

Fluctuations in insurance rates

The market of Amsterdam – if we fall under the spell of the graphic accounts of Jean-Pierre Ricard and Jacques Accarias de Sérionne – was a place of pervasive vitality. Like all centres of trade and finance, the daily round of dealings enlivened an ever-alert concourse of merchants as much in the ebb and flow of business as their entry and exit from the market itself. Yet, however scintillating that activity may have been to observers at the time, the full study of insurance rates seems to carry the badge of all price history: the information available is partial. The problem has already been raised in Chapter 4. Apart from the changing attendance in the market, which varied from day to day and from season to season, the documents themselves are not all they should be. When archives are ready to disgorge prices, they seldom see fit to divulge data on the quantities of commodities or services bought and sold. And all too often promising series are pock-marked with missing lists.

The Amsterdam *prijscouranten*, indeed, are no exception to these shortcomings. The archive is not specifically for insurance, as in the case of the Maatschappij van Assurantie of Rotterdam; and records price not quantity. In the same style, the Kamer van Assurantie in Amsterdam was primarily concerned with settling claims, not predicting risks. In consequence, the periodicities and continuities which emerge from such records must be taken in the wider context of general economic activity, as endogenous to the market rather than as *conjoncture* in the sense used by scholars in France – for example, Fernand Braudel, Ernest Labrousse, René Baehrel – who prefer to define this great reality as exogenous. Since the data cover the years 1766–80, it is possible to isolate fluctuations of duration shorter than this span of fourteen years. The seasonal movement is thus a prime candidate for close study. Beyond this, it would be highly tendentious to look for longer phenomena, such as the Jugular cycle. Moreover, it straddles the intercycle of Ernest Labrousse who detected a *normal* reflux from 1771 and then an *abnormal* continuation of the downswing from 1778 to about 1787.[1] In the still longer term, I attempted in Chapter 2 to find a place for 1766–80 in a secular trend of the seventeenth and eighteenth century, but that too is an undertaking in the margin of precise information.

For all that, the quotations of insurance premiums share a bi-centennial record with commodity prices and finance in the *prijscouranten*.[2] The list begin with pepper, cloves, nutmegs, and cinnamon; then a large section for sugar, followed by the gamut of prime goods for Europe. The lists close with the means of payment and transfer: money, exchanges, and insurance. When a price appeared in the list, it may be inferred that the market was 'made'. For insurance, the same no doubt prevailed: a premium in print meant that dealers were active. When no rate appeared, it seems reasonable to assume (printing errors excluded) that no business was done or on offer. At least that is a possible explanation. Effective supply and demand came together in a printed figure, valid for Amsterdam and, as the *prijscouranten* travelled far afield, for other markets in Europe and beyond.

★

As the years passed, the lists of destinations quoted for insurance lengthened in keeping with the growth of the market and the extension of the range of its trade. The list of 1626, for example, gave ten groups. An important rearrangement came in 1683, that is after the treaty of Nijmegen (1678); and there was another in 1720, in the wake of the peace of Utrecht (1713) and at the time of the financial crises of John Law and the South Sea Bubble (1720). The form of the lists remained much the same during the rest of the century until the fall of the Republic, with two small but notable alterations: in 1737, the entry for *Surinam and Curaçao* divided into *Surinam en Berbiesjes* and *Curaçao*. In 1788 the latter was extended to *Curaçao en St Eustatius*.

This widening range of destinations can readily be seen from three sample lists – for 1626, 1686, and 1728 (see Table 14). In the first period (1626–86), the main alteration is the inclusion of Spain – now more or less in reconciliation after the treaties of Westphalia and Münster (1648) – both for ports in the Mediterranean: Barcelona, Alicante, and Málaga; and for those in the Atlantic: Cádiz, Sanlúcar, and Seville. The same went for Portugal (Lisbon, Setúbal, and Oporto) which in 1640 gained independence after a spell of sixty years under the Spanish crown. The

---

[1] C.-E. Labrousse, *La crise de l'économie française à la fin de l'Ancien Régime et au début de la Révolution* (Paris, 1944), pp. xxii et seq.

[2] N. Posthumus, *Inquiry into the history of prices in Holland* (2 vols., Leiden, 1946–64), I, pp. xxxvi–xxxix. In 1686, 550 commodities were listed; in 1777, 700; the comparable figure for Rotterdam in 1788 was 216: Joh. de Vries, *De economische achteruitgang der Republiek in de achttiende eeuw*, 2nd edn (Leiden, 1968), pp. 36–37.

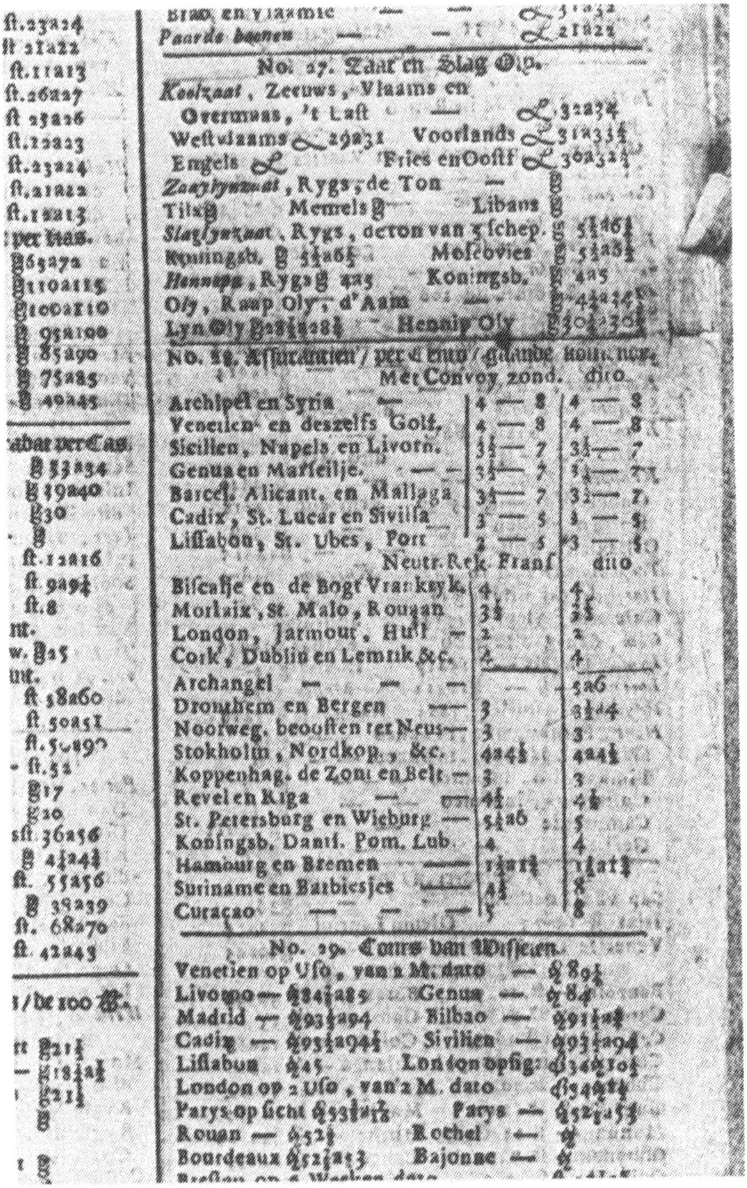
No. 27. Zaat en Slag Oly.
Koolzaat, Zeeuws, Vlaams en Gvermaas, 't Last
Westvlaams Voorlands
Engels Fries en Oostf
Zaadlynzaat, Rygs, de Ton
Tilsit Memels Libaus
Slaglynzaat, Rygs, de ton van 5 schep.
Koningsb. Moscovies
Hennep, Rygs Koningsb.
Oly, Raap Oly, d'Aam
Lyn Oly Hennip Oly

No. 28. Assurantien / per Cento / gaande Hollander

	Met Convoy	zond. dito
Archipel en Syria	4 — 8	4 — 8
Venetien en deszelfs Golf	4 — 8	4 — 8
Sicilien, Napels en Livorn.	3½ — 7	3½ — 7
Genua en Marseilje	3½ — 7	3½ — 7
Barcel. Alicant. en Mallaga	3½ — 7	3½ — 7
Cadix, St. Lucar en Sivilia	3 — 5	3 — 5
Lissabon, St. Ubes, Port	3 — 5	3 — 5
	Neutr. Rek. Fransf	dito
Biscasje en de Bogt Vrankryk	4	4
Morlaix, St. Malo, Rouaan	3½	3½
London, Jarmout, Hull	2	2
Cork, Dublin en Lemrik &c.	4	4
Archangel		5a6
Dronthem en Bergen	3	3½a4
Noorweg. beoosten ter Neus	3	3
Stokholm, Nordkop. &c.	4a4½	4a4½
Koppenhag. de Zont en Belt	3	3
Revel en Riga	4½	4½
St. Petersburg en Wiburg	5a6	5
Koningsb. Dantz. Pom. Lub.	4	4
Hamburg en Bremen	1½a1¾	1½a1¾
Suriname en Barbiesjes	4½	8
Curaçao	5	8

No. 29. Cours van Wisselen.
Venetien op Uso, van 2 M. dato
Livorno Genua
Madrid Bilbao
Cadix Sivilien
Lissabon London op sigt
London op 2 Uso, van 2 M. dato
Parys op sicht Parys
Rouan Rochel
Bourdeaux Bajonne

Plate 7. Insurance section of the Amsterdam *prijscourant* for 10 October 1757 (enlarged photograph by kind courtesy of A. J. Looijenga)

Table 14. *Destinations quoted for insurance in the* prijscouranten *for 1626, 1686, 1728*

1626	1686	1728
Smyrna, Constantinople, Alexandria	Smyrna, Constantinople	Archipelago, Syria
Venice, Candia	Venice, Zante, Bari, Apuleia	Venice, Gulf
Zante, Bari, Malta	Messina, Naples	Sicily, Naples
Toulon Leghorn, Genoa, Marseilles	Leghorn, Genoa	Leghorn, Genoa, Marseilles
Barbary	Marseilles, Barcelona, Alicante, Málaga	Barcelona, Alicante, Málaga
Bordeaux, La Rochelle, St Jean de Luz	Cádiz, Sanlúcar, Seville	Cádiz, Sanlúcar, Seville
St Malo, Nantes	Lisbon, Setúbal, Oporto	Lisbon, Setúbal, Oporto
Rouen, Calais, Dieppe	Nantes, La Rochelle, Bordeaux	Biscay, French Bay
Riga, Königsberg, Danzig, Stettin	St Valéry	Morlaix, St Malo, Rouen
Hamburg	St Malo	London, Yarmouth, Hull
	Rouen, Calais, Dieppe, Somme	Cork, Dublin, Limerick
	Archangel	Archangel
	Copenhagen, Sound	Trondheim, Bergen
	Stockholm, Reval, Riga	Norway east of Naze
	Königsberg, Danzig, Stettin, Lübeck	Copenhagen, Sound
	Hamburg, Bremen	Stockholm, Norrköping
	Curaçao	Reval, Riga
		St Petersburg, Viborg
		Königsberg, Danzig, Pomerania, Lübeck
		Hamburg, Bremen
		Surinam, Curaçao

revised lists also extended to sailings to the North with entries for Copenhagen, Stockholm, and Archangel – the latter not the least important since it gave access to Russian trade. The trade in north-western France gained recognition with the inclusion of the Somme and St Valéry. Bremen joined Hamburg. At the same time, the West Indies put in an appearance with the inclusion of Curaçao. However, the changes were not all gains: the dealings for Barbary disappear; so too for Alexandria.

Between 1686 and 1728, are further significant changes. The Somme and St Valéry disappear; as also Smyrna and Constantinople, replaced by a general listing for the Archipelago and a new entry for Syria. This may have been a response to the growing reorganisation faced by Netherlands trade in the eastern Mediterranean. In compensation, the connection opened to England (after the change in monarchy in 1688) with London, Hull, and Yarmouth; and to Ireland with Cork, Dublin, and Limerick. The listings for the northern trade lengthened. There were now eight sections, including Russia (St Petersburg and Viborg); and Norway after the independence of the Northern war (1700–21), both to the south and to the north (Bergen and Trondheim). In the West Indies, Surinam claimed a separate entry – it had been ceded in 1667; and the West-Indische Compagnie was reorganised (1674), sharing ownership in a tripartite arrangement with Amsterdam and Cornelis van Aerssen (1683).

In the insurance sections of the *prijscouranten* for 1766–80, twelve of the twenty-two sets of destinations are located in temperate Europe (Hamburg/Bremen and to the south); eight are in the Baltic and North; two in the West Indies. Nineteen of these twenty-two groups have been arranged into eight pages of graphs, as given below (Graphs 11–18). It is clear at once that the amplitude of the fluctuations has decided the arrangement – there are four series to a page in the cases of Hamburg/Bremen, France, and the British Isles; two for the Baltic, northern Europe, and the West Indies. The format of the page (that is, the ratio of the horizontal scale to the vertical) has meant, regrettably, that the graphs have not been printed horizontally. The eight pages are as follows:

1. *The Mediterranean:*
    (a) Archipelago and Syria
    (b) Venice and the Gulf
    (c) Genoa, Marseilles

2. *Spain, Portugal, and France*
    (a) Cádiz, Sanlúcar, Seville
    (b) Lisbon, Setúbal, Oporto
    (c) Biscay, French Bay

3. *The North Sea, Channel, and British Isles:*
    (a) London, Yarmouth, Hull
    (b) Morlaix, St Malo, Rouen
    (c) Hamburg, Bremen
    (d) Cork, Dublin, Limerick

4. *Denmark and southern Norway:*
   (a) Copenhagen, Sound, Belt
   (b) Norway, east of the Naze

5. *The south Baltic and Sweden:*
   (a) Stockholm, Norrköping
   (b) Königsberg, Danzig, Pomerania, Lübeck

6. *Norway and the North Cape:*
   (a) Trondheim, Bergen
   (b) Archangel

7. *The east Baltic:*
   (a) Reval, Riga
   (b) St Petersburg, Viborg

8. *The Dutch West Indies:*
   (a) Curaçao
   (b) Surinam, Berbice

Each graph gives four sets of premiums:
(a) outward
(b) return
(c) convoy outward
(d) convoy return

Taking each region in turn:

1. *The Mediterranean.* The shuttle trade to both the western Mediterranean and the Levant – the traditional *Straatvaart* – once so lucrative, and still dangerous,[3] was probably facing difficulties, even decline, in the closing years of the eighteenth century, not least from competition from France as well as from Denmark and Sweden during the winter months.[4] This became a matter for comment in the uncertain days after the bankruptcies of 1772–73. Moreover, although piracy may have generally diminished in the Levant in the eighteenth century, it continued to present dangers off North Africa, where Algerian marauders preyed on

---

[3] J. A. Faber, 'De achttiende eeuw', in J. H. van Stuijvenberg (ed.), *De Econo-misch-geschiedenis van Nederland*, 2nd edn (Groningen, 1979), p. 139; for the early network of trade-routes see A. Christensen, *Dutch trade to the Baltic about 1600* (The Hague, 1941), pp. 17–19. See also J. Accarias de Sérionne, *La Richesse de la Hollande* (2 vols., Amsterdam, 1779), I, pp. 45–46; J.-P. Ricard, *Le Négoce d'Amsterdam*, p. 274; and Vergouwen, *De geschiedenis der Makelaardij*, p. 73. In the commentaries which follow the first destination in a group is frequently used to designate premiums quoted for the region. For example, 'Königsberg' indicates this port as well as 'Danzig, Pomerania, and Lübeck' which are listed together in the *prijscouranten*.

[4] J. V. Th. Knoppers, 'De vaart in Europa', in G. Asaert et al., *Maritieme geschiedenis der Nederlanden*, III, p. 250.

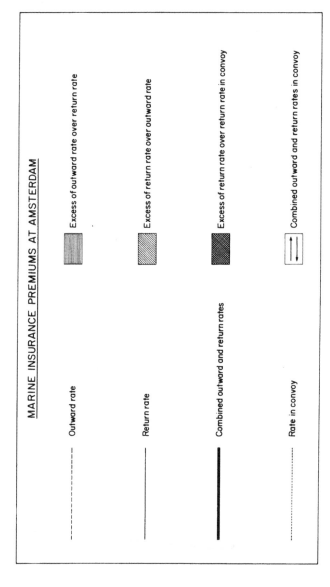

Graphs 11–18: Key

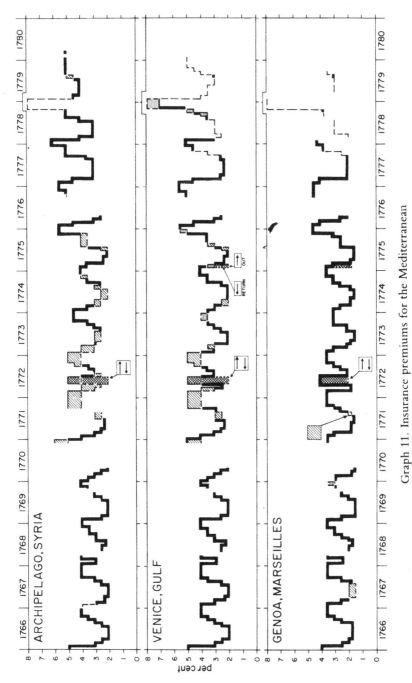

Graph 11. Insurance premiums for the Mediterranean

169

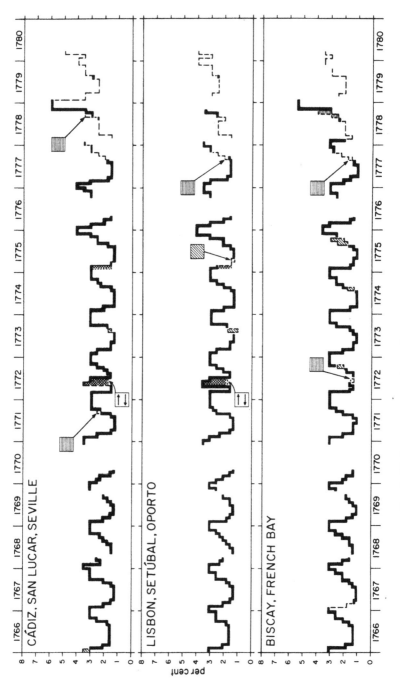

Graph 12. Insurance premiums for Spain, Portugal, and France

170

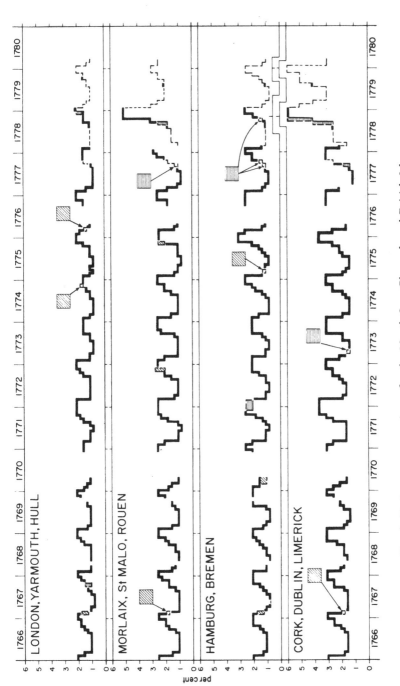

Graph 13. Insurance premiums for the North Sea, Channel, and British Isles

171

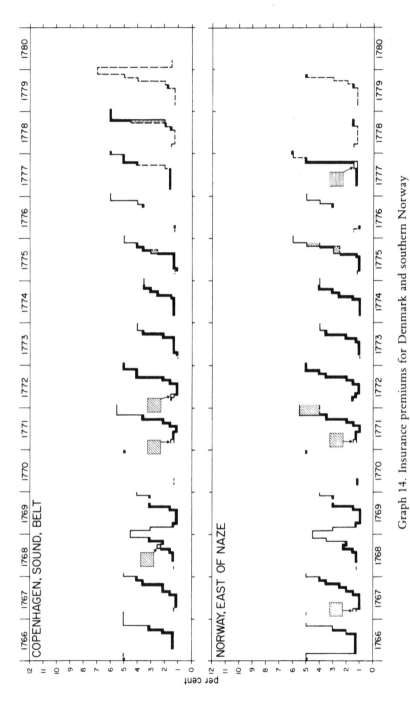

Graph 14. Insurance premiums for Denmark and southern Norway

172

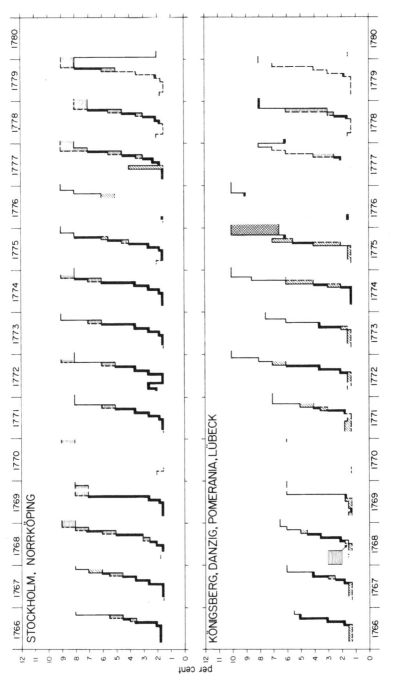

Graph 15. Insurance premiums for the south Baltic and Sweden

173

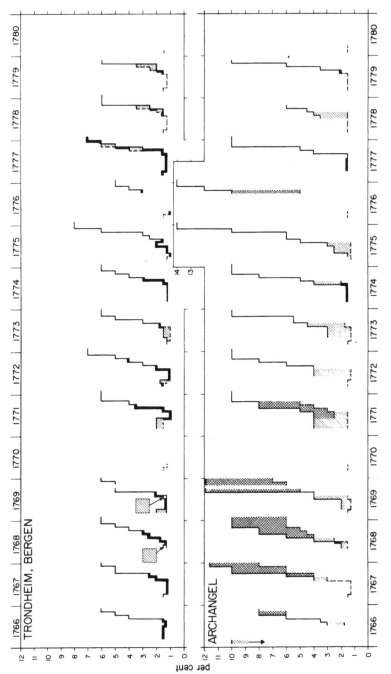

Graph 16. Insurance premiums for Norway and the North Cape

174

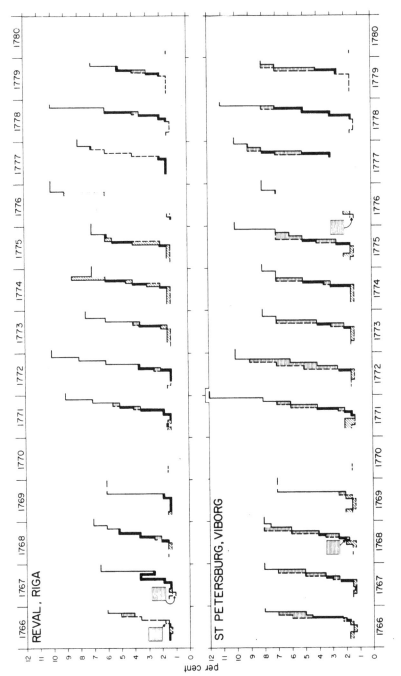

Graph 17. Insurance premiums for the east Baltic

175

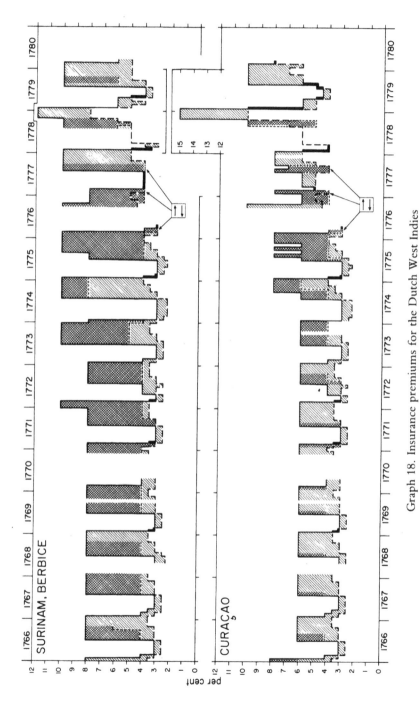

Graph 18. Insurance premiums for the Dutch West Indies

ships and cargoes, enslaving crews. The States General was constantly alert to the problem and took special care to regulate the size of ships and their armament, and to provide for convoy protection.[5]

The longest voyages quoted for insurance were to the Levant, firstly to the Archipelago and Syria; and secondly to Venice and the Gulf. In terms of distance there was not much difference between them. Netherlands ships brought cargoes of grain, textiles, colonial wares; and collected returns either produced locally or delivered overland by the immemorial caravans to the key markets of Tripoli, Iskenderun/Aleppo, and Smyrna with its majestic harbour. The last, specially important, exported wax, gall-nuts, leather, drugs, musk, amber, carpets, and above all the cotton grown in the valleys of the hinterland,[6] which joined in the early expansion of textile industries in the eighteenth century. The ships returned with bulging sails and equally bulging cargoes. Thus the *Azia*[7] departed from Smyrna on 9 February 1767 – a winter sailing – with a cargo of raw cotton, some carpets and a case of opium, valued with the ship at f.137,675; and the *Cornelia Petronella*[8] sailing a month later on 14 March with a mixed cargo but principally raw cotton and cotton goods, some other cloth and carpets valued at f.123,975. At other times, there were cargoes from other ports, The *Vrouw Catharina*[9] sailed from Gallipoli on 6 October 1767, for example, with 290 casks of oil.

There was, of course, the matter of the balance of outward cargoes. Even with colonial products (spices, sugar, coffee, indigo, cochineal) there was sometimes a large deficit, which demanded settlement in cash. Such transfers were complex, since they often relied on a chain of credit and forward buying. As for bullion and specie, the settlements could require two commercial links, first with cargoes for the Italian market to take on specie in the great *porto franco* of Leghorn; and then on to the Levant.[10] The Dutch had been quick to appreciate the highly specialised nature of this trade, which relied on the acumen of centuries. Until the early eighteenth century (1713), the mints in The Netherlands produced a special silver trade-coin for this market, the famous *leeuwendaalder* (weighing 27.68 gr. and at a fineness of 0.75).[11] It was the least valuable of the great trade-coins of The Netherlands, but they circulated widely in

---

[5] See above, Chapter 3, p. 105. For the history of the *Admiraliteiten* in the eighteenth century, see J. R. Bruijn, *De admiraliteit van Amsterdam in de rustige tijd* (Amsterdam, 1970).

[6] A. Justice, *A General Treatise of Monies and Exchanges* (London, 1707), p. 107.

[7] *KVA*, XV, 3493.   [8] *KVA*, XV, 3507.   [9] *KVA*, XV, 3558.

[10] A. Justice, *A General Discourse of Commerce*, 1707, bound with *A General Treatise of Monies and Exchanges*, p. 198; Accarias de Sérionne, *La Richesse de la Hollande*, I, p. 48; S. Ricard, *Traité*, I, p. 604.

[11] H. Enno van Gelder, *De Nederlandse munten*, 6th edn (Utrecht, 1965), pp. 221, 263. The mints coined the *leeuwendaalder* in Holland in 1575 and in The Netherlands generally from 1606.

the Levant, and established themselves as a standard currency under the name of *esedîgurus.*[12]

For these destinations, the 'insurance year' followed the general movement of premiums in the market: the rates dropped in February, and markedly in March. This favourable season lasted until September, when an upward movement began to set in. This strong seasonal movement appears to have been within the limits of 2 and 4 percent. In 1770, a new decade opened with sharp shocks from the Russo-Turkish War (1768–74). Off the coast at Cesme, near Chios and some 70 kilometres from Smyrna, Count Orlov's fleet with aid from Britain defeated the Turks supported by France (6 July 1770). The tensions were widespread. There had been few of the dealers in London in the autumn of 1769 willing to write policies for Constantinople, even at 50 percent.[13] In Amsterdam, convoy rates were quoted in May–June 1772 (these brought premiums back to a more normal 2 percent). The protracted fighting eventually led to the opening of the Bosphorus to the Russian merchant marine, confirmed in the treaty of Kuchuk Kainarji (Cainargeana Mica) of 21 July 1774. It opened a further period in the development of the Black Sea, marked by the later establishment of Odessa (1794). The situation, however, deteriorated after 1775 and markedly in the winter of 1777–78. Premiums moved into a band of 3 to 6 percent, and went still higher when war broke out between France and Britain (1778). The outward rate was at 8 percent from November 1778 to January 1779; and no return was quoted. Throughout this period of tension, the gap between outward and return rates tended to widen, especially in December 1770, July 1771 to July 1772, October 1772 to July 1773, March–August 1774, November 1744, July–November 1775, and August 1779.

Venice remained a focal entrepôt for southern Europe, in spite of the inference of economic decline in Italy and a reputation of dozing in the blandishments of former wealth. In 1751, Venice received a fifth of the total value imported from The Netherlands, France and Britain. The soaring trade of the latter two carried the day: between 1756 and 1789, their tonnage trebled.[14] The return cargoes from Italy were silk, alum, nuts, oil, and fruits. We find the ship *De jonge Jacob*[15] sailing from Venice and Zante on 18 August 1774 with a lading of rice, garnets, coral, wine, currants, and various drugs – not an easy trip as it turned out, for on

---

[12] The name *gurus* covered a wide range of silver coins current in the Ottoman empire.
[13] *Simancas, Estado,* Leg. 6973 (10, ⁰/1703), letters, Mazerano to Grimaldi, London, 12 and 15 September 1769.
[14] A clear statement of the case for decline in C. R. Boxer, *The Dutch economic decline* in C. Cipolla (ed.), *The Economic Decline of Empires* (London, 1970); G. Luzzatto, *Introduzione* in L. Candida, *Il porto di Venezia* (Naples, 1950), p. 22.
[15] *KVA,* XVIII, 634.

arrival at Texel, she was put in quarantine. On the west side of Italy, the trade was no less important. The western basin of the Mediterranean showed signs of sharp competition from the different ports. Genoa gathered in the trade of Liguria and hinterland; southern France and Catalonia gave clear evidence of industrial progress. All these ports struggled over the years to establish *porto franco* status. In Leghorn, it had been from the start (1593); in Genoa (from 1595, with the 'porto franco, libero, generale, e generalissimo' finalised in 1623); in Venice (in limited form, 1661), more recently in Ancona (1732) and Nice (1749).[16]

Amsterdam drew southern fruits and other mixed cargoes. Thus the *St Catharina*[17] sailing from Leghorn on 13 April 1761 carried candied orange peel, fruits, oil, marble, and silk textiles. The ship *De Juffr. Johanna Geertruyda*[18] left Leghorn via St Remo on 11 January 1773 – a winter trip – for St Petersburg with lemons, fruits, raisins, currants, sal-ammoniac, oil, and cheese. After storms and quarantine she finally reached her destination on 13 August, still in the summer season for the northern trade. In return, The Netherlands ships above all filled the granaries of the Italian peninsula. *De Eendragt*[19] left Amsterdam for Leghorn on 5 November 1766 with a single cargo of some 51 lasts of wheat; and two days later the *Maria Theresia*[20] bound for Civitavecchia, similarly laden only with wheat, 150 lasts. Both were, in effect, winter sailings. The same type of trade held for Marseilles: ships such as the *Ernst Gustaff*[21] which sailed 2 January 1767 brought wheat; the *Flecee*[22] sailed 22 December 1766 taking away soap and fruits.

The growth in trade from Germany created a further line of development, consignments from the fairs of Leipzig and Breslau, deliveries of manufactures from Silesia in linens and other textiles, from Bavaria and southern Germany. By the end of the eighteenth century, Saxony had managed to deal extensively with the Spanish peninsula: this destination was said to claim about a tenth of her exports in 1771 and the share was rising.[23] Nevertheless, The Netherlands traders did not let such competition pass without reply; important trade treaties were signed with the Kingdom of the Two Sicilies in 1753; and Venice in 1771.

---

[16] Luzzatto, *Introduzione*, pp. 22, 25–27, and 'Per la costruzioni navali a Venezia nei secoli XV e XVI', *Scritti storici in onore de Camillo Manfroni* (Padua, 1925). For Genoa, the collection of laws in *AC*, Genoa, *Brignole Sale, Decreti*, 108.A.9, p. 81 vo., 108.E.5; A. Brusa, *Il Portofranco della Repubblica di Genova* (Genoa, 1948), p. 141.

[17] *KVA*, XV, 3545. [18] *KVA*, XVIII, 526. [19] *KVA*, XV, 3489.

[20] *KVA*, XV, 3500. [21] *KVA*, XV, 3487. [22] *KVA*, XV, 3504.

[23] The ramifications of this trade are shown in the extensive bibliography given by J. G. van Bel, *De linnenhandel van Amsterdam in de achttiende eeuw* (Amsterdam, 1940); see also E. Hasse, *Geschichte der Leipziger Messe* (Leipzig, 1885); E. Schmitz, *Leinengewerbe und Leinenhandel in Nordwestdeutschland, 1650–1850* (Cologne, 1967); A. Zimmerman, *Blüthe und Verfall des Leinesgewerbes in Schlesien* (Breslau, 1885); W. Zorn, *Handels- und Industriegeschichte Bayerische-Schwabens, 1648–1870* (Augsburg, 1961).

The insurance premiums for Venice and the Adriatic followed closely those for the Levant. Between 1766 and 1769, they normally ranged between 2 and 4 percent. Special risks required convoy rates in May–June 1772 at a differential of 2 percent. In February 1775, this moved to 2 percent outward and 2½ for the return, and conditions tended further to deteriorate. In December 1775, the rates were at 5½ percent; from November 1778 to January 1779 at 8 percent outward and 7½ percent return. These reflected the rising risks of war. In July 1779, the attack began on Gibraltar, the gateway to the Mediterranean.

For Genoa and Marseilles, there was a similar performance, but with two important differences. Firstly, the disturbances in 1770–72 had less effect, so that these can be seen related particularly to disturbances in the eastern Mediterranean. And secondly, the war between Britain and France (March 1778) had more serious results. This interrupted quotations: only outward rates were given and even these disappeared after October 1779.

Such disturbances generally affected the summer outward rates: those for the Archipelago and Syria showed an increase to 2 percent; for Venice 7 percent; for Genoa–Marseilles 1½ percent. The return rates, usually the same as those outward, began under the stress of war to show a differential, with the return rate higher than the outward, as follows:

	difference in percentage points
December 1770	1
July–August 1771	½
October 1771 to June 1772	1
November 1772 to February 1773	1

The situation deteriorated still further after 1777–78. No return rates were quoted at all from November 1778 to January 1779 as war in the different theatres, in North America, in western Europe, and in the area of the Black Sea began to sap the façade of stability adopted by the *ancien régime*.

2. *Atlantic Spain, Portugal, and south-west France.* This group includes a wide variety of ports and regional economies, but together belonged to the 'southern group' with which The Netherlands had important trading connections. The second half of the eighteenth century passed, generally, under the sign of a rising flow of silver from America. Cádiz turned once more into the great terminal of the Atlantic trade to Central and South America,[24] open to view when along with others the Dutch traded in the *vloot uit Spanien*, or secretly when bullion and specie were smuggled to

[24] A. García-Baquero Gonzalez, *Cádiz y el Atlantico* (2 vols., Seville, 1976).

Amsterdam and other money markets of Europe.[25] The *Casa de la Contratación* moved there officially in 1718. A new and splendid Customs House was built in 1764–73. Goods poured in from the colonies – dyestuffs and leather; produce from the plantations. However, although in the long term the trend was favourable, the short-term performance of Cádiz in the 1770s was not clear. If we are to believe Samuel Ricard, 1,215 ships of foreign nations left the Bay in 1775, but only 793 in the war-year of 1779, a falling trend which reduced the movement by 34.7 percent in six years.[26]

Southern Spain sent northwards fruits, nuts, salt, wine, and brandy from Andalusia; and produce from the colonies. Thus, the *Pieter en Wilhelmina*[27] sailed from Cádiz on 15 September 1767 with salt, cochineal, and pieces of eight to the tune of f.172,775. And the *Vrouw Geertruyda*[28] sailed on 24 November 1774 with wool, indigo, cochineal, hides, wine and specie, in which Hope and Company had their share. Amsterdam joined in the general exports of the nations to Cádiz, manufacturers from the industries of Europe, spices and colonial products from Asia, thus linking the continents in trade. The *Abraham en Jacob* [29] sailed from Amsterdam on 8 September 1767 with a mixed cargo valued at f.122,200 and including spices from the Far East; *De Stad Cadix*,[30] with cinnamon to stir the hot chocolate of Central America, and other mixed cargo; and *De Hoop van Vlissingen*,[31] sailing from Ostend on 17 June 1767 but insured in Amsterdam, with a cargo almost all of linen textiles valued with the ship at f.258,100. In the entrepôt trade to America, Andalusia retained its place with the produce of the farms; but the northern merchants scooped the trade with commodities of high industrial input: manufactured metals; textiles (the linens of the North suitable for hot climates).[32] In the shipment of spices, particularly pepper and cinnamon, the rôle of The Netherlands was clear.

Portugal too had a significant part. The Brazil trade continued to pour in cargoes after the end of the official fleets in 1765.[33] Lisbon, like Cádiz, was a commercial hub. In the second half of the eighteenth century, the port movement doubled, with British ships predominating; but The Netherlands still recognised the value of this trade:[34] sugar, gold (though

[25] J. G. van Dillen 'Amsterdam als wereldmarkt der edele metalen in de 17e. en 18e. eeuw', *De Economist*, LXXII (1923); M. Morineau, 'Des métaux précieux américains au XVIIe. et au XVIIIe. siècles', *Bulletin de la Société d'Histoire Moderne*, LXXVI (1977).

[26] S. Ricard, *Traité*, I, p. 581.   [27] *KVA*, XV, 3525.   [28] *KVA*, XVIII, 615.

[29] *KVA*, XV, 3532.   [30] *KVA*, XV, 3514.   [31] *KVA*, XV, 3677.

[32] Faber, 'De achttiende eeuw', p. 139.

[33] For a discussion of the development of trade and related reforms, see J. Muñoz Pérez, 'Los proyectos sobre España e Indias en el siglo XVIII', *Revista Estudios Políticos*, LIV (1955), and 'La publicación del reglamento de comercio libre de Indias de 1778', *Anuario de Estudios Americanos*, IV (1947).

[34] J. Bacellar Bebiano, *O porto de Lisboa* (Lisbon, 1960), pp. 43–45, 107.

now on the decline),[35] diamonds, and dyewoods; and other commodities from the Atlantic islands, such as the rich Madeira wines. And from Portugal itself the highly-prized salt from the pans of Setúbal.[36] This was not an easy trade, for access to the latter had.to find a way through shelving sandbanks.[37] However, there was no shortage of ships to brave the venture. *De jonge Neletta*[38] which arrived there in ballast sailed on 19 February 1774 (winter sailing) direct for Viborg with a single cargo of salt. Or *Le Roy Stanislaus August*[39] which left Setúbal on 14 April 1775 with salt for the Baltic. As for Oporto, there were the wines of the Douro valley, surviving Pombal's policies of destroying vineyards. The *Vrouw Adriana*[40] sailed on 25 October 1775 for Hamburg with sugar, citrous fruits, orange peel and wine – Oporto was probably her last port of call. Amsterdam sent mixed cargoes: the *Vrouw Johanna*[41] which left for Lisbon on 30 September 1764; or the *Porto Galey*[42] for Oporto on 22 November 1776.

The Biscay ports included both those in Spain and in France. Santander and above all Bilbao, through the agency of merchants in Burgos, provided outlets for north Castile, deprived by history, so it was sometimes claimed, of the natural outlet of the Douro valley.[43] The Spanish ship *Nuestra Señora de Begona*,[44] insured in Amsterdam, left Bilbao on 13 December 1767 (winter sailing) with a single cargo of tobacco; the *Anthony*[45] from Santander on 1 January 1776 (winter sailing) with a single cargo of wool, in which Hope and Company had about an eighth share. Other ships carried iron.

As for the French ports, they offered a special attraction to merchants from The Netherlands: Lorient, Bayonne, the naval dockyards of Brest and Rochefort, (the latter established in 1661–64)[46] required naval stores and construction materials. There were wines, brandies, prunes, and chestnuts from Bordeaux (the wine often mixed with that from Spain brought via Sète and the Canal du Midi); from La Rochelle (an outlet for cognac); and from Nantes, with its hinterland in the Loire valley.[47] And

---

[35] See above, Chapter 2, note 134.
[36] See *Comercio de Portugal* in Simancas, *Estado, Portugal*, Leg. 7291, Cap. 6; *AS, Genoa*, AS.2292, letter, Ageno to Serenissima, London, 29 June 1770; for the earlier trade, V. Rau, 'Os holandeses e a exportação do sal de Setúbal nos fins do século XVII', *Revista Portuguesa de História*, IV, (1951); J. V. Th. Knoppers, 'De vaart in Europa', in G. Asaert et al., *Maritieme geschiedenis der Nederlanden*, III, pp. 244, 258.
[37] See *Zeecaert van de Rivier van Lisbon en de bancken voor St. Uves* in J. R. Bruijn, 'De vaart in Europa', in G. Asaert et al., *Maritieme geschiedenis der Nederlanden*, II, p. 233.
[38] *KVA*, XVIII, 679.   [39] *KVA*, XVIII, 696.   [40] *KVA*, XIX, 764.
[41] *KVA*, XV, 3488.   [42] *KVA*, XV, 3491.
[43] V. Palacio Atard, *El comercio de Castilla y el puerto de Santander en el siglo XVIII* (Madrid, 1960), p. 24.
[44] *KVA*, XV, 3570.   [45] *KVA*, XIX, 834.
[46] J. W. Konvitz, *New Port Cities of Louis XIV's France: Brest, Lorient, Rochefort and Sète, 1660–1715* (Ann Arbor, 1974), p. 254.   [47] Faber, 'De achttiende eeuw', p. 138.

then, too, there was the lucrative trade from the salt-pans in the Bay. All this could flourish in the open; but in secret there were also transfers of bullion from Spain and Portugal, quietly across the Pyrenees or discreetly along the coast, through the subtle hands of traders and couriers. Not without good reason did the mints of Bayonne and Pau in the sixty years 1726–85 alone churn out a third of the silver coined in France.[48] However, the trade increasingly by-passed Amsterdam and fell into the hands of foreign shippers.[49]

The key ports were nevertheless Bordeaux and Nantes, for they acted as entrepôts for colonial products from both sides of the world. Thus, we find the *Pieter en Anna*[50] leaving Bordeaux on 12 July 1777 (summer sailing) bound for St Petersburg with a cargo of coffee and wine; and the *Apollo*[51] left Nantes on 21 November 1767 bound for Hamburg with a cargo of sugar, coffee, indigo, and tea. And what proved the case for Bordeaux and Nantes, prevailed in La Rochelle, Lorient and elsewhere – relay-points for the valuable cargoes as much from the plantations of America as from Asia. The region of Biscay and the French Bight was probably one of the middling zones for ship-ton kilometres in the insurance market of Amsterdam.[52]

For Portugal and southern Spain, the year of insurance began to move in February and clearly improved in March. The rates remained relatively stable for April–July, but followed a progressive rise from August. For Cádiz (1766–75), these normally ranged between 1¼ and 3 percent; and the same generally applied to Lisbon and the other ports in Portugal. For Biscay, the rates were usually between 1 and 3 percent in the period 1766–75.

The threat and then onset of war dramatically changed this situation. The open anchorage of Cádiz was vulnerable and this affected the valuable trade from America. Even before the open war between Spain and England (June 1779), conditions were often difficult and ready to deteriorate. There had been the earlier trouble over the Falkland Islands when convoy rates were quoted: in May–June 1772 at 1–1½ percentage points and again in February 1775, a month of alert which stretched from Portugal to the Levant;[53] and this protection reduced the rate to 1¾ percent and 1½ percent respectively. After that, the situation regressed still further. The return rates which had been 1¼–1½ percent in the 1760s moved to 2–2½ percent; and from September 1777 were quoted only occasionally: from Cádiz only in November 1777 to January 1778,

---

[48] From my forthcoming study of coinage and monetary structures in France, 1726–1785.

[49] J. V. Th. Knoppers, 'De vaart in Europa', in G. Asaert et al., *Maritieme geschiedenis der Nederlanden*, III, p. 258.

[50] *KVA*, XIX, 972.   [51] *KVA*, XV, 3550.

[52] See above, Chapter 4, pp. 147–148 and Graph 9.

[53] See below, Chapter 6, p. 238.

August–December 1778, and August 1779. In the period November 1778 to January 1779, the rates were specially high at 6 percent. For Lisbon in December 1775 and January 1776 the maximum rate passed to 4 percent. Premiums were also high in November 1777 to January 1778; September–October 1778 and August 1779.

Finally, the return rates from Cádiz were higher than those outward in January 1766 at ½ percent; and again in August 1773 at ¼ percent. However, the reverse applied in September 1771 at ¼ percent and in September 1778 at ½ percent. For Lisbon, these excess rates appeared in August 1773 and April 1775. In the Biscay ports and south-west France: in October 1772, August 1774 and September–October 1775; but the reverse appeared in May 1772, September 1777 and September–October 1778, the last after the declaration of war between France and Britain (March 1778).

3. *The North Sea, Channel, and British Isles.* This region had special commercial importance for The Netherlands, thriving in time of peace; but fragile in war. The Channel was a bottleneck through which much of the subsistence, industry and navigation of Europe could pass. From Hamburg and Bremen came sheet copper and the manufactures of Germany, carried by river and canal. The ship the *Zeerob*[54] sailed from Hamburg on 19 October 1774 with a mixed cargo valued at f.102,175, composed in particular of linen cloth, notably from Silesia. From western France, the manufactures and products of Brittany (Morlaix and St Malo); of the north-west (Calais and St Valéry gave entry to the privileged Somme valley); and of the Seine valley where Rouen gave access to the metropolis Paris and continental France. From the latter, among other products, wine from Champagne already bottled for the tipplers of the North.[55] The ship *De Zeevrugt*,[56] for example, sailed from Rouen on 27 November 1774 for Amsterdam with a mixed cargo including 300 bottles of champagne valued at f.400. The striking feature about the French trade, as in the case of the Biscay ports, was the huge and growing transfers of colonial products, predominantly from the West Indies. In the mid eighteenth century, these provided half the exports from France and by the eve of the Revolution had reached four-fifths.[57] Little surprise then to find the *Vrouw Margaretha*[58] sailing on 10 February 1774 from Le Havre with a cargo of coffee and sugar. Or *De twee Gezusters*[59] from the same port on 15 March 1777 with a cargo composed principally of sugar with some coffee and indigo. The Nether-

---

[54] *KVA*, XVIII, 607.   [55] S. Ricard, *Traité*, I, pp. 511–515.   [56] *KVA*, XVIII, 591.
[57] Knoppers, 'De vaart in Europa', in G. Asaert et al., *Maritieme geschiedenis der Nederlanden*, III, pp. 255–256.
[58] *KVA*, XVII, 522.   [59] *KVA*, XIX, 829.

lands often sent grain in return: *De Juffrouw Elizabeth*[60] sailed on 13 November 1774 for Rouen with 60 lasts of wheat and 15 of rye. In 1789, a dearth year, 38 percent of the imports of France was in grain. Some, no doubt, could have found its way into the famous brioches.[61]

The trade with Britain combined the manufactures and raw materials of the provincial ports and the complex entrepôt trade of London and Bristol. The ship *De Nieuwe Republicq*[62] sailed from Truro on 6 November 1774 with 550 ingots of tin; the *Sara Johanna en Jacoba*[63] left St Ives on 14 November 1777 bound for Venice with a cargo of pilchards; the ship *Het Brugges Welvaren*[64] left Hull on 15 April 1782 with a mixed cargo of manufactures including pottery, perhaps from Stoke-on-Trent, and bound for Amsterdam, not the least remarkable when this was supposedly in the middle of war. The *Emanuel*[65] sailed on 3 November 1774 from Liverpool direct for Rostock with a single cargo of salt. Other ships brought coal from the Tyne and the Wear. And from Bristol came tobacco: the *Elton*[66] which left the port on 14 July 1768 carried 230 casks of leaf. However, the London traffic was the most interesting and complex. It provided in part manufactures, but also transfers of colonial products: *The Indian Trader*,[67] for example, sailed from the Thames for Amsterdam on 29 November 1774 with a mixed cargo including wool, sugar, coffee, tobacco, rice, gum, pottery – the produce as much of the plantations as of the craftsman's shop. And the *St James*[68] sailing for Amsterdam on 2 February 1775 with mainly tobacco, some sugar and a few other items. Other ships carried bullion in their cargoes.[69] From Ireland (Dublin, Cork, Limerick) the main shipments were dairy products and preserved meats.

For this zone, the year opened in February when the rates dropped sharply and carried into a 'long summer' from March to September. For Hamburg/Bremen, the premiums ranged between $\frac{3}{4}$ and 2 percent, moving to $\frac{3}{4}$–$2\frac{1}{2}$ percent after 1774. For London and the subsidiary ports, the range was between $\frac{3}{4}$ and 2 percent over most of the period. For Ireland, $1\frac{1}{2}$ to 3 percent, which continued until the winter of 1777–78. For Morlaix and the Brittany ports, 1 to $2\frac{1}{2}$ percent until 1777. The premiums for Ireland and France then altered indicating the deterioration in political security and imminent war.

Indeed, war disrupted this scene, but the effects were uneven. For Hamburg/Bremen, the changes were unspectacular in the perod 1776–80 – but then Hamburg, the imperial city of the Elbe, was an *alter ego* of

---

[60] *KVA*, XVIII, 628.
[61] Knoppers, 'De vaart in Europa', in G. Asaert et al., *Maritieme geschiedenis der Nederlanden*, III, p. 255.   [62] *KVA*, XVIII, 606.   [63] *KVA*, XIX, 997.
[64] *KVA*, XXI, 1491.   [65] *KVA*, XVIII, 660.   [66] *KVA*, XV, 3645.
[67] *KVA*, XVIII, 558.   [68] *KVA*, XVIII, 611.   [69] Faber, 'De achttiende eeuw', p. 137.

Amsterdam, and one which aimed to maintain the strictest neutrality. When trouble loomed ahead ships from The Netherlands were not slow to transfer registration to the Hamburg flag. Return rates reflected some difficulties with war declared between Britain and France (March 1778), and the same applied to premiums for London. There, insurance premiums soared, reaching 6 per cent from October 1778 to January 1779, and from December 1779 to January 1780. There was no break in the outward rates during the whole period from 1776 to 1780; and convoy rates were not quoted. For Brittany and north-west France, the outbreak of war brought fewer signs of serious change than might have been anticipated, although premiums reached 5 percent in November 1778 to January 1779. For Ireland, however, the deterioration of sailing conditions was clear from September 1778; and return rates were quoted only in August 1778 to January 1779 and in August 1779.

As for the ratio of outward to return rates, the group presented a changing picture. The return exceeded the outward rate in February 1767 in all four sub-groups. The reverse was the case, however, for Hamburg (December 1771 to February 1772; September–October 1777 and October 1778); for London and France (December 1778); and for Ireland (April 1773, September 1777 and September–October 1778).

4. *Denmark, south Norway, east of the Naze.* This important region combined, on the one hand, the trade of south-west Scandinavia: Denmark, both Copenhagen and the peninsula; southern Norway with the fiord to Christiania/Oslo; a part of Sweden with Gothenburg, founded in 1618, a port to escape the heavy ice of the Baltic and the difficulties of the Sound. It grew in opulence in the second half of the eighteenth century with herring fisheries, trade in Asiatic commodities, and exports from the hinterland (although Stockholm continued to retain control of the main trade in bar-iron).[70] On the other hand, the region commanded the strategic entrance to the Baltic and the movement of shipping through the Sound: the Skagerrak with the Kattegat to the North Sea, the dangerous shoals off Jutland and the Sound under the watchful guns of the fortress Kronborg: all these faced navigation with serious hazards. It was an important market for valuable commodities and the returns were often bulky. A simple port such as Drammen with access to forests could export timber. The *Anna Maria*[71] sailed from there on 28 November 1768 with just such a cargo for Amsterdam. The great entrepôts, however, had a more complex trade. When the ship *De jonge Gesina*[72] left Copenhagen for Amsterdam on 23 September 1765, she

---

[70] S. Högberg, *Utrikeshandel och sjöfart på 1700-talet* (Stockholm, 1969), pp. 238–242; see also I. Lund, *Göteborgs Handel och Sjöfart, 1637–1920* (Gothenburg, 1923).
[71] *KVA*, XV, 3684.   [72] *KVA*, XV, 3520.

carried a cargo predominantly of tea, with some porcelain wares and drugs. The *Anna Sophia*[73] on the same line on 14 October 1774 with tea, *nankings*, linens, and porcelain. The ship *De twee Gezusters*[74] sailed from Gothenburg on 2 December 1767 again with tea, some porcelain, silk goods, and drugs, but in addition 896 bars of iron brought across the ice-bound hinterland. Similarly, *De twee Gebroeders* [75] sailing on the same route on 29 September 1775 with tea (consigned mainly to Horneca, Fizeaux en Compagnie and Jean (Jan) Fizeaux en Zoonen who were concerned in the loans to Sweden), with some iron and steel. Thus, Asiatic mingled with domestic trade. But it could also offer on occasion herring and other fish from the northern waters; whale-oil from Greenland and the Davis Strait; hides and tallow; timber and furs.

The seasonal cycle became clear in March; but summer nagivation already showed signs of closing in August–September. The quotations usually ended in November–December – rates for the latter tended to be high. They ranged between 1 and 5 percent; after 1776, the upper level moved to 6 percent, and in December 1779 to January 1780 to 7 percent. However, the mounting tensions made for devious networks of trade: in 1775, for example, the Danish authorities asked the States General for tobacco from Glasgow and Liverpool to be routed to Denmark via Holland in Norwegian ships and to be exempted from paying customs.[76]

Indeed, hostilities at once aggravated the problems of this area for it held the key to the transit trade in war supplies and naval stores. From the autumn of 1777, return rates were quoted only in October 1777 to January 1778; September 1778 to January 1779; and August 1779. The return rate exceeded the outward on four occasions: in September 1768, in March 1771; April 1772; and September 1775. In October 1778, the reverse was the case, when the outward rate was set at a differential of 2½ percent.

5. *The south Baltic and Sweden: Stockholm and Norrköping; Königsberg, Danzig, Pomerania, and Lübeck.* The Baltic was a great heartland of trade for Amsterdam. The navigation to the coast from Königsberg to Lübeck – at least if we accept the ship-ton kilometres of returns in 1778 – was the largest single assignment among the groups listed for insurance in the *prijscouranten*.[77] In agrarian Europe, most regions were well supplied with the produce of farms, but the Baltic had the strategic commodities: a surplus of grain (Poland was a land free from serious famines except in time of war);[78] high-grade metals for industry (iron

---

[73] *KVA*, XVIII, 568. [74] *KVA*, XV, 3583. [75] *KVA*, XVIII, 707.
[76] *Simancas, Estado, Holanda,* Leg. 6367, letter, Herreria to Grimaldi, The Hague, 9 May 1775. [77] See above, Chapter 4, pp. 147–148 and Graph 9.
[78] W. Kula, *An economic theory of the feudal system* (London, 1976), p. 163.

and steel, copper and brass); masts and timber, pitch and tar for ships; industrial raw materials – wool, hemp, flax for textiles.[79] However, the climatic range was wide, and hard winters meant difficult navigation, particularly in the pack ice of the Gulf of Bothnia. And economic structures, too, were changing. In Sweden, the *Produktplakaat* of 1724 gave a mercantilist thrust to the domestic carrying trade during the century, although the number of Dutch ships flying the Swedish flag is not clear.[80] The Leipzig fairs and the expanding trade of the Oder via the Berlin canals to the Elbe and Hamburg created alternative lines of growth. There were the prestigious caravans of merchants from Poland/Lithuania (Rzeczpospolita) and the growing overland trade to Italy.[81] The power of Prussia in the Partition of Poland (1772) overshadowed the prosperity of Danzig, while Königsberg provided an alternative outlet for east Prussia. It enjoyed a prestigious surge of trade in the 1760s and 1770s.[82] These factors combined growth and stagnation in reshaping the region.

From the southern Baltic, the movement of commodities was clear. In the first place, for the export of grain: *De jonge Koopmans*[83] sailed on 8 October 1767 from Königsberg for Amsterdam with most of the cargo in 100 lasts of rye; the *Vreedelust*[84] on 7 November 1774 from the same port for Marseilles with 100 lasts of wheat. From Danzig, *De Vrijheyd*[85] sailed on 26 September 1767 for Plymouth, no doubt for the naval dock-yard, with oak planks, timber and barrel staves; the *Koninginne Carolina Mathilde*[86] on 27 September 1773 for Amsterdam with 75 lasts of rye and some other grain. From Stettin, the *Amsterdamse Koopman*[87] sailed on 5 October 1774 for Amsterdam with a cargo of oak planks. Hemp and hempseed, flax and flax-seed, wool, ashes, bristles, also made the voyage from the Baltic, providing a flow of prime raw materials for industry.

Sweden had command of high-grade metals and forestry products. The *Vigilantie*[88] left Stockholm for Amsterdam on 8 October 1766 with iron and timber. Likewise *De Eenigheid*[89] on 18 July 1767 with bar-iron

---

[79] S. Ricard, *Traité*, I, pp. 392–395; P. W. Klein, 'De zeventiende eeuw', in J. H. van Stuijvenberg (ed.), *De Economische-geschiedenis van Nederland*, 2nd edn (Groningen, 1979), p. 103; Faber, 'De achttiende eeuw', ibid., p. 133; R. Davis, *The rise of the Atlantic economies* (London, 1973), p. 191.

[80] Knoppers, 'De vaart in Europa', in G. Asaert et al., *Maritieme geschiedenis der Nederlanden*, III, p. 229.

[81] J. J. Oddy, *European Commerce* (2 vols., Philadelphia, 1807), I, pp. 215–218; F. H. Heller, *Die Handelswege Inner-Deutschlands im 16., 17., und 18. Jahrhundert und ihre Beziehungen zu Leipzig* (Dresden, 1884), pp. 35–36; J. Reinhold, *Polen-Litauen auf den Leipziger Messen des 18. Jahrhunderts* (Weimar, 1971), pp. 62–63.

[82] S. Ricard, *Traité*, I, p. 346.   [83] *KVA*, XV, 3551.   [84] *KVA*, XVIII, 650.

[85] *KVA*, XV, 3576.   [86] *KVA*, XVIII, 497.   [87] *KVA*, XVIII, 556.

[88] *KVA*, XV, 3529.   [89] *KVA*, XV, 3534.

and pitch. From Norrköping the *Hetwig Beata*[90] sailed for Amsterdam on 3 September 1767 with 65 iron cannon and bar-iron. If anything the advent of war and the break in North America brightened the prospects of this trade for Sweden. Horneca, Fizeaux en Compagnie consigned a cargo of tar, pitch and planks to the French naval dock-yard at Rochefort, this in the *Margareta*,[91] sailing from Stockholm on 18 July 1777. As for Britain, deprived of the tar of the American forests, she turned to Sweden first, and then to Russia: the reversal in source of supply in 1776 was both dramatic and clear. War raised risks . . . but also profits.

The insurance year usually began in March for this region, in the southern Baltic as much as in Sweden. The shift from summer rates was already showing in July–August, with steep rises in September and high rates in November–December. In the normal course, no quotations were listed in February. For Stockholm, the rates ranged between 1½ and 8 percent; for Danzig and the southern Baltic between 1¼ and 6 percent. For the first, the effects of war after 1776 acted as a stimulus; but in the latter, the Partition (1772) and power-politics left an early mark. In 1772, the upper limit moved to 10 percent; and this re-appeared in 1774–76. Convoy rates were quoted from November 1775 to January 1776.

As for the ratio of outward to return rates, Stockholm appears as an exceptional case. Although the return rate was higher in November 1767, October 1775, October 1776, and June 1777, the reverse became a regular feature in the autumn months. For Königsberg, there were no great differences between the two rates, at most perhaps ½ or 1 percent. This changed in October 1774 and again in November 1775, when a differential opened of 3½ percent. For both these destinations, convoy rates were given only once: in the three months November 1775 to January 1776 at a differential of 3½ per cent. In 1776–77, convoy rates were given occasionally for both Stockholm and Königsberg; for the former this difference was only 1 per cent and lasted three months; but for the latter, the differential in October 1778 was as wide as 3 percent.

6. *Northern Norway and the North Cape: Bergen, Trondheim, and Archangel.*
This important group provided cargoes from fisheries, trapping, and the forests: fish, whale-oil, furs, timber, masts, and spars. The old Hanseatic wharf – the *Tyskenbryggen* – of Bergen remained an important collecting station, even when the famous *Kontor* was wound up (1774).[92] Among the *Noordvaarders*, we find the ship *De Elkswaardige Jufvrouw*[93] sailing

---

[90] *KVA*, XV, 3519.   [91] *KVA*, XIX, 906.
[92] P. Dollinger, *The German Hansa*, Eng. trans. (London, 1970), p. 369; Klein, 'De zeventiende eeuw', p. 104; Faber, 'De achttiende eeuw', p. 135.
[93] *KVA*, XIX, 824.

from Bergen on 7 October 1776 freighted direct to Venice with a valuable cargo of fish. There was the *Catharina Elizabeth*[94] which sailed from Trondheim for Amsterdam on 23 July 1776 with copper-plates, whale-oil, tar, and stockfish. And the *Anna Margaretha*[95] from Kristiansund for Amsterdam on 8 November 1766 with whale-oil, stockfish, and furs.

As for the North Cape trade, the long-established market in Archangel (1584) held the no less famous fairs in August, which usually continued to 10 September. This port offered access to the Vologda and the overland caravans from the Urals and Siberia.[96] A rich hinterland provided industrial raw materials and naval stores: pitch and tar, flax and hemp, ship-building timber, tallow, besides grain and furs. Its fortunes revived somewhat in the second half of the eighteenth century, when in 1762 trading privileges were granted similar to those of St Petersburg. The trade was varied. The ship *De twee jonge Jannen*[97] sailed for Amsterdam on 11 July 1767 with 1,911 barrels of tar, *matten*, hides, candles, and walrus tusks. The *Amsterdam* similarly routed on 18 October that year with tar, *matten*, tallow, and flax-seed. War also brightened the outlook. Hope and Company had a consignment of hemp in the mixed cargo of the *Koning van Groot Brittanyen* sailing on 27 September 1776.[98] While Jan Texier en Compagnie (in the Sligtenhorst lists as an insurer) had 2,869 barrels of tar in the *Vrouw Catharina*[99] sailing on 10 October 1779 for Texel 'met orders' – perhaps in this instance destined to be re-routed for France. However, the harsh winter made sailing conditions treacherous, and the access channel was free from ice hardly six months of the year. This, therefore, made navigation to Archangel subject to high risk and the sailing year was accordingly restricted.

For Bergen/Trondheim, the outward quotations usually began in March and ended in September; for Archangel, the period was even shorter, March to July (or August in 1767, 1773, 1778, and 1779). For the first, the rates ranged between 1 and 6 percent; but for the latter between 1¼ and 10 percent. In the exceptional years of 1767, 1769, 1775, and 1776, they went still higher. In the difficult months from December 1775 to January 1776, the rate for Bergen/Trondheim rose to 8 percent; and for Archangel to 14 percent. The latter premium re-appeared in the lists from December 1776 to January 1777.

The advent of war clearly affected the strategic returns (and dangers) of naval stores. No return rate was quoted for Bergen and Trondheim in

---

[94] *KVA*, XV, 3509. [95] *KVA*, XV, 3492.
[96] S. Ricard, *Traité*, I, pp. 275–279; P. J. Blok, *History of the People of The Netherlands* (5 vols., London, 1898–1912), IV, p. 514; A. Attman, *The Russian and Polish markets in international trade* (Gothenburg, 1973), pp. 151–153; Klein, 'De zeventiende eeuw', pp. 104–105; Faber, 'De achttiende eeuw', p. 135.
[97] *KVA*, XV, 3518. [98] *KVA*, XIX, 835. [99] *KVA*, XXI, 1298.

March–July in 1778 and 1779. As for Archangel, no rate appeared in November 1778 to January 1779. An excess ratio of return over outward rates appeared for Norway in March and July 1769, March–May 1771, April 1722, and April–July 1773. However, the reverse was the case when open hostilities were declared: there were no quotations in October–November 1777, September–October 1778, and September–October 1779.

For Archangel, an excess return rate appears to have been normal for the period from April to August, although not always for the full five months. Convoy rates were not quoted for Trondheim, but they were frequent for Archangel: in 1767 the differential was 4 percent; in September 1769, 7 percent; and in September–October 1771, 3 percent. Threat of war brought them back in October 1776 at a differential of 5 percent.

7. *The East Baltic: Reval and Riga; St Petersburg and Viborg.* This important region – an area of development in the eighteenth century with the founding of St Petersburg (1703) and Russia's advance to enjoy the outlook of her 'window' – comprised a number of ports listed by name in the *prijscouranten*: Reval, Riga, St Petersburg, Viborg. And others also came into the commercial network from the type of commodities they produced: Libau and Windau perhaps; certainly Arensburg, Narva, Helsingfors/Helsinki, Åbo/Turku. Riga, set in its gulf, held by name the key to the strategic naval stores – the best masts (although a declining asset) and the best hemp for ropes and sails.[100] The strategic trade could hardly be in doubt when on 23 August 1778 *De jonge Elias* [101] left with a cargo of hemp bound for Cádiz; or when Hope and Company shipped a consignment of masts and spars on 11 November 1779 to Amsterdam. And there were other commodities for export: the *Jonkvrouw Catharina*[102] left Arensburg on 25 September 1774 on the island of Ösel – probably the last port of call for the island itself had little to offer – with a cargo of rye freighted for Amsterdam.

St Petersburg comprised in reality a complex of harbours, the great west-port of Kronstadt being open for only some six or seven months. Early preparations for return cargoes were therefore necessary and orders were usually placed in January–February. The opening of the port with the thaw became an event: in the two centuries 1706–1899, the earliest recorded was on 18 March and the latest 12 May; the earliest closing on 28 October and the latest 9 January.

The port handled increasing numbers of ships: 288–387 in the 1760s,

---

[100] S. Ricard, *Traité*, I, pp. 300–301, 307; see also A. Attman, 'The Russian market in world trade, 1500–1860', *Scandinavian Economic History Review*, XXIX (1981), 184–190.
[101] *KVA*, XX, 1114.   [102] *KVA*, XVIII, 572.

more than 700 in the 1770s. It is evident that Amsterdam was losing some of its monopoly of the Baltic ports of Russia: it accounted for 97.7 percent of Holland's ships in the trade in 1724–25, but only 67.6 percent in 1784–85.[103] The cargoes, however, were important: leather and hides, wax and caviar, furs, above all grain, from farms and fisheries; iron from the mines of the Urals. And for the expectant mercantile marines and navies of Europe, again strategic naval stores: hemp, flax, cordage, sail-cloth; and forestry products. Travellers marvelled at the clusters of sawmills along the River Neva.[104] Thus, we find the *Vrouw Anna Catharina*[105] leaving Kronstadt on 19 October 1774 for Barcelona with a cargo of wheat. And with the onset of war, hemp, and iron bars: on 2 October 1778 Jan Texier en Compagnie freighted such a cargo for Amsterdam; or another cargo ten days later this time bound for the naval dock-yard at Brest, the hemp again for Texier but the iron bars for Jan en Theodor van Marselis.[106]

Viborg, across the gulf and set on a peninsula, was the prime timber outlet of Finland. Most of this trade was in pine-planks, more suitable for carpentry than ship-building.[107] Dutch ships predominated in the port, although the merchants in the city were of German origin. And further still the port of Åbo an outlet for metals and forestry products: the *Patientie*[108] sailed on 31 August 1765 for Amsterdam with a mixed consignment of bar-iron, tar, pitch, boards, 60 balks of timber, and – *mirabile dictu* – 2,000 *contanten*, perhaps even from the local silver mines.

War, which darkened the political horizons of Europe, at once brightened the commercial outlook of these ports and their products. Tar was an example to which we have referred in the context of Sweden. Before independence, North America was the major supplier to England – 84.27 percent in 1764; with Russia providing 0.62 and Sweden 12.30. War in 1775 reversed this. By 1778, 2.84 percent came from America, 40.86 from Russia, and 44.75 from Sweden. By the end of the war, the major supplier was Russia,[109] and continued to be so into the nineteenth century.

Such cargoes were composed of prime raw materials; but the deliveries from the Netherlands were a mirror of Dutch trade and industry. One example must suffice for this complex reality. The *Werkhoven*[110] left Amsterdam/Texel on 4 September 1773 (a late sailing) bound for

---

[103] J. V. Th. Knoppers, *Dutch trade with Russia from the time of Peter I to Alexander I* (diss., 3 vols., Montreal, 1976), I, p. 335.
[104] S. Ricard, *Traité*, I, pp. 279–291; Faber, 'De achttiende eeuw', p. 135; G. E. Munro, *The development of St. Petersburg as an urban center during the reign of Catharine II (1762–1796)* (Ann Arbor, 1974), p. 207.   [105] *KVA*, XVIII, 691.
[106] *KVA*, XX, 1115.   [107] S. Ricard, *Traité*, I, p. 300.   [108] *KVA*, XV, 3510.
[109] K. Hautala, *European and American tar in the English market during the eighteenth and early nineteenth centuries* (Helsinki, 1963), esp. pp. 105–106.

St Petersburg. The mixed cargo valued at f.160,100 included Spanish and other wine, cochineal, indigo, paper, cloth, linen, camelhair wool, and four sacks of *rijksdaalders* (each containing 500). As it turned out, there was a penalty for risking the luck of the weather: the *Werkhoven* ran into storms, put into Copenhagen for repairs, was obliged to 'overwinter' and managed finally to sail again on 12 April in the following year.

★

The insurance year usually began in March but for outward policies ended early and before the freeze. For Reval, the rates began to rise in August; for St Petersburg, this often started in July, with a substantial upward shift in August. Peak rates came in November–December; and in February there were no quotations listed at all, in common with most of the northern destinations.

The range of this seasonal movement was wider than for the southern Baltic: $1\frac{1}{4}$ to 8 percent. For St Petersburg, the rates often went higher still, to 10 percent in 1772, 1775, and 1777, 11 percent in November 1778 and 12 percent in the exceptional year of 1771 (when problems of war and plague distorted the flows of trade).

For Reval and Riga, the differential between outward and return rates were similar; with an occasional gap of $\frac{1}{2}$ percent for one or two months in 1771–73; and of 1 percent in October 1776, and November 1779. However, the differences were considerable for St Petersburg. These contrasted with the summer months, sometimes at $\frac{1}{4}$ percent. In the months of August–October the *outward* rate was often quoted at 2–$2\frac{1}{2}$ percent over the return rate, in 1773 at 3 percent. This occurred often enough in the series to be considered a regular feature.

★

Before closing the section on the northern trade, some comments of a general nature are in order. After all, if we follow the analysis of ship-ton kilometres for 1778, the North contributed a good half of the arrivals for Amsterdam.[111] The large commitment of tonnage was an indicator, so too the bulky nature of the valuable and strategic commodities, the seasonal characteristics of the trade – which proved the fortune of the fairs of Archangel or of Tikhvin on the approaches to Lake Ladoga. The trade in high-grade iron was a case in point, crucial for the early development of machines and industrialisation. Between the 1740s and the 1770s exports from the Baltic doubled to some 4 million schippond.[112] When analysed in detail they reveal the growing exports of Russia especially to England. Different from Sweden, there could be a cost

[110] *KVA*, XVIII, 515.
[111] See above, Chapter 4, pp. 147–148 and Graph 9.
[112] Knoppers, 'De vaart in Europa', in G. Asaert et al., *Maritieme geschiedenis der Nederlanden*, III, p. 247.

advantage in the Russian trade with iron used as ballast for cargoes of hemp and flax. Nevertheless, in that trade, The Netherlands share was falling sharply.

Such pressures pointed to keen competition: the Anglo-Russian treaty (December 1734) made Britain the most-favoured nation not least when Article V exempted her traders from settling in *rijksdaalders*, for long a standard currency in the Baltic.[113] In The Netherlands, such pressures of growth spilled over into disputes. From 1753, the control of the Russian trade came under the *Directie van de Moscovische Handel*, leaving the rest of the Baltic to the administration of the *Directie van de Oostersche Handel en Rederijen*. Dutch ships were not the predominant carriers serving St Petersburg during the years 1775–80. In 1784–85, Amsterdam neverthe-less still managed to account for about two-thirds of the Dutch ships trading with the Baltic ports of Russia.[114]

8. *Surinam/Berbice, Curaçao*. This region provided an important flow of colonial products for the markets of The Netherlands. If we take the returning ship-ton kilometres it was one of the four important areas for insurance listed formally on the Amsterdam Bourse. However, simple listings disguise a complex reality of trade and navigation. There was the triangular slave trade via Africa and the returns to Europe, often including gold, ivory and malaguetta pepper routed via the West Indies. The *Nicolaas*[115] left Surinam on 11 July 1773 bound for Amsterdam with the main cargo consisting of coffee, sugar, and cacao but with a supplement of ivory tusks and 10 mark 5 ounces weight of gold.

Secondly, in the trade of Surinam itself – the 'wilde kust' – the early development of timber and tobacco gave way to the plantations: sugar (by 1670), cacao (1700) the most valuable, coffee (1720) the largest crop, cotton (1735). In 1775, for return cargoes to The Netherlands, they still remained roughly in that order of importance.[116] Those plantations generated the demand for the trade in slaves, flourishing until the 1770s. Surinam provided the most important clients after about 1740, although we should not ignore the clandestine trade through Curaçao and, in the 1770s also through St Eustatius. Cornelis de Jong noted in his voyage to the latter in October 1780 that business was brisk on the island and

---

[113] M. Gideonse, *Dutch Baltic trade in the eighteenth century* (diss., Harvard, 1932), pp. 182–183.

[114] Knoppers, 'De vaart in Europa', in G. Asaert et al., *Maritieme geschiedenis der Nederlanden*, III, pp. 233–238.

[115] *KVA*, XVIII, 505; P. C. Emmer, 'De vaart buiten Europa: het Atlantisch gebied', in G. Asaert et al., *Maritieme geschiedenis der Nederlanden*, III, p. 299.

[116] H. J. Korver, 'Twee eeuwen scheepvaart op Suriname', *Ons Zeewezen*, LII, 11 (1963), 23; Emmer, 'De vaart buiten Europa: het Atlantisch gebied', in G. Asaert et al., *Maritieme geschiedenis der Nederlanden*, III, pp. 307–310.

indeed in the whole Caribbean.[117] But in this the planters of Surinam may not have wholly shared. Heavily in debt with the proliferation of loans, constrained to usurious share-cropping, unable to retain the confidence of Amsterdam investors after the 1773 crisis, the Surinam planters began to lose out to competition from other islands.[118] And not least among the problems, was one of government. The plantation charters had set norms for the ratio of black to white settlers, but they were overlooked in the large inflow of slaves from Africa.[119] Fugitive slaves took to the tropical forest, and as *bosnegers* – the *aucaners* freed in 1761, the *saramaccaners* in 1762 – remained a remote source of disturbance and insurrection. This problem remained endemic from the time of acquisition (Treaty of Breda, 1667), through the revolts as in 1772 and 1774, until an uneasy settlement in 1778.[120]

Surinam, then, had an uneven performance. Sometimes, as we have seen in the case of the *Haast U Langzaam*, the proceeds of the sale of slaves in unfavourable years were returned by bill of exchange, or in cargoes loaded in St Eustatius collected from the Caribbean. Thus we find the *Resolutie*[121] left Surinam on 20 October 1773 with a cargo mainly of coffee – 102 bales for that outstanding entrepreneur of Rotterdam, Ferrand Whaley Hudig – and some cacao. Or the *Petrus Alexander*[122] valued at f. 122,750, mainly from the cargo of coffee, also bound for Amsterdam. Often the slave-ships were not used for returning cargoes; there was an important, direct shuttle from The Netherlands to the colonies.

As for Curaçao, it had a special place. Declared a free port in 1675,[123] it had enjoyed a century of trade through loop-holes to the Spanish settlements in which officials often connived: commodities and specie mingled in the holds of returning ships. There were some ten a year in the late 1770s, such as the *Vrouw Maria*[124] which left the island on 26 February 1774 for Amsterdam. She carried f. 66,950 in coffee, tobacco, timber, cacao, and hides; and for good measure another consignment valued at f.5,775 in 26 lots of specie both silver and gold.

St Eustatius, as we have seen, was not idle. It had a commercial catchment area which included the French islands of St Domingo and

---

[117] C. de Jong, *Reize naar de Caribische eilanden in de jaren 1780 en 1781* (Haarlem, 1807), p. 113.

[118] J. P. Van der Voort, *De Westindische plantages van 1720 tot 1795: financiën en handel* (Eindhoven, 1973), esp. Chapter 1.

[119] PRO, SP, 84.502, letter, Yorke to Halifax, The Hague, 22 July 1763, estimating the ethnic ratio of 36,000 to 1,300 white inhabitants.

[120] C. de Jong, *Reize naar de Caribische eilanden*, pp. 121–123; and see above p. 89.

[121] *KVA*, XVIII, 499.   [122] *KVA*, XVIII, 596.

[123] Emmer, 'De vaart buiten Europa: het Atlantisch gebied', in G. Asaert et al., *Maritieme geschiedenis der Nederlanden*, III, p. 305.

[124] *KVA*, XVIII, 536.

Haiti; and the trade flourished when war broke out with Britain. Coffee and sugar were the prime returns, as on *De Jonge Clemens Hendrik*[125] which sailed from the island on 28 March 1774; but there were also some small consignments of cacao and indigo, and sometimes gold and silver both in bullion and specie. This island was listed in the *prijscouranten* for insurance from 1788 in conjunction with Curaçao. However, for the purposes of the 1770s in general, and 1778 in particular, the routes of the returning ships seemed to link it more with Surinam. At least, it came second after Surinam in the numbers of ships routed for Amsterdam in the registrations of Texel and Vlieland.[126]

There is some evidence that in the direct sailings to and from the West Indies, the outward cargoes were low in value compared with the returns.[127] This was not always the case for those en route for St Eustatius. The *Harmonie*[128] sailing on 8 December 1773 for the Golden Rock was valued (hull and cargo) at f.160,050 and the latter catered discreetly for the needs of colonial settlers: gin, wine, and beer; spices, paper-books, linen, and cotton cloth; rope and anchors.

★

Against such outlays, most return cargoes could be classed as high-value consignments. Although the long distances in this trade imposed heavy wear and tear on the ships, the value of the cargoes appreciated on the way to Europe. Under such circumstances, the seasonal movement was markedly in evidence. The premiums dropped in February and March and continued until July (sometimes earlier, as in 1766 and 1769, when the summer rates ended in June). This strong seasonal movement ranged from $2\frac{1}{2}$ to 6 percent for Curaçao and from $2\frac{1}{2}$ to 8 percent for Surinam. One possible explanation could point to the protection of valuable cargoes returning from the mainland plantation, especially in view of the steep rise in return rates in July–August, continuing through until January–February. In 1766–73, the spread of rates in July–February from Curaçao increased from 3 to 6 percent; while those from Surinam went up from 3 to 8 percent. Then came the build-up to war. The rate for Curaçao started to rise in October 1774, reaching 8 percent; and for Surinam starting in July 1773 to reach 10 percent. The situation deteriorated seriously in November 1778 to January 1779 with active war between France and England. The position of the two colonies reversed: the more exposed and vulnerable Curaçao, closer to the Isthmus of

---

[125] *KVA*, XVIII, 544.
[126] See above, Chapter 4, pp. 147–148 and Graph 9.
[127] S. Ricard, *Traité*, II, p. 468; Emmer, 'De vaart buiten Europa: het Atlantisch gebied', in G. Asaert et al., *Maritieme geschiedenis der Nederlanden*, III, p. 302.
[128] *KVA*, XVIII, 539.

Panama, reached 15 percent; while the premium for Surinam remained at 10 percent.

The varying types of return cargo no doubt accounted for these disparities, and for the differential use of convoys. Until 1771, the convoy rates for Curaçao usually appeared for one month, at the beginning or at the end of a period of high return rates (that is, either in July or in February). This protection brought a reduction of 2 percent. From 1772, however, the protection assumed an increasingly important rôle. This can be seen in the lengthening period of convoy rates quoted:

year	number of months of convoy rates
1772	4
1773	7
1774	6
1775	9
1778	2

With the onset of open war, convoy rates disappeared, leaving exceptionally high premiums (12–15 percent in November 1778 to January 1779).

The return voyages from Surinam initially received longer convoy protection. In 1766–75, this usually started in July or August and continued through until January or February. From 1776, however, the periods were restricted to two to four months (usually August–September or September–October), and coincided with the returning autumn fleets. The convoy rate started at a differential of 4 percent, and then rose to 5 percent. In 1774, it was at 2, but in 1775 and 1777 reached 6, and then in the war of 1778–79, fell back to 4 percent.

*

What closing comments can we make on the profile of these fluctuations, dominated as they were by a powerful seasonal movement? None, to be sure, without referring again to the validity of the material. The premiums listed in the *prijscouranten* must be considered as a 'going rate' but individual instances brought considerable variety. The problem was clear in a Rouen price-current of 9 April 1757, when insurance premiums were listed to alter 'according to the size and strength of the ships . . .'[129] It is all too evident that ships varied in tonnage and design but in Amsterdam the premiums averaged the market, and are silent on the variations in the operating ships. No need to look for special categories used at Lloyd's in early nineteenth-century London, which put ships of teak, not more than sixteen years old, at the top of the list; and then down the scale of timbers and ages.[130] Such qualities could rank the

---

[129] Price-current for Rouen, *EHA, Amsterdam, Prijscouranten*, Rouen, 9 April 1757.
[130] R. G. Albion, *Forests and Seapower* (Cambridge, Mass., 1926), p. 37.

sailing vessels of Europe. Beyond these requirements were the merits of a captain with a blameless record; of not 'hazarding' his ship; of maintaining the morale of his crew. A cursory glace at the documents suffices to give the stature of the master – his name·was often enough. He personified the ship.

However, as second comment, the data demonstrate clearly the strength of the seasonal movement. In the relative calm of the late 1760s, the rhythm is striking, as if the market had long since come to terms with these conventional risks in the constraints of climate. Low insurance rates in Amsterdam from March to July, even to September in some cases, coincided (lagged for sailings by a month or two) with commercial conditions at an optimum. All passed for the best: fair weather and fair winds filled the sails and smoothed the seas more often than at other times. Winter brought a different tale. Gales could drive ships to look for harbours or sheltered coasts; ice could close ports; poor conditions meant delays in handling cargoes when often they had to be sent in lighters to waiting vessels. In agrarian Europe, such considerations carried weight in moving products from the land to warehouse and market. Insurance premiums passed from the lows of June to the highs of November–February. This rhythm of the seasons permeated the life of the continent, and navigation paid homage to the immemorial rule.

The seasonal movement was differentiated by the regional organisation of Amsterdam's trade. Each destination had its own characteristics and scalars of risks. Access to the Mediterranean passed a gauntlet of pirates, and demanded well-armed, well-manned ships, often under convoy. The Bay of Biscay was notorious for capricious, rough weather. The Baltic, Scandinavia and White Sea brought winter hazards which were legion. In such a system, it was necessary to assign priorities and it seems that for The Netherlands the northern trade was the 'risk leader'. The Baltic produced and assembled strategic raw materials for collection in the optimum months of summer. To meet this order of sailing, the trade of the South was the dependent variable. For example, the wines of France travelled best from January to May. In this context, it is worth noting that the numbers of policies registered in the Paris *Chambre d'assurances* (1668–80) reach a peak in January–March and a trough in June–August.[131] Then, too, there was the trade from further south and the Mediterranean – the salt of Biscay, the bullion trade of Cádiz and Lisbon. Cargoes from these more temperate zones could be shipped easily into the North during the better months of the summer. Those cargoes required preparations in the South well in advance. The alterna-

---

[131] J. Delumeau, 'Exploitation d'un dossier d'assurances maritimes au XVIIe. siècle', in *Mélanges en l'honneur de Fernand Braudel* (2 vols., Toulouse, 1973), I, p. 141.

tion of seasons accentuated regional disparities and the allocation of commercial resources.

Finally, the fluctuations in insurance rates point to the changing scenario of peace and war. Political security created the necessary conditions for the navigation of The Netherlands. The themes in Hugo Grotius' *Mare liberum* and the polemics for neutrality carried weight and purpose. The convergence of markets, however, served to sharpen competition in Europe. During the seventeenth and eighteenth centuries insurance rates improved as other markets grew in competence. If the quotations in the *prijscouranten* were accurate indicators, the low period reached during the years 1765 to 1774 marked a turning-point. Spacious years were followed by tension and rising premiums, the indicators of the increasing risks during armed neutrality and the wars which closed the century.

CHAPTER 6

A differential geography of marine insurance

So far, this study has taken in turn the salient components of the system of navigation and its risks. In years of relative equilibrium (1765–74), the seasonal movement left a clear and characteristic presence. The bio-mass of the continent lived in an annual rhythm, producing with the warmth of the sun, the resources of the soil, the benevolence of nature itself. Distance offered linearity of growth on the high seas. Events grew into market turbulence. These elements differentiated insurance for the various lines of ship movements. How can we bring this discussion of Amsterdam together as a matrix of trade and risk-aversion?

A solution can be found in the spatial setting. The destinations[1] in the *prijscouranten* – twenty in Europe and two in the West Indies – set formal horizons for navigation and shaped the range of premiums on offer. Thus it is possible to formulate the spectrum of insurance dealings in much the same way as the continuities around the ideal market of Johann Heinrich von Thünen.[2] This would envisage a model with 'broad bands' – in the terminology of topologists – concentric on Amsterdam. They would co-ordinate season and climate, distance and political obligation into a dynamic system which converged during the optimal months of spring and summer. The spatial setting, therefore, formulates the interdependence of different categories of uncertainty, both structural and event. In other lines of enquiry, the concepts are well-established: there are isobars for atmospheric pressure, isotherms for temperature, isobaths for depth. Isochrones give the time-scale of communications, and this perspective of Amsterdam's Atlantic can be seen in Map 1.[3]

---

[1] In this context, 'destination' is used as a term of convenience to designate ports of both destination and departure, see above Chapter 5, note 3.

[2] See the edition by P. Hall, *Von Thünen's Isolated State* (Oxford, 1966), Introduction, pp. 20 et seq.

[3] For isochrones, see the maps of T. Hossinger in F. Heidrich and R. Sieger (eds.), *Karl Andree's Geographie des Welthandels* (4 vols., Vienna, 1910–21), IV (end maps), and G. Schott, *Geographie des Atlantischen Ozeans*, 2nd edn (Hamburg, 1926), pp. 308–309. The concept has been extensively and effectively used in the publications of the *Annales*, and

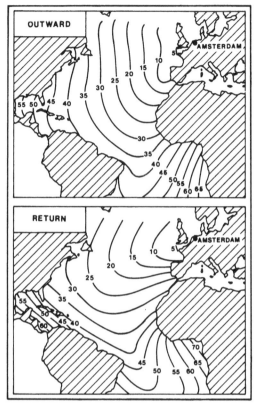

Map 1. Isochrones of Atlantic voyages to and from Amsterdam (in sailing days)

However, in mapping uncertainties, I should like to offer another category: *isokindunes*. These mark out 'broad bands' of risk concentric on Amsterdam. If the volumes of insurance taken out were available for this enquiry, it would be possible no doubt to establish more accurately the numbers of steps involved. However, in the following chapter I propose to take up this problem within the geography of maritime Europe, and adopt the method of an atlas of monthly maps.

★

The publication of any visual material rarely escapes technical difficulties, and this particular sequence has had more than its fair share. The limitations of format and the ratio of reduction in printing have restricted the full use of the quantitative data. After a number of trials with different symbols and shading, I opted for circles divided vertically. The

in particular P. Sardella, *Nouvelles et spéculations à Venise au début du XVIe. siècle* (Paris, 1948); F. Braudel, *La Méditerranée et le monde méditerranéen à l'époque de Philippe II*, 2nd edn (2 vols., Paris, 1966), I, pp. 336–337.

Risks at Sea

left half shows the outward rate; the right half the return. The premiums quoted have been divided into eight bands with divisions ranging between 1.5 and 14 percent. Each band has a shading graduated from light stipple to solid black. An asterisk designates a ninth band for premiums of 14 percent and above. The visual effect is that as premiums rise the circles darken. Since all degrees of shading are positive quotations, a blank circle indicates that no rate was given in the particular *prijscourant*. This may be considered in its own way a statement of the market. Where whole lists are missing in the archives, the maps have a label 'no information'. Each page of maps has a scale of reference; a full key is placed at the beginning of the atlas.

The final – and perhaps most difficult problem – has been the ratio of reduction. The number of suitable shadings has decided the number of bands. And in order to use as large a frame as possible, the locations of Archangel, Surinam/Berbice, and Curaçao have been moved, the first to the top right corner; and the others to the left margin. For the same reasons, it has not been possible to include convoy rates. However, the space in the top left-hand corner of each map has been used for a compass-rose, giving the prevailing monthly wind direction at Deal, based on the daily reports in Lloyd's List.[4]

The groups of destinations, in the order given in the *prijscouranten*, are as follows (the numbers appear in the appropriate circles in the key map):

1. Archipelago, Syria
2. Venice, Gulf
3. Sicily, Naples, Leghorn
4. Genoa, Marseilles
5. Barcelona, Alicante, Málaga
6. Cádiz, Sanlúcar, Seville
7. Lisbon, Setúbal, Oporto
8. Biscay, French Bight
9. Morlaix, St Malo, Rouen
10. London, Yarmouth, Hull
11. Cork, Dublin, Limerick
12. Archangel
13. Trondheim, Bergen
14. Norway, east of Naze
15. Stockholm, Norrköping

[4] The daily reports are in *Lloyd's Lists* (repr., 6 vols., Farnborough, 1969). Some lists for the period have not survived – for example, those for 1778, the first year of war with France in the Channel; and in 1770 there is a gap for November–December, so that only 285 reports remain. The data were assembled for me by Michael Turner. The *prevailing wind* is the median of wind directions recorded for the month. The arrow on the compass-rose points to the origin; where two statistics are of the same size giving a split result, both directions are marked. See below, p. 240.

16. Copenhagen, Sound, Belt
17. Reval, Riga
18. St Petersburg, Viborg
19. Königsberg, Danzig, Pomerania, Lübeck
20. Hamburg, Bremen
21. Surinam, Berbice
22. Curaçao

The atlas has the purpose of co-ordinating the *uncertainties* listed in Chapter 3 with the conventional risks of the type-year set out in Chapter 4.[5] The annual sequences of monthly premiums (January to December) display a calendar year on two facing pages, and so contrast the optimal season of navigation during spring and summer with the rising hazards of winter. Naturally enough, the reader must keep constantly in mind that these are insurance quotations and form part of the *preparations* for navigation. The actual sailing year was lagged by days, even weeks. These delays reflected stochastic variables about which the data are silent. They were weighty enough for outward voyages; and highly speculative for the returns, when the news of the departure for the home port sometimes arrived at the same time as the ship itself.

A SYNOPSIS OF INSURANCE MAPS

Taking the years in sequence:

1766. With the series beginning in January, it is soon evident, as in other years, that this month belonged more often than not to the preceding year. Conditions clearly improved in March and gathered way into the fine month of June. From March to August for both the axis of the North Sea as well as for other destinations, navigation achieved a certain measure of unity. Archangel was an exception: here the 'insurance year' apparently did not start until the summer – the first reported premium appeared in the July. Then with the approach of autumn, the circles gradually darken. For Archangel: an outward rate in July was a singleton, followed only by returns. Outward rates virtually ended for Bergen and Trondheim from September; and for the Baltic generally from November. The year ended with a void in the North: Scandinavia, the Baltic and Russia. At the other end of Europe, affairs seemed quiet: the arrival of Ali Bey as ruler of Egypt, at once ready to declare independence from the Sultan, seems to have left little sign of disturbance in the Levant. As for the West Indies, the sailings appeared to share the spacious days in Europe, at least in the months from March to June.

[5] See above, Chapter 4, pp. 122–124.

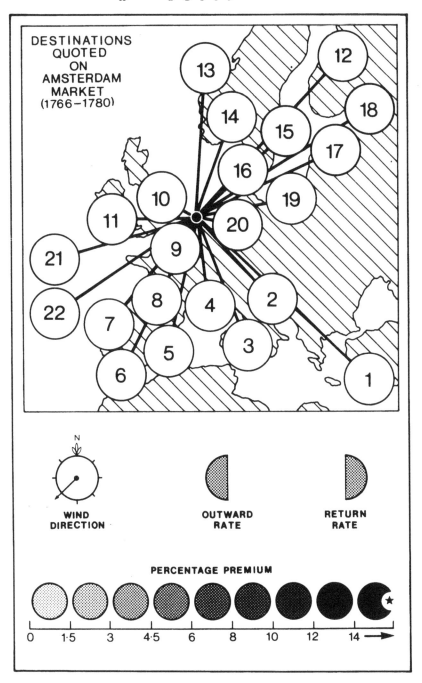

DESTINATIONS
QUOTED
ON
AMSTERDAM
MARKET
(1766–1780)

WIND
DIRECTION

OUTWARD
RATE

RETURN
RATE

PERCENTAGE PREMIUM

0   1·5   3   4·5   6   8   10   12   14 ⟶

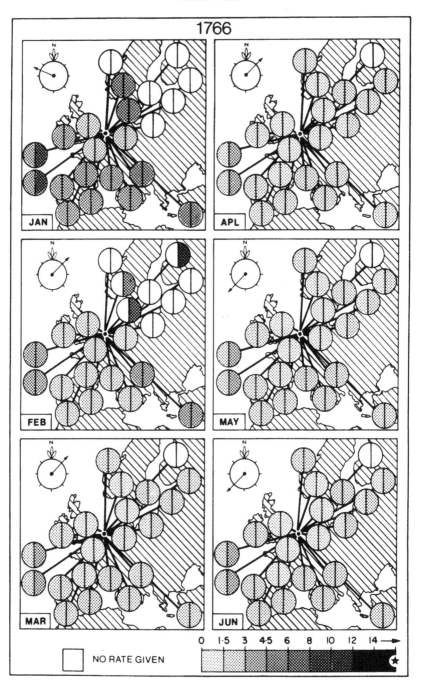

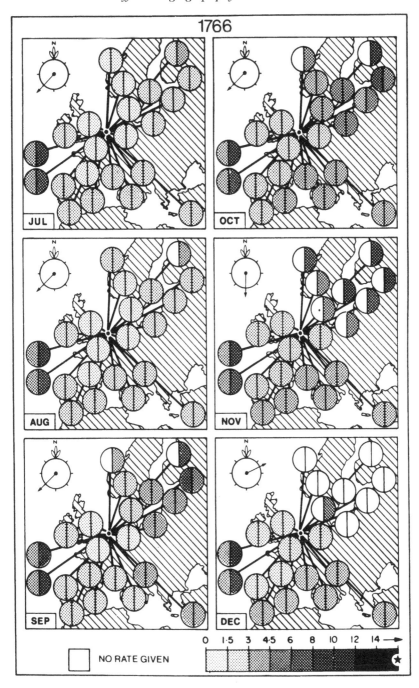

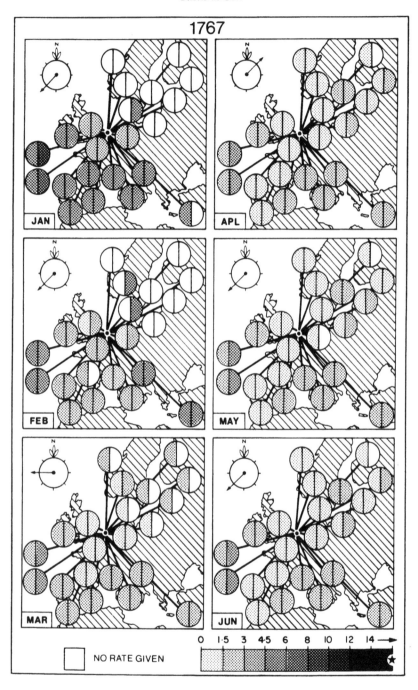

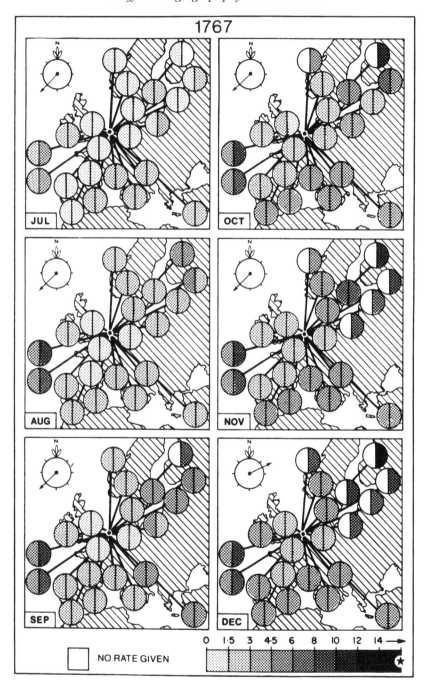

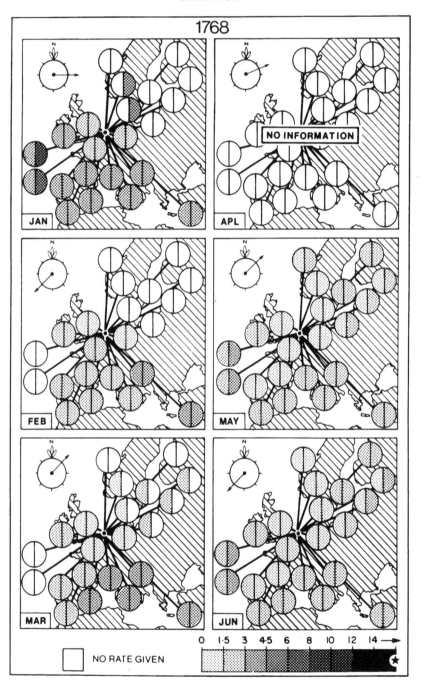

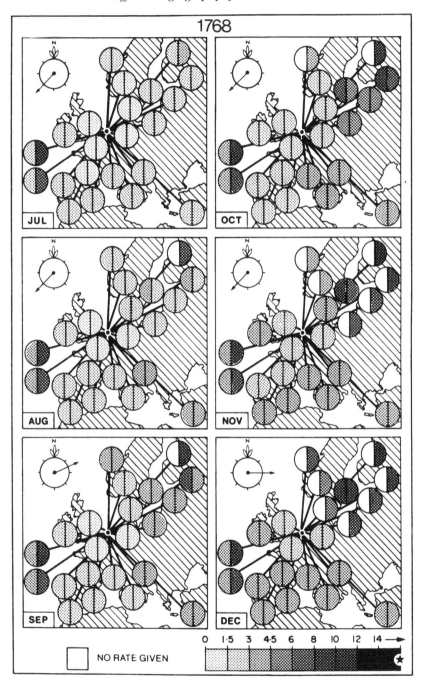

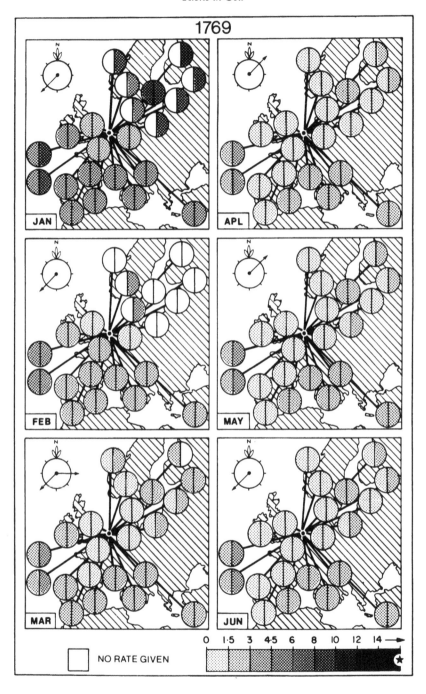

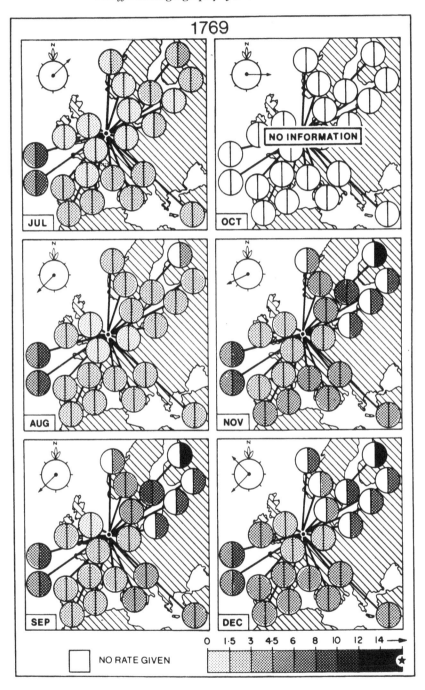

1769

JUL

OCT   NO INFORMATION

AUG

NOV

SEP

DEC

0   1·5   3   4·5   6   8   10   12   14 →

NO RATE GIVEN

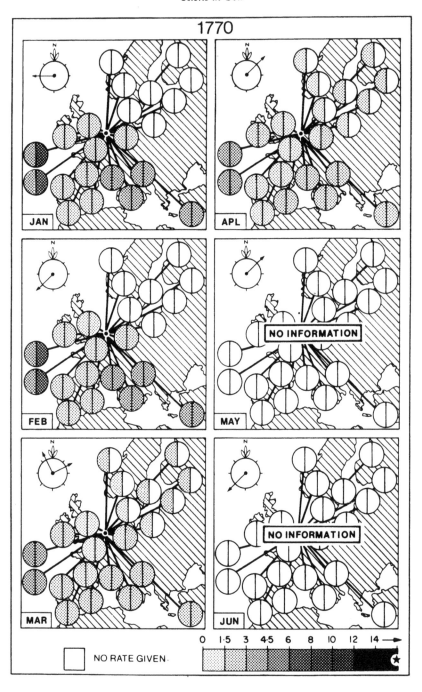

1770

JAN   APL

FEB   MAY   NO INFORMATION

MAR   JUN   NO INFORMATION

0   1·5   3   4·5   6   8   10   12   14 ⟶

NO RATE GIVEN.

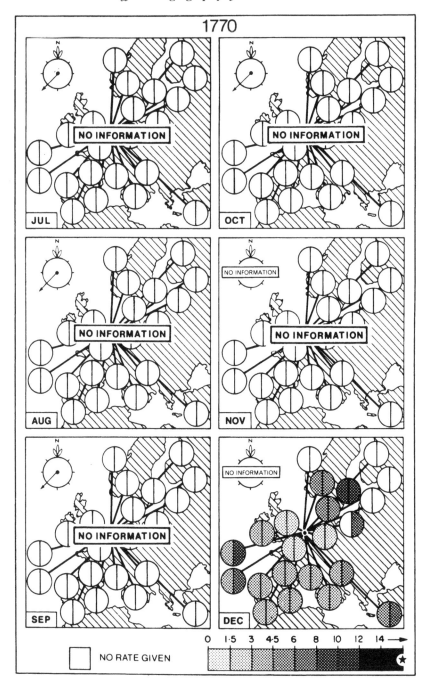

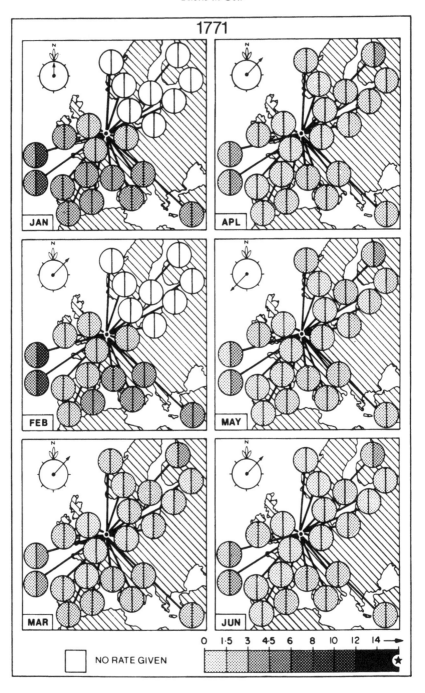

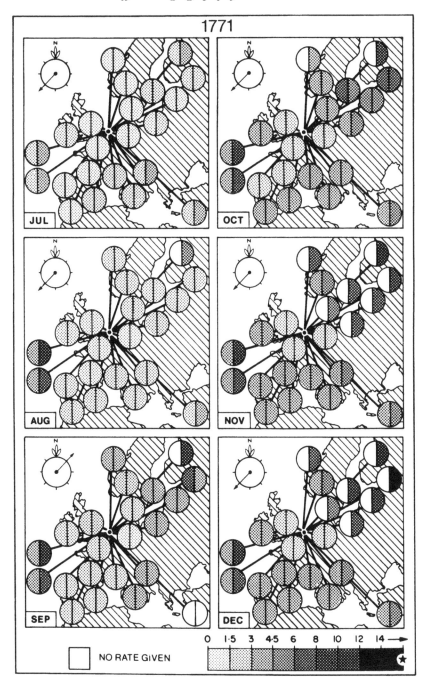

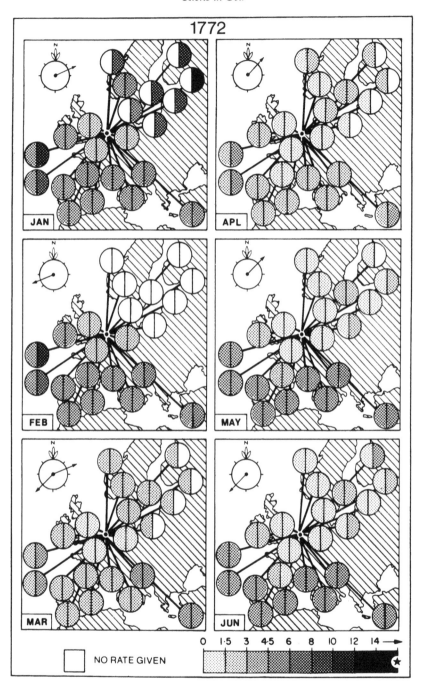

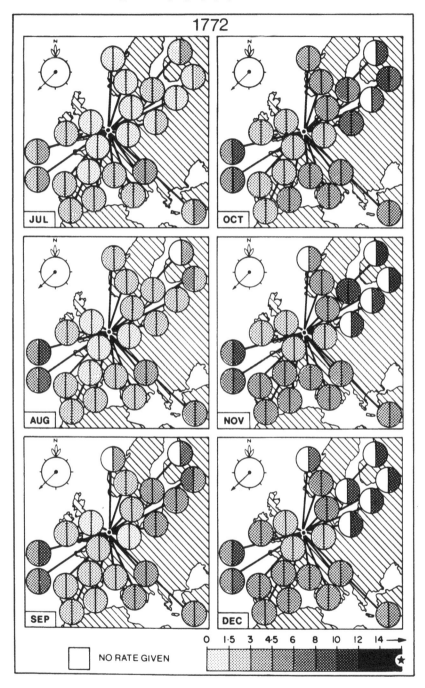

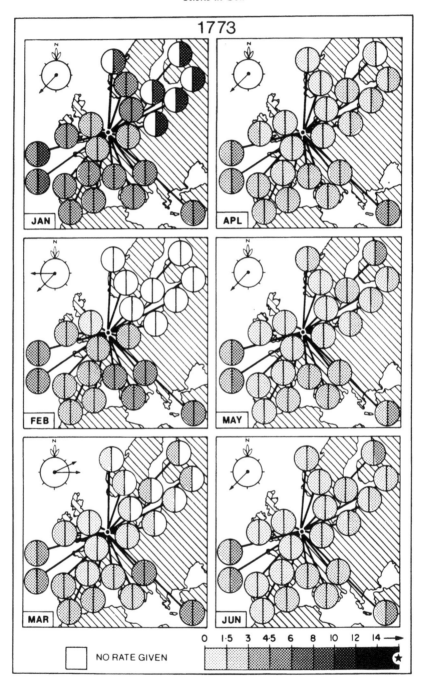

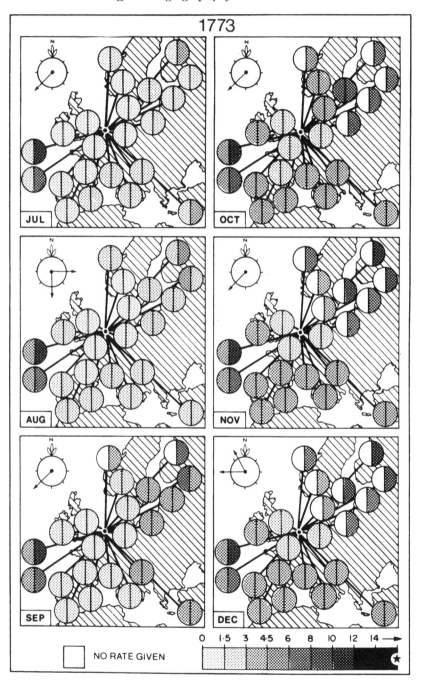

1773

JUL

OCT

AUG

NOV

SEP

DEC

NO RATE GIVEN

0 1·5 3 4·5 6 8 10 12 14 ——➤

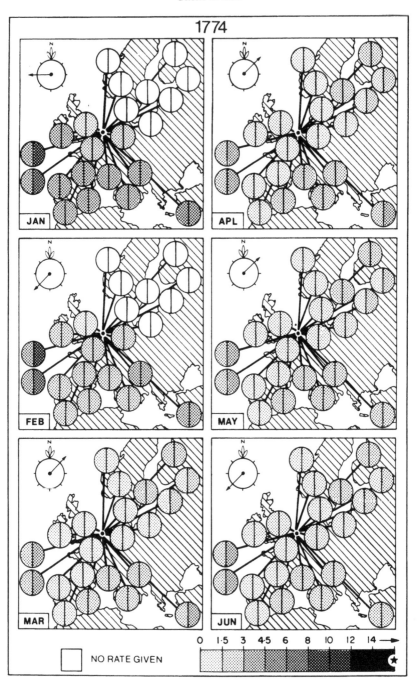

1774

JAN

FEB

MAR

APL

MAY

JUN

NO RATE GIVEN

0   1·5   3   4·5   6   8   10   12   14 →

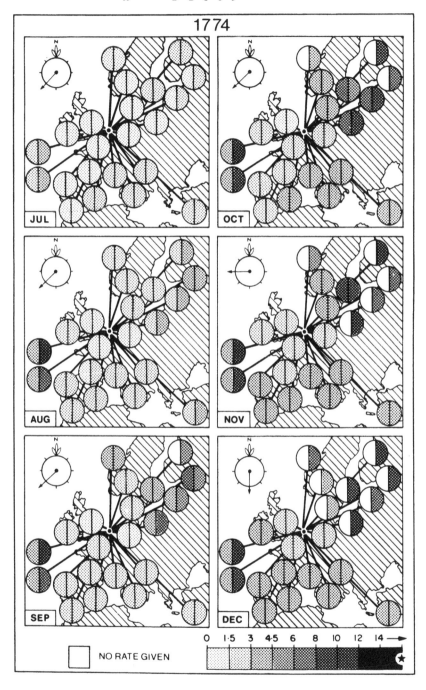

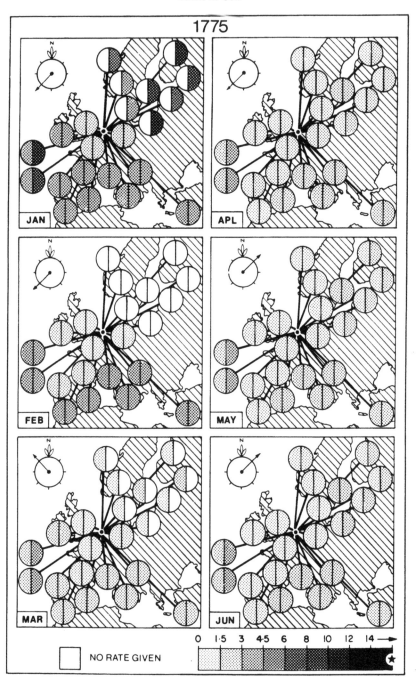

1775

JAN APL

FEB MAY

MAR JUN

NO RATE GIVEN

0   1·5   3   4·5   6   8   10   12   14 →

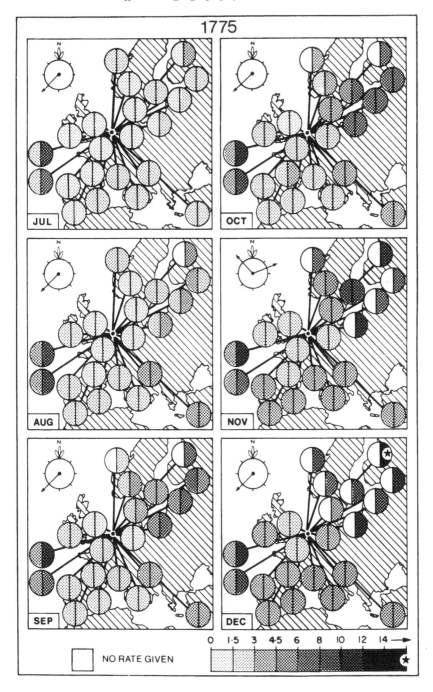

1775

JUL   OCT
AUG   NOV
SEP   DEC

0 1·5 3 4·5 6 8 10 12 14 ⟶

NO RATE GIVEN

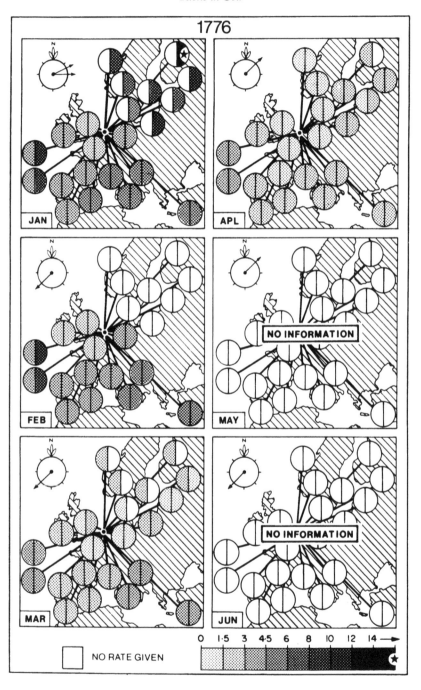

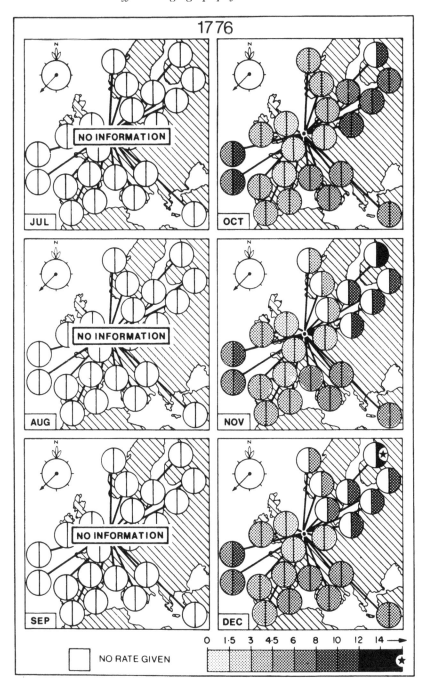

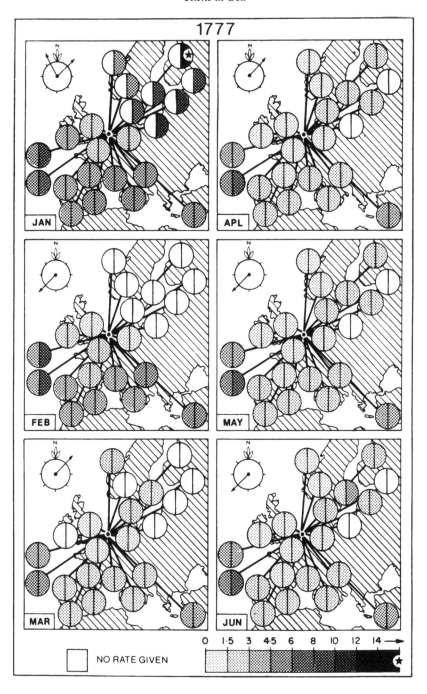

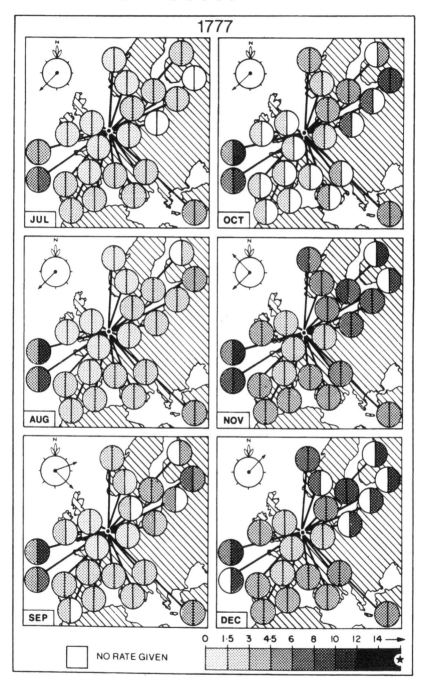

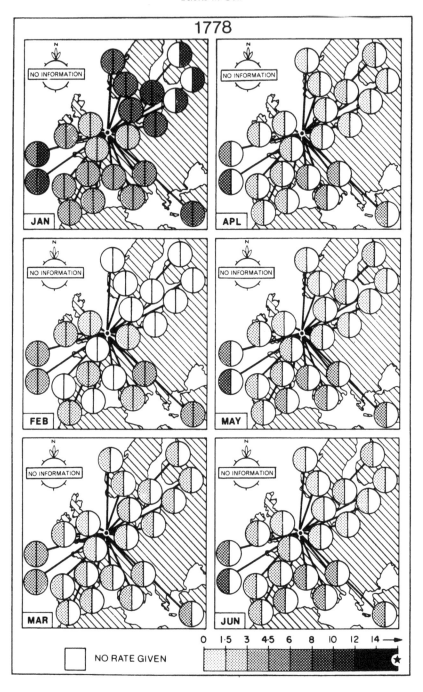

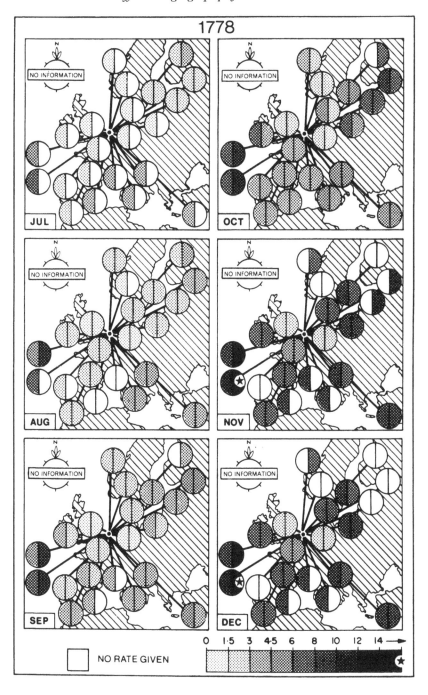

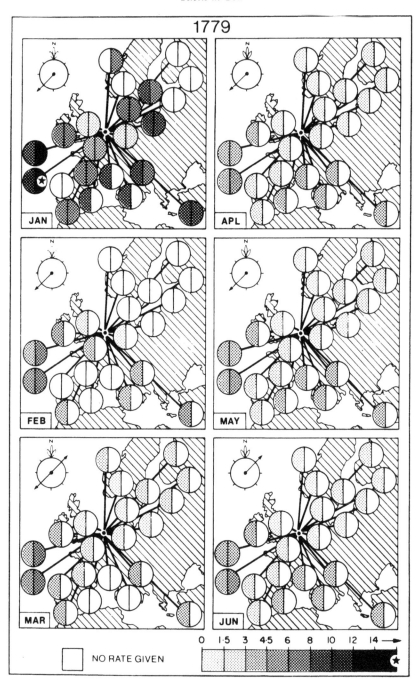

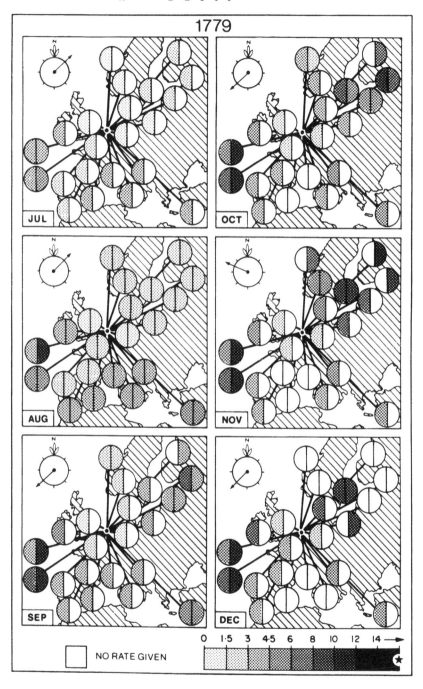

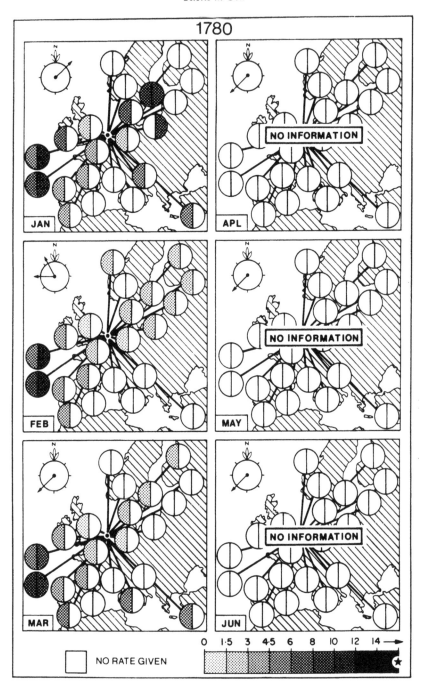

1780

JAN

APL — NO INFORMATION

FEB

MAY — NO INFORMATION

MAR

JUN — NO INFORMATION

NO RATE GIVEN

0 1·5 3 4·5 6 8 10 12 14 ⟶

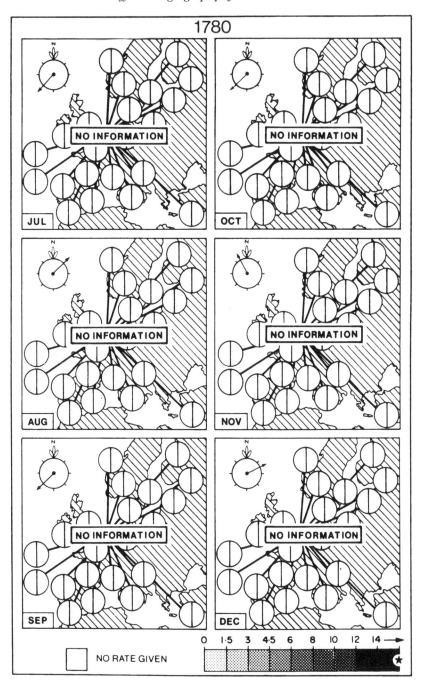

1767. Quotations for Archangel and the Baltic began again in March; and the rates for other destinations quickly improved. An optimal season stretched from April to July. The reversal from this also developed quickly in the North. In September, outward rates to Archangel were not listed, but continued until November for Stockholm/Norrköping. Most returns nevertheless were given but were increasingly high: in the case of Archangel they reached an upper limit of 12 percent in December. For the West Indies, favourable rates stretched from April to July.

1768. The *prijscourant* for April is missing. The earliest start for the optimal season could have been in this month. However, premiums for Archangel and Bergen/Trondheim do not appear until May. The general movement is then clear and continues until July – and for London, Yarmouth and Hull until September. While outward rates for most destinations in the Baltic were at an end in November, with the exception of Stockholm/Norrköping, which with other returns continued into January. In the south-east, there were few signs as yet of the gathering disputes which filled the gazettes, when dominant Russian armies pursued Polish insurgents into Ottoman lands; and the Sultan with the aid of France began the series of confrontations which were to drag on until the uneasy peace of 1774. For the West Indies, there are no quotations in February–March, so that the first list appears in May and together with June made a summer 'low'.

1769. The year opened well: most ports, including the Baltic and North, made the lists in March. In this year, the optimal season was somewhat shorter – April to June, with London, Yarmouth, Hull, surviving until August. In the North, the reverse trend tended to gather rapid momentum. The upper range of returns from Archangel was quoted at 12 percent in September–December. There is no information for October but in November the outward rates had already disappeared for St Petersburg/Viborg and the ports along the southern Baltic. As for returns, these lasted until December. For the West Indies, the quotations in March–June promised a season of favourable navigation.

1770. The year appeared to open promptly. Preparations for the Baltic and North were in full swing in March and this appeared to usher in the optimal season. However, the lists are missing for May–November. When they start again in December the eastern Baltic, Gulf of Finland and northern Norway have already closed. Quotations for Stockholm/Norrköping and for southern Sweden and southern Norway (both outward and return) and the southern Baltic (returns) continued. In the south-east of Europe, however, there was tension. The Russian fleet had sailed from the Baltic, through the Straits of Gibraltar, and with the aid of English officers on 6 July grappled off Cesme with the Turkish fleet, which in turn was supported by France.[6] The rates for the Archipelago and Syria probably soared during the autumn: already in December they were up by half. Other destinations in the Mediterranean shared the disturbance. By the new year, calmer affairs returned, and provided relative relief in the winter recess. In the West Indies, rates were slightly higher in March–April; but it would be difficult to attribute these to the rising dispute over the Falkland Islands (1771).

1771. After such commotions, the year seemed to open as usual in March, with quotations outward for all destinations. An optimal season stretched from April to July, with specially low rates for London–Hull and for western France in June–July. The autumn and early winter showed growing tensions: in November, there are no outward rates for northern Norway, Archangel, and the Baltic – which this time included Stockholm/Norrköping. In December, a 10 percent return premium appeared for voyages from Archangel and 12 percent from St Petersburg/Viborg. There were high rates from the other Baltic ports, which carried over into January. Can some of this excitement be attributed to the alarm over the threat of plague to the ports, for it had already caused panic in Moscow in February? Through 1771 and 1772 the maritime nations of western Europe took increasing precautions, setting aside areas for quarantine, as much in Hamburg as in Holland and elsewhere.[7] And in the Levant, too, further alarm as Russian troops moved through the Crimea. In September, there were no quotations for the Archipelago; in October and on into February, the premiums were up by about a quarter. For the West Indies, return premiums included convoy rates in February–March (which brought them down by half). In the Falkland Islands dispute, the unwillingness of France to implement the *pacte familiale* promoted a relatively peaceful settlement.

1772. The atmosphere of disturbance carried into the new year, bringing a fresh crop of troubles: financial crises which were particularly acute in Amsterdam and London; partition in Poland; conflict in south-eastern Europe; hurricane disaster in the West Indies. These combined to push up premiums. The traces of tension experienced and pending had not disappeared from the lists when activity picked up in March. For much of western Europe, the optimal season was from April to July; for London Yarmouth, and Hull, it went on until September. Areas of special tension, however, revealed themselves in the Mediterranean *en*

---

[6] See above, Chapter 5, p. 178.
[7] See above, Chapter 3, pp. 88–89.

bloc. South-western Spain (Cádiz–Seville) and Portugal were provided with convoy rates in May–June, which halved the going premiums. Even in the autumn and on into January, the market remained above normal. As for the North and the Baltic, another sensitive zone, late summer had already brought a brisk change, finalising months of tension. On 5 August, Austria, Prussia and Russia clawed away large tracts of Polish territory. The trading positions of Baltic ports were altered. Premiums for the southern group (Königsberg, Danzig, Pomerania, and Lübeck) leapt 2 points above the normal outward rate and 3 for the return. Quotations disappeared for Reval/Riga and for most of the Baltic in November; and even for Stockholm/Norrköping in December. By then, the return rates from Archangel and from the east and south Baltic (reaching from St Petersburg/Viborg to Lübeck) were unusually high – all in December–January were listed at 10 percent. While Europe bristled, the West Indies seemed to follow its own interests: even the August hurricane, so disastrous to those in its path, did not seem to unhinge insurance forecasts in the Amsterdam market.

1773. As the new year opened, more than a few financiers gasped at the news of the procession of bankruptcies in Amsterdam, London, and elsewhere. Even so, the outlook for insurance dealings did not seem to depart from the norm. The 'year' may have started somewhat later, but by May all was in its place and in full swing. Optimal conditions prevailed in May–July; for London, Yarmouth, and Hull an exceptionally low rate (¾ percent) from April to July. The year in the North closed finally in December and with generally reduced rates – but the returns remained high for St Petersburg/Viborg (8 per cent) and Archangel (10 percent). And with the new year, offers for these destinations were not in sight. For the Levant, high rates at 5 percent continued into January. And in the West Indies, an optimal season from March to June, then rising quotations: from Surinam the upper rate was 10 percent, and this lasted from July to December.

1774. The year began under the sign of financial recovery and started briskly in March, with all outward rates listed. An optimal season lasted until August (for London from February to September, with specially low rates of ¾ percent from March to July). The treaty of Kuchuk Kainarji (21 July 1774) gave Russian merchant ships access to the Black Sea so that one point of tension at least was resolved for the time being. A measure of safety returned to the eastern Mediterranean. In the north of Europe, however, it appeared that conditions of the previous year continued. Tension marked the southern Baltic: from Königsberg, Danzig, Pomerania, and Lübeck the returns were at 10 percent in

November–January. The same applied from Archangel. Even for Stock-
holm/Norrköping, outward rates disappeared in December; and the
returns reached 8 percent in November–January. The West Indies were
not exempt: return premiums from Surinam reached an upper 10 percent
in August and stayed there until January.

1775. The carry-over into January set a tense note for the beginning of
the new year. And the dark foreboding of the battles of Lexington and
Concord (19 April) promised major troubles ahead. The stress did not
abate: in February, an unusual instance, convoy rates were listed for all
destinations from Portugal to the Levant. These disappeared in March
when preparations as usual seemed to be underway. An optimal season
ensued from April to July (for London, February to October with
premiums of ¾ percent from May to July). However, the confrontations
and rising tensions in North America soon made their presence felt. The
Baltic, a reservoir of the strategic materials of war, soon responded to
both growing demand and increasing uncertainty: by December the
return rates from Russia were high – 10 percent from St Petersburg/
Viborg, 14 per cent from Archangel – which continued into January.
Stockholm/Norrköping were not listed outward in December and then
the return was at 9 percent. In the eastern Mediterranean, too, premiums
were above the norm – at 5½ percent outward and return in December–
January. And again the West Indies, where the return rates from Surinam
moved to an upper range of 10 percent in September and remained there
until the following February.

1776. This was a year of both decision and contradictory movements.
The declaration of independence in Philadelphia was a time for colonial
Spain to found the settlement of San Francisco, for Adam Smith to
publish his *Wealth of Nations*, for Robert Turgot to issue the liberating
Six edicts. However, the evidence of insurance is far from clear: the
Amsterdam *prijscouranten* are missing for the five crucial months May–
September. When they start again, high premiums were the rule – in the
Mediterranean, the premiums for the region from Syria to Venice were
at 5 percent moving to 5½ in December and January. By December the
rate to and from Cádiz was 4 percent, returns from the Baltic from Reval
to Lübeck at 10, from Archangel at 14. From November, Stockholm/
Norrköping were without return rates. However, the West Indies
appeared to show nothing out of the ordinary, as if the islands were
basking in the sun in the lull before the storms to come.

1777. For the basin of the North Sea the year progressed without too
much commotion – an optimum season from March–April to July–
August which for London was prolonged into September (the low ¾

percent premium lasted until July). As summer gave place to autumn and winter, the quotations appeared to have less and less co-ordination. This prevailed in the North and Baltic which commanded strategic materials and naval stores. The destinations St Petersburg/Viborg and from Königsberg to Lübeck were not listed at all in February–July – the former reached 10 percent in December–January 1778. Returns from Archangel were listed at this level from November to January. Cádiz/Seville in September and all the destinations from Venice to Ireland in October were without return premiums. The West Indies were not excluded, for the upper return rate went to 10 percent in August (convoys were at 4 percent) and stayed at this level until January. If anything, the quotations in the insurance market were beginning to show signs of faltering.

1778. The rising level of tension in Europe carried into open conflict in March with war between France and England: it was the storm cloud which the Spanish ambassador in The Hague observed stretching across half the world from Azov to Boston.[8] In the basin of the North Sea, the optimal season can be discerned in March–September (for Hamburg/Bremen) and February–September (for London, Yarmouth, and Hull); but smooth days were perhaps over when premiums for the latter group did not fall below 1 percent. Evidence of the growing tension came with the absence of quotations of return rates: in many instances they re-emerged only in August, and in some cases hardly at all until the end of the series in March 1780. For Cádiz/Seville, the outward summer rates were up at 2½ percent (2 percent in August) and went to 6 percent in November–December. In the Mediterranean, there was further tension. No rates were given in August for the coast from Genoa to Málaga; while by November navigation outward to the Mediterranean *en bloc* went at premiums of 8 percent. Perhaps most telling were the rates for the West Indies, where the island colonies of The Netherlands turned into depots for smugglers. While in happier days the navigation to and from Surinam seemed more vulnerable, Curaçao, the smuggler's haunt, now moved into front place: in November returns from the former went at 12 percent and from the latter at 15 percent. These rates continued into January.

1779. Again, exceptional conditions pointed to the widening impact of war. In February, there were no listings for Biscay, Portugal and the Mediterranean coast from Genoa to Málaga. In the last case, this continued and was joined by Sicily, Naples, and Leghorn – in effect, the western basin of the Mediterranean. For the whole range of destinations,

[8] See above, Chapter 3, pp. 96–97.

with the exception of the West Indies, no return premiums were quoted from February to July. In June, Spain and Britain were finally at open war. By July the official despatch had reached the fortress of Gibralter and the siege (1779–83) was on. From Genoa to Málaga there were no listings from October to the end of the series. Cádiz/Seville and Lisbon, Setúbal and Oporto went at 4 percent in December–January. By December, the listings were sporadic, and for Archangel, Norway, and the Baltic only a quarter of the slots were filled. In the West Indies, the upper levels for returns settled at 10 percent for Surinam/Berbice (August–February) and Curaçao (November–January).

1780. The lists for the quarter January–March confirm the uncertainties of the market in time of spreading war. Return premiums were given only from the West Indies. For the Mediterranean as a whole, only two rates in March (outward for the Archipelago/Syria and Sicily, Naples, Leghorn) and then at 5 percent compared with 2 and $1\frac{3}{4}$ respectively in 1769. Premiums for Cádiz were on offer in March at 5 percent and Lisbon at 4 (both at $1\frac{1}{2}$ in 1769). For the Baltic and the North, there were large gaps in March with only outward rates for Archangel (a normal $1\frac{1}{2}$ percent as in 1769), Stockholm/Norrköping at 2 percent ($1\frac{1}{2}$ in 1769), and Copenhagen, the Sound and Belt at $1\frac{1}{2}$ ($1\frac{1}{4}$ in 1769). But this was the time of discussions for Armed Neutrality. By the end of the year, The Netherlands found itself at war with Britain, the culmination of five years of growing disruption in trade and investment, which cast so much into doubt and mutual dispute.

PREVAILING WINDS AT DEAL

The atlas of monthly maps has a final sequence of data: the prevailing wind directions at Deal. The grand days of sail and the growth of London had brought fortune to this coastal town. The excellent open anchorage gave reprieve from the tortuous estuary of the Thames – already Samuel Pepys (1660) had noted the numerous wrecks there in the fairway, their masts standing from the water like navigation marks. The famous Deal luggers – fine-lined, deep-keeled, and with three masts, in the eighteenth century – were designed for launching from the shelving gravel beach to make speedy trips to ships at anchor and in most weather conditions. Little surprise then that Deal became a preferred out-port for London. Ships homeward-bound from the oceans to the North Sea could discharge passengers in a hurry to reach the city, or send off urgent news and letters. On the outward voyage, they could pick up last orders and assignments. Lloyd's List reported the daily wind direction there with an assiduous regularity.[9] The winds at Deal served as key information for ship movements.

A first essay on the data gives prevailing winds. These are the median monthly wind directions and have been placed in the top left-hand corner of each map in the Atlas.

A second essay on the same material gives the combined result for the whole period 1766–80 (see Map 2). Little surprise when the data show that winds from the south-west quarter (SSW, SW, and WSW) predominated: these occupied about a third of the reports. The north-east (NNE, NE, and ENE) came in second place with a fifth. Set against the map of Europe, the annual aggregate of these wind directions mark out a corridor coasting the profile of the continent from Portugal to the Skaggerak. It held a central core of maritime economies – above all, the Netherlands, France, and England. Little wonder that national interest sometimes overrode more pragmatic considerations when it came to depend on that fickle element. Early in 1780 a fierce gale scattered the English fleet returning home from Jamaica, which the French agent in Amsterdam, Grand, reported to Vergennes in Paris: 'It is the first time', he wrote with rueful satisfaction, 'that the winds have failed to be English.'[10]

Around the coasts of Europe, the location of registry had perhaps more than a passing word to say in the scheme of navigation. Sailings could benefit from this natural axis of south-west/north-east, but changes in course also called for special skills. Entering and sailing in the Baltic presented challenges with which Dutch captains successfully contended, clearly enjoying an accumulated fund of experience in shipbuilding and ship-handling.

There were, of course, variations in the pattern during the season of navigation. Here we must turn again to the problem raised in Chapter 4 that the Baltic could best be served by summer voyages, receiving cargoes from the South assembled in less favourable months. How did the winds prevail over the season as a whole? Taking the data of wind direction at Deal for the twenty years 1763–82, the prevailing (median) winds by months are (results almost equal are split; a substantial number but less than half the mentions are in brackets):

---

[9] See above, note 4. Records of wind directions also exist for Zwanenburg near Amsterdam (1743–78), which present a number of difficult problems in interpretation; and for wind-force at Franeker, Friesland, established by J. H. van Swinden: see F. J. B. d'Alphonse, *Eenige Hoofdstukken uit het Aperçu sur la Hollande* in *Bijdragen tot de Statistiek van Nederland*, Nieuwe Volgreeks, I (1900), pp. 30–35.

[10] *AAE, CP, Hollande*, 540, fo. 296 vo., letter, Grand to Vergennes, Amsterdam, 23 March 1780; but see also, six months earlier, ibid., 537, fo. 330 ro., same correspondents, Amsterdam, 9 September 1779, when he had reported 'les voilà enfin Français'.

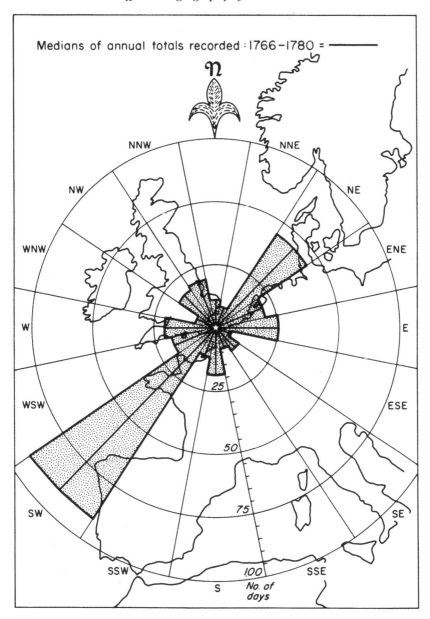

Map 2. Wind directions at Deal

Month	Prevailing wind direction
January	(SW)
February	SW
March	SW/NE
April	NE (SW)
May	NE/SW
June	SW (NE)
July	SW
August	SW
September	SW
October	SW
November	(SW)
December	(SW)

In going south in the spring, were ships sailing before the north-easters; and returning in June, taking advantage of changes to the south-west? The policies registered in the Rotterdam Maatschappij van Assurantie gave pride of place to the Baltic in the summer months. And voyages there, so it seems, could enjoy winds from the south-westerly quarter.

It need hardly be emphasised that these data refer to Deal, located at a critical site in the Channel to be sure, yet still a special case. Indeed, it would be contentious to pass from conditions prevailing at Deal to those in other ports in Europe; and even more from variations in wind direction to fluctuations in crops and seasonal movements. It is possible that the grain shortages in 1772 and 1773[11] coincided with longer spells of south-westerly and north-easterly winds at Deal; but the association has little rigour to carry conviction. In 1777, 112 out of 365 reports listed south-westerly winds – this in the year of extensive spring flooding in St Petersburg: ice floating downstream could become a serious problem when met by persistent winds from the south-west. Again, the information is too partial and Deal too far from the Zuiderzee to carry decisive weight on the floor of the Amsterdam Bourse.

★

In the wider context, what can be said to close this discussion of the atlas of maps? The twenty-two groups of destinations listed in the *prijscouranten* are overwhelmingly biased to the continent of Europe; only two are for Surinam and Curaçao, and these are still in the northern hemisphere. Trade flowed from the four corners of the world, but the great city, Amsterdam, often cited as an outstanding example of an early world-economy, still showed a marked partiality for the old world with all its limitations.

[11] See above, Chapter 3, p. 87.

Yet, set in this matrix of Europe, the optimum season for navigation is clear enough. The sequence is striking for the convergence in the summer months. All – or almost all – the sailings conformed to this benign pattern. Days which were favourable for harvesting were generally kind to navigation, and an agrarian world showed its best countenance in moving the produce of the land. Sailors and masters could join with peasants and yeomen in a moment of garnering and feasting the incomes of Michaelmas.

In the series of some fourteen years, the last five fall from the point and counterpoint of the seasonal movement and into the grasping vice of war. Unlike the universality of the former, armed conflict brought the regions to respond in varying measure. High premiums, gaps in quotations, absence of insurance on return cargoes – all these point to the rising risks in crossing the paths of warring nations. The Netherlands hankered after neutrality – indeed it was *de rigueur* in some strata of the society. What could be more logical in assigning priority to the northern trade, when it commanded strategic materials and a large share of the ton-kilometres at sea.

Lastly, the atlas sets out the rôle of The Netherlands to co-ordinate commercial flows around the coasts of Europe. That rôle had already contributed much in the convergence of the continental economy. However, it is necessary to distinguish between fluctuations around the equilibrium of the market, and a shift in the economic structures themselves. The seasonal movement can be placed in the first category; but the tensions and deteriorations of war were not so much a repetition of annual events, rather a profound change in the polity of Europe. What seemed a phase of equipoise carried price-tags of risk, and the 1770s evolved in a way progressively different from the years immediately after the Seven Years' War. The growth of Britain and the powerful interests of France created an axis of tension. At the same time, the rich endowments of the north-east of Europe deteriorated into the instability of change: a *coup d'état* in Sweden; expansionist tactics in Prussia; the carve-up of Poland; conflicts facing Russia in the Baltic, Turkey and the Cossack Steppes. As it turned out, the rift in North America decanted the issues in an Anglo-French war (March 1778), involving Spain (June 1779) and Armed Neutrality (August 1780), and The Netherlands (1780–84). These were bench-marks in reshaping for a spell the limits of security in navigation.

In Amsterdam, both insurers and insurance market, as we have seen,[12] bore heavy penalties for the political and economic uncertainties of 1778–84 and 1786–87. In such conditions, shippers and ship-owners did

[12] See above, Table 1 and Graph 1.

not hesitate too long in adopting the solution of disguise under a neutral flag. Well-placed ports, such as Hamburg, enjoyed windfall gains. So, too, Copenhagen, where the Sø-Assurance Kompagni found itself in the happy position of being able to hand out extraordinary dividends of 8 percent on underwriting during the war (1781–83).[13] We have only to put this into contrast with the gloomy losses turned in by the Maatschappij van Assurantie in Rotterdam (see Graph 3) during these very years to appreciate the unwelcome facets of national hostilities in international insurance.

[13] C. Thorsen, *Det Kongelig Oktroierede Sø-Assurance Kompagni, 1726–1926* (Copenhagen, 1926), pp. 234–235.

CHAPTER 7

~~~~~~

Conclusions

What reflections should close this study? My initial purpose was to study the provision of marine insurance in Amsterdam during a particular period: 1766–80. For this serial history, the *prijscouranten* offered an excellent observation point and the advantage of simultaneous reporting on a market with domestic ramifications. At the same time, in the spatial setting of an international economy, splendid Amsterdam coped on the one hand with the fertile heritage of a golden age, and on the other hand, as the decades passed, with inclinations to maturity in that activity. Clearly the eighteenth century hardly hesitated for a moment in assigning it a place of outstanding prestige among the markets of Europe. It enjoyed access to broadly based capital but the very nature of that democracy of wealth held impediments to easy expansion in new directions. Samuel Ricard[1] put a pertinent finger on its complex structure – perhaps there were fewer guilder millionaires than often supposed, but the wealthy nevertheless disposed of funds outside the immediate requirements of their business and these were ready for further investment. Nothing was simpler, he maintained, than to set up an enterprise on the Dam; but nothing more difficult than to hold out there without substantial assets. If anything, the performance of the insurance market tended to bear this out. The lines written in the policies for the *Haast U Langzaam* were for moderate amounts and consistent – about half were for f.1,000, giving the impression of an assured capacity to shift risks through the numbers of underwriters in the market and the diversity of their resources. The other side of the picture pointed to limitations: the tardy acceptance of corporative companies to broaden the capital base; and not least, the remarkable turnover among active underwriters themselves – a loss-rate of some 7 percent a year on average when times were good, and higher still under the shocks of war (1780–84) and political upheaval (1786–87).

---

[1] S. Ricard, *Traité*, I, p. 207.

Such internal problems went *pari passu* with external pressures from economic growth at the international level, where marine insurance found both freedom of manoeuvre and profit. When considered with the dispassionate eye of history, it is evident that early success left Amsterdam with vintage commitments to the past, and these were often burdens to resolve as Europe edged towards industrialisation. These frontiers of growth – they were also frontiers of risk, both technological and spatial – set the problem in a larger format and necessarily enter caveats on simple interpretations. Before closing this study, however, three dimensions to marine insurance and its market in Amsterdam call for special comment: the dynamic aspects and periodicities of marine protection; the structural problems of steady state in distance on the high seas and in coastal waters; and the spatial problems of Amsterdam in the wider context of economic growth in The Netherlands which conditioned the climate of risk-taking.

★

Firstly, the periodicities in the evolution of insurance premiums. In the short-term, the seasonal movement showed a distinct form, with affinities to other price fluctuations. This was the characteristic and dominant cycle of agrarian Europe; and the signing of policies, allowing for varying delays, was closely associated with the movement of ships and the transfers of commodities. The alternation of summer and winter made an indelible imprint on the risks of navigation.

In the long-term, progressive convergence in the market system of Europe was marked by a secular fall in insurance premiums through the seventeenth and eighteenth centuries, at least to the years 1765–74. This decade found a place in the trough of the protracted movement. The fall in premiums was most striking in the case of the Mediterranean and Levant, but all regions showed similar tendencies. They shared in the centuries of interdependence under the Republic.

The reversal from this downward trend into growing tension passed along a road sign-posted to war. It was long in preparation: the First Partition of Poland (1772); the re-opening of war in North America (1775–76), between Britain and France (1778) and Spain (1779); Armed Neutrality, and the Russian fleet setting course for the Mediterranean (1780), and the Fourth (and longest) Anglo-Dutch War (1780–84). In the closing decades of the eighteenth century, the rise in the level of premiums was small by comparison with the long-term fall which preceded it. In explanation, we should consider the conjuncture of both increasing risks from hostilities and of profound and liberating structural changes in the economy of Europe itself – convergence in markets, improvements in the capital base, and growth into industrialisation. These served to reinforce the access to wealth, but at the same time such widespread growth offered multipolar competition to Amsterdam from other centres such as Hamburg and Bremen, London and Rouen, Rotterdam and Antwerp. The absence of a clear hierarchy detracted from the efficiency of the market as referee. It often abandoned the outcome to the arbitrage of war. And that, for a time, introduced risks which escaped the competence of normal business activity.

*

A second set of comments relates to the structural interdependence of the system of navigation, and in particular the continuities and discontinuities of distance on the high seas and in coastal waters. The array of premiums shows a remarkable *linearity*. At least in 1769, a sample year of relative calm. Then, in the benign month of June, all regions seemed prompt to commune in summer harmony. The system tended to equilibrium in the short-term – the season; and in the long-term – the secular trend. Yet, in that relative equilibrium there remained a deep-seated dichotomy, which penetrated to the core of navigation in early modern Europe. On the one hand, there were the life and acquisitions of the high seas. In an agrarian world, the spatial freedom of navigation enjoyed significant continuity and opened the way for colonial plantations to cascade commodities onto the markets of Europe. At the same time, the linearity of premiums quoted followed a slope which promised economies of scale, for they did not double with twice the distance. Sailing on the high seas offered high growth potential.

On the other hand, this linearity of distance contended with a significant discontinuity. The regression of insurance premiums did not start from zero. The freedom of the high seas did not begin with casting off the mooring-lines, or manning the capstan to raise the anchor. There were the manoeuvres to leave harbour and set course along the coast, when ships' masters contended with risks of a different order. Often too, there were hazards in transferring cargoes by lighter from wharves to ships in the fairway: Dutch insurance policies were explicit in providing cover from the hour and day the consignments arrived on the quay rather than on the ship. And that completed, they faced the perils of setting sail and navigating close inshore.

Much of the navigation by Netherlands ships around the coasts of Europe was 'in soundings', not least in the North Sea, that hub of growth so similar in many respects to the western basin of the Mediterranean. Such sailing called the crew to different tasks: the watch in the bows; the look-out in the crow's nest; the duty-hand in the chains on the weather-side to heave the lead, test the bottom from the imprint on the tallow, 'singing', as Samuel Pepys recalled, the deeps and fathoms to the duty officer in the stern. Harbours and estuaries created what I have preferred to define as a risk-trap below which premiums rarely fell.

Organised pilotage and shipping industrialised with steam and steel in time offered a way to escape from the circle of obstacles. The need was there, and the inventions came early. We have only to turn to the steam tug of Jonathan Hulls (or Hull), a stern-wheeler patented on 12 December 1736, of which the details emerged in print in London the following year: '*Description and Draught of a new-invented Machine for carrying Vessels and Ships out of or into any Harbour, Port, or River against Wind and Tide, or in a Calm . . .*' At first a failure, success in tug and tow came later, virtually the original function of the steam-ship in the early nineteenth century. The full triumph of steam navigation in confined waters came perhaps with the Suez Canal,[2] when it was possible to fuse the categories of maritime risks at sea and in harbour, and create an effective continuity in trade, that great 'engine of growth'.[3] For the eighteenth century, the story was different. The spectrum of risks can be susceptible to explanations in a version of the 'turnpike theorem' – the system offered an initial stage of high costs in order to reach the 'turnpike' with its alternative high rates of return.[4] Yet in agrarian Europe the mariner had little choice in the matter. Ports were key transit-points which gave access to inland waterways, to the continental mass and its striving populations. The Dutch in their prime dominated the intricacies of coasting better than most. After all, twenty out of the twenty-two groups of destinations listed in the *prijscouranten* were in Europe. They created a co-ordinated web of risk and enterprise.

At the time, the problem did not emerge precisely in these terms, but was rather sensed, debated, even determined at another level. What proved to be an innovatory polemic for Hugo Grotius in *Mare liberum* (1609), a defensive contest for John Selden in *Mare clausum seu de dominio maris* (1635), continued into the definition of claims in Cornelis van Bynkershoek's *De dominio maris dissertatio* (1703 and 1744). Later it lay in the economic heartland of Adam Smith's *Wealth of Nations* (1776), in the marginal sovereignty of Ferdinando Galiani's *De' doveri de' principi neutrali verso i principi guerreggianti* (1782), and indeed, too, in the thesis of Admiral Mahan's *The influence of seapower on history* (1890). *Super altum mare*, the competing claims of national economies were variations on a theme, undetermined but rich in promise. Perhaps only the equanimity of a Jean-Jacques Rousseau (1712–78) could compose maritime liberties with the liberty of theory and obligation.

★

Thirdly, there are comments on the rôle of Amsterdam in the spatial

[2] F. C. Spooner, 'The Suez Canal and the growth of the international economy, 1869–1914', in *Mediterraneo e Oceano Indiano*, ed. M. Cortelazzo (Florence, 1970).

[3] D. Robertson, 'The future of international trade', *EJ*, XLVIII (1938), p. 5.

[4] See above, Chapter 4, note 39.

range of The Netherlands economy. The Dam inherited, scooped up the traditional flux and reflux of trade between North and South. As a focus of growth, in the sense of François Perroux's *pôle de croissance*, or as a network of development blocks, in the import of Erik Dahmén's *utvecklingsblock*,[5] it came to prosper in co-ordinating transactions when all the sea-lanes seemed to lead to the prestigious but dangerous Zuiderzee. In the eighteenth century this focal activity, this *world-system*, to return to Immanuel Wallerstein's apt terminology,[6] still resisted determined challenges to coasting across climatic zones and freighting regional flows of commodities.[7] The implicit opportunities accordingly developed all the appropriate devices and techniques: corporations and flexible *rederijen*; markets, *wisselbanken*, and mechanisms; and not least the tentacles of a wide-ranging, international currency system. To supplement the famous *piezas de a ocho reales* which poured through Spain, The Netherlands mints produced three great trade coins, no less famous in their way, since they conformed to the design of navigation. There was the *leeuwendaalder* (1606–1713) for the Levant; the silver *dukaat* (1659) for the Baltic, where it gradually assumed the older name of *rijksdaalder* or *rixdalder*; and the silver *rijder* or *ducaton* (1659) for the Far East, exported by the VOC along with other bullion and specie. The consignments more often than not travelled by ship with attendant risks. Impetus to growth came, as the documents said, *uit de Zee*, in a substantial expansion of the maritime sector. This international dimension was long held apart from the domestic economy. A wisselbank charged an agio or differential between bank (or international) money and domestic currency. The *negotiepenningen* of *leeuwendaalder*, *dukaat* and *ducaton* contrasted with the *standpenningen* of silver *gulden* (1680 for Holland, 1694 for the Republic) and gold *rijder* (1606 and with face-value fixed on the coin in 1749) strictly for use as domestic payments and assets. The international bias of growth was all too evident.

Initially, the risks in navigation over a season were high, especially to the North. The Baltic straddled some of the best resources and naval stores available; the temperate regions of the continent could assemble cargoes of commodities and specie, even in the difficult months of winter and early spring, so that the potential market could clear. The basic tenet was to take time by the forelock, and so during the clement months of summer ships could maximise the profits of trade in those areas with

---

[5] F. Perroux, 'Economic space: theory and application', *QJE*, LXIV (1950), p. 95, and 'Note sur la notion de pôle de croissance', *Économie appliquée*, VIII (1955); E. Dahmén, *Svensk industriell företagarverksamhet: kausalanalys av den industriella utvecklingen, 1919–1939* (2 vols., Stockholm, 1950), I, pp. 66–71, which was happily drawn to my attention and explained by Alexander Gerschenkron.

[6] I. Wallerstein, *The modern world-system* (New York, 1974), pp. 8–10.

[7] Accarias de Sérionne, *La Richesse de la Hollande*, I, p. 58.

high elasticities of risk. The system could be said to converge in the short-term. In the matrix of trade, transactions tended to symmetry in the sense that in optimal conditions risks to the south approximated to those to the north. However, in order to take advantage of the favourable months for navigation in northern waters, it appears to have been necessary to sail southwards in some of the more difficult months. The *risk-averaging* of such a strategy tended then to include rates above the warranted minima of bilateral relations.

Winter, decisive in the North, came to explode that system and transform the spectrum of risks for the insurers of Amsterdam. Perhaps, as in the case of war, the market was not always fully willing to cope, for during the autumn dealers showed an inclination to withdraw from insurance business and leave Admiral Winter in command. The market was imperfect in that it did not always stretch to full cover. But high risks in the early days of expansion were covered by the profits of wide monetary and price differentials between regional markets.

The Republic in the splendour of its golden age can be said to have found its *métier* in a powerful surge to commercial convergence between continental markets.[8] This required an exceptional expansion of the coasting trade – the *grand cabotage* so aptly described by Balthazar-Marie Emerigon – in which Dutch mariners excelled. They coped as entrepreneurs and innovators with a frontier of risks and uncertainties. Monetary and price convergence progressively eroded commercial profitability. And the culmination of this profound structural change may be said to have contributed in no small measure to the dilemma which The Netherlands faced in retaining as much a relative place in international trade, as the customary profile of its domestic economy.

★

The spatial dimension of the economy of the Republic surfaces in the well-ventilated problems of stagnation and growth, and more recently in the rôle of the efficiencies – or inefficiencies – of capital markets as factors in retarding industrialisation in The Netherlands. Joel Mokyr has admirably stressed the structural shortcomings of those capital markets in directing flows of wealth and investment into modern industrial undertakings.[9] James Riley equally admirably has pointed to the extraordinary propensity to save and accumulate – at some 10 percent he

---

[8] See the report by L. H. Klaassen, P. W. Klein, and J. H. P. Paelinck on 'Relations between regions of uneven development', with accompanying discussion, *Proceedings of the Sixth International Congress on Economic History* (1974) (Copenhagen, 1978), Themes, esp. pp. 104–105, and Proceedings, pp. 149–163; see also above, Chapter 2, note 138.

[9] J. Mokyr, *Industrialization in the Low Countries, 1795–1850* (New Haven, Conn., 1976), pp. 203–230; and his important review of conceptual problems in 'Industrialization in two languages', *EcHR*, XXXIV (1981).

suggests for most of the life of the Republic.[10] Both have proposed much to explain the complexity of the problem. In the long perspective, the degrees of freedom of the economy and their attendant risks may fall into three phases of growth. Each, in spite of the small size of the country and its extraordinary internal communications,[11] imposed heavy demands in re-location. There were the opulent days of Hansa cities in Ijsselstreek: Kampen, Zwolle and Deventer hosting fairs of repute, visited and furnished with cargoes from the 'best-practice' cogs of the northern trade.[12] The adventure of the Atlantic opened a second phase and passed the main chance to Amsterdam: the urban prodigy flexed its muscle in 1527 by taking the marker-buoys in the treacherous Zuiderzee from the grasp of Kampen.[13] Half a century later with independence declared from Spain, the mature eastern *foci* managed to claim their place in the federal democracy of the young Republic. However, the second phase of growth continued to accelerate, on into the golden days of the early seventeenth century, to give Amsterdam and Holland a good half share in all that was done. A third phase can be said to have begun in the eighteenth century, although this may appear paradoxical after so much has been written about decline, at least in the relative sense. It appears to have gathered momentum slowly by the mid eighteenth century and continued into the nineteenth. At the same time, it did not pass without gloomy days – for example, in the *Noorderkwartier*, which A. M. van der Woude has so admirably shown.[14] But the federal Republic in the mutation of revolution emerged into a unitary state under monarchy, in which Amsterdam asserted its acquired weight. The formal capital for the nation moved to the Dam (1808).[15]

[10] J. C. Riley, *International government finance and the Amsterdam capital market, 1740–1815* (Cambridge, 1980), pp. 11–12, 27, 96, 239.

[11] Jan de Vries, *The Dutch Rural Economy, 1500–1700* (New Haven, Conn., 1974), pp. 208–209.

[12] For the rôle of these cities and the co-ordination of the Hanseatic trade with the Venetian *galere da mercato*, see the map I contributed to *The Times Atlas of World History* (London, 1978), p. 144. For the Hanseatic *Kogge* (1380) in the Deutsches Schiffahrtsmuseum, Bremerhaven, see M. Schnyder, 'Die Bremer Hansakogge', *Neue Zürcher Zeitung*, 239 (1978), p. 75, and P. Heinsius, *Dimensions et caractéristiques des 'Koggen' hanséatiques dans le commerce baltique*, in *Le navire et l'économie maritime du nord de l'Europe du Moyen Age au XVIIIe. siècle* (Paris, 1969).

[13] Audrey Lambert, *The making of the Dutch landscape* (London, 1971), p. 149, citing E. Rijpma, *De ontwikkelingsgang van Kampen tot omstreeks 1600, vooral in de laatste jaren der 16e. eeuw* (Groningen, 1924).

[14] A. M. van der Woude, *Het Noorderkwartier. Een regionaal historisch onderzoek in de demografische en economische geschiedenis van westelijk Nederland van de middeleeuwen tot het begin van de negentiende eeuw*, AAG, Bijdragen, XVI (Wageningen, 1972).

[15] E. H. Kossmann, *The Crisis of the Dutch State, 1780–1813: Nationalism, Federalism, Unitarism*, in J. S. Bromley and E. H. Kossmann (eds.), *Britain and the Netherlands* (The Hague, 1971); S. Schama, *Patriots and Liberators: Revolution in the Netherlands, 1780–1813* (London, 1977), p. 586.

This long digression has the object of pointing to a defect of the system in which Amsterdam insurance operated. It was, after all, implicitly concerned with the short-term end of the capital market. The federal structure of the Republic failed to make a capital city out of Amsterdam in the sense that decision-making at all levels was co-ordinated. The States General met in The Hague; academe found its grove in Leiden; coinage for Holland was centred in Dordrecht; Utrecht retained an earlier prestige; Rotterdam mounted the watch on the Rhine. And perhaps more relevant to our purpose, the debts of the Republic remained – unevenly, to be sure – assigned to provincial administrations. It created flaws in co-ordinating the flow of funds to the financial centre, and defects in the capital markets on which Joel Mokyr has placed a heavy responsibility for poor industry-investment.[16] In unitary England, such accumulations of tax-payments in the provinces meshed into the seasonal flows of funds in the agricultural sector, through the agency of the famous country banks, inland bills of exchange, and the London money market. The Bullion Report of 1810 made it explicit that these funds reinforced commercial credit. All too often early industrial undertakings faced problems not so much in financing production as in finding markets. Such shortcomings in the heavily urbanised and high-wage Netherlands found slow solutions but did not leave the system of the insurance market untouched. As we have seen, the cohort of insurance dealers in Amsterdam bore the characteristics of private rather than corporate capital. This revealed itself in an assessment in 1851 when Amsterdam had more dealers and companies but capital resources on average inferior to those of Rotterdam.[17]

In the last phase of the Republic at the onset of a new and industrial epoch, Britain – and to some extent France – had an advantage among the nations of the North Sea hub in navigating with ships built bigger and designed for the oceans. These brought economies of scale and high potential in international trade, a sector for growth so well observed by Kenneth Berrill.[18] Such navigation could splice into the proven, persevering competence of Dutch coasting services which continued the old *beurtdiensten* to Bremen, Hamburg, Rouen, London, or refurbished the traditions of the Hanseatic *umlandsfarer*. A fast-growing port such as Rotterdam, admirably placed to promote trade with both Britain and

---

[16] See above, note 9; and R. T. Griffiths, *Industrial retardation in the Netherlands, 1830–1850* (The Hague, 1979), pp. 185–189.

[17] F. J. A. Broeze, 'Rederij', in G. Asaert et al., *Maritieme geschiedenis der Nederlanden*, III, p. 127.

[18] K. Berrill, 'International trade and the rate of economic growth', *EcHR*, XII (1960); R. Davis, *The rise of the English shipping industry* (Newton Abbot, 1962), pp. 71–73, 78–79: ships of 50–99 tons carried 11 tons per man and ships of 300 tons, 20 tons.

France, could thrive on new opportunities. In the eighteenth century, it acquired the nickname of 'Little London'. Little surprise then to find the Rotterdam Coffee House in the shadow of the London Stock Exchange collecting orders in 1778 for passengers and freight to cross the North Sea.[19] Or later, the General Steam Navigation Company carrying off the first postal contract for steam on the shuttle service from London to Rotterdam.[20] Indeed, national labels limit – distort even – a subtle reality. Distribution in Europe relied so much on coasting, and the masters of Dutch ships were able to offer an undeniable service. Even in the early twentieth century, cargo-ships returning to Britain from the Far East continued to receive sailing instructions marked 'Holland for orders'. These paid tribute to older practices and skills in navigating along the shores of the continent.

Such considerations focus on great zones of trade in deficit; the Baltic, the Levant, the Far East. The Amsterdam market offered insurance (at least officially in the *prijscouranten*) for the first two, and above all the Baltic. The last – the Far East – remained largely in the hands of the VOC, with the capacity to 'internalise' protection. Each, in different ways, was a form of risk-shifting in the mature opulence of a periwig age. Each, too, offered sidelights on the great and continuing debate about the economic decline of The Netherlands, for which the evidence is both voluminous and persuasive. When assessed by sectors, the performance of the economy in the international context – shipping against shipping; industry against industry; finance against finance – clearly revealed growing shortfalls in relative standing. Yet, at two levels, the conclusions that the economy of the Republic closed in decline must leave misgivings. On the one hand, a nation of two millions, and adaptable for that, placed at one of the junctions of Europe and endowed with the fortunes of business acumen could hardly run consistently counter to a tide of growth which already for half a century or more suffused the nations bordering on the North Sea or with access to the Atlantic. And on the other hand, there is the subsequent performance of the economy: in order to attain the high rates of increase in national income, coupled with substantial structural change between agricultural and non-agricultural sectors – both these shifts being evident in the mid

---

[19] *Simancas, Estado*, Leg. 7000, letter, Escarano to Floridablanca, London, 24 February 1778; see also R. H. Kraus (ed.), *Clio betaalt premie: historisch tafereel der verzekeringen* (Rotterdam, 1975), p. 41.

[20] H. C. Bos, *Economic growth in the Netherlands* (MS., Rotterdam, 1959), p. 10; J. H. van Stuivenberg, 'Economische groei in Nederland in de negentiende eeuw: en terreinverkenning', in *Bedrijf en samenleving. Economisch-historische studies over Nederland in de negentiende eeuw aangeboden aan Prof. Dr. I. J. Brugmans* (Alphen aan den Rijn, 1967), pp. 195–225; J. Teijl, 'Nationaal inkomen van Nederland in de periode 1850–1900', *EHJ*, XXXIV (1971), p. 262.

nineteenth century[21] – it seems necessary to have had some commensurate development in the last phase of the Republic. If the destiny of modern industrialisation in The Netherlands came late in the nineteenth century, set new patterns of risk, and favoured fresh pioneers, it should not obscure other possible forms of dependent wealth-making. In 1775, on the verge of great events, the enlightened Abbé Desnoyers can have a pertinent if not final word: 'the last bankruptcy in the world', he said,[22] 'will be that of Holland, and it will come when there are no longer either seas around the globe, or luxury among other peoples'.

---

[21] R. Weber, 'De paketboot Harwich–Hellevoetsluis legde de basis voor de rechtstreekse bootdienst op Engeland', *Ons Zeewesen*, L, 6 (1961); W. A. Engelbrecht, 'Het onstaan van den Hoek van Holland', *Rotterdamsch Jaarboekje*, 4e. R., II (1934).

[22] *AAE, CP, Hollande*, 528, fo. 14 vo., letter, Desnoyers to Vergennes, The Hague, 8 September 1775.

Monthly insurance premiums in Amsterdam
(January 1766 to March 1780)

The lists of premiums which follow have been taken from the *prijscouranten* of the Amsterdam Bourse. Usually one list exists for each month, occasionally two. In the latter case, the list given is the one closest to the fifteenth day of the month. Where a particular list gives a small 'spread' in the premiums, the upper figure is given, and indicated by an asterisk. Where possible, convoy rates are included; these are specially important in the case of voyages from the West Indies (Surinam/Berbice and Curaçao). The abbreviations 'Conv' = with convoy; 'Noco' = without convoy.

Risks at Sea

AMSTERDAM: MARINE INSURANCE RATES

Year: 1766

Month Outward/Return voyage	January Out	Ret	February Out	Ret	March Out	Ret	April Out	Ret	May Out	Ret	June Out	Ret
Archipelago, Syria	5*	5*	3*	3*	2½	2½	2	2	2	2	2	2
Venice, Gulf	5*	5*	3*	3*	2½	2½	2	2	2	2	2	2
Sicily, Naples, Leghorn	4	4	2½	2½	2	2	1¾*	1¾*	1¾*	1¾*	1¾*	1¾*
Genoa, Marseilles	4	4	2½	2½	2*	2*	1¾*	1¾*	1¾*	1¾*	1¾*	1¾*
Barcelona, Alicante, Malaga	3½	3½	2¼*	2¼*	1¾*	1¾*	1½	1½	1½	1½	1½	1½
Cádiz, San Lucar, Seville	3	3½*	2	2	1½	1½	1½*	1½*	1½*	1½*	1½*	1½*
Lisbon, Setúbal, Oporto	3	3	2*	2*	1½*	1½*	1½*	1½*	1½*	1½*	1½*	1½*
Biscay, French Bight	3	3	1¾*	1¾*	1¼*	1¼*	1¼*	1¼*	1¼*	1¼*	1¼*	1¼*
Morlaix, St Malo, Rouen	2½	2½	1½	1½	1	1	1	1	1	1	1	1
London, Yarmouth, Hull	2	2	1½*	1½*	1*	1*	1*	1*	1*	1*	1*	1*
Cork, Dublin, Limerick	3*	3*	1¾	1¾	1½	1½	1½	1½	1½	1½	1½	1½
Archangel	—	—	—	10* (b)	—	—	—	—	—	—	—	—
Trondheim, Bergen	—	—	—	—	1½	1½	1½	1½	1½	1½	1½	1½
Norway, East of Naze	5	5	—	5*	1¼	1¼	1¼	1¼	1¼	1¼	1¼	1¼
Stockholm, Norrköping	—	—	—	—	1¾	1¾	1¾	1¾	1¾	1¾	1¾	1¾
Copenhagen, Sound, Belt	5	5	—	5*	1¼	1¼	1¼	1¼	1¼	1¼	1¼	1¼
Reval, Riga	—	—	—	—	1½*	1½	1½*	1½	1¼	1½*	1¼	1½*
St Petersburg, Viborg	—	—	—	—	1½*	1¾*	1½*	1¾*	1¼	1½*	1¼	1½*
Königsberg, Danzig, Pomerania, Lübeck	—	—	—	—	1¼	1½	1¼	1½	1¼	1½	1¼	1½
Hamburg, Bremen	2	2	1¼	1¼	1*	1*	1*	1*	1*	1*	1*	1*
Surinam, Berbice	3½	8	3*	4*	2½	3	2½	3	2½	3	2½	3
Curaçao	3½	6-8 (a)	3	4*	2½	3	2½	3	2½	3	2½	3

(a) 6-8   (b) 8-10

258

Appendix

AMSTERDAM: MARINE INSURANCE RATES
Year: 1766

Month Outward/Return voyage	July (14) Out	Ret	August Out	Ret	September (15) Out	Ret	October (13) Out	Ret	November Out	Ret	December Out	Ret
Archipelago, Syria	2	2	2½*	2½*	3*	3*	3½*	3½*	4*	4*	4*	4*
Venice, Gulf	2	2	2½*	2½*	3*	3*	3½*	3½*	4*	4*	4*	4*
Sicily, Naples, Leghorn	1¾*	1¾*	1¾	1¾*	2½	2½	3	3	3½*	3½*	3½*	3½*
Genoa, Marseilles	1¾*	1¾*	1¾	1¾*	2½	2½	3	3	3½*	3½*	3½*	3½*
Barcelona, Alicante, Malaga	1½	1½	1½	1½	2	2	3*	3*	3	3	3	3
Cádiz, San Lucar, Seville	1½*	1½*	1½	1½	2*	2*	2½	2½	3*	3*	3*	3*
Lisbon, Setúbal, Oporto	1½*	1½*	1½	1½	1¾*	1¾*	2½*	2½*	2½	2½	2½	2½
Biscay, French Bight	1¼*	1¼*	1¼	1¼	1½	1½	2	2	2½*	2½*	2½*	2½*
Morlaix, St Malo, Rouen	1	1	1	1	1¼	1¼	1¾*	1¾*	2*	2*	2*	2*
London, Yarmouth, Hull	1*	1*	1*	1*	1¼*	1¼*	1½	1½	1¾*	1¾*	1¾*	1¾*
Cork, Dublin, Limerick	1½	1½	1½	1½	1¾	1¾	2	2	2½*	2½*	2½*	2½*
Archangel	1¾*	3*	—	3½*	—	6* (a)	—	6-8 (b)	—	8	—	—
Trondheim, Bergen	1¼	1¼	1½	1½	—	4	—	5	—	6	—	—
Norway, East of Naze	1¼*	1¼*	1¼	1¼	2	2	3	3	—	5*	—	—
Stockholm, Norrköping	1¾	1¾	2	2	4	3½	5½	4½	—	8	—	—
Copenhagen, Sound, Belt	1¼	1¼	1¼	1¼	2	2	3	3	—	5*	—	5
Reval, Riga	1½*	1½*	1¾*	1½	3½	3½*	5	4	—	6*	—	—
St Petersburg, Viborg	1½	1¾*	2¼*	2	6	4½*	7	5	—	8*	—	—
Königsberg, Danzig, Pomerania, Lübeck	1¼	1½*	1¾*	1¾	3	3	5	5	—	5½*	—	—
Hamburg, Bremen	1*	1*	1*	1*	1¼*	1¼*	1½	1½	2	2	2	2
Surinam, Berbice	3*	4-8	3	4-8	3	4-8	3	6-8	3½*	8	3½*	8
Curaçao	3	4-6	3	4-6	3	6	3	6	3½*	6	3½*	6

(a) 5-6   (b) 6-8, (?) convoy or 8*

259

Risks at Sea

AMSTERDAM: MARINE INSURANCE RATES   Year: 1767

Month / Outward-Return voyage	January Out	Ret	February Out	Ret	March Out	Ret	April Out	Ret	May Out	Ret	June Out	Ret
Archipelago, Syria	4	—	3	3	2¼*	2¼*	2	2	2	2	2	2
Venice, Gulf	4	4	3	3	2¼*	2¼*	2	2	2	2	2	2
Sicily, Naples, Leghorn	4*	4*	2½	2½	2	2	1½*	1½*	1¾*	1¾*	1¾	1¾
Genoa, Marseilles	3½	3½	2½	2½	2*	2*	1½	2*	1½	2*	1½	2*
Barcelona, Alicante, Malaga	3½*	3½*	2½	2½	1¾*	1¾*	1½*	1½*	1½*	1½*	1½*	1½*
Cádiz, San Lucar, Seville	3	3	2	2	1½	1½	1¼	1¼	1¼	1¼	1¼	1¼
Lisbon, Setúbal, Oporto	3	3	2*	2	1½*	1½*	1¼*	1¼*	1¼	1¼	1¼	1¼
Biscay, French Bight	3*	3*	1¾*	—	1¼*	1¼*	1	1	1	1	1	1
Morlaix, St Malo, Rouen	2½*	2½*	1¾*	2*	1	1	1*	1*	1*	1*	1*	1*
London, Yarmouth, Hull	2	2	1¼	1¾*	1*	1*	¾	¾	¾	¾	¾	¾
Cork, Dublin, Limerick	3*	3*	1¾	2*	1½	1½	1½*	1½*	1½*	1½*	1½*	1½*
Archangel	—	—	—	—	1½	—	1¼	—	1¼	—	1¼	—
Trondheim, Bergen	—	—	—	—	1½*	—	1¼	1¼	1¼	1¼	1¼	1¼
Norway, East of Naze	—	—	—	5*	1¼	1½*	1	1	1	1	1	1
Stockholm, Norrköping	—	—	—	—	1½	—	1½	1½	1½	1½	1½	1½
Copenhagen, Sound, Belt	—	5	—	5*	1¼	—	1	1	1	1	1	1
Reval, Riga	—	—	—	—	1½*	—	1¼	1	1¼	1½	1¼	1¼
St Petersburg, Viborg	—	—	—	—	1½	—	1¼	1½*	1¼	1¼*	1¼	1½*
Königsberg, Danzig, Pomerania, Lübeck	—	—	—	—	1¼	—	1¼	1½*	1¼	1½*	1¼	1½*
Hamburg, Bremen	2	2	1¼	1¾*	1*	1*	¾	¾	¾	—	¾	¾
Surinam, Berbice	3½*	8	3*	4	2½	3½*	2½	3	2½	3	2½	3
Curaçao	3½*	6	3	4	2½	3½*	2½	3	2½	3	2½	3

Appendix

AMSTERDAM: MARINE INSURANCE RATES — Year: 1767

Month	July		August		September		October		November		December	
Outward/Return voyage	Out	Ret	Out	Ret	Out	Ret	Out	Ret	Out	Ret	Out	Ret
Archipelago, Syria	2	2	2½*	2½*	3*	3*	4*	4*	4*	4*	4*	4*
Venice, Gulf	2	2	2½*	2½*	3*	3*	4*	4*	4*	4*	4*	4*
Sicily, Naples, Leghorn	1¾*	1¾*	1¾	1¾*	2½	2½	3½	3½	3½	3½	3½	3½
Genoa, Marseilles	1½	2*	1¾	1¾*	2½	2½	3½	3½	3½	3½	3½	3½
Barcelona, Alicante, Malaga	1½*	1½*	1½	1½	2	2	3½*	3½*	3½*	3½*	3½	3½
Cádiz, San Lucar, Seville	1¼	1¼	1½	1½	2*	2*	3	3	3	3	3	3
Lisbon, Setúbal, Oporto	1¼	1¼	1½	1½	1¾*	1¾*	2½	2½	2½	2½	3*	3*
Biscay, French Bight	1	1	1¼	1¼	1½*	1½*	2	2	2	2	2½	2½
Morlaix, St Malo, Rouen	1*	1*	1	1	1¼*	1¼*	1¾*	1¾*	1¾	1¾	2¼	2¼
London, Yarmouth, Hull	¾	¾	1*	1*	1¼*	1¼*	1½	1	1½	1½	1¾	1¾
Cork, Dublin, Limerick	1½*	1½*	1½	1½	1¾	1¾	2½*	2½*	2½*	2½*	3*	3*
Archangel	1¼	—	3	4*	—	4-6	—	6-10*	—	6-10*	—	8-12
Trondheim, Bergen	1¼	1¼	2*	2*	2½	2½	—	5	—	5	—	6
Norway, East of Naze	1	1	1½*	1½*	2	2	2½	2½	3½	3½	4*	4*
Stockholm, Norrköping	1½	1½	2½	2½	3½*	3½*	5½	4½	7	6	—	8
Copenhagen, Sound, Belt	1	1	1½*	1½*	2	2	2	2	3½	3½	4*	4*
Reval, Riga	1¼	1¼	1¾	1¾	3½	3½	2½	2½	—	6½*	—	6½*
St Petersburg, Viborg	1¼	1½*	3*	2½	5	3½*	7*	5*	—	8*	—	8*
Königsberg, Danzig, Pomerania, Lübeck	1¼	1½*	1¾	1¾	3*	2½*	4*	4	—	6	—	6
Hamburg, Bremen	¾	¾	1	1	1¼*	1¼	1½	1½	2	2	2	2
Surinam, Berbice	2½	3	3	4-8	3	4-8	3	4-8	3	4-8	3½	8 (a)
Curaçao	2½	3	3	4-6	3	6	3	6	3	6	3½	6

(a)   no entry but probably 4-8

261

Risks at Sea

AMSTERDAM: MARINE INSURANCE RATES Year: **1768**

Month Outward/Return voyage	January Out	January Ret	February Out	February Ret	March Out	March Ret	April Out	April Ret	May Out	May Ret	June Out	June Ret
Archipelago, Syria	4	4	3*	3*	4	4	No Information		2½	2½	2½	2½
Venice, Gulf	4	4	3*	3*	4	4			2½*	2½*	2*	2*
Sicily, Naples, Leghorn	4*	4*	2½	2½	3½*	3½*			2*	2*	2*	2*
Genoa, Marseilles	3½	3½	2½	2½	3½*	3½*			2*	2*	2*	2*
Barcelona, Alicante, Malaga	3½	3½	2½*	2½*	3½*	3½*			1¾*	1¾*	1¾*	1¾*
Cádiz, San Lucar, Seville	3½*	3½*	2¼	2¼	2½	2½			1½*	1½*	1½*	1½*
Lisbon, Setúbal, Oporto	3	3	2¼*	2¼*	2	2			1¼*	1¼*	1¼	1¼
Biscay, French Bight	3*	3*	2*	2*	1½	1½			1¼*	1¼*	1¼*	1¼*
Morlaix, St Malo, Rouen	2½*	2½*	1½	1½	1¼	1¼			1*	1*	1*	1*
London, Yarmouth, Hull	2	2	1	1	1	1			1*	1*	1*	1*
Cork, Dublin, Limerick	3	3	2*	2*	1¾*	1¾			1½*	1½*	1½*	1½*
Archangel	—	—	—	—	—	—			1½*	2	1½*	2
Trondheim, Bergen	—	—	—	—	—	—			1¼*	1½	1¼*	1¼*
Norway, East of Naze	—	5*	—	—	1¼	—			1¼*	1¼*	1¼*	1¼*
Stockholm, Norrköping	—	—	—	—	1¾	—			1½	1½	1½	1½
Copenhagen, Sound, Belt	—	5*	—	—	1¼	—			1¼*	1¼*	1¼*	1¼*
Reval, Riga	—	—	—	—	1½*	—			1¼	1½*	1¼	1½*
St Petersburg, Viborg	—	—	—	—	1½*	—			1¼	2*	1¼	2*
Königsberg, Danzig, Pomerania, Lübeck	—	—	—	—	1½*	—			1¼	1½*	1¼	1½*
Hamburg, Bremen	2	2	1	1	1	1			¾	¾	¾	¾
Surinam, Berbice	3½	4-8	—	—	—	—			2¼	3	2¼	3
Curaçao	3½	6	—	—	—	—			2½	3	2½	3

Appendix

AMSTERDAM: MARINE INSURANCE RATES   Year: **1768**

Month / Outward/Return voyage	July Out	July Ret	August Out	August Ret	September Out	September Ret	October Out	October Ret	November Out	November Ret	December Out	December Ret
Archipelago, Syria	2¼	2¼	3*	3*	3	3	3½*	3½*	3½	3½	4*	4*
Venice, Gulf	2¼	2¼	3*	3*	3	3	3½*	3½*	3½	3½	4*	4*
Sicily, Naples, Leghorn	2*	2*	2¼*	2¼*	2½	2	3*	3*	3	3	3½*	3½*
Genoa, Marseilles	1¾*	1¾*	2	2	2½*	2½*	3*	3*	3	3	3½*	3½*
Barcelona, Alicante, Malaga	1¾*	1¾*	2*	2*	2¼	2¼	2½*	2½*	3*	3*	3	3
Cádiz, San Lucar, Seville	1½	1½	1¾	1¾	2	2	2¼*	2¼*	3*	3*	3	3
Lisbon, Setúbal, Oporto	1½	1½	1¾*	1¾*	2*	2*	2¼*	2¼*	2½	2½	3*	3*
Biscay, French Bight	1¼	1¼	1½	1½	1½	1½	2*	2*	2½*	2½*	3*	3
Morlaix, St Malo, Rouen	1	1	1¼*	1¼*	1¼	1¼	1¾*	1¾*	2*	2*	2½	2½
London, Yarmouth, Hull	1*	1*	1	1	1	1	1½	1½	1¾*	1¾*	2	2
Cork, Dublin, Limerick	1¾	1¾	1¾	1¾	1¾	1¾	2¼*	2¼*	3*	3*	3	3
Archangel	2½*	4*	—	4-6	—	4½-8*	—	5-8*	—	6-10*	—	6-10*
Trondheim, Bergen	1¾*	1¾*	2½*	2½	3	3	—	4	—	5	—	6
Norway, East of Naze	1¼	1¼	1½	1½	2¼	2¼	2	2	—	3½*	—	4½*
Stockholm, Norrköping	2*	2*	3*	2½	3½	3½	6	5	8	7	9	8
Copenhagen, Sound, Belt	1¼	1¼	1½	1½	2¼*	2½*	2	2	3	3	—	4½*
Reval, Riga	1½	1½	2½*	2	3½*	3½*	5	5*	—	6*	—	7*
St Petersburg, Viborg	2*	1¾*	3½*	2½	6*	4*	8*	6*	—	7½*	—	8*
Königsberg, Danzig, Pomerania, Lübeck	1¾*	1½*	2	2	3½*	3½*	4½	5*	—	6*	—	6½*
Hamburg, Bremen	1*	1*	1	1	1¼	1¼	1½	1½	1¾*	1¾*	2	2
Surinam, Berbice	2½	4-8	3	4-8	3	4-8	3	4-8	3½*	8	3½	8
Curaçao	2½	4-6	3	6	3	6	3	6	3½*	6	3½	6

263

Risks at Sea

AMSTERDAM: MARINE INSURANCE RATES Year: 1769

Month Outward/Return voyage	January Out	Ret	February Out	Ret	March Out	Ret	April Out	Ret	May Out	Ret	June Out	Ret
Archipelago, Syria	4*	4*	2½	2½	2	2	2	2	2	2	2	2
Venice, Gulf	4*	4*	2½	2½	2	2	2	2	2	2	2	2
Sicily, Naples, Leghorn	3½*	3½*	2½*	2½*	1¾	1¾	1¾*	1¾*	1¾*	1¾*	1¾*	1¾*
Genoa, Marseilles	3½*	3½*	2½*	2½*	1½	1½	1½	1½	1½	1½	1½	1½
Barcelona, Alicante, Malaga	3	3	2	2	1½	1½	1½	1½	1½	1½	1½	1½
Cádiz, San Lucar, Seville	3	3	2*	2*	1½*	1½*	1¼	1¼	1¼	1¼	1¼	1¼
Lisbon, Setúbal, Oporto	3*	3*	1¾	1¾	1½*	1½*	1¼	1¼	1¼	1¼	1¼	1¼
Biscay, French Bight	3*	3	1¾*	1¾*	1¼*	1¼*	1	1	1	1	1	1
Morlaix, St Malo, Rouen	2½	2½	1½*	1½*	1*	1*	1*	1*	1*	1*	1*	1*
London, Yarmouth, Hull	2	2	1¼*	1¼*	1*	1*	1*	1*	1*	1*	1*	1*
Cork, Dublin, Limerick	3	3	1¾	1¾	1½*	1½*	1¼	1¼	1¼	1¼	1¼	1¼
Archangel	—	6-10*	—	—	1½*	—	1¼	2	1¼	2	1¼	2
Trondheim, Bergen	—	6	—	—	1¼*	2	1¼	1¼	1¼	1¼	1¼	1¼
Norway, East of Naze	—	4½*	—	3	1¼*	1¼*	1	1	1	1	1	1
Stockholm, Norrköping	9	8	—	—	1½	1½	1½	1½	1½	1½	1½	1½
Copenhagen, Sound, Belt	—	4½*	—	3	1¼*	1¼*	1	1	1	1	1	1
Reval, Riga	—	7*	—	—	1¼	1½*	1¼*	1¼*	1¼*	1¼	1¼*	1¼
St Petersburg, Viborg	—	8*	—	—	1½*	2*	1¼	1½	1¼	1½	1¼	1½
Königsberg, Danzig, Pomerania, Lübeck	—	6½*	—	—	1¼	1½	1¼	1¼	1¼	1½*	1¼	1½*
Hamburg, Bremen	2	2	1¼	1¼	1*	1*	¾	¾	¾	¾	¾	¾
Surinam, Berbice	3½	8	3*	3	2½	3	2½*	3	2½*	3	2½*	3
Curaçao	3½	6	3*	3	2½	3	2½*	3	2½*	3	2½*	3

Appendix

AMSTERDAM: MARINE INSURANCE RATES

Year: 1769

Month Outward/Return voyage	July Out	July Ret	August Out	August Ret	September Out	September Ret	October Out	October Ret	November Out	November Ret	December Out	December Ret
Archipelago, Syria	2	2	2½*	2½*	3	3	No Information		3½	3½	4*	4*
Venice, Gulf	2	2	2½*	2½*	3	3			3½	3½	4*	4*
Sicily, Naples, Leghorn	1¾*	1¾*	2¼*	2¼*	3*	3*			3	3	3½*	3½*
Genoa, Marseilles	1½	1½	2	2	2½	2½			3	3*	3½*	3*
Barcelona, Alicante, Malaga	1½	1½	2*	2*	2½	2½			3	3	3	3
Cádiz, San Lucar, Seville	1½*	1½*	1¾*	1¾*	2	2			3*	3*	3	3
Lisbon, Setúbal, Oporto	1½*	1½*	1½	1½	2*	2*			2½	2½	3*	3*
Biscay, French Bight	1¼*	1¼*	1½*	1½*	1¾*	1¾*			2½*	2½*	3*	3*
Morlaix, St. Malo, Rouen	1*	1*	1¼*	1¼*	1½*	1½*			2*	2*	2½*	2½*
London, Yarmouth, Hull	1*	1*	1	1	1¼	1¼			1¾*	1¾*	2	2
Cork, Dublin, Limerick	1¼	1¼	1¾*	1¾*	2*	2*			2½	2½	3	3
Archangel	1½	4*	—	4	—	5-12*			—	6-12	—	7-12
Trondheim, Bergen	1¼	1½	2*	2*	—	5			—	5	—	6
Norway, East of Naze	1	1	1½	1½	3	3			3	3	—	4
Stockholm, Norrköping	1¾	1¾	2½	2½	8	7			8	7	—	8
Copenhagen, Sound, Belt	1	1	1½	1½	3	3			3	3	—	4
Reval, Riga	1¼	1¼	1¾*	1¾*	—	6*			—	6*	—	6
St. Petersburg, Viborg	1½	2*	2½*	2	—	7			—	7	—	7
Königsberg, Danzig, Pomerania, Lübeck	1¼	1¾*	1¾*	1¾*	—	6*			—	6*	—	6*
Hamburg, Bremen	¾	¾	1	1	2*	2*			2*	2*	2	2
Surinam, Berbice	3*	4-8	3	4-8	3	4-8			3	4-8	3½*	4-8
Curaçao	3*	4-6	3	6	3	6			3	6	3½*	6

Risks at Sea

Month Outward/Return voyage	January Out	January Ret	February Out	February Ret	March Out	March Ret	April Out	April Ret	May Out	May Ret	June Out	June Ret
Archipelago, Syria	3½*	3½*	3	3	2½	2½	2	2	No Information			→
Venice, Gulf	3½*	3½*	3	3	2½	2½	2	2				
Sicily, Naples, Leghorn	3	3	3*	3*	2	2	1¾*	1¾*				
Genoa, Marseilles	3	3	3*	3*	1¾*	1¾*	1½	1½				
Barcelona, Alicante, Malage	2½	2½	2½	2½	1½	1½	1½	1½				
Cádiz, San Lucar, Seville	2½	2½	2¼*	2¼*	1½	1½	1¼	1¼				
Lisbon, Setúbal, Oporto	2½*	2½*	2*	2*	1½*	1½*	1¼	1¼				
Biscay, French Bight	2	2	1¾*	1¾*	1¼*	1¼*	1¼*	1¼*				
Morlaix, St Malo, Rouen	1¾	1¾	1½	1½	1	1	1	1				
London, Yarmouth, Hull	1½	1½	1¼	1¼	1*	1*	1*	1*				
Cork, Dublin, Limerick	2½*	2½*	2*	2*	1½	1½	1½	1½				
Archangel	—	—	—	—	1½	—	1½	—				
Trondheim, Bergen	—	—	—	—	1½	—	1¼	—				
Norway, East of Naze	—	—	—	—	1¼	—	1¼	—				
Stockholm, Norrköping	—	—	—	—	2*	—	1½	—				
Copenhagen, Sound, Belt	—	—	—	—	1¼	—	1¼	—				
Reval, Riga	—	—	—	—	1½	—	1½	—				
St Petersburg, Viborg	—	—	—	—	1½	—	1½	—				
Königsberg, Danzig, Pomerania, Lübeck	—	—	—	—	1¼	—	1¼	—				
Hamburg, Bremen	2	2	1½*	1½*	1	1½*	1	1½*				
Surinam, Berbice	3½	4-8	3*	4*-6	3*	4*	3*	4*				
Curaçao	3½	6	3*	4*-6	3*	4*	3*	4*				

Appendix

AMSTERDAM: MARINE INSURANCE RATES   Year: 1770

Month	July		August		September		October		November		December	
Outward/Return voyage	Out	Ret	Out	Ret	Out	Ret	Out	Ret	Out	Ret	Out	Ret
Archipelago, Syria	No Information										5*	6*
Venice, Gulf											4	5*
Sicily, Naples, Leghorn											4*	4*
Genoa, Marseilles											3½	3½
Barcelona, Alicante, Malaga											3½*	3½*
Cádiz, San Lucar, Seville											3½*	3½*
Lisbon, Setúbal, Oporto											3½*	3½*
Biscay, French Bight											3	3
Morlaix, St Malo, Rouen											2½	2½
London, Yarmouth, Hull											1½	1½
Cork, Dublin, Limerick											3	3
Archangel											—	—
Trondheim, Bergen											—	—
Norway, East of Naze											5	5
Stockholm, Norrköping											9	8
Copenhagen, Sound, Belt											5	5
Reval, Riga											—	—
St Petersburg, Viborg											—	—
Königsberg, Danzig, Pomerania, Lübeck											—	6
Hamburg, Bremen											2	2
Surinam, Berbice											3½	4·8
Curaçao											3½	6

AMSTERDAM: MARINE INSURANCE RATES **Year: 1771**

Month	January		February		March		April		May		June	
Outward/Return voyage	Out	Ret	Out	Ret	Out	Ret	Out	Ret	Out	Ret	Out	Ret
Archipelago, Syria	4	4	3	3	2½*	2½*	2¼*	2¼*	2¼*	2¼*	2¼*	2¼*
Venice, Gulf	4*	4*	3	3	2½*	2½*	2¼*	2¼*	2¼*	2¼*	2¼*	2¼*
Sicily, Naples, Leghorn	3½	3½	3*	3*	1¾	1¾	1¾	1¾	1¾	1¾	1¾*	1¾*
Genoa, Marseilles	3½*	3½*	3*	3*	1¾	1¾	1¾*	1¾*	1¾*	1¾*	1½	1½
Barcelona, Alicante, Malaga	3½*	3*	3*	3*	1½*	1¾* (sic)	1½	1½	1½	1½	1½	1½
Cádiz, San Lucar, Seville	3½*	3½*	2½*	2½*	1½	1½	1¼	1¼	1¼	1¼	1¼	1¼*
Lisbon, Setúbal, Oporto	3	3	2¼*	2¼*	1½	1½	1¼	1¼	1¼	1¼	1¼	1¼
Biscay, French Bight	3	3	2	2	1¼	1¼	1¼	1¼*	1¼*	1¼*	1	1
Morlaix, St Malo, Rouen	2½	2½	2	2	1	1	1	1	1*	1*	¾	¾
London, Yarmouth, Hull	1½	1½	1½*	1½*	1*	1*	1*	1*	1*	1*	¾	¾
Cork, Dublin, Limerick	3	3	2½	2½	1½	1½	1½	1½	1½	1½	1½*	1½*
Archangel	–	–	–	–	1½	4*	1½	4*	1½*	4*	1½*	2½-4*
Trondheim, Bergen	–	–	–	–	1½	2	1½*	2	1½*	2	1	1
Norway, East of Naze	–	–	–	–	1¼	1½	1¼*	1¼*	1¼*	1¼*	1	1
Stockholm, Norrköping	–	–	–	–	1½	2*	1½	1½	1½	1½	1½	1½
Copenhagen, Sound, Belt	–	–	–	–	1¼	1½	1¼*	1¼*	1¼*	1¼*	1	1
Reval, Riga	–	–	–	–	1¼	1½*	1½	1½	1¼	1½	1¼	1¼
St Petersburg, Viborg	–	–	–	–	1½	2*	1¼	2	1¼	2	1¼	1¼
Königsberg, Danzig, Pomerania, Lübeck	–	–	–	–	1¼	1¾*	1¼	1¾*	1¼	1¾*	1¼	1½
Hamburg, Bremen	2½*	2½*	2	2	1	1	1*	1*	1*	1*	¾	¾
Surinam, Berbice	4*	Conv 4 / Noco 8	3½*	Conv 3 / Noco 8*	2½	3	2½*	3	2½*	3	2½*	3
Curaçao	4*	? / Noco 6	3½*	Conv 3 / Noco 6	2½	3	2½*	3	2½*	3	2½*	3

Appendix

AMSTERDAM: MARINE INSURANCE RATES   Year: 1771

Month	July		August		September		October		November		December	
Outward/Return voyage	Out	Ret	Out	Ret	Out	Ret	Out	Ret	Out	Ret	Out	Ret
Archipelago, Syria	2½*	3*	2½	3	–	–	4	5	4	5	4	5
Venice, Gulf	2½*	3*	2½	3	3	3	4*	4*	4	5	4	5
Sicily, Naples, Leghorn	1¾*	1¾*	2*	2	3*	3*	3	3	4*	4*	4*	4*
Genoa, Marseilles	(a) (1½)	(1½)	1¾	2*	2½	2½	3	3	3½	3½	3½	3½
Barcelona, Alicante, Malaga	1½	1½	1¾*	1¾*	2½	2½	3*	3*	3½	3½	3½	3½
Cádiz, San Lucar, Seville	1¼	1¼*	1½	1½	2½*	2¼*	3*	3*	3	3	3	3
Lisbon, Setúbal, Oporto	1¼	1¼	1½	1½	2½*	2½*	2¾*	2¾*	3	3	3	3
Biscay, French Bight	1	1	1¼	1¼	2	2	2½	2½	3*	3	3	3
Morlaix, St Malo, Rouen	¾	¾	1	1	1¾	1¾	2¼	2¼	2½	2½	2½	2½
London, Yarmouth, Hull	¾	¾	1*	1*	1½*	1½*	1¾*	1¾*	2*	2*	2*	2*
Cork, Dublin, Limerick	1½*	1½*	1½*	1½*	2½*	2½*	3*	3*	3½	3½	3½	3½
Archangel	1½*	2½-4*	–	3-5*	–	4-8*	–	5-8*	–	10*	–	10*
Trondheim, Bergen	1	1	1½*	1½ⁱ	3½*	3½*	–	4	–	6	–	6
Norway, East of Naze	1	1	1½*	1½*	2*	2*	3½*	3½*	4	5½*	4	5½*
Stockholm, Norrköping	1¾	1¾	2½	2½	3½	3½	6	5	–	8	–	8
Copenhagen, Sound, Belt	1	1	1½*	1½*	2*	2*	3½	3½	–	5½	–	5½*
Reval, Riga	1¼	1¼	1¾	1¾	4*	3½	5½*	5*	–	7*	–	9*
St Petersburg, Viborg	1½*	1½	2½*	2	6*	4	7	6	–	8	–	12*
Königsberg, Danzig, Pomerania, Lübeck	1¼	1½*	1¾	1¾	3	3½*	4	5*	–	7*	–	7
Hamburg, Bremen	¾	¾	1	1	1¼	1¼	1¾*	1¾*	2½*	2½*	2½*	2
Surinam, Berbice	2½*	3	3	3-8*	3	3-8*	3½*	4-8	3½	4-8	3½	4-8
Curaçao	2½*	3	3	3-6	3	6	3½*	6	3½	6	3½	6

(a)   Damaged MS

269

AMSTERDAM: MARINE INSURANCE RATES   Year: 1772

Month / Outward/Return voyage	January Out	Ret	February Out	Ret	March (16) Out	Ret	April (30 March) Out	Ret	May Out	Ret	June Out	Ret
Archipelago, Syria	4	5	4	5	3*	4*	2½	4*	Conv 2 / Noco 4	Conv 2 / Noco 5*	Conv 2 / 4	Conv 2 / 5*—
Venice, Gulf	4	5	4	5	3*	4*	2½*	2½*	Conv 2 / Noco 4	Conv 2 / Noco 5*	Conv 2 / Noco 4	Conv 2 / Noco 5
Sicily, Naples, Leghorn	4*	4*	4*	4*	2	2	2*	2*	Conv 2 / Noco 4	Conv 2 / Noco 4	Conv 2 / Noco 4	Conv 2 / Noco 4
Genoa, Marseilles	3½	3½	3½	3½	1¾	1¾	1¾*	1¾*	Conv 2 / Noco 4	Conv 2 / Noco 4	Conv 2 / Noco 4	Conv 2 / Noco 4
Barcelona, Alicante, Malaga	3½	3½	3½	3½	1½	1½	1½	1½	Conv 2 / Noco 4	Conv 2 / Noco 4	Conv 2 / Noco 4	Conv 2 / Noco 4
Cádiz, San Lucar, Seville	3	3	3	3	1½*	1½*	1½	1½	Conv 1¾ / Noco 3½	Conv 1¾ / Noco 3½	Conv 1¾ / Noco 3	Conv 1¾ / Noco 3*
Lisbon, Setúbal, Oporto	3	3	3	3	1½*	1½*	1½*	1½*	Conv 1¾ / Noco 3½	Conv 1¾ / Noco 3½	Conv 1¾ / Noco 3	Conv 1¾ / Noco 3*
Biscay, French Bight	3	3	3	3	1½*	1½*	1¼	1¼	1½*	1½*	1½*	1¼*
Morlaix, St Malo, Rouen	2½	2½	2½	2½	1¼	1¼	1	1	1*	1*	1*	1*
London, Yarmouth, Hull	2*	2*	2*	2*	1	1	1	1	1*	1*	1*	1*
Cork, Dublin, Limerick	3½	3½	3½	3½	1¾	1¾	1½	1½	1½*	1½*	1½*	1½*
Archangel	—	10*	—	—	1½	—	1½*		1¼	—	1¼	4*
Trondheim, Bergen	—	6	—	—	1½*	1½	1¼	1¾	1	1	1	1
Norway, East of Naze	4	5½*	—	—	1½*	1½	1¼*	1¼*	1	1	1	1
Stockholm, Norrköping	—	8	—	—	2	2	2½	2½	1½	1½	1½	1½
Copenhagen, Sound, Belt	—	5½*	—	—	1½*	1½*	1¼*	1½*	1	1	1	1
Reval, Riga	—	9*	—	—	1½*		1¼	—	1¼	1¼	1¼	1¼
St Petersburg, Viborg	—	12*	—	—	1½*		1½*	—	1¼	1½	1¼	1½
Königsberg, Danzig Pomerania, Lübeck	—	7	—	—	1½*		1¼	—	1¼	1½	1¼	1½
Hamburg, Bremen	2½*	2	2½*	2	1*	1*	1*	1*	¾	¾	¾	¾
Surinam, Berbice	3½	4-10*	3½	4-10*	2½	3	2½	3	3	4	3	4
Curaçao	3½	6	3½	6	2½	3	2½	3	3	4	3	4

AMSTERDAM: MARINE INSURANCE RATES Year: 1772

Month Outward/Return voyage	July Out	Ret	August Out	Ret	September Out	Ret	October Out	Ret	November Out	Ret	December Out	Ret
Archipelago, Syria	2½	3*	3	3	3½	3½*	4	4½*	4	5*	4	5*
Venice, Gulf	3*	3*	3*	3*	3½	3½*	4*	4½*	4	5*	4	5*
Sicily, Naples, Leghorn	2	2	2	2	3*	3*	3	3	3½*	3½*	3½	3½
Genoa, Marseilles	2	2	2	2	2½	2½	3	3	3½*	3½*	3½	3½
Barcelona, Alicante, Malaga	2	2	2*	2*	2½*	2*	3	3	3½*	3½*	3½*	3½*
Cádiz, San Lucar, Seville	1½	1½	1¾	1¾	2	2	2½	2½	3	3	3	3
Lisbon, Setúbal, Oporto	1½	1½	1½	1½	2	2	2½	2½	3	3	3	3
Biscay, French Bight	1¼	1¼	1¼	1¼	1¾	1¾	2	2½*	3*	3	3	3
Morlaix, St Malo, Rouen	1*	1*	1	1	1½	1½	2*	2*	2	2¾*	2½	2½
London, Yarmouth, Hull	1*	1*	1*	1*	1	1	1½*	1½*	1¾*	1¾*	2*	2*
Cork, Dublin, Limerick	1½*	1½*	1¾*	1¾*	2	2	2½	2½	2½	2½	3	3
Archangel	1¼	4*	—	4*	—	6*	—	8*	—	10*	—	10*
Trondheim, Bergen	1	1	2	2	—	3*	4	4	—	5	—	7*
Norway, East of Naze	1	1	1½	1½	2	2	3½*	3½*	4	4	5*	5*
Stockholm, Norrköping	1½	1½	2½	2½	3½	3½	6	5	9	8	—	8*
Copenhagen, Sound, Belt	1	1	1½	1½	2	2	4*	4*	4	4	5*	5*
Reval, Riga	1¼	1¼	2½*	2	3½	3½*	—	6*	—	8*	—	10*
St Petersburg, Viborg	1¼	1½	5	2½*	7*	4*	9*	6	—	10*	—	10
Königsberg, Danzig, Pomerania, Lübeck	1¼	1½	2*	2	3½	3½*	6*	7*	—	8	—	10*
Hamburg, Bremen	¾	¾	1	1	1	1	1½*	1½*	2*	2*	2	2
Surinam, Berbice	2½	4*	3	4-8	3	4-8	3½*	4-8	3½	4-8	3½	4-8
Curaçao	2½	4*	3	3-6	3	4*-6	3½*	4-6	3½	6	3½	6

Risks at Sea

Month Outward/Return voyage	January Out	January Ret	February Out	February Ret	March Out	March Ret	April Out	April Ret	May Out	May Ret	June Out	June Ret
Archipelago, Syria	4	5*	3	4*	3*	4	3*	3*	2½	3*	2½	3*
Venice, Gulf	4	5*	3	3	3*	3½*	2	2	2	2	2	2
Sicily, Naples, Leghorn	3½	3½	3*	3*	2	2	1¾	1¾	1½	1½	1½	1½
Genoa, Marseilles	3½	3½	3*	3*	2	2	1¾*	1¾*	1½	1½	1½	1½
Barcelona, Alicante, Malaga	3½*	3½*	2½	2½	2*	2*	1½	1½	1½	1½	1½	1½
Cádiz, San Lucar, Seville	3	3	2½*	2½*	1½	1½	1½	1½	1¼	1¼	1¼	1¼
Lisbon, Setúbal, Oporto	3	3	2½*	2½*	1½	1½	1½	1½	1¼	1¼	1¼	1¼
Biscay, French Bight	3	3	2	2	1¼	1¼	1¼	1¼	1	1	1	1
Morlaix, St Malo, Rouen	2½	2½	2*	2*	1	1	1	1	1*	1*	1*	1*
London, Yarmouth, Hull	2*	2*	1	1	1*	1*	¾	¾	¾	¾	¾	¾
Cork, Dublin, Limerick	3	3	2*	2*	1½	1½	1½*	1¼	1¼	1¼	1¼	1¼
Archangel	—	10*	—	—	1½*	—	1¼	—	1¼	3	1¼	3
Trondheim, Bergen	—	7*	—	—	1¼	—	1	1¼	1	1½	1	1½
Norway, East of Naze	5*	5*	—	—	1	—	1	1	1	1	1	1
Stockholm, Norrköping	—	8	—	—	1½	—	1½	1½	1½	1½	1½	(1½)
Copenhagen, Sound, Belt	5*	5*	—	—	1	—	1	1	1¼	1¼	1¼*	1¼*
Reval, Riga	—	10*	—	—	1¼	—	1¼	1½	1¼	1½	1¼	1½
St Petersburg, Viborg	—	10	—	—	1½	—	1¼	1½	1¼	1½	1¼	1½
Königsberg, Danzig, Pomerania, Lübeck	—	10*	—	—	1¼	—	1¼	1½	1¼	1½*	(1¼)	1½
Hamburg, Bremen	2	2	2*	2*	1*	1*	1*	1*	¾	¾	¾	¾
Surinam, Berbice	3½	4-8	3	4*	2½	3	2½*	3	2½*	3	2½*	3
Curaçao	3½	6	3	4*	2½	3	2½*	3	2½	3	2½	3

Appendix

AMSTERDAM: MARINE INSURANCE RATES Year: **1773**

Month	July		August		September		October		November		December	
Outward/Return voyage	Out	Ret	Out	Ret	Out	Ret	Out	Ret	Out	Ret	Out	Ret
Archipelago, Syria	2½	3*	2½	2½	3	3	3½	3½	5*	5	5*	5
Venice, Gulf	2	2	2½*	2½*	3*	3*	3½	3½	4*	3½	4*	3½
Sicily, Naples, Leghorn	1½	1½	2*	2*	2	2	3	3	3½	3½	3½	3½
Genoa, Marseilles	1½	1½	2*	2*	2	2	3	3	3	3	3	3
Barcelona, Alicante, Malaga	1½	1½	1¾	1¾	2	2	3	3	3	3	3	3
Cádiz, San Lucar, Seville	1¼	1¼	1½	1¾*	1¾	1¾	3*	3*	3*	3*	3*	3*
Lisbon, Setúbal, Oporto	1¼	1¼	1	1¾*	1¾	1¾	3*	3*	3*	3*	3*	3*
Biscay, French Bight	1	1	1¼	1¼	1½	1½	2½	2½	3*	3*	3*	3*
Morlaix, St Malo, Rouen	1*	1*	1	1	1¼	1¼	2¼*	2¼*	2½*	2½*	2½*	2½*
London, Yarmouth, Hull	¾	¾	1	1	1	1	1½*	1½*	1½*	1½*	1½*	1½*
Cork, Dublin, Limerick	1¼	1¼	1¾	1¾	1¾	(a) (1¾)	3*	3*	3	3	3	3
Archangel	1¼	3	1¾	5*	—	6*	—	6	—	10*	—	10*
Trondheim, Bergen	1	1½	1¾*	1¾	—	3*	—	5*	—	6*	—	6*
Norway, East of Naze	1	1	1¼	1¼	2*	2*	3½*	3½*	—	4	—	4
Stockholm, Norrköping	1¾	1¾	2½	2½	3½	3½	7	6	—	9	—	9
Copenhagen, Sound, Belt	1¼*	1¼*	1¼	1¼	2*	2*	3½*	3½*	—	4	—	4
Reval, Riga	1¼	1½	1½	2*	4*	3½*	—	6	—	7½*	—	7½*
St Petersburg, Viborg	1¼	1½	3*	2	7*	4	—	7*	—	8*	—	8*
Königsberg, Danzig, Pomerania, Lübeck	1¼	1½	1½	2*	3½*	3½*	—	6	—	7½*	—	7½*
Hamburg, Bremen	¾	¾	1	1	1¼*	1¼*	2*	2*	2	2	2	2
Surinam, Berbice	2½	5*-10	3	5*-10	3	5*-10	3½*	5*-10	3½	5-10	3½	5-10
Curaçao	2½	4*-6	3	4-6	3	4-6	3½*	6	3½	4-6	3½	4-6

(a)   printed as 1¼ but probably in error

273

Risks at Sea

AMSTERDAM: MARINE INSURANCE RATES — Year: 1774

Month	January		February		March		April		May		June	
Outward/Return voyage	Out	Ret	Out	Ret	Out	Ret	Out	Ret	Out	Ret	Out	Ret
Archipelago, Syria	5*	5	3½	3½	2½	3	2½	3	2	2½	2	2½
Venice, Gulf	3½	3½	3	3	2	2½	2	2½	2*	2*	2*	2*
Sicily, Naples, Leghorn	3	3	2½	2½	1¾	1¾	1¾	1¾	1½	1½	1½	1½
Genoa, Marseilles	3	3	2½	2½	1¾	1¾	1¾	1¾	1½	1½	1½	1½
Barcelona, Alicante, Malaga	3	3	2¼	2¼	1½	1½	1½	1½	1½	1½	1½	1½
Cádiz, San Lucar, Seville	3*	3*	2	2	1¼	1¼	1¼	1¼	1¼	1¼	1¼	1¼
Lisbon, Setúbal, Oporto	3*	3*	2	2	1¼	1¼	1¼	1¼	1¼	1¼	1¼	1¼
Biscay, French Bight	3*	3*	1½	1½	1	1	1	1	1	1	1	1
Morlaix, St Malo, Rouen	2½	2½	1½*	1½	1*	1*	1*	1*	1*	1*	1*	1*
London, Yarmouth, Hull	1½*	1½*	1	1	¾	¾	¾	¾	¾	¾	¾	¾
Cork, Dublin, Limerick	3*	3*	1¾	1¾	1¼	1¼	1¼	1¼	1¼	1¼	1¼	1¼
Archangel	—	—	—	—	1½	1½	1½	1½	1½	1½	1½	1½
Trondheim, Bergen	—	—	—	—	1¼	1¼	1¼	1¼	1¼	1¼	1¼	1¼
Norway, East of Naze	—	—	—	—	1	1	1	1	1	1	1	1
Stockholm, Norrköping	—	—	—	—	1½	1½	1½	1½	1½	1½	1½	1½
Copenhagen, Sound, Belt	—	—	—	—	1¼	1¼	1¼	1¼	1¼	1¼	1¼	1¼
Reval, Riga	—	—	—	—	1¼	1½	1¼	1½	1¼	1½	1¼	1½
St Petersburg, Viborg	—	—	—	—	1¼	1½	1¼	1½	1¼	1½	1¼	1½
Königsberg, Danzig, Pomerania, Lübeck	—	—	—	—	1¼	1¼	1¼	1¼	1¼	1¼	1¼	1¼
Hamburg, Bremen	2	2	1½*	1½*	¾	¾	¾	¾	¾	¾	¾	¾
Surinam, Berbice	3	4-8	2½	3	2¼	3	2¼	3	2¼	3	2¼	3
Curaçao	3	4-6	2½	3	2¼	3	2¼	3	2¼	3	2¼	3

AMSTERDAM: MARINE INSURANCE RATES Year: 1774

Month Outward/Return voyage	July		August		September		October		November		December	
	Out	Ret	Out	Ret	Out	Ret	Out	Ret	Out	Ret	Out	Ret
Archipelago, Syria	2	2½	2½	3*	2½	2½	3½	3½	3½	4*	4*	4*
Venice, Gulf	2*	2*	2	2	2½	2½	3½*	3½*	3½	3½	4*	4*
Sicily, Naples, Leghorn	1½	1½	1¾	1¾	2½*	2½*	3	3	3½	3½	4*	4*
Genoa, Marseilles	1½	1½	1¾	1¾	2½*	2½*	3*	3*	3	3	3½*	3½*
Barcelona, Alicante, Malaga	1½	1½	1¾	1¾	2¼	2¼	3*	3*	3	3	3½*	3½*
Cádiz, San Lucar, Seville	1¼	1¼	1½	1½	2¼*	2¼*	2½	2½	3*	3*	3	3
Lisbon, Setúbal, Oporto	1¼	1¼	1½	1½	2	2	2½	2½	3*	3*	3	3
Biscay, French Bight	1	1	1¼	1¾*	2*	2*	2½*	2½*	2½	2½	3*	3*
Morlaix, St Malo, Rouen	1*	1*	1	1	1½	1½	2	2	2	2	2½	2½
London, Yarmouth, Hull	¾	¾	1*	1*	1	1	1¼	1¼	1½	1¾	1½*	1½*
Cork, Dublin, Limerick	1¼	1¼	1½	1½	1¾*	1¾*	2½	2½	2½	2½	3*	3*
Archangel	1½	1½	2	4*	—	5*	—	8*	—	10*	—	10*
Trondheim, Bergen	1¼	1¼	1½	1½	3*	3*	—	4*	—	5	—	6*
Norway, East of Naze	1	1	1½	1½	2½*	2½*	3*	3*	4	4*	—	4*
Stockholm, Norrköping	1¾	1¾	2½	2½	3½*	3½*	6	5	9	8	—	8*
Copenhagen, Sound, Belt	1¼	1¼	1½	1½	2½*	2½*	3*	3*	4	4*	—	4*
Reval, Riga	1¼	1½	2	3*	4	4½*	6*	8½*	—	7*	—	7*
St Petersburg, Viborg	1¼	1½	3½*	3*	7	5*	—	7*	—	7*	—	8*
Königsberg, Danzig, Pomerania, Lübeck	1¼	1¼	2	3*	4	6*	6*	8½*	—	10*	—	10*
Hamburg, Bremen	¾	¾	1	1	1¼	1¼	1¾*	1¾*	2	2	2½*	2½*
Surinam, Berbice	2¼	3	3	(a) 8*-10	3	(a) 8*-10	3½	(a) 8*-10	3½	8*-10	4*	8-10
Curaçao	2¼	3	3	4-6	3	4-6	3½	(b) 4-8*	3½	6*-8	4*	6-8

(a) 4, 6, 8 or 10   (b)   4 or 6-8

275

AMSTERDAM: MARINE INSURANCE RATES Year: **1775**

Month Outward/Return voyage	January		February with or without convoy		March		April		May		June	
	Out	Ret	Out	Ret	Out	Ret	Out	Ret	Out	Ret	Out	Ret
Archipelago, Syria	4*	4*	2-3½	2-3½	2¼*	2¼*	2¼*	2¼*	2	2	2	2
Venice, Gulf	4*	4*	2-3½	2½-3	2¼*	2¼*	2¼*	2¼*	2	2	2	2
Sicily, Naples, Leghorn	4*	4*	1¾-3	1¾-3	2	2	2*	2*	1¾*	1¾*	1¾*	1¾*
Genoa, Marseilles	3½*	3½*	1¾-3	1¾-3	1¾	1¾	1½*	1½*	1½	1½	1½	1½
Barcelona, Alicante, Malaga	3½*	3½*	1¾-3	1¾-3	1¾*	1¾*	1½*	1½*	1½	1½	1½	1½
Cádiz, San Lucar, Seville	3	3	1½-3	1½-3	1½	1½	1¼	1¼	1¼	1¼	1¼	1¼
Lisbon, Setúbal, Oporto	3	3	1½-2½	1½-2½	1½	1½	1¼	1½	1¼	1¼	1¼	1¼
Biscay, French Bight	3*	3*	1½*	1½*	1¼*	1¼*	1¼	1¼	1	1	1	1
Morlaix, St Malo, Rouen	2½	2½	1¼*	1¼*	1*	1*	1*	1*	¾	¾	¾	¾
London, Yarmouth, Hull	1½*	1½*	1	1	¾*	¾*	1*	1*	¾	¾	¾	¾
Cork, Dublin, Limerick	3*	3*	1¾*	1¾*	1½*	1½*	1¼	1¼	1¼	1¼	1¼	1¼
Archangel	—	10*	—	—	1¼	—	1¼	1½	1¼	2½*	1¼	2½*
Trondheim, Bergen	—	6*	—	—	1¼	—	1	1	1¼*	1¼*	1¼*	1¼*
Norway, East of Naze	—	4	—	—	1¼	—	1*	1*	1	1	1	1
Stockholm, Norrköping	—	8	—	—	2*	—	1½	1½	1½	1½	1½	1½
Copenhagen, Sound, Belt	—	4	—	—	1¼	—	1*	1*	1¼*	1¼*	1¼	1¼
Reval, Riga	—	7*	—	—	1¼	—	1¼	1½*	1¼	1½*	1¼	1½*
St Petersburg, Viborg	—	8	—	—	1½*	—	1¼	2*	1¼	1½*	1¼	1½
Königsberg, Danzig, Pomerania, Lübeck	—	10*	—	—	1¼	—	1¼	1½*	1¼	1½*	1¼	1½*
Hamburg, Bremen	2½*	2½*	1¼*	1¼*	1	1¼*	1*	1*	¾	¾	¾	¾
Surinam, Berbice	4*	8-10	3*	3 (a)	2½	3	2½*	3	2¼*	3	2¼*	3
Curaçao	4*	6-8	3*	3 (a)	2½	3	2½*	3	2¼	3	2½*	3

(a)   Probably convoy rate only

AMSTERDAM: MARINE INSURANCE RATES   Year: 1775

Month	July		August		September		October		November		December	
Outward/Return voyage	Out	Ret	Out	Ret	Out	Ret	Out	Ret	Out	Ret	Out	Ret
Archipelago, Syria	2	2½	3½*	4*	3½	4*	3½	4*	3½	4*	5½*	5½*
Venice, Gulf	2	2½	3	3½	3½	3½	3½	3½	3½	3½	5½*	5*
Sicily, Naples, Leghorn	1¾	2*	2½	2½	2½	2½	2½	2½	3½*	3½*	5½*	5½*
Genoa, Marseilles	1½	1½	2½*	2½*	2½	2½	2½	2½	3	3	4½	4½
Barcelona, Alicante, Malaga	1½	1½	2	2	2½	2½	2½	2½	3	3	4½	4½
Cádiz, San Lucar, Seville	1¼	1¼	1¾	1¾	2½	2½	2½	2½	3*	3*	4	4
Lisbon, Setúbal, Oporto	1¼	1¼	1½	1½	2	2	2	2	3*	3	4	4
Biscay, French Bight	1	1	1¼	1¼	1¾*	2½*	2	3*	2½	2½	3½	3½
Morlaix, St Malo, Rouen	¾	¾	1	1	1½	1¾*	1½	1½*	2	2½	2½	2½
London, Yarmouth, Hull	¾	¾	1*	1*	1	1	1	1	1½	1½	2	2
Cork, Dublin, Limerick	1¼	1¼	1¾	1¾	2	2	2	2	2½	2½	3½	3½
Archangel	1¼	3*	—	5*	—	6*	—	6*	—	10*	—	14*
Trondheim, Bergen	2*	2*	1½	1½	—	2½	—	3*	—	6	—	8*
Norway, East of Naze	1	1	1¼	1¼	2½	3*	2½	3*	4	5	—	6
Stockholm, Norrköping	1¾	1¾	2½	2½	4½	4	5½	6	8	8	—	9
Copenhagen, Sound, Belt	1¼*	1¼*	1¼	1¼	2½	3*	3½	3½	4	4	—	5
Reval, Riga	1¼	1½*	2*	4*	5½	6*	6	6*	—	7*	—	7
St Petersburg, Viborg	1½	1½*	4*	2½*	7	5	7	6	—	7*	—	10*
Königsberg, Danzig, Pomerania, Lübeck	1¼	1½*	2*	4*	5½	(a) 7*	6	(b) 6*	—	(c) 6½-10*	—	6½-10*
Hamburg, Bremen	¾	¾	1	1	1¼	1¼	1½	1½	2	2	3	3
Surinam, Berbice	2½	3*-8	3*	3*-8	3	4-10*	3½	4-10*	3½	4-10*	4	4-10*
Curaçao	2½	3-6	3*	3*-8	3	4-6	3½	4-8	3½	4-6	4	4-8

(a)   Probably convoy "6, 5½ and 7"   (b)   Probably convoy "5½, 6 and 5"   (c)   Probably convoy "6½, 7½ and 10"

AMSTERDAM: MARINE INSURANCE RATES   Year: **1776**

Month / Outward/Return voyage.	January Out	Ret	February Out	Ret	March Out	Ret	April Out	Ret	May Out	Ret	June Out	Ret
Archipelago, Syria	5½*	5½*	4½*	4½*	3	3	2½	2½	No Information	→		
Venice, Gulf	5½*	5½*	4½*	4½*	3	3	2½	2½				
Sicily, Naples, Leghorn	5½*	5½*	4½*	4½*	3	3	2½	2½				
Genoa, Marseilles	4½	4½	4	4	2½	2½	2	2				
Barcelona, Alicante, Malaga	4½	4½	4	4	2½	2½	2	2				
Cádiz, San Lucar, Seville	4	4	3½	3½	2	2	1¾*	1¾*				
Lisbon, Setúbal, Oporto	4	4	3	3	2	2	1½	1½				
Biscay, French Bight	3½	3½	3*	3*	1½	1½	1¼	1¼				
Morlaix, St Malo, Rouen	2½	2½	2½*	2½*	1¼	1¼	1	1				
London, Yarmouth, Hull	2	2	1¾*	1¾*	1¼	1½	1	1				
Cork, Dublin, Limerick	3½	3½	2½	2½	1½	1½	1½	1½				
Archangel	—	14*	—	—	1½	—	1½	—				
Trondheim, Bergen	—	8*	—	—	1½	—	1	1				
Norway, East of Naze	—	6	—	—	1½	—	1	1				
Stockholm, Norrköping	—	9	—	—	1½	—	1½	1½				
Copenhagen, Sound, Belt	—	5	—	—	1¼	—	1¼	1¼				
Reval, Riga	—	7	—	—	1¼	1¼	1¼	1½				
St Petersburg, Viborg	—	10*	—	—	1½	1¼	1½*	2				
Königsberg, Danzig, Pomerania, Lübeck	—	6½-10*	—	—	1½	1½	1½	1½				
Hamburg, Bremen	3	3	2½	2½	1¼	1¼	1	1				
Surinam, Berbice	4	4-10*	3	4-10*	3	3-4	3	3				
Curaçao	4	4-8	3	4-8	3	3-4	3	3				

Appendix

AMSTERDAM: MARINE INSURANCE RATES

Year: **1776**

Month	July		August		September		October		November		December	
Outward/Return voyage -	Out	Ret	Out	Ret	Out	Ret	Out	Ret	Out	Ret	Out	Ret
Archipelago, Syria	No Information					→	5*	5*	5*	5*	5½*	5½*
Venice, Gulf							5*	5*	5*	5*	5½*	5½*
Sicily, Naples, Leghorn							5*	5*	5*	5*	5	5
Genoa, Marseilles							4½*	4½*	4½*	4½*	4½*	4½*
Barcelona, Alicante, Malaga							4	4	4	4	4½*	4½*
Cádiz, San Lucar, Seville							3½*	3½*	3½*	3½*	4*	4*
Lisbon, Setúbal, Oporto							3	3	3	3	3½	3½
Biscay, French Bight							2½	2½	2½	2½	3	3
Morlaix, St Malo, Rouen							1¾	1¾	1¾	1¾	2½*	2½
London, Yarmouth, Hull							1½	1½	1½	1½	2	2
Cork, Dublin, Limerick							3	3	3	3	3	3
Archangel							—	(a) 5-10	—	12*	—	14*
Trondheim, Bergen							3	3	—	4	—	5
Norway, East of Naze							3	3	—	4	—	5
Stockholm, Norrköping							5	6	—	8	—	9
Copenhagen, Sound, Belt							3½	3½	—	4	—	6
Reval, Riga							6	9	—	10	—	10
St Petersburg, Viborg							7	7*	—	8	—	8
Königsberg, Danzig, Pomerania, Lübeck							9	9	—	10	—	10
Hamburg, Bremen							2½	2½	2½	2½	2½	2½
Surinam, Berbice							4½	(b) 10*	4½	(c) 4-8	5*	(c) 4-8
Curaçao							4½	(b) 10*	4½	4-6	5*	4-6

(a) "5 and 10" (b) "9 and 10" (c) "4 and 8, 4 and 6"

AMSTERDAM: MARINE INSURANCE RATES — Year: 1777

Month / Outward/Return voyage	January Out	Ret	February Out	Ret	March Out	Ret	April Out	Ret	May Out	Ret	June Out	Ret
Archipelago, Syria	5½*	5½*	4½	4½	3*	3*	3*	3*	3*	3*	3*	3*
Venice, Gulf	5½*	5½*	4½	4½	2½*	2½*	2¼*	2¼*	2¼*	2¼*	2¼*	2¼*
Sicily, Naples, Leghorn	5	5	4	4	2*	2*	2*	2*	2*	2*	2*	2*
Genoa, Marseilles	4½*	4½*	4*	4*	2*	2*	2*	2*	2*	2*	2*	2*
Barcelona, Alicante, Malaga	4½*	4½*	4*	4*	2*	2*	2*	2*	2*	2*	2*	2*
Cádiz, San Lucar, Seville	4*	4*	3	3	1¾*	1¾*	1½*	1½*	1½	1½	1½	1½
Lisbon, Setúbal, Oporto	3½	3½	3	3	1¾*	1¾*	1½*	1½*	1½*	1½*	1½*	1½*
Biscay, French Bight	3	3	2*	2*	1½*	1½*	1	1	1	1	1	1
Morlaix, St Malo, Rouen	2½*	2½	1¾	1¾	1	1	¾	¾	¾	¾	¾	¾
London, Yarmouth, Hull	2	2	1¼	1¼	¾	¾	¾	¾	¾	¾	¾	¾
Cork, Dublin, Limerick	3	3	2	2	—	—	1	1	1	1	1	1
Archangel	—	14*	—	—	—	—	1½	1½	1½	1½	1½	1½
Trondheim, Bergen	—	5	—	—	1½*	(1½*)	1¼*	1¼*	1¼*	1¼	1¼*	1¼*
Norway, East of Naze	—	5	—	—	—	—	1¼*	1¼*	1¼	1¼	1¼*	1¼*
Stockholm, Norrköping	—	9	—	—	1½	1½	1½	1½	1½	1½	1½	4
Copenhagen, Sound, Belt	—	6	—	—	1½*	1½*	1½*	1½*	1½*	1½*	1½*	1½*
Reval, Riga	—	10	—	—	—	—	1½*	1½*	1½*	1½*	1½*	1½*
St Petersburg, Viborg	—	8	—	—	—	—	—	—	—	—	—	—
Königsberg, Danzig, Pomerania, Lübeck	—	10	—	—	—	—	—	—	—	—	—	—
Hamburg, Bremen	2½	2½	1¼	1¼	1*	1*	¾	¾	¾	¾	¾	¾
Surinam, Berbice	5*	4-8	4*	4-8	4	4	4	4*	4	4*	4	4
Curaçao	5*	4-6	4*	4-8	5	5	5	6*	5	6*	5	6*

AMSTERDAM: MARINE INSURANCE RATES — Year: 1777

Month / Outward/Return voyage	July Out	July Ret	August Out	August Ret	September Out	September Ret	October Out	October Ret	November Out	November Ret	December Out	December Ret
Archipelago, Syria	3*	3*	3	3	3½*	3½*	5*	5*	5*	5*	5	5
Venice, Gulf	2¼*	2¼*	2¼*	2¼*	2½	2½	3½*	—	4½	4½	4½	4½
Sicily, Naples, Leghorn	2*	2*	2*	2*	2	2	3	—	4*	4*	4*	4*
Genoa, Marseilles	2*	2*	2*	2*	2	2*	2½	—	3¾	3¾	3¾	3¾
Barcelona, Alicante, Malaga	2*	2*	2*	2*	2	2*	2¾*	—	3½	3½	3½	3½
Cádiz, San Lucar, Seville	1½	1½	1¾*	1¾*	2*	—	2½*	—	3	3	3½	3½
Lisbon, Setúbal, Oporto	1½*	1½*	1½	1½	2*	1¾*	2½*	—	3*	3*	3	3
Biscay, French Bight	1	1	1¼*	1¼*	1¾*	1½	2¼*	—	2¾	2¾	2¾	2¾
Morlaix, St Malo, Rouen	¾	¾	1*	1*	1¼*	1	1¾	—	2	2	2½*	2½*
London, Yarmouth, Hull	¾	¾	¾	¾	1	1	1½	—	1½	1½	1½	1½
Cork, Dublin, Limerick	1	1	1¼	1¼	1¾*	1¼	2½	—	3*	3*	3	3
Archangel	1½	1½	—	1½	—	4*	—	5	—	10* (a)	—	10* (b)
Trondheim, Bergen	1¼	1¼	1¼	1¼	1½	1½*	4	3	6*	5	6*	6*
Norway, East of Naze	1¼*	1¼*	1¼	1¼	1½*	1¼	1½*	1¼	5*	5*	6*	—
Stockholm, Norrköping	1¾	1¾	2¼	2¼	3½	3	5½	4½	9	7	9	8
Copenhagen, Sound, Belt	1½*	1½*	1½	1½	2*	—	4*	4*	5	5	5	5
Reval, Riga	1½*	1½*	2	2	4	—	6	—	7	7	—	8
St Petersburg, Viborg	—	—	3	3*	7*	5	9	8*	—	9* (c)	—	10*
Königsberg, Danzig, Pomerania, Lübeck	—	—	2*	2*	4	2½*	6	—	7	7	—	8
Hamburg, Bremen	¾	¾	1*	1*	1¼	1	1½*	1¼*	2	2	2	2
Surinam, Berbice	4	4	4	4-10	4	4-10	4	10	5	10	5	10
Curaçao	5	6*	4	4-8	4	4-7	5	8	6*	8	—	8

(a) "7 and 10"   (b) "9 and 10"   (c) "7 and 9"

Risks at Sea

| Month | January | | February | | March | | April | | May | | June | |
Outward/Return voyage	Out	Ret	Out	Ret	Out	Ret	Out	Ret	Out	Ret	Out	Ret
Archipelago, Syria	6*	6*	4*	4	3*	—	3	—	3	—	3	—
Venice, Gulf	5	5	3	3	2½*	—	3*	—	3	—	3	—
Sicily, Naples, Leghorn	4¼	4¼	2½	2½	2*	—	3*	—	3*	—	3*	—
Genoa, Marseilles	4¼	4¼	—	—	2*	—	3*	—	3	—	3	—
Barcelona, Alicante, Malaga	3½*	3½*	—	—	2*	—	2½	—	3*	—	3*	—
Cádiz, San Lucar, Seville	3¾	3¾	2¼	2¼	1¾	—	2½	—	2½	—	2½	—
Lisbon, Setúbal, Oporto	3½	3½	—	—	1½	—	2½	—	2½*	—	2½*	—
Biscay, French Bight	3	3	2*	2*	1½*	—	2	—	2	—	2	—
Morlaix, St Malo, Rouen	2¾	2¾	—	—	1*		1½	—	1½	—	1½	—
London, Yarmouth, Hull	1½	1½	1*	1*	1*	—	1	—	1*	—	1*	—
Cork, Dublin, Limerick	3	3	2*	2*	1½	—	2½*	—	2½*	—	2½*	—
Archangel	—	10*	—	—	1½	—	1½	—	1½	—	1½	—
Trondheim, Bergen	7*	7*	—	—	1½	—	1¼	—	1¼	—	1¼	—
Norway, East of Naze	6	6	—	—	1½	—	1¼	—	1¼	—	1¼	—
Stockholm, Norrköping	9	8	—	—	2*	—	1½	—	1½	—	1½	—
Copenhagen, Sound, Belt	6	6	—	—	1½*	—	1¼	—	1¼	—	1¼	—
Reval, Riga	—	8	—	—	1½*	—	1¼	—	1¼	—	1¼	—
St Petersburg, Viborg	—	10	—	—	1½*	—	1¼	—	1¼	—	1¼	—
Königsberg, Danzig, Pomerania, Lübeck	6	6	—	—	1½*	—	1¼	—	1¼	—	1¼	—
Hamburg, Bremen	2½	2½	1¼	1¼	1*	—	1*	—	1*	—	1*	—
Surinam, Berbice	5	10	3½	3½	3	4*	5	—	5	—	5	—
Curaçao	6*	8	4	4	4*	4	6	—	6	—	6	—

Appendix

Month	July		August		September		October		November		December	
Outward/Return voyage	Out	Ret	Out	Ret	Out	Ret	Out	Ret	Out	Ret	Out	Ret
Archipelago, Syria	3	—	4	4	5*	4	5	5	8*	8*	8*	8*
Venice, Gulf	3	—	3½	3½	4	3½	5*	4½	8*	7	8*	7
Sicily, Naples, Leghorn	3*	—	3	3	4	3	4½	4	8*	—	8*	—
Genoa, Marseilles	3	—	—	—	4	—	4	4	8*	—	8*	—
Barcelona, Alicante, Malaga	3*	—	—	—	4	—	4	4	8*	—	8*	—
Cádiz, San Lucar, Seville	2½	—	2½	2½	3½	3*	3½	3½	6	6	6	6
Lisbon, Setúbal, Oporto	2½*	—	2	—	2½	2½	3½	3½	—	—	—	—
Biscay, French Bight	2	—	2½*	2½*	3	2½*	4*	3	6	6	6	6
Morlaix, St Malo, Rouen	1½	—	1¾*	1¾*	2½	1¾*	3*	3*	5	5	5	5
London, Yarmouth, Hull	1*	—	1*	1*	1	1	1½	1½*	1½	1½	2*	1½
Cork, Dublin, Limerick	2½*	—	2½*	2½*	4	2½*	6	4	6	6	6	6
Archangel	1½	3½*	1½	4	—	4½*	—	6	—	—	—	—
Trondheim, Bergen	1¼	—	1½*	1½*	2*	1½*	3½	2½	—	6	—	6
Norway, East of Naze	1¼	—	1¼	—	1½*	1½*	1½*	1½*	—	—	—	—
Stockholm, Norrköping	1¾	1¾	2	2	3½	3	5½	4½	8	7	8	7
Copenhagen, Sound, Belt	1¼	—	1½	1½	2	2*	4½	2	6	6	6	6
Reval, Riga	1½*	1½	2	2	4	3½*	6	6	—	10	—	—
St Petersburg, Viborg	1½*	1½*	3*	3*	5*	5*	8	7	—	11*	—	—
Königsberg, Danzig, Pomerania, Lübeck	1¼	—	1½*	1½*	3	2½*	6	3	8	8	8	8
Hamburg, Bremen	1*	—	1	1	1	1	1½	1¼	2	2	2½	2½
Surinam, Berbice	5	—	5	6-10	5	5-10	6*	5-10	8	12	8	12
Curaçao	6	—	6	—	7*	5-10	7*	5-10	10	15	10	15

Risks at Sea

AMSTERDAM: MARINE INSURANCE RATES Year: **1779**

Month Outward/Return voyage	January Out	Ret	February Out	Ret	March Out	Ret	April Out	Ret	May Out	Ret	June Out	Ret
Archipelago, Syria	8*	8*	4½	—	4*	—	4*	—	4*	—	4*	—
Venice, Gulf	8*	7	4	—	3½	—	3½	—	3½	—	3	—
Sicily, Naples, Leghorn	8*	—	4*	—	—	—	3	—	3*	—	3*	—
Genoa, Marseilles	8*	—	—	—	—	—	3	—	3*	—	3*	—
Barcelona, Alicante, Malaga	8*	—	—	—	—	—	3	—	3*	—	3*	—
Cádiz, San Lucar, Seville	6	6	3½	—	3½*	—	2½	—	2½	—	2½	—
Lisbon, Setúbal, Oporto	—	—	—	—	3*	—	2½	—	2½*	—	2½*	—
Biscay, French Bight	6	6	—	—	2½	—	2	—	2	—	2	—
Morlaix, St Malo, Rouen	5	5	3	—	2½	—	2*	—	2*	—	2*	—
London, Yarmouth, Hull	2	2	1½	—	1¼*	—	1	—	1	—	1	—
Cork, Dublin, Limerick	6	6	5	—	4	—	3*	—	3*	—	3*	—
Archangel	—	—	—	—	1½	—	1½	—	1½	—	1½	—
Trondheim, Bergen	·	6	—	—	1½	—	1¼	—	1¼	—	1¼	—
Norway, East of Naze	—	—	—	—	1¼	—	1¼	—	1¼	—	1¼	—
Stockholm, Norrköping	8	7	—	—	1¾	—	1½	—	1½	—	1½	—
Copenhagen, Sound, Belt	6	6	—	—	1¼	—	1¼	—	1¼	—	1¼	—
Reval, Riga	—	—	—	—	1½	—	1½*	—	1½*	—	1½*	—
St Petersburg, Viborg	—	—	—	—	1½	—	1½*	—	1½*	—	1½*	—
Königsberg, Danzig, Pomerania, Lübeck	8	8	—	—	1¼	—	1¼	—	1¼	—	1¼	—
Hamburg, Bremen	2½	2½	1¼	—	1*	—	¾	—	¾	—	¾	—
Surinam, Berbice	8	12	5*	6	4	6	5*	6	3½	4	3½	4
Curaçao	10	15	5*	6	5	6	5*	6	4	4½*	4	4½*

Appendix

AMSTERDAM: MARINE INSURANCE RATES Year: **1779**

Month	July		August		September		October		November		December	
Outward/Return voyage	Out	Ret	Out	Ret	Out	Ret	Out	Ret	Out	Ret	Out	Ret
Archipelago, Syria	4*	—	4½*	5*	5	5	5	—	5	—	5	—
Venice, Gulf	3	—	3	3	4	—	4½	—	5*	—	5*	—
Sicily, Naples, Leghorn	3*	—	3*	3*	3½	—	4*	—	4	—	—	—
Genoa, Marseilles	3*	—	3*	3*	3½	—	—	—	—	—	—	—
Barcelona, Alicante, Malaga	3*	—	3*	3*	3½	—	—	—	—	—	—	—
Cádiz, San Lucar, Seville	2½	—	3*	3*	3½*	—	3½	—	3½*	—	4	—
Lisbon, Setúbal, Oporto	2½*	—	2½*	2½*	3	—	3	—	3	—	4*	—
Biscay, French Bight	2	—	2	2	3*	—	3	—	—	—	3½*	—
Morlaix, St Malo, Rouen	2*	—	2*	2*	2	—	2½	—	2½	—	3*	—
London, Yarmouth, Hull	1	—	1¼*	1¼*	1¼*	—	1½	—	1½	—	2	—
Cork, Dublin, Limerick	3*	—	4*	4*	5*	—	5*	—	5	—	6	—
Archangel	1½	—	2*	2*	—	3½	—	6*	—	10	—	—
Trondheim, Bergen	1¼	—	1½*	1½*	2½*	2	3½	2	—	6	—	—
Norway, East of Naze	1¼	—	1½*	1½*	2	—	3	—	5	5	—	—
Stockholm, Norrköping	1¾	—	2	2	3½	—	6	5	9	8	9	8
Copenhagen, Sound, Belt	1¼	—	1¾	1¾	2	—	4	—	5*	—	7	—
Reval, Riga	1½	—	2	2	4	3	5	5	7	—	—	—
St Petersburg, Viborg	1½	—	2½	2½	7	4*	8	7*	—	8	—	—
Königsberg, Danzig, Pomerania, Lübeck	1¼	—	1¾*	1¾*	3	—	4	—	7*	—	—	8
Hamburg, Bremen	¾	—	1	1	1¼	—	1½	—	2*	—	2½*	—
Surinam, Berbice	3½	4	4*	10	4	6-10	5*	6-10	5*	10	5*	10
Curaçao	4	4½	5	5	6*	4% rest	6*	4% rest	6	10	7	10

285

Risks at Sea

Month	January		February		March	
Outward/Return voyage	Out	Ret	Out	Ret	Out	Ret
Archipelago, Syria	5	—	—	—	5	—
Venice, Gulf	5*	—	—	—	—	—
Sicily, Naples, Leghorn	—	—	—	—	5*	—
Genoa, Marseilles	—	—	—	—	—	—
Barcelona, Alicante, Malaga	—	—	—	—	—	—
Cádiz, San Lucar, Seville	4	—	3½*	—	5*	—
Lisbon, Setúbal, Oporto	4*	—	3	—	4	—
Biscay, French Bight	3½*	—	3	—	3½*	—
Morlaix, St Malo, Rouen	3*	—	2½*	—	2½	—
London, Yarmouth, Hull	2	—	1¼	—	1	—
Cork, Dublin, Limerick	6	—	3*	—	3	—
Archangel	—	—	1½*	—	1½*	—
Trondheim, Bergen	—	—	1½*	—	—	—
Norway, East of Naze	—	—	—	—	—	—
Stockholm, Norrköping	9	8	2	—	2	—
Copenhagen, Sound, Belt	7	—	1½*	—	1½*	—
Reval, Riga	—	—	1½*	—	—	—
St Petersburg, Viborg	—	—	1½	—	—	—
Königsberg, Danzig, Pomerania, Lübeck	—	8	1½*	—	—	—
Hamburg, Bremen	2½*	—	1¼*	—	1*	—
Surinam, Berbice	5*	10	5*	10 "met"	5*	6
Curaçao	7	10	6	4% rest (a)	8*	8

(a)   for those ships which sailed after 31 December

INDEX

Index

Asiatisk Kompagni, *see under* East India Company, Danish
Assekuranz-Compagnien, Hamburg, 49
Assekuranzkammer, Berlin, 43
Assekuranz- und Havereiordnung (1731), Hamburg, 43
Assurantie Compagnie, Brussels, 27
Assurantie Compagnie, Ghent, 46
Assurantie Compagnie, Middelburg, 25 and n. 46, 27, 38
Assurantie Compagnie (Spain), 46
Assurantie Maatschappij, Bruges, 46
Assurantie Maatschappij op Brand, Amsterdam, 41
Assurantie Compagnie voor Brand, Amsterdam, 41
Assurantie Compagnie, Trieste (Camera mercantile dell' assicurazione marittima, 1779), 46
Assurantie Societeit, Brussels, 46
Atlantic economy, development in early modern Europe, 3
attorneys, use of, 65
aucaners, in Surinam, 195
auctions of ships, as prizes, 110; as wrecks, 140
Austria, loans raised in Amsterdam, 65, 92; loans (1766, 1768, 1769) through Cesar Sardi and Company, 93; loans outstanding (1775), 70–71; loan (1779) raised in Amsterdam and The Hague, 72; loans raised in Genoa, 61; Partition of Poland (1772), 238; acquires salt trade of Wieliczka (1772), 88; purchase of arms in Namur (1773), 98–99; War of Austrian Succession, 59
average, general, 142–153; definition by Lord Mansfield, 18

Bacon, E., captain, sailing from Amsterdam to Boston, Mass. (1782), 114–115
Badin y Compañia, Madrid, 62, 67
Baehrel, R., 161
Baggen, P. C. van, 29
Bakker, H., 28
Baltic, 186–187, 193, 198, 203, 236–242, 244, 255; difficulties in 1763, 79; power struggle, 87; dealers on Amsterdam Bourse, 19; trade, 48, as *moeder commercie*, 48, 50; ships sailing to, 147; climatic conditions, 188; navigation in summer, 12, in winter, 251; as 'risk leader', 126
Balue, De la, et Compagnie, Paris, in bankruptcy, 86
Banda, 149

Bank of Berlin, established (1763), 85; branches in Prussia and Silesia, 85
Bank of England, check to discounting bills of exchange (1772), 90
bankruptcies, and insurance market in Amsterdam, 11; of De Neufville Gebroeders (1763), 82–83; in Britain (1772), 91; in Scotland (1772), 94; of Neale, James, Fordyce and Downe (1772), 90; of Clifford and Sons (1772), 91–92; of Varese e Compagnia, Genoa (1773), 94
Barbary, 165, 166
Barbour, Violet, 1, 18
Barcelona, 163, 165; trade in war munitions, 98, sales to American agents, 99
Bari, 165
Bartelse, J., 32, 161
Bavaria, loan raised in Amsterdam (1772), 70; succession crisis, 96; textile trade, 179
Bayonne, 182; mint in, 183
bearer bonds, France, arbitrage in, 63; reforms (1764), 63; registered before notaries in Paris, 66
Beautemps-Beaupré, C. F., 139
Belt, Denmark, 167, 241
Bensa, E., 1
Berbice, 148, 159, 163, 167, 202, 241
Berckel, E. F. van, grand pensionary, Amsterdam, 103; submits *Memorie* to States of Holland, 103
Berens, H., and Sons, London, 45
Berens, R., agent in London for J. Texier en Compagnie, 110
Berg (Berge) Wz., D. van, Middelburg, 27, 155 '
Bergen, 124, 148, 165, 166, 167, 190, 203, 236; the Hanseatic wharf (*Tyskenbryggen*) in, 189
Berkel, D. E. van, 29
Berlin, canals, 188; as *Hafenstadt*, 43; *Assekuranzkammer*, 43; arrival of crisis of 1763, 84
Berrill, K., 254
beurtdiensten, 254; to Antwerp, 53; Bremen, 53; Cologne, 53; Dordrecht, 53, 54; Düsseldorf, 53; Hamburg, 53; London, 53; Rhineland, 54; Rotterdam, 54
beunhazers, 22, 119
Beveridge, Lord, evidence of high prices of grain (1772–74), 87
Bibber, Abraham van, Maryland agent in St Eustatius, 102
Bilbao, 182

Index

Index

Ehrenberg, R., 1
Eickhoff, J. H., 21
Elbe river, 188; lighthouses, 138; dredging
    to improve port of Hamburg, 134; link
    with Oder trade to Hamburg, 79
Elbing, monopoly of trade following
    Partition of Poland (1772), 87–88
Elias, J. E., 1
Elink Schuurman, W. H. A., 1
Emden, as port, 137
Emerigon, B.-M., 7, 46, 89, 118, 252
Engelen, P., en Compagnie, 32
Enkhuizen, economic difficulties, 109
entrepreneurs, as underwriters of public
    loans, 74
epoch, in industrialisation, 10–11
Ephraim, Veitel Heine, as farmer of mints
    in Prussia, 81
equilibrium in insurance rates, in the
    short-term, 249, in the long-term, 249;
    evidence in favour of the year 1769,
    127
esedîgurus (leeuwendaalders), 178 and n. 12
Essequibo, 159; plantation loans, 27, 61,
    raised in Middelburg, 68; effects of
    exchange on Netherlands, 69
Europe, international loans, 61
Europe, shipping, share of Britain, 50
event uncertainties, *see under* uncertainty
Everitt, A., 22
exchange rate, West Indies on Amsterdam
    (1774), 69; France on Amsterdam
    (1771), 70; London on Amsterdam
    (1780), 110 n. 179

Faesch en Compagnie, 21
Fagel, Hendrik, greffier of the Republic,
    103
fairs, Archangel, 190, 193; Breslau, 179;
    Deventer, 253; Frankfurt am Main, 62,
    193; Leipzig, 62, 79, 179, 188; Tikhvin,
    193
Falkland Islands, 96, 99, 183, 237
Far East, 255; voyages, innavigability, 148
Fayle, C. E., 2
Febvre, L., 5
Felloni, G., 2, 61
Finland, Gulf of, 236
fire, on board ship, 140
fishing, 186; insurance in Amsterdam, 145
Fizeaux, J., en Zoonen, 140, 187
Fizeaux, J. E., 33
flags, of neutral ships, 113
fluit, 9, 117, 137; dimensions, 48–49,
    132–133; advantages, 48–49
Flushing, 113
Fordyce, A., leaves for France, 90

forms, 'catastrophic' and random in
    insurance markets, 120
fortune de mer, innavigability defined by
    R.-J. Pothier, 143
Fouquet, P., 17 n. 8
Fourth Anglo-Dutch War, *see under* wars
France, 186, 190, 237; Ordonnance de la
    Marine (1686), 44; support for Turks
    against Russia, 178, 237; secret treaty
    with United States (1778), 103; silver
    currency, 66–67, and exchange on
    Amsterdam, 70; public finance, 86;
    food riots (1774–75); foreign loans, 66,
    in the Netherlands, 70, 71, in Genoa,
    61; trade with the Netherlands, 103,
    dealers, 19, cloth, 53, salt, 165–166,
    colonial products, 33, 184; munitions
    and gunpowder to Spain, 99, to
    United States, 100; restrictions on
    trade with Netherlands, 107–109
Frankfurt am Main, fairs, sale of
    Amsterdam bonds, 62; crisis of 1763,
    84
Frederick II (the Great), of Prussia, 80, 82;
    establishes companies, 85
freight, in combination with credit and
    insurance, 12, 16; trends, 58–59
Friedman, M., 5, 116
Friesland, shipping, 50

Galiani, Ferdinando, Abate, 250
galjoot, 49
Gallitzin, Dmitri, Prince, 112
gambling and insurance, 59, 118–119
games theory, 6
Gaspée affair, 97
General Steam Navigation Company, 255
Genoa, 165, 166, 180, 240, 241;
    improvement of port, 133; trade, 179;
    porto franco, 179; seasonal movement,
    121; market for bonds, 65; investments
    in Austria, 61, France, 61, Naples, 61,
    Russia, 61, Spain, 61, Venice, 61;
    bankruptcy of Varese e Compagnia
    (1773), 94
Germany, 66, 179
Gerschenkron, A., 5
Ghent, canal (1760), 53, 137; Gendse
    Societeit, 46
Gibraltar, 180, 237, 241
Gildemeester (Gil de Meester), J., and
    Company, 99
Gillingham, H. E., 2
Giro-Bank, Hamburg, in crisis of 1772–73,
    95
Glasgow, trade in war munitions, 98
Glückstadt, 137

294

Index

Lightning Source UK Ltd.
Milton Keynes UK
UKHW010632020221
378106UK00001B/17